The
DEFENDER'S DILEMMA

Identifying and Deterring Gray-Zone Aggression

ELISABETH BRAW

AMERICAN ENTERPRISE INSTITUTE

ISNB-13: 978-0-8447-5039-2   Hardback
ISNB-13: 978-0-8447-5040-8   Paperback
ISNB-13: 978-0-8447-5041-5   eBook

© 2022 by the American Enterprise Institute for Public Policy Research. All rights reserved.

The American Enterprise Institute (AEI) is a nonpartisan, nonprofit, 501(c)(3) educational organization and does not take institutional positions on any issues. The views expressed here are those of the author(s).

American Enterprise Institute
1789 Massachusetts Avenue, NW
Washington, DC 20036
www.aei.org

Contents

Introduction 1

    I. Defining and Identifying Gray-Zone Aggression 8

    II. 2014: A Decisive Year 20

    III. Gray-Zone Aggression, a National Security Threat 26

    IV. Is Sponsorship an Act of Aggression? Use of Licit Means
        in the Gray Zone 38

    V. Subversive Economics: When Business as Usual Enters
        the Gray Zone 56

    VI. Coercion, Bullying, and Subversion of Civil Society 83

    VII. Gradual Border Alterations and Surreptitious Fishing:
        Use of Illicit Means 109

    VIII. Producing Fear in the Enemy's Mind: Adapting Cold War
        Deterrence for Gray-Zone Aggression 142

    IX. Cold War Swedish and Finnish Total Defense
        as Deterrence 168

    X. Building a Wall of Denial Against Gray-Zone Aggression 185

    XI. Deterrence by Punishment 221

Concluding Reflections 250

Notes 252

About the Author 313

Index 315

Introduction

In March 2021, the United States was reeling from COVID-19's continuing devastation, not to mention Donald Trump's campaign to invalidate Joe Biden's election victory. The latter had culminated in an assault on the US Capitol that resulted in five deaths and global shock that the president of the United States would incite supporters to attack Congress. In the background, another devastating turn of events continued to fester. On the same day Trump supporters stormed the Capitol, Chinese hackers launched a devastating cyber intrusion, infiltrating an estimated 30,000 Microsoft Exchange servers in the United States and hundreds of thousands worldwide.[1] Russian cyber operators had already accessed large parts of the US government by digitally breaking into the software firm—and government contractor—SolarWinds. In the UK, Chief of the Defence Staff Gen. Nick Carter warned that clandestine activity by hostile states that does not reach the threshold for war could quickly "light a fuse" if it were misunderstood or escalated.[2]

Less than two months before, in November 2020, Australian winemakers lost their largest export market after China imposed tariffs so punitive as to make Australian wine unsalable in China. While officially a response to alleged Australian "wine dumping" in China, the tariffs were a de facto Chinese retaliation against the Australian government, which had decided to exclude the Chinese mobile-technology giant Huawei from its 5G network and backed an international inquiry into the origins of COVID-19.[3] Around the same time, the CEO of Ericsson, Börje Ekholm, sent a string of text messages to a Swedish minister, pleading with the Swedish government to reverse its ban on Huawei. He did so after having been pressured by the Chinese government, whose market Ericsson depends on.[4]

Spring 2020 had, in turn, brought news of not just COVID-19's catastrophic march through the world but also a less conspicuous event: a major investment in Norwegian Air Shuttle, the world's fifth-largest budget carrier.[5] The investor, BOC Aviation, now owns a 12.67 percent stake in the company, which makes it one of Norwegian's largest shareholders.[6] On the face of it, this was just one of millions of daily commercial transactions taking place worldwide. BOC Aviation's ultimate owner is, however, an investment arm of the Chinese state-owned Bank of China. By means of a fully legal transaction, the Chinese government acquired a significant chunk of one of Europe's largest airlines.

Until recently, a Chinese takeover of a Norwegian airline would have been considered positive news, and a Russian cyber intrusion involving most of the US government would have seemed unlikely. But while global business transactions have continued to increase and cyber-penetration techniques have reached ever-higher levels of sophistication, relations between the West and China, Iran, North Korea, and Russia have deteriorated.[7]

The most commonly cited juncture is Russia's 2014 annexation of Crimea and covert military activities in eastern Ukraine. As a result of these events, European countries have increased their defense spending. Between 2015 and 2019, every European NATO member state except Croatia and Belgium increased its defense spending, in some cases dramatically. (Lithuania more than doubled its defense expenditures.[8]) NATO now has multinational battalions in each Baltic state and Poland. At the time of writing, 1,525 troops from 10 NATO member states are helping Latvia's armed forces deter Russian aggression. Sweden, a non-NATO member state that joined many others in slashing defense spending from the 1990s onward, is likewise trying to rebuild its armed forces in response to Russia's behavior.

These reactions to Russia's aggression toward Ukraine are logical: If Russia could engage in subversive military activities against Ukraine, which country will be next? National leaders have a responsibility to protect their countries against armed attacks. But what if aggression comes in a completely different guise? What if it is not even carried out by the attacking country's armed forces? The concept of gray-zone warfare is age-old, but for the past several years, it has been comprehensively used by China, Russia, and, with a more limited focus, Iran and North Korea. Regarding China, Michael Mazarr notes,

> In its "gray zone" tactics and elaborate economic investment programs, China gives every indication of intending to pursue its goals short of the use of force. China's dominant strategies, in short, are not built around conquest; the competition is not likely to be resolved by military power.[9]

While much of the West worries about an invasion, gray-zone aggression is taking place every day—and it is hard to detect because it often looks like the normal bustle of daily life.

Gray-zone aggression is happening because it is exceedingly easy to attack liberal democracies in the gray zone between war and peace. Indeed, it is distinctly advantageous to use nonmilitary means of aggression. Doing so brings the attacking side the benefits it seeks, which may be industrial prowess rather than territorial gains. It makes the defender's task harder; indeed, the aggression is extremely difficult to deter. For years, Western governments and businesses have worked to strengthen their defense against cyberattacks. Many have strengthened their offensive cyber capabilities. Governments and the wider public in Europe and North America have experienced the effects of disinformation campaigns against their societies, and myriad government and civil-society initiatives are trying to limit the spread of disinformation and make the public more resilient to such content. Yet the aggression continues, often by simply taking on new guises.

In a global environment of constant aggression in the gray zone between war and peace, in which any tool and area can be used to weaken an adversary, the defender is by definition one step behind. The COVID-19 pandemic put this changing security environment into sharp focus. Although Mother Nature almost certainly caused the most severe crisis to hit many Western countries since World War II, it was exacerbated and exploited by the Chinese government, which obfuscated when the virus was first discovered and then used European countries' early misery for propaganda purposes.

COVID-19 also forced a significant rethink on relations with Beijing. Until the pandemic, many Western governments had tried working with Beijing on a basis of partnership or even trust. However, China's actions in 2020—including not just "Bad Samaritanism" and obfuscation over COVID-19 but also punishment and coercion directed against Western businesses and governments—made citizens and policymakers alike conclude that their assessments of China might have been clouded by optimism bias.

COVID-19, in a sense, was China's Crimea: the moment when the world found itself forced to reevaluate its approach. The Pew Research Center's October 2020 report *Unfavorable Views of China Reach Historic Highs in Many Countries* delivered staggering figures: 73 percent of Americans held negative views of China, up from 47 percent three years before. In Australia, the rate skyrocketed from 32 to 81 percent; in the UK, from 37 to 74 percent; in Canada, from 40 to 73 percent; in Sweden, from 49 to 85 percent; and in the Netherlands, from 42 to 73 percent. Even in Italy, a long-standing object of Chinese overtures in Europe, the negativity rate rose in 2020, the year when China tried to win Italian affections at the expense of Italy's allies by delivering COVID-19 supplies.[10]

Even before COVID-19, it was no secret that China was taking advantage of Western economies through, for example, intellectual property theft and strategic acquisitions by Chinese companies. But little had been done to counter the practice. It was often seen as a nuisance, not a national security threat.

In addition to highlighting Western countries' relative lack of pandemic preparedness, COVID-19 brutally demonstrated to decision makers and ordinary citizens alike how vulnerable their societies are to different forms of disruption. Until then, governments had focused most of their attention on cyberattacks and disinformation by China, Iran, North Korea, and Russia and on military threats. Those efforts resulted in better cyber defense by businesses, individuals, and governments. The US government and others had also tried to stem China's systematic cyber theft of intellectual property, while some governments had begun tackling disinformation by, for example, adding information literacy to school curricula.

The West's rivals also engage in gray-zone aggression using entirely legal means. During the chaotic first weeks of COVID-19 in Europe, when Italy's pleas for aid from its European allies went unheeded, China delivered medical supplies to Italy and successfully used the event as propaganda intended to weaken EU solidarity. It violated no laws in doing so. Acquiring cutting-edge Western technology has until now mostly been legal, though countries' legislation is beginning to change. Dalian Wanda Group's 2012 acquisition of the AMC movie theater chain in the United States, the world's largest movie theater empire, was not illegal.[11] Nor is the fact that Western movies are censored before being shown in China, which in reality means global audiences watch movies that have been adjusted to suit Chinese censors. Yet apart from the Trump administration, which went to bat against China over unfair practices, Western governments that took modest steps to limit their countries' vulnerabilities to Chinese subversion—for example, Germany, which strengthened its foreign direct investment rules in 2018—did so quietly. In 2020, that began to change.

During the early stages of World War II, when Switzerland seemed destined to meet the same fate that Belgium, Denmark, France, the Netherlands, Norway, Poland, and the UK did, the country's defense minister, Rudolf Minger, kept a note attached to his office door: "In case of war, please ring twice."[12] Today, it would be nearly impossible to know when to ring the bell.

In the increasingly busy gray zone between war and peace, even seemingly menial actions directed against civil society can cause considerable harm to the targeted country. As Yevgeny Vindman points out, "International law limits the basis for resort to war, *jus ad bellum* in Article 2(4) of the U.N. Charter, to an illegal 'use of force' or armed attack."[13] While countries could certainly choose to define gray-zone attacks as "use of force" or "armed attacks" and retaliate in-kind, that would lead to escalation that is not in their interest. Yet not signaling a forceful response likewise is not a sustainable strategy. As long as the West lacks effective defense and deterrence against these activities, they will continue to grow and morph. Indeed, they will connect with other legal and illegal forms of aggression. The West's adversaries are limited only by their imaginations.

This book maps today's gray-zone landscape, evaluating selected forms of gray-zone aggression. These forms are less well-known than are cyberattacks and disinformation, which have already been extensively discussed in academia and politics. Part of the defender's dilemma is that almost any area of life in a liberal democracy can be targeted by gray-zone aggression. Therefore, the issues I discuss in this book illustrate risks and solutions, rather than providing a complete inventory of gray-zone aggression.

6   THE DEFENDER'S DILEMMA

I use empirical evidence in the form of interviews with leading practitioners in select Western countries: business leaders, military officials, politicians, and senior government officials. Many agreed to speak with me on the record, specifically for the purpose of this book. All quotations and comments denoted in the endnotes as interviews belong to this category. Any conclusions drawn from their observations are, of course, mine alone. Although existing academic literature—from which this book also benefits—is an important source of information, practitioners on the front line of gray-zone aggression form an unparalleled resource in this constantly morphing environment.

The Defender's Dilemma also outlines how gray-zone aggression can be deterred. Because the armed forces alone cannot counter all forms of gray-zone aggression, any defense against—and deterrence of—it must involve wider society. What should deterrence against gray-zone threats comprise, how does civil society fit into the framework, and how can existing deterrence models be adopted and adapted for this purpose?

Some countries, notably in the Nordic-Baltic region, have a history of total defense involving all parts of society and have for the past few years updated it to better include gray-zone aggression. Others, including the United States, have built up impressive cyber defense and offense. Yet even though there is a lively academic debate about gray-zone threats, no country has so far come close to establishing comprehensive defense and deterrence against them. The evidence of this is, of course, that gray-zone aggression takes place and continues to expand. Part of the defender's dilemma is that the aggression may not always be obvious. Gray-zone defense and deterrence must also counter activities that have not yet been carried out. Because deterrence is primarily about psychology, not the tools used, traditional deterrence models can be highly useful if adapted to gray-zone aggression.

I am grateful to Charlotte Salley, the book's editor, and to Laila Hanandeh and Áine Josephine Tyrrell. I am also enormously grateful to colleagues who have read and commented on early versions of one or more chapters: Ewan Lawson, Brig. Gen. Gerhard Wheeler (ret.), Chris Brannigan, Air Commodore Andrew Hall (ret.), Richard Utne, George Robertson, Maj. Gen. Pekka Toveri (ret.), Maj. Gen. Mitch Mitchell (ret.), Robert Dalsjö, Gen. Riho Terras (ret.), Jerker Hellström, Lt. Gen. Arto

Räty (ret.), Maj. Gen. Jim Keffer (ret.), Balkan Devlen, Col. Bo Hugemark (ret.), Derek Scissors, Sven-Christer Nilsson, Marcus Kolga, Timothy Dowse, Amb. Håkan Malmqvist, Amb. René Nyberg, Stefan Forss, Madeleine Moon, Amb. Cameron Munter, and especially Rear Adm. David Manero (ret.).

This book is intended as a resource for policymakers, members of the armed forces, industry leaders, and wider civil society. Western governments cannot simply impose gray-zone deterrence. Instead, it is in the interest of all members of society to play a role in gray-zone defense and deterrence, as everyone stands to benefit. By extension, so does each country.

I
Defining and Identifying Gray-Zone Aggression

In the legend of the Trojan War, the Achaeans realized that the best—perhaps only—road to victory against the tenacious Trojans depended on not a military onslaught but subterfuge. The Trojans had to be lulled into a false sense of security, a sense that the war had ended. The Achaean soldiers pretended to depart, leaving only Sinon, who persuaded the Trojans that the Achaeans had given up and generously bequeathed them a gigantic horse, a gift to the goddess Athena that would make the city impenetrable. Cassandra's warnings went unheeded.

What happened next is taught to every schoolchild today. After the grateful Trojans brought the unexpected horse inside the city walls, Achaean soldiers leaped out and opened the city's gates from the inside, allowing fellow soldiers hiding outside the walls to capture the city. The Trojans' failure to consider their adversary's creativity cost them their freedom.

Even though the Trojans did not use the term "gray-zone attack," they were early victims of one. Indeed, the attack against them could have remained in the gray zone. Instead of hiding soldiers in a horse, the Achaeans could have convinced some Trojans to subtly spread falsehoods—perhaps in exchange for money—and could thus have sown discord among the Trojans to cause them to lose faith in their society, especially in their abilities vis-à-vis the Achaeans. The Achaeans did what some countries do today: use deception and other nonmilitary means to weaken opponents. The horse was merely a tool used in the gray zone between war and peace to allow the Achaeans an advantageous return to armed conflict.

As defined by the US special forces community, gray-zone aggression comprises "competitive interactions among and within state and non-state actors that fall between the traditional war and peace duality."[1] (Emphasis omitted.) In current discourse, especially since Russia's annexation of Crimea in 2014, another term often used to describe aggression between traditional war and peace is "hybrid warfare." The term was introduced to the general public by then-Gen. James Mattis in a 2005 speech and expanded on by Frank Hoffman in a 2007 book that established the term among a wider audience. In Hoffman's wording,

> Hybrid threats incorporate a full range of different modes of warfare including conventional capabilities, irregular tactics and formations, terrorist acts including indiscriminate violence and coercion, and criminal disorder. Hybrid Wars can be conducted by both states and a variety of non-state actors [with or without state sponsorship]. These multi-modal activities can be conducted by separate units, or even by the same unit, but are generally operationally and tactically directed and coordinated within the main battlespace to achieve synergistic effects in the physical and psychological dimensions of conflict.[2]

Erik Reichborn-Kjennerud and Patrick Cullen note,

> In military terms, [hybrid warfare] is designed to fall below the threshold of war and to delegitimize (or even render politically irrational) the ability to respond by military force....
> Hybrid warfare breaks down the distinction between what is and what is not part of the battlefield.[3]

Hybrid warfare, in other words, is a conflict involving persistent use of military force and non-armed aggression and can occur between both countries and substate entities that are at war with each other and those that are not. Ewan Lawson proposes that "hybrid" can also be divided between hybrid warfare and hybrid threats: "In the case of Ukraine, for example, some of the activity in Donbas is hybrid alongside conventional military activity—this is hybrid warfare. The broader campaign to destabilize Ukraine can be described as hybrid threats."[4] This distinction solves a dilemma that too liberally using the term "hybrid warfare" will by definition create: The targeted side, feeling pressured to tackle what public discourse labels "warfare," may be tempted to escalate in response.

Definitions matter, because, below the threshold of war, not everything is hybrid warfare. In contrast, gray-zone aggression is, by my definition, the use of hostile acts outside the realm of armed conflict to weaken a rival country, entity, or alliance.

In a 2013 article for the *Military-Industrial Courier*, Russia's Chief of the General Staff Valery Gerasimov noted that "in the 21st century we have seen a tendency toward blurring the lines between the states of war and peace. Wars are no longer declared and, having begun, proceed according to an unfamiliar template."[5] Although Gerasimov's comment concerned Arab Spring revolutions and color revolutions in former Soviet republics and was not presented as a new Russian doctrine, it subsequently became known as the "Gerasimov doctrine." But Mark Galeotti, who coined the term, has frequently pointed out that Gerasimov's article should not be read as a statement of a new Russian doctrine. Indeed, Gerasimov himself does not refer to the article as a new doctrine, and his points in the article could instead be described as a summary of current conditions in intrastate competition rather than a statement of how Russia should operate.

"Wars [that] are no longer declared and [which], having begun, proceed according to an unfamiliar template" is, in fact, an accurate description of recent developments in the interactions between any two nations, certainly in the developed world. While developed countries have, as Scott Shapiro, Oona Hathaway, and others document, moved away from formal wars against one another,[6] today fierce competition characterizes the relationship between Western countries and Russia and China. The Westphalian system, in which countries alternately cooperate and jockey for power, has not been replaced—as many had predicted—by a system of global governance. Instead, it has taken on a new guise.

Referring to hybrid warfare, Reichborn-Kjennerud and Cullen speak of "synchronized attack packages," a helpful label that can also be applied to forms of aggression conducted entirely in the gray zone.[7] In recent years, authoritarian countries—especially Russia and China—have perfected the use of such synchronized attack packages. This should come as no surprise. In hybrid and gray-zone aggression, authoritarian regimes have a fundamental advantage vis-à-vis their liberal democratic rivals: The latter feature not only small governments but also independent private sectors and citizenry that cannot easily be commandeered by the government. Reichborn-Kjennerud and Cullen note,

> While the West is largely stuck in an instrumentalist, technicist, battle-centric and kinetic understanding of war, its opponents have been busy redefining war. . . .
>
> States with highly centralized abilities to coordinate and synchronize their instruments of power (government, economy, media, etc.) can create synergistic force multiplying effects. Specifically, state [hybrid warfare] allows for operations that "target and exploit the seams" in Western-style liberal democratic societies that do not have similar coordinating offices or capabilities.[8]

Put more colloquially, hybrid and gray-zone aggression can be likened to cooking a soup. The West's rivals can cook a soup more easily than Western countries can, but they also use a wider range of ingredients. In fact, the targeted country has no way of predicting which ingredients will be used on any given occasion. It is, for example, conceivable that a hostile state could try to unleash a highly contagious virus.

The definitions of gray-zone and hybrid warfare demonstrate the clear difference between them: Gray-zone warfare does not involve persistent use of military force, while hybrid warfare does. Indeed, one can argue that all wars are hybrid, as they involve persistent use of force with one or more of the elements Hoffman describes. The major difference between traditional past wars on one hand and Russia's conflict with Ukraine and potential future hybrid wars on the other may simply be that today's and tomorrow's wars have a much stronger component of gray-zone aggression and a much smaller component of conventional warfare than do traditional wars. In addition, gray-zone aggression is less likely to be formally acknowledged by the attacking country.

Hoffman's definition of hybrid warfare—which has become standard—notably does not include civilian activities conducted without any connection to military confrontation. In common parlance, however, hybrid warfare is often used to describe exactly such non-armed acts of aggression (e.g., disinformation campaigns). For example, the European Centre of Excellence for Countering Hybrid Threats in Helsinki, Finland, (which was set up in 2017) states that "the term hybrid threat refers to an action conducted by state or non-state actors, whose goal is to undermine or harm a target by influencing its decision-making at the local, regional, state or institutional level."[9]

NATO's Strategic Communications Centre of Excellence in Riga, Latvia, has the following list of what it considers hybrid threats, perhaps because the list also includes traditional territorial violation:

- Territorial violation,
- Nongovernmental organizations,
- Government-organized nongovernmental organizations,
- Espionage and infiltration,
- Exploitation of ethnic or cultural identities,
- Media,
- Lawfare,
- Agitation and civil unrest,
- Cyber operations,
- Religious groups,
- Academic groups,
- Coercion through threat or use of force,
- Energy dependency,
- Political actors,
- Economic leverage, and
- Bribery and corruption.[10]

It is not clear that influence through media and nongovernmental organizations should count as hybrid aggression, as it can also be used legitimately. Indeed, Western governments have long used it. Disinformation is, however, indisputably a form of gray-zone aggression.

Lyle Morris et al., in turn, list the following forms of Russian gray-zone activities in Europe: "military measures, information operations, cyber-attacks, legal and diplomatic measures, economic coercion, and political influence [such as manipulating population groups and funding individuals or parties]."[11]

They list the following Chinese gray-zone measures in East and Southeast Asia: "military intimidation, paramilitary activities [maritime militia and maritime law enforcement over disputed territories breaking norms of good seamanship], co-opting of state-affiliated businesses, manipulation of borders, . . . lawfare and diplomacy, and economic coercion."[12]

Notably, Morris et al. do not mention strategic investments in, and venture capital funding of, cutting-edge technology companies, arguably one of China's currently most successful gray-zone activities. This absence illustrates the novel nature of gray-zone aggression, which includes activities so far from traditional national security thinking that they may simply not be noticed by the affected countries until a relatively late stage.

Identifying Gray-Zone Aggression

While most average citizens in Western countries may be unfamiliar with the term "gray-zone aggression," most of them have perhaps unwittingly encountered it in their daily lives. Until Russian gangs brought down Colonial Pipeline in the US, the Irish national health care system, meat-processing giant JBS, and many other providers of vital services in spring and summer 2021,[13] most ordinary citizens were unaware of the increasingly sophisticated cyberattacks directed, every day, against companies they rely on for the conveniences of daily life. The CEO of a major European telecoms infrastructure company said,

> Attacks on my company have increased, and they're directed both against our staff and against our infrastructure. A disproportionate share of the attacks originates in China. According to our law enforcement authorities, the attacks directed against us are very sophisticated. It's clear why we're being targeted: If you harm us, you limit other people's access to communication. And if you knock us out, you knock out the government's ability to issue public-service announcements.[14]

Like virtually all companies attacked, the telecoms firm does not highlight the amount of aggression directed toward it—even though attacks to date have not been successful—as highlighting the aggression would undermine public confidence in the company.

This relative absence of public discourse regarding gray-zone aggression exacerbates the public's lack of awareness and even dismissive attitude toward the possibility that hostile states may be engaging in aggression. Most US Facebook users who, during the 2016 election campaign, liked or shared posts placed by Russian proxies likely did not consider they might be unwitting participants in gray-zone aggression. Ordinary citizens rarely pay attention to investments in companies that are not household names. They do not study the input into academic research or its funding or energy supply conditions. But these are not ordinary times: Just as cyberattacks can bring a country to its knees, acquisitions undertaken by companies based in countries with hostile intentions can dangerously weaken the targeted countries. That is why the ransomware attacks on Colonial Pipeline, the Irish health service, and JBS—attributed to criminal gangs thought to be tolerated by the Russian government—were so important in raising the public's awareness to new dangers.

Indeed, almost any aspect of daily life in a liberal democracy can be turned into a weapon against it. In gray-zone competition, Western countries' openness and the limited size and powers of their governments form a distinct disadvantage. That Russia and China, despite having large armed forces at their disposal, are trying to weaken the West through gray-zone means should come as no surprise. The West's rivals use non-weapon tools precisely because the price of attacking the West with military means would be extremely high and, equally importantly, would, in the case of NATO member states, be met with such force that NATO would likely win eventually. Any clever leaders of rival states seeking to weaken the West would likely use non-armed means of aggression, which are not only much less risky and costly but also likely to encounter minimal resistance and punishment.

Indeed, while Russia and China (and to a lesser extent, Iran and North Korea) are today's main practitioners of gray-zone aggression, the West's vulnerabilities and the lack of comprehensive defense and deterrence against gray-zone aggression mean that any country or non-state actor wishing to engage in gray-zone aggression against the West could do so.

Not all forms of gray-zone aggression are illegal. Throughout 2020, for example, Beijing engaged in wide-ranging coercive diplomacy directed at governments of whose—entirely legal—behavior it disapproved. (In traditional diplomacy, countries or groups of countries issue threats against countries that break international laws or conventions.) While the Chinese diplomats' threats were addressed to governments, the targets were often private companies.

When Sweden decided not to include Chinese telecoms giant Huawei in its 5G network, China's Foreign Ministry spokesman Zhao Lijian immediately announced that "Sweden should assume an objective attitude and address its erroneous decision in order to avoid negative consequences for Swedish companies in China."[15] The statement could only be seen as a threat to Swedish companies and the Swedish government, considering Swedish businesses' extensive operations in China and exports to the Chinese market. Yet a diplomat simply warning of consequences—even if the warning is intended as a threat and understood as such—does not engage in illegal behavior.

When the UK made the same decision regarding Huawei, Chinese officials responded with similarly ominous language, and after the UK offered a path to British citizenship for Hong Kong residents born while the city was a British crown colony, the Chinese government demanded that it "immediately correct its mistakes" and warned there would be consequences.[16] It was immediately clear to British companies with significant operations in China, such as the banks HSBC and Standard Chartered, that any consequences were likely to hit them.[17] In 2020, Chinese diplomats' use of such coercive language increased so much that analysts began labeling it "wolf warrior" diplomacy.[18]

The utility of different forms of gray-zone aggression is precisely that so much of it operates in the realm of legality. In addition, the aggressor can keep inventing new forms of legal and seemingly illegal aggression, leaving the targeted country permanently on the back foot.

In late 2020, an expert panel convened by the US National Academies of Sciences, Engineering, and Medicine released its findings regarding a mystery illness that had befallen US diplomats working in Cuba and China. The expert commission concluded that the cause of the diplomats' illness was pulsed radio frequency energy. While the commission did not identify the perpetrator of the attacks, it noted that the Soviet Union had researched the effects of pulsed radio frequency energy.[19] This suggests Russia may be the perpetrator.

Which innovative tool of aggression will the West's rivals next use? It is impossible to predict. In gray-zone aggression, the only limitation is the aggressor's imagination. When the Achaeans could not defeat the Trojans with traditional military means, they used their imagination and built a wooden horse. While the gray zone has, of course, always been available to attackers—including Western democracies—globalization has immeasurably increased opportunities for aggressors. The Chinese government can issue ominous warnings to the Swedish and UK governments over their 5G decisions because these countries are home to so many businesses reliant on Chinese suppliers and the Chinese market. Indeed, today's globalized economy, with its long supply chains and technology-dependent operations, forms a significant opportunity for gray-zone aggression and is an amplifier of it. Previously, factory production and civilian shipping could be disrupted, but today it can be done at scale, with less effort and to more devastating effect. The more convenient life in liberal democracies becomes, the more vulnerable such countries become to gray-zone aggression. I refer to this as the "convenience trap."

Gray-zone aggression thus differentiates itself from aggression involving persistent use of armed force in that its form is nearly impossible for the targeted country to predict and thus prepare for. Admittedly, history is full of military surprises, such as Nazi Germany's invasion of the Soviet Union in 1941, but the basic principles of military aggression are not in doubt. Each time, military attacks involve service personnel and military equipment operating in ways that the defender has a chance of trying to predict. Gray-zone aggression can use any tool against any target.

Deterring Gray-Zone Aggression

The second challenge facing targeted countries is response, retaliation, and deterrence. Since gray-zone aggression is so amorphous that it is not even clear whether an act is a hostile one directed by a foreign government, response is infinitely more complicated than with traditional armed aggression. Even when an act is clearly hostile, it is not by definition an act of gray-zone aggression. On the contrary, it can be part of competitive statecraft practiced even among allies. During the 1970s' so-called cod wars between Iceland and the UK, Iceland deployed decidedly rough tactics that included ignoring judgments by multilateral institutions, threatening to withdraw from NATO—thus depriving NATO of its crucial airbase at Keflavík—and cutting trawler nets.[20]

When China, a country with a recent history of subversive acts and a population some 4,000 times larger than Iceland's, engages in hostile activities, these clearly must be judged differently. In December 2020, China's Ministry of Commerce signed an agreement to build a massive fish-processing plant on the Torres Strait island of Daru, which is close to Australia but administered by Papua New Guinea.[21] Since the area is not known for abundant fish stocks, the construction suggests the facility may have a purpose other than processing fish.

A similar reality is true regarding Russia. In the mid-2010s, Finnish authorities began noticing a string of purchases, by Russian citizens, of properties near Finnish strategic installations such as ports and military bases.[22] If, say, Swedes had bought the properties, it would have raised no concerns. In this case, the Finnish government decided it had to restrict opportunities for non-EU citizens to buy properties in Finland.[23]

As with Finland's property purchases, China's fish-processing plant close to Australia is legal—and raises gray-zone fears. It does so because legal commercial activities can also be used to weaken another country.

Over centuries of warfare, countries have built and refined highly complex deterrence strategies that have, since the creation of nuclear weapons, also included nuclear deterrence. Such strategies are of no use against gray-zone aggression. Because no liberal democracy would retaliate against, say, diplomatic threats against its businesses with military strikes, the West's formidable collective military might has minimal impact on gray-zone aggressors. As Dr. Strangelove might have said, the presence of the United States' nuclear arsenal produces fear to attack in the mind of an enemy contemplating a nuclear attack, but it produces no fear in the mind of an enemy contemplating the imposition of punitive wine tariffs.

And even when the targeted country identifies the aggression and wants to take clear action, doing so is difficult without escalating. To date, Western governments have largely contented themselves with naming and shaming governments they have found to sponsor cyberattacks, disinformation, and other forms of gray-zone aggression including the poisoning of Sergei and Yulia Skripal in Salisbury, England, in 2018. Many countries and their businesses have strengthened cybersecurity and introduced offensive cyber capabilities, most recently demonstrated by the UK's creation of the National Cyber Force.[24]

Meanwhile, some countries—for example, Finland, Latvia, and Sweden—have gone to great lengths to begin training segments of their populations in information literacy and (in Latvia's case) general resilience.[25] The United States, in turn, increasingly indicts individuals who have perpetrated cyberattacks against American and other Western targets on behalf of foreign governments.[26] Yet as the spate of ransomware attacks and subversive corporate takeovers throughout 2021 demonstrates, hostile activities in the gray zone continue, often in new guises. Even when a country manages to plug its vulnerability in one area, aggressors can move to a different area or new type of aggression. Matching defensive efforts with a specific mode of aggression—say, disinformation—does not create comprehensive gray-zone defense, let alone deterrence.

What makes gray-zone aggression even more difficult to counter is that even if the mode of aggression is licit, its effect is ultimately to weaken the targeted country, which means the activity needs to be countered before the aggressor succeeds in establishing faits accomplis. China's construction of artificial islands in the South China Sea is a good example of the dilemmas involved in countering gray-zone aggression. When China first began building illegal infrastructure in the disputed atolls, the United States and its allies in the region considered the action so minor that trying to prevent the construction was not worth the standoff with China that would inevitably result. This repeated itself at every stage as China continued to build. Today, the construction has yielded artificial islands featuring military installations that change the geopolitical balance in the South China Sea.[27]

Rear Adm. Mark Montgomery (ret.) of the US Navy, who, during part of the period when the islands were built, served as director of operations at US Pacific Command and commander of Carrier Strike Group 5 embarked on the USS *George Washington* stationed in Japan, explained China's construction of the islands.

> It was definitely a campaign of strategic ambiguity. That's a very dangerous path for a major country. You can be operationally

ambiguous, of course, and in fact that's often an advantage. But you shouldn't be strategically ambiguous. The US understands that, and we try not to be strategically opaque.[28]

This is a central point. During an armed conflict, obscuring information vis-à-vis the adversary regarding tactical plans such as troop movements is not only permissible but indeed vital; providing the adversary with knowledge about the plans would render them pointless. Indeed, as the Trojans discovered too late, deception is part of any armed conflict. Writing in the fifth century BC, Sun Tzu advised,

> When able to attack, we must seem unable; when using our forces, we must seem inactive; when we are near, we must make the enemy believe we are far away; when far away, we must make him believe we are near.[29]

In gray-zone aggression, however, deception can also be applied to nonmilitary forms of aggression. Indeed, aggressor countries can—and do—obscure the very nature of their activities. Is a business transaction, a piece of maritime construction, or a diplomat complaining of cognitive fog an inconsequential matter or gray-zone aggression? The targeted country can often only determine much later.

II

2014: A Decisive Year

This book focuses on developments since 2014. Although it may seem like an arbitrary date, observers of geopolitical competition know it is not. While gray-zone aggression took place before 2014, Russia's annexation of Crimea and subsequent war against Ukraine over parts of eastern Ukraine put gray-zone aggression into sharp focus. Russia's war against Ukraine is, of course, not just a gray-zone operation: It is a war. Specifically, it is a hybrid war involving conventional capabilities and irregular tactics and formations, as defined by Frank Hoffman.[1]

In November 2013, Ukrainians started protesting against their government's reversal of its decision to sign an association agreement with the European Union. The government's change of heart was seen as a concession to Russia by President Viktor Yanukovych and was a clear departure from the planned closer cooperation with the European Union. As Patrick Cullen and Erik Reichborn-Kjennerud point out,

> During the period leading up to the conflict the Russians used a combination of political pressure and compensation in the form of cheap gas and loans via the SAPs [synchronized attack packages] to encourage president Yanukovych to abandon the signing of the European Union (EU)–Ukraine Association Agreement.[2]

By early 2014, the protests had expanded, with 100,000 participants in Kyiv and additional protests in other cities. Even though police and security forces used harsh tactics that killed numerous protesters and Yanukovych offered to release arrested protesters and limit presidential power, the government found itself unable to contain the protests.[3]

On February 22, Yanukovych resigned and subsequently fled to Russia; various other government officials likewise left their posts. A provisional government took power and announced its intention to resume

Ukraine's pro-European course. While Crimea's regional government said it would adhere to the new government's policies, members of Crimea's Russian-speaking population organized themselves, sometimes armed, and rebelled against the regional government. On February 27, Russian forces without insignia—soon dubbed "little green men"—occupied Crimea. Following a March referendum that the EU and the United States dismissed as illegal,[4] Crimea acceded to Russia.

The following month, separatists in the Donbas region of eastern Ukraine began protesting for independence; this soon led to skirmishes between the separatist forces and the Ukrainian armed forces. The US Army Special Operations Command notes that

> pro-Russian protesters labeled the Kyiv government as Western fascists and adopted a position that ethnic Russians in Ukraine were in danger. Groups of unidentified armed men began appearing throughout the region, often in coordination with local pro-Russian militias. Both the Ukrainian government and most Western intelligence sources claimed that the "little green men" were Russian operatives.[5]

International media also reported that some militia members were, in fact, Russian soldiers.[6]

However, aggression in the gray zone was insufficient, and Russia resorted to military force, rendering eastern Ukraine a hybrid conflict. Balkan Devlen of the Macdonald-Laurier Institute observed that

> Russian intervention in Donbas in the spring and summer of 2014 went beyond the support for the so-called pro-Russian militias. What turned the tide and prevented a decisive Ukrainian victory in the summer of 2014 was the intervention of regular Russian army troops with heavy armor in the August and September of that year.[7]

The full extent of Russia's involvement in the Donbas region has not yet been fully documented and may never be. Plausible deniability is, of course, a key characteristic of many forms of gray-zone and hybrid aggression. At the time of writing, the conflict between Ukrainian forces and separatists—thought to be aided by Russia—in eastern Ukraine is still ongoing. From January to March 2020, for example, the Organization for Security and Co-operation in Europe's Special Monitoring Mission to Ukraine recorded 60,188 cease-fire violations, 424 weapons in violation of withdrawal lines, 23 casualties, and four fatalities.[8]

Russia's annexation of Crimea and involvement with separatist militias were a dramatic wake-up call for Western governments. It is no exaggeration to say that 2014 forms a demarcation line in Western national security thinking. Despite Russia's 2008 war with Georgia[9] and the crippling cyberattack on Estonia in 2007 that is thought to have originated in Moscow,[10] until 2014 Western governments had preferred to think of Russia as a partner, albeit a flawed one. The events of 2014, however, were so radical that they changed Western policymakers' analyses of their countries' geopolitical realities. Pål Jonson, chairman of the Swedish parliament's defense committee and a member of the center-right Moderate Party, explained that "since 2014, we have had a fundamentally different security environment. We had seen signs before, but in 2014, it became really apparent."[11]

These realizations triggered action: sanctions against Russian businesses and individuals by the EU and the United States,[12] suspension of Russia from the G8, and increased defense spending in nearly all NATO member states[13] and partner countries such as Sweden. NATO established its Enhanced Forward Presence in Estonia, Latvia, Lithuania, and Poland: multinational battle groups intended to help these member states' forces deter Russian military aggression. The alliance also supplemented its existing schedules with new, larger ones such as the 2018 Trident Juncture,[14] and multinational exercises by NATO member states and partners have increased. Defender Europe 2020 was going to be the largest US-led exercise in Europe for a quarter century until the COVID-19 outbreak caused it to be modified.[15] Sweden and Lithuania reintroduced military service using a competitive model similar to ones used in Norway and Denmark.[16]

The most important lesson of 2014 may, however, be completely different: Warfare has morphed. Since World War II, warfare among developed countries has fallen out of fashion.[17] Fighting a war to dominate a country or part of its territory is expensive, and the desired victory adds even more expense and effort. War for territorial conquest is hardly a good investment for a country wishing to strengthen its global or regional position. To raise living standards in Crimea—and thus solidify the population's support of Russia's annexation of the peninsula—Russia has spent considerable sums on infrastructure projects in the region. The 18.1-kilometer Kerch Strait Bridge, which opened in May 2018, cost $3.7 billion to build, and Moscow has also committed sizable amounts to constructing a pipeline supplying natural gas, a new passenger terminal at Simferopol International Airport, and a new highway.[18] In addition to such infrastructure investment expenses, an occupier faces costs associated with administering a territory or country.

The Russo-Ukrainian conflict is thus an exception to the trend toward ever-fewer wars, though a type of exception that clearly cannot be discounted. Russia's government seized Crimea and supported separatists in eastern Ukraine not because it was a preferable choice but because it was, from Russia's perspective, the only one. Other countries may decide in favor of war because they, too, consider it the only option.

Russian gray-zone activities directed against Ukraine, in turn, have immediate relevance for other countries. Indeed, while European countries are still responding to the events in 2014 by increasing spending on their armed forces, the most significant change is instead needed in gray-zone defense. Gray-zone aggression is constantly morphing, but the result is always the same: a disrupted or weakened civil society.

It is therefore illustrative to consider Ukraine's recent experience away from battlefields and little green men. On December 23, 2015, the Ukrainian electricity distribution company Kyivoblenergo was hacked, leaving nearly 250,000 people without power. Ukrainian authorities subsequently attributed the hack to Russia's security services.[19] The following year, hackers—who were subsequently traced to the Russian government—struck Ukrenergo, Ukraine's national grid operator. The attack, more devastating than the one in December 2015, caused a blackout in much of Kyiv.[20] The cyberattacks have since continued and become more sophisticated.

Russia has also directed a continuing stream of disinformation against Ukraine. RT, a television and online news outlet operated by the Russian government, has repeatedly spread misinformation about Ukraine—for example, linking it to the downing of Malaysian Airlines Flight 17 traveling from Amsterdam to Kuala Lumpur in July 2014.[21] In June 2020, Dutch prosecutors charged three Russians and a Ukrainian—who were linked to separatist militias in eastern Ukraine—in connection with the downing.[22] In 2015, a report by the NATO Strategic Communications Centre of Excellence in Riga, Latvia, noted that

> whilst reporting on Ukraine events, journalists of the Russian state controlled media have methodically manipulated video and photo materials in order to produce material visually supporting the prevailing narrative. This includes the use of photographs from the Syria, Kosovo and Chechnya wars, as if they had been taken in East Ukraine, and has proven particularly effective on social networks.[23]

In news interviews, Russian media featured individuals who were incorrectly described as Ukrainian residents; all supported a Russian narrative. The Strategic Communications Centre of Excellence report notes, for example, that "the same woman was used to play the roles of 'Crimean activist', 'resident of Kyiv', 'soldier's mother', 'resident of Odessa', 'resident of Kharkiv', 'participant of Antimaidan', and 'refugee from Donetsk.'"[24]

Even before Russia's annexation of Crimea, Western countries had been targets of disinformation and cyberattacks by not just Russia but also China, Iran, and North Korea. The cyberattack on Estonia in 2007—which was certainly a gray-zone magnum opus, hitting Estonia's presidency, parliament, nearly all government ministries, political parties, news media, and banks[25]—prompted Estonia to radically improve its cyber defense.

But other Western countries did not take decisive action until 2014 or even later. Paradoxically, as many of them now energetically try to improve their defense against cyberattacks and disinformation, other forms of gray-zone aggression are increasing. "With war, if you don't try it, you can't know how it will turn out," Gen. Hideki Tojo—Japan's prime minister during most of World War II—is reported to have said.[26] Today, countries can try doing a little aggression below the threshold of war and see what works, and the targeted country may not even know the aggression is happening or who the aggressor is.

The governments of China, Iran, Russia, and other countries allege that Western states, too, target their countries in the gray zone.[27] Iran could, for example, argue that the United States' assassination of Maj. Gen. Qassem Soleimani in January 2020[28] constitutes gray-zone aggression. Although such Western actions deserve scrutiny, the focus of this book is aggression against Western countries by hostile states and their proxies—and how to deter it. As Ukrainians discovered in 2014, an adversary is likely to keep innovating, leaving the targeted country constantly struggling to defend itself.

III

Gray-Zone Aggression, a National Security Threat

At the time of writing, countries worldwide are still reeling from the COVID-19 pandemic. Nearly one and a half years after the virus first appeared in noticeable case numbers outside China, it has claimed around 4.5 million lives. While some countries in Africa and Asia are painfully acquainted with previous 21st-century epidemics and pandemics, for Western countries, COVID-19 brought a highly uncomfortable realization: Countries can be severely weakened by events that involve no sustained use of military force.

"COVID-19 has reminded us that security threats and tests of national resilience can take many forms," UK Prime Minister Boris Johnson observed in his foreword to the country's March 2021 national strategy, *Global Britain in a Competitive Age: The Integrated Review of Security, Defence, Development and Foreign Policy*.[1] Although the virus appears to have been created by Mother Nature and spread on its own, not through the malice of a hostile government, it nonetheless achieved the same effect as do many forms of gray-zone aggression: colossal disruption. Thanks to its ability to disrupt, undermine, and weaken daily life, gray-zone aggression has, in fact, replaced conventional military conflict as the most urgent national security threat facing liberal democracies' societies today.

Governments have long been aware of the damage nonmilitary crises can cause. The UK government's 2017 national risk register, for example, highlighted pandemic flu, noting that

> consequences may include . . . up to 50% of the UK population experiencing symptoms, potentially leading to between 20,000 and 750,000 fatalities and high levels of absence from work. . . . Disruption to essential services, particularly health

and education; and economic disruption, including disruption to business and tourism.² (Emphasis omitted.)

In 2016, the UK government conducted a pandemic flu exercise set in week seven of an outbreak that, without government intervention, was estimated to kill 200,000–400,000 people.³ When COVID-19 struck, however, the UK government failed to respond decisively. By early 2021, the country reached 100,000 deaths.

Governments have long been aware that, in war, an adversary can target another country's civilian population with tools from propaganda to blockades—and indeed Trojan horses. Many governments, including democratic ones, have themselves engaged in such activity and trained their citizens for such activities by other countries. During World War II, Allied, Axis, and neutral governments alike conducted constant public awareness campaigns to keep their populations vigilant against foreign infiltration and prepared for the disruption bombing raids inflicted.

Today, however, no Western country is experiencing war on its home soil.⁴ Yet all are targeted by gray-zone aggression. This, in a sense, could have been expected. While war-based competition among industrialized countries has faded, other means of competition have often replaced it. The rule-based international order, however, lacks the structure to sufficiently punish bad behavior. While offenders may suffer damage to their reputations, it will not cause a behavioral change if having a poor reputation does not trouble them.

This is certainly the case with China and Russia. In February 2021, China banned BBC World News from broadcasting in the country,⁵ while Russia sentenced the opposition activist Alexey Navalny to prison immediately after he returned from Germany, where he had been treated for a near-lethal poisoning reportedly ordered by the Russian government.⁶ Iran and North Korea are not concerned about damage to their international standings caused by their detention of Westerners. With the international community, alliances, and individual countries lacking structures to punish bad behavior, countries targeted by gray-zone aggression are highly vulnerable.

Maj. Gen. Ed Wilson (ret.) of the US Air Force, deputy assistant secretary of defense for cyber policy in the Donald Trump administration, observed,

> One of our challenges is that the threat is diverse and blending. It's typically associated with revenue-generating individuals, organized crime, hostile states, or a combination of actors and motivations. On the nation-state side, I've seen IP [intellectual property] theft by China across all economic sectors. In the area of disinformation campaigns, Russia is the best in the world. They target institutions of traditional stability and harm people's trust in those institutions.
>
> During the Cold War, the private sector was not attacked very often. That has changed. Today the private sector is frequently attacked, not least because it owns more assets than it used to. What we're seeing is horizontal escalation.[7]

Horizontal escalation, of course, means that the escalation may not even be perceptible to the attacked side. Chris Inglis, a member of the US Cyberspace Solarium Commission and former deputy director of the US National Security Agency, noted that "the cyber aggression has come on with sufficient slowness and subtlety that it has barely registered."[8] Since this interview, Inglis has been appointed the US government's first national cyber director.

Sometimes gray-zone aggression is so subtle that some might argue it is simply part of the tussle in a globalized world. But Giedrimas Jeglinskas, NATO's assistant secretary-general for executive management and a former vice minister of defense of Lithuania, argued that, taken together, gray-zone aggression is as concerning as the traditional kind is, and "when you weave all the elements together, we get a picture that is radically different from that of a typical aggression."[9] Canadian Security and Intelligence Service Director David Vigneault made a similar observation during a presentation in February 2021. Describing China as a "significant danger to Canada's prosperity and sovereignty," he said that the Chinese government "is pursuing a strategy for geopolitical advantage on all fronts—economic, technological, political, and military—and using all elements of state power to carry out activities that are a direct threat to our national security and sovereignty."[10] As previously mentioned, Erik Reichborn-Kjennerud and Patrick Cullen observed in 2016 that "while the West is largely stuck in an instrumentalist, technicist, battle-centric and kinetic understanding of war, its opponents have been busy redefining war."[11] Regrettably, little has changed since then.

China, Russia, and other countries could (and do) also engage in "whataboutism," labeling Western activities relating to their countries as surreptitious. That makes it even harder for the West to conclusively identify, call out, and respond to gray-zone aggression. A senior executive in the Finnish critical national infrastructure (CNI) sector who is also a former senior officer in the Finnish Defence Forces (FDF) explained,

> Several years ago, we did a study at the [Finnish] MOD [Ministry of Defence] about aggression against Finland and identified political pressure, airspace violations, and fake news, including social media and fake bogus claims. We began educating government officials, about 2,000 of them. But political decision makers are uneasy about tackling this issue. They want to have clear-cut things on the table.[12]

Indeed, gray-zone aggression could be called geopolitical gaslighting. While the targeted country's government—and often businesses and ordinary citizens—may notice that something is not right, identifying it as an aggressive act by another country is difficult. The other country, meanwhile, can downplay the targeted country's unease and suggest the country is being paranoid.

The Swedish Security Service, which is in charge of counterintelligence, reported in 2020 on what the reality of a targeted country looks like.

> Around 15 countries currently conduct different forms of espionage against Sweden along with other activities that constitute a threat to Sweden. Russia, China, and Iran constitute the biggest threats. The regimes in these states have as their objective to, in addition to create stability for themselves, strengthen their respective country's status as an economic, political and military major power. Russia, China, and Iran also engage in intelligence activity that constitute a threat to individuals' life and health.[13]

In January 2021, the Netherlands' National Coordinator for Counterterrorism and Security Pieter-Jaap Aalbersberg presented a similar picture: "State actors are focusing on an increasing number of different areas. They not only look at the classic targets, such as the national government and companies within the vital infrastructure, they look broader."[14] His fellow Dutchman Erik Brandsma—who has spent most of his career in Sweden, was at the time of the interview CEO of the regional utility Jämtkraft, and served as director general of Sweden's energy agency, Energimyndigheten—stressed the West's lack of preparation for gray-zone aggression until 2014.

> Until Russia's actions in Ukraine, there was a naiveté about the kind of security we needed. Today there are much clearer responsibilities. There's also better cooperation between the government and the private sector, whereas five years ago there was virtually none. The government and the private sector lived in two different worlds. Also, pre-2014 most parts of society didn't want to have discussions about preparedness.[15]

The interviews in this book cover a range of countries and sectors. Despite this variety, the blended nature of gray-zone aggression stands out as a common theme. This blend can at any given time comprise one or more elements of licit or illicit methods to weaken the targeted country, often with the associated objective of benefiting the aggressor country. The CEO of a major European telecommunications infrastructure company, for example, pointed out that

> the methods of gray-zone cyberattacks are becoming more and more sophisticated. In the past, you had to click on a link in order to inadvertently trigger cyber intrusion; now simply receiving the email is enough.
>
> Our home country is one of the world's most connected countries, measured in the number of people connected to the internet. That also makes us a country where criminals and hostile states first test their attacks.[16]

For all the similarities, though, there are also clear differences. In the Baltic states, there is considerable concern regarding Russian subversive actions in key sectors such as energy. Jeglinskas explained that

> Russia's attempts to keep the lid on the energy market, either through support of the Astravets nuclear plant buildup by Belarus or the construction of Nord Stream 2, are the most obvious form of pressure on Lithuania. Our dependency on Russia for energy sources is a vulnerability, but it can be resolved.[17]

Dominykas Tučkus, at the time of the interview director of infrastructure and development for the Lithuanian energy company Ignitis Group, provided an illuminating account of the reality of leading a company in the intersection between pure business and gray-zone aggression. His comments are worth quoting at length.

> We've experienced cyberattacks focused mostly on the interface with our clients. Nobody was able to pinpoint where the attacks originated, but we're a state-owned company, and other Lithuanian companies were attacked at the same time as us, so from the context, we could tell that the attacks originated with Russia.
> Overall, though, the situation in the energy sector is better today than it was until December 2014, when Lithuania's LNG [liquefied natural gas] terminal was inaugurated. It means that Gazprom is not our sole gas supplier anymore. In fact, the situation has changed completely. There's fierce competition between Gazprom and LNG suppliers, mostly from the US. We're not at risk of being exploited by unfair pricing anymore.
> In electricity, it's a different situation, though. Rosatom [the Russian electricity giant] is constructing a new nuclear power plant 50 kilometers from Vilnius [the Lithuanian capital]. From a technical point of view, the location is odd. There are better sites for such a plant farther from the Lithuanian border.
> In addition, they're undercutting us by offering very cheap electricity. They can produce it very cheaply because they don't have to follow EU safety standards and don't have to pay the

CO_2 [carbon dioxide] levy that EU companies have to pay. That, in combination with the Russians selling natural gas below market prices, means that Lithuanian energy providers struggle to compete. They'd probably say they're competitive because they're not paying taxes, while we think CO_2 levies encourage CO_2 reduction, which is a good thing. Either way, Russia and also Belarus don't apply the same environmental standards to their energy production, so the reality is that they can undercut our energy generators.

When it comes to power generation, the Russians' objective is to dominate the industry, be it through gas or through electricity generation. That could come in handy as a political instrument as well. Russian and Belarusian companies undercut our prices, which weakens our energy companies and could force them out of business. That would obviously make us more dependent on Russian and Belarusian providers. It's hard to prove that they're doing this to weaken the Baltic states, but that's the effect.

We've appealed to the European Commission, suggesting that the EU should impose an equalizer tax equivalent to the CO_2 levy on energy imports from outside the EU. That would make Russian and Belarusian energy less cheap and help us compete on a more level playing field. The Lithuanian government is also trying to bring attention to the CO_2 levies within the EU, but it's not going very well. We're a small country at the edge of the EU, and other EU member states are less connected to Russian energy, so the issue doesn't concern them as much. It's mostly the Baltic states that face this problem, as well as, to a lesser extent, Finland and Hungary.

We're also very concerned about Russian and Belarusian safety standards. If there were an accident in the nuclear power plant they're building near our border, Lithuania would obviously be seriously exposed to the radiation. We can see the Belarusian nuclear power plant from Vilnius high-rise buildings. The fact that they don't pay a CO_2 levy means they're causing more harm to the environment, and as discussed, to our energy companies as well.[18]

Does dirty energy from a strategic rival that undercuts cleaner domestic energy constitute gray-zone aggression? Or is it simply international business as usual? How about exposing a neighbor to potentially catastrophic radiation by building a nuclear power plant close to the border? Such questions illustrate the elusive nature of gray-zone aggression and how easily targeted countries can be gaslighted.

In spring and summer 2021, Lithuania was targeted by a string of activities by Belarus that unequivocally constitute gray-zone aggression. On May 23, Belarusian air traffic control— alleging it had received a bomb threat—instructed a Ryanair flight that was in Belarusian airspace en route from Athens to Vilnius to divert to Minsk, the Belarusian capital. A Belarusian fighter jet escorted the passenger airliner, which landed in Minsk, where no bomb was found on board. However, Belarusian authorities seized Belarusian opposition blogger Roman Protasevich and his Russian girlfriend, Sofia Sapega, whereupon the other passengers were allowed to continue to Vilnius.[19] Protasevich was living in Poland but frequently visiting Vilnius, where many Belarusian opposition members—including 2020 presidential candidate Sviatlana Tsikhanouskaya—are based.

The Lithuanian government responded to Belarus' unprecedented act of aviation piracy by banning inbound and outbound flights from using Belarusian airspace. The European Union and the UK responded similarly. Belarus' president, Alexander Lukashenko, in turn threatened to flood Europe with "migrants and drugs"[20]—not an empty threat given Belarus' extensive land border with Lithuania.

The following month, Canada, the EU, the UK, and the US imposed coordinated sanctions on key Belarusian politicians.[21] Belarus escalated, implementing Lukashenko's threat. By July 1, 672 people—mostly claiming to be Iraqis—had tried to illegally enter Lithuania from Belarus. That compares to 81 undocumented migrants entering Lithuania from Belarus in 2020 and 46 in 2019.[22] This prompted Lithuania to call for assistance from the EU's external border force, Frontex, which normally patrols the EU's southern border. By July 7, another 779 undocumented migrants had crossed the Belarus-Lithuania border.[23] Independent news outlets found that the Belarusian government was arranging for Iraqis to travel from Baghdad to Minsk by quickly issuing them tourist visas.[24]

In the Baltic states, the proximity of Russian and NATO forces is not a matter of gray-zone aggression but must briefly be highlighted as it is an undeniable national security concern. Jeglinskas stressed that Lithuania's proximity to Kaliningrad, Russia, "the most militarized district in the world, can only be managed through cooperation with our NATO and EU partners and building up the basic level of deterrence with capabilities, pre-positioned defense assets, and on-the-ground allied troop presence."[25]

NATO's activities in the Baltic states demonstrate an important reality: In analyzing gray-zone and conventional aggression, it is imperative to try to view activities from the other side's perspective. In many cases, activities that seem aggressive to the West are seen by the West's rivals as simply a response to actions the West considers entirely defensive and commonsense. It does not mean that the West's rivals' assessments are sincere or correct, and it certainly does not mean that the targeted country and its allies should tolerate the activities. Nevertheless, viewing actions from the other side's perspective helps build a better understanding of rivals' motivations. I discuss this further in Chapter VIII.

The 2018 US National Defense Strategy highlights the reality of blended gray-zone aggression.

> In competition short of armed conflict, revisionist powers and rogue regimes are using corruption, predatory economic practices, propaganda, political subversion, proxies, and the threat or use of military force to change facts on the ground. Some are particularly adept at exploiting their economic relationships with many of our security partners. We will support U.S. interagency approaches and work by, with, and through our allies and partners to secure our interests and counteract this coercion.[26]

The UK MOD's Development, Concepts and Doctrine Centre (DCDC) makes a similar point in a 2019 joint doctrine note.

> Threats to UK security may come in any form, from any sector and may impact on an entirely different sector. They may be economic, political, societal or military in nature; they may originate from the cyber or space domains and they may

GRAY-ZONE AGGRESSION, A NATIONAL SECURITY THREAT   35

involve the competition for information superiority. Two examples could be:

- a threat that impacts on global positioning systems . . . or communications satellites would have a major effect across the whole globe; or
- in the UK, a threat to the energy industry (for example, electricity supply) would impact on all aspects of society.[27]

Gray-zone aggression is made easier because it can be conducted by state actors and proxies alike and because daily life in liberal democracies—which are often also advanced economies—offers considerable opportunities for such aggression. As DCDC notes,

> Technology-enabled globalisation has caused supply chains, communications networks and social awareness to become highly complex. Second and third order effects may be magnified, even if they are not immediately apparent or understood. Stakeholders are more numerous, feel a greater sense of empowerment and are not necessarily bound by traditional (and predictable) conventions of statehood.[28]

In most Western countries, large parts of CNI are no longer government owned, which compounds the challenge. Telecommunications companies, railways, airlines, airports, water utilities, and other CNI providers have, to different extents, been privatized, which has undoubtedly contributed to better service and more choice for consumers. It does, however, make society more vulnerable to hostile acts: As private companies' first responsibility is to their customers and shareholders, investing in resilience and backup plans has until now not been a priority. There is also little legislation in place to compel businesses to prepare for contingencies short of war.[29]

The ransomware attack against Colonial Pipeline in 2021, which left large parts of the US East Coast struggling to find gasoline, dramatically illustrated this state of affairs. In February 2021, Texans likewise experienced how seriously gray-zone aggression could affect them and others.

An unexpected cold freeze disabled power plants, forcing energy companies to slash production to avoid monthslong blackouts. Millions of residents were left without power.[30] While Mother Nature caused the Texan disruption, the attacks against Colonial Pipeline and the meat-processing giant JBS demonstrate how hostile actors can cause similar harm.

The lack of legislation is understandable, given that it is unclear how such legislation should be designed without disadvantaging the companies it covers vis-à-vis their competitors, including foreign ones. Nevertheless, the lack of cooperation between government and companies in a range of essential sectors presents a vulnerability that even NATO Secretary-General Jens Stoltenberg felt compelled to articulate: "For large operations, around 90% of military transport relies on civilian ships, railways and aircraft."[31]

In addition, since the end of the Cold War, new sectors have emerged that today must be considered CNI: internet, mobile telephony, and even social media platforms. At the time of writing, there is virtually no consensus on what these sectors' obligation to national resilience should be and how any legislation should be designed.[32] Social media in particular dovetails with the gray-zone area of disinformation. Indeed, disinformation can be used in combination with every other form of gray-zone aggression.

Dependency on foreign supplies and global supply chains, too, has increased over the past three decades as globalization has accelerated. The United States, for example, imports 95 percent of coffee and fish products and about half of fresh fruits.[33] Of pharmaceuticals sold in the United States, 80 percent are produced in China. Indeed, China is also the largest supplier of medical devices used in the United States.[34] But finished products are only one small part of global trade: Components provided and added by first-, second-, and sometimes third-tier suppliers form a much larger part. Products often cross many borders during the assembly process, an arrangement that works well when there is no disruption.

The West is not alone in such dependency on imports; virtually every country has been pursuing globalization as a strategy toward more prosperity. Nevertheless, global supply chains pose a particular vulnerability to the West, as its rivals may be willing to disrupt supply chains in a way that a liberal democracy would not.[35] The supply chains include everything from footwear to sophisticated technology. In Europe, for example, as of

February 2021, 44 percent of mobile telephony travels via equipment of which 40 percent is made by Huawei.[36]

Identifying a problem is only the first step. The final chapters of this book outline strategies Western governments—in cooperation with their private sectors and wider civil societies—can adopt to better protect their countries. Precisely because gray-zone aggression is so elusive and because too forceful a response could cause escalation, strategies must deter the aggression without creating a gray-zone arms race or a gray-zone equivalent of mutually assured destruction, which would dangerously harm the constant interaction among countries on which today's prosperity is based.

The goal of these deterrence efforts, involving all parts of society, should be to create a combined shield against gray-zone aggression that can appear in any combination. "We need to talk about these issues more widely, educate our kids about them. The holistic view is key," the Finnish executive and former FDF officer said.[37] Educating youth about gray-zone aggression is not as flippant as it sounds. Indeed, considering that celebrities who teenagers look up to may be sponsored by companies that work with hostile governments and considering that the services ordinary citizens take for granted may be disrupted by a hostile state or its proxies, gray-zone aggression is a reality every member of a Western society should be aware of. It can directly affect their lives in a way conventional warfare is unlikely to do, precisely because conventional wars are unlikely to occur on Western soil.

Today, however, liberal democracies' weaknesses practically invite the West's adversaries to not just engage in aggression but also develop new forms of aggression. Just like countries throughout history that have decided to launch conventional military attacks, countries engage in gray-zone aggression because they consider it a rational choice, one from which they expect a bottom-line gain. The following chapters analyze selected forms of this aggression.

IV

Is Sponsorship an Act of Aggression? Use of Licit Means in the Gray Zone

On August 4, 2020, the Swedish pop star Zara Larsson told a TV program that she had ended her sponsorship deal with Huawei.[1] "From a professional and also a personal perspective it was not the smartest deal I've done in my career. We know that the Chinese state is not a nice state. I don't want to support what they do," Larsson added. The singer, who has a large following in Sweden and abroad, had come under increasing scrutiny over her sponsorship deal with Huawei,[2] and she realized the deal made her appear to be a tool of the Chinese government. Sponsorship deals with Western artists and top athletes are legal and common even when the companies involved pose national security concerns. Yet, like many other legal practices, they can be used in gray-zone aggression.

Unlike high-profile attacks such as Russia's 2017 NotPetya cyberattack on Ukraine, gray-zone aggression using legal means takes place without many people noticing—because it looks like daily life in a liberal democracy. Liberal democracies, in effect, unwittingly host activities designed to weaken or undermine them. While some forms of this aggression—such as sponsorships between Western celebrities and firms linked to hostile regimes—may seem largely innocuous, other forms—such as takeovers of the West's most cutting-edge firms—may look more like aggression. All are, however, legal and used in combination with illegal forms of aggression to create a soup with constantly changing ingredients.

In its list of types of gray-zone aggression, the NATO Strategic Communications Centre of Excellence includes several forms that could be considered legal:

- Nongovernmental organizations,
- Government-organized nongovernmental organizations,
- Exploitation of ethnic or cultural identities,

- Media,
- Agitation and civil unrest,
- Religious groups,
- Academic groups,
- Energy dependency, and
- Political actors.[3]

Some of these categories, especially support of religious groups, academic groups, media, and political actors, can also be conducted outside the gray zone as entirely legitimate activities. This is certainly how Western governments and organizations view their support of human rights groups, pro-democracy news outlets, and academics in emerging democracies. The regimes in those countries may perceive the activities as interference—that is, gray-zone aggression.

Either way, in the West it is often legal for foreign entities to financially support nongovernmental organizations or even political parties; it is also legal to acquire the vast majority of companies (though this is changing) and sponsor celebrities. Indeed, precisely because liberal democracies are open societies, they offer myriad opportunities for hostile regimes—sometimes aided by proxies—to engage in gray-zone aggression without violating any laws. As a result of the West's increasing focus on digital threats—especially cyberattacks and online disinformation—it is easy to underestimate the effect of slow-moving analogue threats.

Sometimes it is even unclear whether gray-zone aggression is taking place. It is, for example, difficult to discern when Russian and Chinese friendship societies are completely benign and when they pose a concern. The same is true for activities by China's Confucius Institutes,[4] which offer language classes like the British Council and Germany's Goethe-Institut do, but are also thought to censor their Western academic partners.[5] In addition, "China offers attractive courses for Baltic and Western students in general, to attract them to Chinese universities," notes Vytautas Leškevičius, a Lithuanian former ambassador to NATO.[6]

This, again, highlights the difficulty in identifying gray-zone aggression, as Western countries have for decades offered precisely the same opportunities through academic exchange programs (but with less government involvement). So does Moscow's use of so-called Moscow Houses, cultural and business centers in foreign capitals. "They're supposed to be for cultural exchange, but we have our thoughts on what they're really for," Leškevičius notes.[7] In Vilnius, Lithuania, the construction of a Moscow House has been delayed multiple times over national security concerns.[8]

Performances by artists from hostile countries pose yet another challenge. While such visits are welcome on an artistic basis, some Western countries are concerned that the artists will use their visits for propaganda purposes, as has been the case with Venezuela's Simón Bolívar Youth Orchestra (now Simón Bolívar Symphony Orchestra). Yet artistic links can offer opportunities for diplomacy during otherwise frozen periods; this was the case during the Cold War.

There are, in fact, unlimited ways an adversary could undermine liberal democracies using only legal means. While Russia and China are best equipped with intent and capability, as long as target countries unwittingly offer the opportunity, other countries may also use it. This chapter highlights one less-discussed and one much-discussed opportunity. Chapters V and VI discuss in detail selected forms of gray-zone aggression using legal means.

Sponsorship of Western Artists and Athletes

Before canceling her sponsorship deal, Larsson had been criticized for staying silent on Huawei's involvement with authorities in the Xinjiang region—home to some 12 million Uyghurs, a minority ethnic group—while giving the firm and thus the Chinese government a presentable face in Sweden.[9] In December 2020, French soccer star Antoine Griezmann followed Larsson in canceling his sponsorship deal with Huawei, similarly citing the firm's involvement in government surveillance of Uyghurs.[10] That same month, Western news media reported that the telecoms giant—alongside Chinese facial recognition specialist Megvii—was developing a "Uyghur alert" in its facial recognition software capable of determining ethnicity as part of its "face attribute analysis."[11]

Two months before, Sweden's Post and Telecom Authority had announced it would exclude Huawei from its 5G auction on national security grounds.[12] In doing so, it made the same decision as other Western countries did, including the UK and Poland. This led to forceful calls from Chinese officials for Sweden to reverse its decision and explicit threats of consequences if it did not.[13] A globally active business, forcefully backed by its home government but considered a national security concern by the governments of other countries, can legally sponsor artists and athletes in these very countries, thus making its brand attractive among those countries' consumers. This illustrates the reality of gray-zone aggression and the reason it is easy for perpetrators to gaslight targeted countries.[14]

China's ambassador to Sweden, meanwhile, has given interviews to Swedish news outlets that can only be described as bullying.[15] In May 2021, Chinese media reported that Beijing would give Sweden "one last chance" before Ericsson would take a hit in China.[16] When Ericsson presented its quarterly report two months later, worldwide sales were up—except in China, where they had declined.[17]

Sponsorship deals do not have to be part of gray-zone aggression; most often they are not. The UK's Premier League is a good example. At the time of writing, Adidas (a German firm) sponsors seven soccer teams' kits, Nike (a US firm) and Puma (another German firm) each sponsor four teams' kits, and Danish firm Hummel, Italian firm Kappa, and US firm Under Armour each sponsor one team's kit.[18] The league's shirt sponsors include Emirates and Etihad Airways (both based in the United Arab Emirates), Chevrolet, King Power and Tourism Authority of Thailand (both based in Thailand), and sundry betting firms based in countries such as Malta and the Philippines. This clearly does not mean Malta, the United States, or the Philippines is engaging in gray-zone aggression against the UK.

Huawei, meanwhile, for many years sponsored Australia's Canberra Raiders, the only National Rugby League team in the country's capital.[19] Huawei ended the contract in 2020, citing that "the business environment in Australia is very hard for a Chinese company."[20] Nord Stream, the energy consortium majority-owned by Russia's Gazprom, sponsors an elite women's volleyball team in the German state of Mecklenburg–Western Pomerania, where the Nord Stream 2 pipeline will come ashore, and the European Handball Federation's (men's) Champions League.[21] In its most benevolent form, sponsorship is used for image promotion, but as the deals mentioned above illustrate, it is difficult to draw the line between sponsorship as image promotion and part of geopolitics.

Indeed, celebrity sponsorship can be used to influence another country's public to help undermine that country's freedom of action. In addition to, for example, soccer sponsorships of the Champions League, the Saint Petersburg–based Zenit team in Russia, and the Bundesliga team Schalke 04 in Germany,[22] Gazprom also sponsors Serbia's Red Star (Crvena Zvezda) team. It signed the deal with Red Star when Russia was trying to get Serbia's permission to route the South Stream pipeline through the country.[23]

Larsson and Griezmann canceled their deals with Huawei over Uyghur concerns, but many other celebrities maintain their contracts with Huawei and other firms connected to hostile regimes, as is their right. Indeed, there is no guarantee that celebrities will cancel sponsorship deals over ethical or national security concerns. As geopolitical confrontation increases, artists and athletes with their large fan bases could thus increasingly be used to undermine the standing of their home countries—that is, used as a tool of gray-zone aggression.

Disinformation

Although disinformation ("fake news") is not listed separately, it is part of many of the entries on the Strategic Communications Centre of Excellence's list[24] and qualifies as legal because most liberal democracies interpret individuals' freedom of speech liberally. Disinformation has, for example, been used by Russia in the 2016 US presidential election campaign,[25] the UK's 2016 Brexit referendum campaign,[26] and France's 2017 presidential election campaign.[27]

While elections present an attractive target, disinformation never completely subsides; it is, in fact, an age-old tool of geopolitical competition. The Achaeans placing their wooden horse in front of Troy's city walls was disinformation, leading the Trojans to believe their enemy had surrendered. Deception, spread by both sides to deceive the public, later became a mainstay of conflicts. During the Cold War, it was further professionalized. Writing in the *American Journal of International Law* in 1951, John Whitton noted that coincident with the outbreak of the "cold war" the Soviet Union began a series of propagandistic attacks on the United States, its leaders and its policies, using every medium of communication for this purpose, but with special emphasis on radio propaganda. For some time the United States Government suffered these attacks to go unanswered, but in February, 1947, the "Voice of America" began to include among its other foreign programs regular broadcasts in Russian to the Soviet Union. At first these programs were confined almost entirely to music and straight news reports, but gradually more and more time was devoted to answering Soviet attacks.[28]

The situation today magnifies the disinformation opportunities available during the Cold War, not to mention preceding centuries. The ease of information access—especially the un-vetted information disseminated on social media—provides hostile states with enormous opportunities to sow discord in the targeted country, and the disinformation can seize on any subject. In *Industrialized Disinformation: 2020 Global Inventory of Organized Social Media Manipulation*, the Oxford Internet Institute at the University of Oxford reported that activity by cyber troops (which it defines as "government or political party actors tasked with manipulating public opinion online"[29]) continues to increase. The researchers documented cyber troops that use social media to spread propaganda and disinformation about politics in 81 countries, up from 70 countries in their 2019 version of the report. They also identified 48 private firms providing such services, up from 25 in 2019.[30]

The Cold War's organized disinformation has, in a sense, turned into an opportunistic battle in which the least scrupulous participants have a distinct advantage. When Western researchers, at the end of 2020, appeared close to a breakthrough in developing a coronavirus vaccine, Russian news media began publishing stories relating to the pharmaceutical firm AstraZeneca's vaccine development. So did Chinese news outlets. In an April 2021 report, the European Commission highlighted these efforts, noting that

> Russia and China, in particular, continue to intensively promote their own state-produced vaccines around the world. The

so-called "vaccine diplomacy" follows a zero-sum game logic and is combined with disinformation and manipulation efforts to *undermine trust in Western-made vaccines, EU institutions and Western/European vaccination strategies*. Both Russia and China are using state-controlled media, networks of proxy media outlets and social media, including official diplomatic social media accounts, to achieve these goals.[31] (Emphasis in original.)

The 2020 US presidential election is, of course, the most noteworthy example of that. Although it is unclear to what extent hostile powers contributed to the disinformation and misinformation that convinced several thousand Americans to storm the Capitol on January 6, 2021, to prevent what they considered the ratification of a fraudulent election, that information was clearly effective. While the rioters failed to prevent the ratification of Joe Biden as the winner of the 2020 presidential election, they succeeded in soiling America's reputation as a bastion of democracy.

Few newsworthy developments, even those far less significant than a US presidential election, escape attempts at distortion through disinformation. In November 2020—after an Australian investigation established that Australian special forces soldiers had committed crimes against Afghan civilians—Chinese Foreign Ministry spokesman Zhao Lijian tweeted a fake image showing an Australian soldier killing an Afghan child. Despite worldwide condemnation of the fake image, the Foreign Ministry refused to apologize, instead upping its criticism of Australian soldiers' actions in Afghanistan.[32]

Following the discovery of Russia's disinformation campaign during the 2016 US presidential election campaign, the US Senate Select Committee on Intelligence conducted an extensive inquiry into the matter. In August 2020, the committee released its fifth and final report.[33] Before that, following a two-year investigation into alleged collusion between Russia and the Donald Trump campaign during the 2016 presidential election, Robert Mueller—an independent counsel appointed by Congress—delivered a report to Congress. While Mueller found that Russia had tried to influence the election campaign, he could not establish whether Trump had committed a crime.[34]

Russia's use of social media during the campaign is the focus of the committee's second report. The committee notes,

> Masquerading as Americans, [Russian] operatives used targeted advertisements, intentionally falsified news articles, self-generated content, and social media platform tools to interact with and attempt to deceive tens of millions of social media users in the United States. This campaign sought to polarize Americans on the basis of societal, ideological, and racial differences, provoked real world events, and was part of a foreign government's covert support of Russia's favored candidate in the U.S. presidential election.[35]

The 2016 disinformation campaign was so successful partly because Americans had become accustomed to a historically rare lull in disinformation. The re-independent Baltic states are, in turn, a bellwether in identifying disinformation. Speaking of his country's experience, Jānis Garisons, state secretary in Latvia's Ministry of Defence, pointed out that Latvians

> were already used to malign interference in our internal affairs. We first started noticing interference in our information space in 2007, but is has really been around since our re-independence in 1991. So in 2014, when the rest of the world began noticing the practice, we had not only acknowledged it but done something about it.
> *Information warfare has been around throughout history; it's just the technology that has changed.* The West always thought technology could be used for good—for example, democracy—but they didn't realize it could be used against us—for example, to manipulate public opinion.[36] (Emphasis added.)

It is vital for targeted governments to appreciate that disinformation is not a phenomenon limited to today's Russia, China, and perhaps Iran and North Korea, but that it is, in fact, a constant companion of international relations.

Mindaugas Ubartas, a serial entrepreneur who leads Infobalt, Lithuania's information and communication technology industry association, pointed out that Lithuania is constantly exposed to fake news, hacking, spreading of negative opinions—for example, suggestions that Lithuanian democracy is broken, that NATO is broken. For example, a Lithuanian bank went bankrupt . . . and the owner escaped to London. He was subsequently extradited to Lithuania but then fled to Russia. Then a newspaper published an interview with his wife, who claimed that they had lost everything and couldn't afford to eat. That was not true, but the story managed to make Lithuania look chaotic.[37]

Disinformation can be used opportunistically wherever it is deployed, such as in the debate over whether Russia's objective in the 2016 disinformation campaign was to help get Trump elected or simply to sow doubt among Americans regarding a pillar of their democracy. Exploiting citizens' doubts about their democratic systems is, of course, easy in liberal democracies, in which dirty laundry ranging from politicians' misdeeds to unaddressed societal concerns is washed in public.

Ubartas added,

When there was a survey showing that a low percentage of Germans were willing to defend newer NATO member states, that news was used to weaken Lithuanian politicians who want to strengthen defense. Russian news outlets also write or broadcast about Lithuanian Nazi collaborators in their propaganda. That, again, is to show that independence has been a mistake.[38]

Since NATO decided in 2014 to form its Enhanced Forward Presence in the Baltic states and Poland, the battle groups have, like the countries themselves, become targets of Russian disinformation.[39]

In fact, former Warsaw Pact members such as the Baltic states and Poland have long been alert to Russian disinformation in a way that western European countries and especially the United States have not. Ojārs Kalniņš, a member of parliament for Latvia's center-right New Unity party and vice chair of the foreign affairs committee, observed,

What's clear here in Europe is that Russia is undermining our countries by financing radical parties that are sometimes anti-NATO and certainly anti-EU. We're hearing domestic voices in our countries parroting Russian talking points. Here in the Baltic states, we're very aware of who's undermining our democratic order, but in other countries, that's not so. RT [the Russian government-funded outlet formerly known as Russia Today] employs locals as reporters and presenters, native speakers of the respective language, and there are what you might call fake think tanks, outfits that essentially operate as front organizations for Russia. This is an area where the Balts have to educate our friends in western Europe. Russia has been trying to influence our elections for 30 years.[40]

Part of the problem, Ubartas said, is that "journalism in digital media is not about quality but about quantity. The message Russia is sending, with the help of communications channels that are more about quantity than quality, is that democracy is fucked up."[41] Since the interviews with Ubartas, his analysis has been radically borne out by, for example, anti-COVID-19-restrictions protests and COVID-19 vaccine refusal in Europe and the United States and, of course, Trump supporters' rebellion against the 2020 US presidential election results. While it is not clear how much foreign governments contributed to such sentiments, Russia's long-standing efforts to discredit Western democracy generally have helped increase citizen distrust vis-à-vis democratic institutions.

As with other forms of gray-zone aggression, the rest of the world is not blameless regarding disinformation. In a recent report, Diego Martin, Jacob Shapiro, and Julia Ilhardt document 76 foreign influence efforts targeting 30 countries between 2013 and 2019. The researchers characterize foreign influence efforts as

> coordinated campaigns by a state or the ruling party in an autocracy to impact one or more specific aspects of politics at home or in another state ... through media channels, including social media, by ... producing content designed to appear indigenous to the target state.[42]

That is, interference using legal means. The researchers established that 64 percent of the operations were carried out by Russia. China, Iran, Saudi Arabia, and the United Arab Emirates were responsible for most of the rest.[43]

This, again, demonstrates the opportunistic nature of gray-zone aggression, which simply avails itself of an opportunity, whether it is an issue, a technical tool, a political candidate, or a divide in another country. Of the influence efforts documented by the researchers, 26 percent targeted the US, 16 percent targeted multiple countries, 9 percent targeted the UK, 4 percent each targeted Germany and Spain, and 3 percent each targeted Australia, France, the Netherlands, South Africa, and Ukraine.[44]

Combining Gray-Zone Means

In true soup fashion, disinformation is often combined with other forms of gray-zone aggression. Each time, the hostile state considers scale, purpose, and to what ends the aggression will be used. To date, targeted countries react only in cases of serious aggression, thus leaving the initiative squarely with the aggressor. That also gives the aggressor the freedom to consider longer-term aspects, such as whether and how to use proxies, the desired effect in the short and long term, and a timescale that may outwit targeted liberal democracies with their electoral cycle–linked thinking.

In spring and summer 2021, the Biden administration several times warned Russia regarding Russian gangs' ransomware attacks, in what amounted to deterrence messaging. Biden told reporters,

> I made it very clear to [Vladimir Putin] that the United States expects when a ransomware operation is coming from his soil, even though it's not—not—sponsored by the state, we expect them to act if we give them enough information to act on who that is.[45]

If Russia fails to do so, the Biden administration has said the US government will take action through visible and clandestine means.

A striking example of how an adversary can exploit an opportunity through swift action is Chinese and Russian aid to Italy during COVID-19's catastrophic first weeks in the country. Speaking soon afterward, Paolo Alli, formerly a center-right Italian member of parliament and president of the NATO Parliamentary Assembly, noted the chain of events.

> In the first weeks of the coronavirus emergency, when Italy and Lombardy were facing a dramatic situation and the EU was still underestimating the problem and denying any kind of support to Italy, Xi Jinping sent a plane full of masks, and Putin sent a planeload of doctors. Doing so cost Beijing and Moscow virtually nothing, but the timing was so impeccable that Italian support for the EU plummeted within days. If you ask Italians whether Brussels, Moscow, and Beijing is their best friend, there is no doubt that most will still put Brussels last.[46]

China and Russia took advantage of EU member states' failure to assist Italy with urgently needed medical supplies during the dramatic first weeks of the coronavirus crisis.[47] Beijing's small delivery—part of which the Italians had to pay for—and Moscow's large team of military doctors with expertise seemingly unsuited to coronavirus emergencies were intended less to save Italy than to undermine EU cohesion. China in particular used the aid for elaborate publicity, providing a steady stream of slanted information on social media, often on accounts belonging to Chinese diplomats, and through government-linked media organizations such as *China Daily*, the Chinese Communist Party's (CCP) newspaper.[48] The countries were "Bad Samaritans," helpers exploiting another country's misery to discredit and undermine its institutions and allies, destabilize the Western alliance, and win over the public.[49]

The mission was successful. In early April 2020, shortly after Chinese aid arrived in Italy, a survey by pollster SWG found that the number of Italians who considered China a friend had skyrocketed to 52 percent, up from 10 percent only two months previously.[50] In June 2020, 63 percent of Italians said the EU failed their country during the coronavirus crisis; 4 percent said the EU was Italy's best ally during the crisis, while 25 percent called China Italy's best ally.[51]

Gray-zone aggression can, as demonstrated above, be effective even when the aggressor uses only legal tools. Disinformation, for example, has already had a significant effect on liberal democracies. In the United States, a poll by the *Economist* and YouGov in February 2020 showed that a majority (51 percent) of Americans did not believe the country could defend itself against foreign interference in the November 2020 elections.[52] A majority of Americans believes Russia interfered in America's 2016 elections,[53] and a January 2021 poll showed that only 16 percent of Americans believe the country's democracy is working well or extremely well.[54] In the UK, 47 percent of Britons believe Russia interfered in the 2016 Brexit referendum, compared to 23 percent who believe it did not.[55] Americans' lack of trust in the 2020 elections before they occurred was a perfect example of the Thomas theorem, named after the American sociologist William Thomas, who concluded that "if men define situations as real, they are real in their consequences."[56]

Following Russia's annexation of Crimea, subversion of political processes emerged as a major concern in Western capitals. It is yet another form of gray-zone aggression that is not inherently illegal; the Russian government considers Western support of Russian civic organizations as unwelcome interference, as have many other authoritarian regimes over the years. Yet reverse interference—foreign governments meddling with Western groups and political parties—seems to have taken Western societies by surprise. The Soviet Union was a key practitioner of such interference, and in the past several years, Russia has made notable efforts in the area.

In January 2015, I documented Russia's efforts to build relations with increasingly popular European radical parties on the left and right, including Germany's Alternative for Germany and Die Linke, the Freedom Party of Austria, and Italy's Lega Nord (now called Lega).[57] Those efforts included friendly outreach by Russian officials, invitations to Russia, and in some cases, such as France's then–Front National, bank loans. In return, some of the parties' elected representatives traveled to Crimea as observers of the region's disputed referendum on incorporation with Russia and decreed it free and fair.[58]

China has not managed to build similarly lasting connections with political parties in other countries, perhaps because it lacks a convincing narrative to sell to them. Instead, China banks on foreign parties' and governments' interest in its economic strength. Italy, for example, in 2019 became the first major developed economy to endorse China's Belt and

Road Initiative.⁵⁹ The Lega–Five Star Movement coalition government took the step, Alli said, as it felt Italy had "missed the boat on commercial opportunities" in China that France and Germany had been pursuing for a long time.⁶⁰ In addition to such legitimate engagement, however, China also builds foreign influence through Chinese citizens abroad and foreign citizens of Chinese ancestry. As Charles Parton points out,

> The CCP targets ethnic Chinese, seeking to use them to lobby and vote in its interests. In Australia, funding through naturalised citizens with close Party links has influenced politicians' stances. . . . Another tactic is the establishment of associations which do not advertise their UFWD [United Front Work Department] links and which lobby for positions supported by the CCP.⁶¹

The UFWD is the CCP's influence arm and is also active outside the country.

Early Efforts at Creating Resilience

Since 2014, even Western countries that had previously not regarded disinformation as a major concern have taken action to lessen its effect. This makes disinformation the first gray-zone area in which countries have made rigorous efforts to protect themselves. In June 2020, Damian Collins, a British member of Parliament for the Conservative Party and former chairman of the Digital, Culture, Media and Sport Committee (DCMS), noted that

> there's enormous activity around the coronavirus. The UK government has a specialist unit that monitors coronavirus disinformation, and Facebook is willing to take posts down even if they're not illegal. That's a big change since the times of Cambridge Analytica. People are becoming aware that disinformation is a problem that needs to be addressed.⁶²

A DCMS inquiry in 2018 found that Cambridge Analytica, a data-harvesting firm, had interfered with the Brexit referendum two years previously.[63] Maj. Gen. Pekka Toveri (ret.), at the time of the interview the Finnish Defence Forces' chief of intelligence, said that, in Finland, disseminating disinformation is now "relatively difficult because the public is well educated."[64]

Yet such efforts do not mean a country is inoculated against disinformation. In April 2020, 40 percent of British adults said they were "finding it hard to know what is true or false about the [corona]virus."[65] The January 2021 mob storming of the US Capitol, meanwhile, demonstrated that even disinformation that influences a minority of people can cause devastating damage, not just physically but also to a country's image of itself and its standing in the world. The January 6 mob also illustrated how people who may already be confused or angry pose a fertile ground for disinformation; 60 percent of the January 6 attackers had a history of financial troubles, including bankruptcies and unpaid taxes.[66]

Even though knowledge of disinformation does not prevent it, knowledge does eliminate the surprise element. Russia tried to interfere with US elections in 2020 by "push[ing] influence narratives—including misleading or unsubstantiated allegations against President Biden—to US media organizations, US officials, and prominent US individuals."[67] It did so knowing that America was better prepared for such interference efforts than it was in 2016. Yet if the targeted country offers even a small opportunity for gray-zone aggression, the cost is so low that an adversary country with intent and capability would reasonably seize it.

This is important in gray-zone aggression, as skilled gray-zone practitioners exploit gaps in rivals' preparation. Russia followed up its annexation of Crimea not by attempting to annex majority-Russian regions of Estonia and Latvia, a possibility that the West fears, but through interference in US elections. Many countries have tried to build resilience against disinformation through information literacy campaigns and segments in school curricula, while the European Union has created a plethora of task forces, media literacy efforts, and disinformation tracking units. The EU also meticulously prepared for potential interference in its 2019 parliament elections. The European Commission "structured a comprehensive and robust plan to prevent or, at least, reduce the risk of electoral interference and the spread of disinformation in the run-up to the EP [European Parliament] elections," Edoardo Bressanelli et al. note in a June 2020 report prepared for the European Parliament.[68] Facebook and Twitter, meanwhile, have taken modest steps to regulate disinformation.

The 2019 European Parliament elections were considered a test for how well the EU could withstand election interference, especially disinformation. The elections were a success. The June 2020 report by the European Parliament notes that

> interference operations were present and sustained, but did not take the shape of a massive cross-national disinformation campaign or of coordinated cyberattacks. It also seems that false, misleading and ideologically extreme content did not consistently influence the information flow on social media platforms. The Commission thus stated that interference attempts were deterred by the EU measures.[69]

The Irony of Successfully Deterring One Form of Gray-Zone Aggression

"The Commission thus stated that interference attempts were deterred by the EU measures."[70] This matters. If one form of gray-zone aggression can be at least partially deterred—in this case, through resilience—rivals are likely to focus on other forms and innovate. In the interviews conducted for this book, disinformation did not stand out as the interviewees' most important concern.

Kalniņš pointed out that

> here in Latvia, our most significant vulnerability is the economy. If our economy deteriorates, people will leave—but we're a small country and can't afford to lose people. We had a big banking problem with lots of suspicious money coming into the system. We have banks with 80 percent Russian or other foreign capital. There are lots of ways in which you can use that sort of money to undermine a country.[71]

Niklas Karlsson, the vice chair of the Swedish parliament's defense committee, highlighted the risk posed by subversive foreign investments.

> In Sweden, we're currently conducting an investigation into FDI [foreign direct investment]. China's Belt and Road Initiative is not just a project to maintain economic growth in China; it has larger ambitions. How to deal with it is a difficult balancing act. One mustn't be too naive, but not too restrictive either.
>
> I don't have a clear idea of what's the best way forward, but the bottom line is that there are lots of countries in the world that we can trade with. That creates jobs and growth. But we should trade on our own terms. We can't tell the Chinese that they're not welcome. We can't close ourselves off. All this is the democrat's dilemma.[72]

Or, again, the defender's dilemma of being an open society whose openness hostile states can exploit. With legal forms of gray-zone aggression, a key challenge is, as always, to identify it. Toveri provided an illustrative example from Finland.

> When approaching military officers and civilian authorities, our adversaries face challenges. Government officials normally have strict rules regarding whom they can speak with and how to report possible foreign contacts. Politicians and private sector representatives don't have such rules and restrictions. There are very few restrictions on whom they can meet or where a politician can go to work after leaving political office. This provides an opening for Russia and for China too.[73]

This is a crucial point. While enormous attention has been paid to Russian disinformation efforts on official channels such as RT and Sputnik and on social media, the most important avenue for a country wishing to shape a Western country's public debate may, in fact, be through conversations with "influencers" such as business leaders and former politicians. As noted by Toveri, while it is illegal to provide classified information to a foreign country, it is legal for business leaders, former politicians, and other key representatives to hold conversations with representatives of rival countries. Such conversations can be part of an agenda coordinated or even controlled by a hostile government.[74] That senior officials' (and indeed business leaders' and celebrities') interactions with entities representing hostile states is legal reflects the post–Cold War belief in the correcting nature of the globalized economy: the supposition that other countries will adjust to Western standards of behavior once they join the globalized economy and begin benefiting from it.

Globalization has not just introduced new forms of competition among countries—and as a result, new risks of geopolitical friction—but also created new opportunities for gray-zone aggression. The importance of globalization in gray-zone aggression cannot be overstated. Authoritarian countries, of course, also benefit from access to time and consistency, which allows them to play a long game that is much harder for liberal democracies operating in electoral cycles to achieve.

Even though the forms of theoretically legal gray-zone aggression that received the most attention immediately after 2014—disinformation and potential uprisings fueled by Russia—have an aggressive edge, other forms are now becoming a much larger concern. They are of an even less visible nature. This latent gray-zone aggression is fundamentally connected to globalization because it weakens a rival country by undermining its global links. Two forms of this are analyzed in depth in the following chapters: subversive economics and coercion, bullying, and subversion of civil society.

While China appears to use gray-zone aggression to reinforce its national priorities, Russia seems to focus on sowing chaos. Other current or future rivals may develop additional strategies. That makes it even more vital for liberal democracies to understand their vulnerabilities and address them. Toveri pointed out that "as defenders, we should learn to know ourselves better. Which are the weak points in our government, legislation, and society? We think that we know ourselves well, but we haven't looked at ourselves from others' perspective."[75] This, too, is part of the defender's challenge: seeing oneself as the gray-zone aggressor would.

V

Subversive Economics: When Business as Usual Enters the Gray Zone

Many people have heard of SolarWinds. Far fewer are familiar with Romaco Group or Silex Microsystems. Although cyberattacks are the subject of intense public discussion, they are—as we have seen—just one of many non-kinetic ways countries seek to weaken liberal democracies. Indeed, the focus on cyberattacks means less attention is given to an even more damaging form of gray-zone aggression: subversive economics. It is not only a major strategic threat to Western countries but also one against which the West has minimal protection.

What Is Subversive Economics?

The premise of globalization is that countries agree to open their markets and participate in a global economy with few barriers because they believe doing so will benefit all countries involved, through increased trading opportunities, more specialization, and lower costs and prices. This will, in turn, increase prosperity.

Countries can, however, exploit globalization as part of a strategy to increase their power and weaken that of their rivals. Subversive economics, by my definition, is the systematic undermining of liberal democracies' open markets by hostile governments, their businesses, or a combination of the two, with the goal of weakening the targeted country, strengthening the perpetrating country, or both.[1]

US officials have frequently referred to "predatory economics." US Secretary of State Rex Tillerson used the term during the first year of the Donald Trump administration,[2] and it subsequently became a key US foreign policy theme under his successor, Mike Pompeo. The 2018 US National Defense Strategy also featured the term.[3] "Predatory," however, implies visibility that is often not present. Subversive economics is so dangerous precisely because it typically does not protrude above the parapet of everyday business practices in the globalized economy. It is thus harder to detect, let alone counter.

Indeed, the fact that subversive economics concertedly exploits the globalized economy makes it fundamentally different from economic foul play during the Cold War and previous eras, when the world was far less interlinked. Subversive economics is also different from everyday business activities in the globalized economy, which may be cutthroat and frequently aggressive but do not collectively exploit a country's economy.

Subversive economics may pose a more significant threat to liberal democracies than cyberattacks do because the latter cause damage that can be repaired, while the former causes lasting damage by undermining the very functioning of a country's economy. It does so by exploiting liberal democracies' openness, the ease of doing business in them, and the fact that they mostly adhere to international rules while their rivals sometimes do not.

Trade Disputes and Subversive Economics

A country trying to gain advantages by targeting another country's industry is not a new phenomenon. As John Conybeare observed in 1988, "International trade conflicts have been occurring at least since the times of classical Greece."[4] Indeed, as Conybeare noted in the same article, "During the past twenty years, trade issues have become part of the realm of 'high politics,' the subject of major inter-state threats, negotiations, and occasionally even trade wars."[5] Trade issues have, in fact, entered high politics at various points throughout history. In the 1930s, for example, Herbert Hoover sought to strengthen the domestic US economy by placing tariffs on some 20,000 foreign goods—the so-called Smoot-Hawley Tariff Act—which unsurprisingly triggered counter-tariffs by the targeted countries and contributed to a global economic downturn.[6]

The signing of the General Agreement on Tariffs and Trade in 1947 and the creation of the World Trade Organization (WTO) in 1995 were supposed to limit trade disputes through firm rules and adjudication. That countries have continued to join the WTO since its founding—including China in 2001—highlights its importance. Despite its inability to punish offending member states, the WTO maintains an important role in world trade by adjudicating and citing violations of WTO rules.[7] Since the WTO's founding, member states have filed some 500 complaints with its dispute settlement body.[8]

These complaints include one submitted by the EU after President Trump made good on his threats to address what he considered the unfair trade imbalance between the United States and the EU and after he imposed tariffs of 25 and 10 percent on steel and aluminum, respectively, from the EU.[9] The Trump administration justified the tariffs with national security concerns. Subsequently, Trump called the EU "worse than China" and suggested that America's friends are, in fact, sometimes its enemies.[10]

Yet even though the EU and the United States have over the years filed additional WTO complaints against each other, China's trade practices pose concerns of a far more serious nature. Between 2009 and 2017, the Barack Obama administration brought 25 cases to the WTO, the largest number of any country during that period. Sixteen of the complaints alleged wrongdoing by China.[11] At the time of writing, the United States has won seven of these cases. The EU has likewise filed complaints against China. It did so, for example, regarding stainless steel—a key component in products from aircraft to medical devices—alleging that Beijing has unfairly supported domestic producers at the expense of foreign ones.[12]

The limitations of the WTO's power to punish bad behavior have come into stark relief through the stainless steel case. In 2017, the Chinese stainless steel company Tsingshan opened a plant in Indonesia, which has the world's largest nickel reserves, a key component of stainless steel.[13] The plant's construction was supported by the Chinese government[14] and was an important step for Tsingshan as more than two-thirds of the world's nickel is used to make stainless steel.[15] With the plant operating for less than two years, the Indonesian government suddenly announced it would ban exports of nickel, which caused global nickel prices to skyrocket. Thanks to its Indonesian plant, Tsingshan was shielded from the nickel hike,[16] with a resulting increase in exports of Indonesian-made stainless steel to Europe.

In 2015, the European Union had responded to Chinese price dumping of stainless steel by imposing tariffs. In August 2019, the European stainless steel industry filed another dumping complaint with the European Commission, this time also involving Indonesia. The EU followed up, imposing

17 percent duties on stainless steel made by Tsingshan and its Indonesian subsidiaries and 18.9 percent duties on another Chinese firm.[17] China, however, preempted the Europeans by raising its antidumping duties on European stainless steel from 18.1 percent to a staggering 103.1 percent.[18] This is exactly the kind of dispute the WTO was set up to solve. Without stronger global structures to punish wanton tariff usage, it is hard to see how such practices can be curtailed.

The solar panel sector, once dominated by Western businesses, demonstrates the risks involved when another country's government-supported manufacturers undercut competitors and, as a result, edge them out of business. Thanks to government support, between 2006 and 2013, China's share of photovoltaic-cell production—solar panels' key component—grew from 14 to 60 percent. Western economies seeking to wean themselves off fossil fuels now find themselves at the mercy of Chinese solar panel manufacturers.[19]

Subversive economics, however, extends far beyond unfair trade practices. In an October 2020 speech, German Minster of Defence Annegret Kramp-Karrenbauer provided a summary that every Western country would certainly agree with.

> As a leading export nation, we Germans are greatly concerned about how China has positioned itself in international trade matters. Our concerns include
> - currency manipulations that have been going on for a long time;
> - aggressive appropriation of intellectual property;
> - unequal investment conditions;
> - state-subsidized distortion of competition.[20]

Foreign Investments as Gray-Zone Aggression

In December 2018, Swedish media reported that three cutting-edge Swedish semiconductor firms—Imego, Norstel, and Silex Microsystems—had been sold to Chinese buyers.[21] Even though there was no government approval process for non-EU takeovers of Swedish firms at the time, the government could have intervened to prevent the sale based on the technologies' sensitivity. In 2018, the German government intervened in a business transaction on similar grounds, thwarting an investment by the State Grid Corporation of China in the high-voltage energy operator 50Hertz by instructing the government-owned bank KfW to buy the stake. In March 2021, the German government again used KfW to buy a stake in a crucial firm; this time the transaction involved a controlling stake in Hensoldt, which makes components for Eurofighter Typhoon aircraft. The German government had announced in December 2020 that it would make the investment to prevent "unfriendly powers" from acquiring matériel such as sensors and encryption technology.[22]

Yet despite the sensitivity of the three firms' expertise, the Swedish government did not intervene. In the case of Silex, which specializes in accelerometers, gyroscopes, and other microscopic sensors, its buyer—aviation, satellite, and defense enterprise NavTech—announced soon afterward that "it would build a $300m plant in Beijing 'relying on Silex's technology' in micro-electromechanical systems . . . the components embedded in chips that are increasingly central to everything from mobile phones and medical devices to self-driving cars."[23]

The case of the three Swedish semiconductor firms illustrates a general picture: Until recently, most Western governments regularly approved the vast majority of sales of domestic firms to foreign buyers, if they scrutinized the sales to begin with.[24] Giving evidence to the UK Parliament's Defence and Business, Energy and Industrial Strategy Committees in October 2018, Alex Chisholm, permanent secretary of the Department for Business, Energy and Industrial Strategy, stated that under the UK's 2002 Enterprise Act there had been eight government "interventions" on national security grounds. Richard Harrington, the department's parliamentary undersecretary (and an elected member of parliament), added that

> there have been eight interventions, but that has to be put into the context of literally thousands of M&A [mergers and acquisitions] transactions. I don't think anyone could say that foreign investment in this country is anything other than welcome, and that will remain the case.[25]

Eight government interventions on national security grounds out of thousands of M&As is an exceptionally low number and demonstrates the UK's eagerness to attract foreign investment, which, in the 21st century, has meant a special focus on attracting Chinese investment. Perhaps the most obvious demonstration of that eagerness came in 2017 when former Prime Minister David Cameron launched the UK-China Fund, an investment fund promoting UK-China cooperation in sectors including energy, technology, and health care.[26]

It is symptomatic that, after the Cold War, belief in the benefits of global business was so profound that most Western countries slashed or even removed scrutiny of foreign direct investment (FDI). Pål Jonson, a member of the Swedish parliament for the center-right Moderate Party and chairman of its defense committee, observed,

> We were caught rather flat-footed when China began acquiring companies in Sweden. We used to have strict legislation regarding FDI, but it was abolished in 1993. Now we're trying to pass a new, similar law. And we're trying to make technology supply chains more secure. Sweden has a very advanced tech sector, so securing the supply chain is vital. Today, China is a substantial threat to Sweden's economic competitiveness.[27]

While the benefits of globalized markets may be obvious, globalization is open to exploitation by governments that are willing to violate the rules of fair play and that are unconcerned by the resulting reputational damage. Because China is the main practitioner of such exploitation, it forms the focus of this chapter. Among subversive investments by other countries, the February 2021 acquisition of Bergen Engines is a descriptive case. The Norwegian engine manufacturer was sold by Rolls-Royce to TMH International, a Swiss-based fully owned subsidiary of the Russian firm TMH Group. Because Bergen Engines, which specializes in large ship engines, is a major supplier to the Norwegian coast guard, the acquisition created immediate concerns in Norway.[28]

For the past several years, Beijing has been pursuing economic great-power status. The Made in China 2025 plan was launched in 2015 and forms the framework for transforming China into a leading manufacturing power by focusing on technologically sophisticated production.[29]

To reach this goal, Beijing concluded early on that it could not count on its domestic firms' capabilities, especially since Chinese companies have lower levels of automation and digitization than do firms in highly industrialized countries.[30] The strategy instead relies on Chinese firms acquiring cutting-edge Western firms. As Jost Wübbeke et al. pointed out in 2016, Made in China 2025

> targets virtually all high-tech industries that strongly contribute to economic growth in advanced economies: automotive, aviation, machinery, robotics, high-tech maritime and railway equipment, energy-saving vehicles, medical devices and information technology to name only a few. Countries in which these high-tech industries contribute a large share of economic growth are most vulnerable to China's plans.[31]

Wübbeke et al. noted that this "creates an enormous demand for smart manufacturing products like industrial robots, smart sensors, wireless sensor networks and radio frequency identification chips," and they identified as particularly vulnerable a string of countries including Denmark, Finland, Germany, Japan, South Korea, Sweden, and the United States.[32] Indeed, just months before their report was published, the Chinese firm Midea Group had acquired the cutting-edge German industrial robot maker KUKA. Although KUKA was considered a crown jewel among German robotics firms, the considerable price Midea paid surprised many market watchers, who surmised that Midea did not just have a regular business deal in mind. Within two years of KUKA's takeover, its highly respected CEO left the company, which had shifted its attention to China.[33] Today, KUKA is de facto no longer a German firm.

The generous price paid for KUKA is part of a larger trend. A 2019 report by Mikko Huotari and Agatha Kratz describes the wide range of credits and national and subnational subsidies provided to Chinese firms by various Chinese government entities. The authors conclude that this panoply of financing benefits empowers Chinese companies with advantages over foreign competitors not only at home but also when they engage in foreign takeovers, with relative disregard for commercial risks, allowing them to offer premiums for foreign assets if necessary.[34]

Such apparent generosity can be especially attractive during national crises. In January 2021, it emerged that Shenzhen-based BGI Group, the world's largest genome-sequencing company, had offered to build and operate COVID-19 testing centers in six American states. BGI had even offered to make donations. US intelligence agencies, however, warned the states against accepting the offer based on concerns over BGI's close links to the Chinese government, which include operating China's national genetic database. In its stock filings, BGI says it aims to help the Chinese Communist Party (CCP) achieve its goal to "seize the commanding heights of international biotechnology competition."[35] BGI also works directly with the Chinese armed forces, for which it conducts genetic research.[36] The US intelligence agencies' concerns focused on the risk of the Chinese government accessing US residents' genetic information. Ultimately, all six states declined the offer.[37]

However, Sweden's leading medical research institute, the Karolinska Institute, partners with BGI for COVID-19 tests. In 2020, Vivien Yang Swartz, BGI's head of business development in the Nordic countries, said that no genetic information collected by BGI in Sweden was being sent to China. "They're not interested in that," she told the *Times*.[38] That interest could, of course, change.

Extent of Investments

It is unclear how many Chinese acquisitions of cutting-edge technology firms (and large-stake investments in such firms) have taken place over the past decade, as there is no publicly accessible database listing all foreign investments. Even if such a database were created, it would be unlikely to document all foreign (or non-EU, non–Five Eyes, and non-NATO) ownership. This is because information regarding the investing party's name and address may not reveal the ultimate beneficial owner. As Jerker Hellström notes in the case of the three Swedish semiconductor firms, the Swedish government's seemingly hyper-permissive approach could be because the buyers obfuscated their identities.[39] (Two of the Swedish firms' buyers were later found to have links to the Chinese armed forces.)

Hellström suggests that, given the difficulty in establishing the full identity of these buyers, many more Western firms than have anecdotally been identified may have been acquired by companies owned by Chinese entities. Firms in all developed economies examine prospective partners ahead of mergers, acquisitions, and investments for business viability and compliance with due diligence laws; indeed, a whole sector specializes in conducting such research. By contrast, governments do not require commercial partners to present for government scrutiny such investigations ahead of commercial deals involving foreign investment, including venture capital (VC) funding. While the acquired entity may know the identities of the acquirer and any ultimate beneficial owners, there is no requirement to inform the government.

Investments in the United States have declined in total amount, shifting away from legacy businesses in traditional sectors toward smaller firms in technology-focused ones. Indeed, in recent years, Chinese FDI patterns in industrialized countries have shifted significantly. During the years soon after China's accession to the WTO in 2001, Chinese investment and acquisition activity involving US and other Western firms primarily occurred in more-traditional sectors such as energy, real estate, automotive manufacturing (including Volvo), and tourism.[40] However, Agatha Kratz et al. calculate that "Chinese FDI transactions in the EU-28 dropped by 33 percent [in 2019], from EUR 18 billion in 2018 to EUR 12 billion in 2019, bringing the total back to 2013 levels."[41]

The decreased investment volume should come as no surprise. For roughly the past half decade, Chinese firms have been pursuing more inconspicuous acquisitions than they did at the beginning of the 21st century, but this may pose a significantly larger risk to Western countries. Instead of primarily making high-profile investments in traditional sectors, Chinese firms have been buying more small- and medium-size enterprises, especially in tech-heavy sectors such as biotech and artificial intelligence (AI) that are central to Made in China 2025.[42]

Deals in 2019, for example, included National Electric Vehicle Sweden[43] and France's Maxeon Solar Technologies, in which state-owned Tianjin Zhonghuan Semiconductor acquired a 29 percent stake and three board seats.[44] Deals in 2018 included the acquisition by Shanghai's Will Semiconductor of California-based OmniVision Technologies, one of the world's top makers of image sensors and chips for smartphone and tablet cameras.[45] Around the same time, state-owned Chinese firms bought several other US chipmakers.[46]

Also in 2019, US tech firm Spigot sold itself to a Chinese buyer, and the firm's founder then launched a consultancy focused on steering more US tech startups to Chinese buyers.[47] While the launch of the consultancy is one of thousands of business transactions taking place every day, it again illustrates the elusive nature of gray-zone aggression. Steering cutting-edge US startups to Chinese buyers is not illegal, yet the loss of these startups could weaken the US economy and strengthen that of a competitor that uses acquisitions as a strategy.

Although limited to Sweden, another good indicator of the shift in Chinese investments is a November 2019 report by the Swedish Defence Research Agency.[48] The authors identify 51 acquisitions of Swedish firms and 14 significant investments below a majority stake; the acquisitions have also given the Chinese buyers control of some 100 subsidiaries. The transactions accelerated after 2014, and about half involve Swedish companies in sectors that are part of Made in China 2025. The authors caution that there may be many more cases that they have not been able to identify.

The China Global Investment Tracker maintained by the American Enterprise Institute and the Heritage Foundation also documents this shift.[49] Since 2016, Chinese firms have bought more companies in, for example, the biotech sector than they did during the aughts. In 2016, for example, Chinese firms acquired Finnish silicon wafer maker Okmetic,[50] Imagination Technologies (a world-leading British semiconductor chipmaker),[51] Linxens (a French maker of smart-chip components for contactless payment technology),[52] US biomedical firm MP Biomedicals,[53] and German data-streaming startup Data Artisans.[54] Chinese firms also bought majority stakes in many other European and North American firms, including German pharmaceutical technology firms Romaco Group[55] and Biotest[56] and NMS Group, which is an Italian group of companies focused on oncology drug discovery, preclinical research, clinical development, and manufacturing.[57]

Along with the shift in thematic focus, the investments' geographical focus also seems to be shifting, from large European countries to tech-focused smaller ones. The research firm Datenna notes that, in Germany, the annual number of acquisitions accelerated in 2014, peaked in 2016, and has since slowed.[58] Kratz et al. likewise document a decline in volume of capital invested in Germany (and France and the UK) between 2015 and 2019. By contrast, during the same period, investments in smaller, technology-heavy northern European countries increased.[59] The Lithuanian serial entrepreneur Mindaugas Ubartas, for example, pointed out that, even though Lithuania is not a major target market in general, the country has a strong laser sector and is a target for Chinese takeover attempts in that area: "Chinese companies are trying to buy Lithuanian laser firms. And because we have businesspeople who think in short terms and who want the investments, there's nothing the government can do."[60]

Despite the slowdown in larger European countries, Chinese acquisition activity is considerable. Indeed, it is imperative to assess it by the number of deals, not just the total amount spent. As David Cogman, Paul Gao, and Nick Leung note, "The big-ticket deals that make the headlines are . . . not representative of the majority of transactions. These are mostly middle-market deals: the median deal size over the past three years was only $30 million."[61] For this reason, even though compilations of Chinese investment trends in Europe and North America (and other liberal democracies such as New Zealand and Australia) tend to show declining activity in recent years, when measured by total value, this should certainly not be understood as declining Chinese interest.

In a further iteration of the shift from legacy industries to cutting-edge ones, during the 2010s, the share of Chinese state-owned enterprises in aggregate Chinese investment in the EU dropped from an average of 70 percent to a mere 11 percent.[62] Datenna's China-EU FDI Radar, however, highlights that many ostensibly private Chinese firms involved in M&As have close links to the Chinese government. For example, the radar contains 174 significant investments in Germany between 2010 and 2020. In 18 percent of the acquisitions, the acquired German firm is now owned by the Chinese government,[63] and in another 51 cases, the

Chinese acquirers have considerable links to the Chinese government. The China-EU FDI Radar's figures raise the question of how many acquisitions in the EU and other Western countries involve ultimate Chinese ownership without the respective governments being aware, let alone being able to intervene.

Know Your Buyer

Lack of knowledge regarding investors' ultimate beneficial owners is a weakness of most Western regulations. While companies are expected to conduct due diligence before major commercial transactions to identify any financial improprieties or other illegal actions committed by the prospective partner, due diligence does not require investigations into legal behavior. While a to-be-acquired party may be interested in learning an acquirer's ultimate owner, it does not have to decline the takeover offer if the ultimate owner is a foreign government, nor do Western regulators routinely screen potential acquisitions over such links.

The Dutch semiconductor company Ampleon's acquisition by Chinese investor Beijing Jianguang Asset Management in 2015 demonstrates what such government links can look like.

> Jianguang Asset Management (JAC Capital) is a joint venture between China State Construction Investment Management (JIC Capital) and Wise Road Capital (Jianping Science and Technology Information Consulting). JIC Capital owns 51% of the shares. . . . Through 4 layers of investment vehicles JIC is fully owned by the State Council.[64]

Yet given many private Chinese firms' extensive cooperation with Beijing, the ownership structure may make little difference regarding the harm that could result from an acquisition. Even if the acquiring party has no connections to Chinese security apparatuses, it may shift its new asset's activities toward China, as was the case with KUKA. President Xi Jinping has also strengthened the government's power over private enterprises. China's 2017 National Intelligence Law, for example, states,

> Any organization and citizen shall, in accordance with the law, support, provide assistance, and cooperate in national intelligence work, and guard the secrecy of any national intelligence work that they are aware of. The state shall protect individuals and organisations that support, cooperate with, and collaborate in national intelligence work.[65]

This is a change in policy compared to the pre-Xi era. Richard McGregor points out that

> from the Mao era onwards, Chinese state firms have always had a predominant role in the economy, and the Communist party has always maintained direct control over state firms. For more than a decade, the party has also tried to ensure it played a role inside private businesses. But in his first term in office, Xi has overseen a sea change in how the party approaches the economy, dramatically strengthening the party's role in both government and private businesses.[66]

The French contactless payment firm Linxens illustrates the steps involved during a typical takeover of a Western firm by a Chinese one. After being sold to a Luxembourg-based private equity investor, in 2018 Linxens was sold to Ziguang Liansheng, an entity founded that year for the specific purpose of acquiring Linxens. As documented by Datenna, Ziguang Liansheng is controlled by Tsinghua University, which in turn ultimately reports to China's Ministry of Education. At the time of writing, Linxens is building a state-the-art facility in Tianjin, China, that will become its largest facility worldwide.[67] While none of this is illegal, it raises the questions of whether Linxens' intellectual property (IP) is leaving France for good and whether every advanced-technology majority-stake investment by non-EU firms poses a risk of significant IP loss. Without comprehensive scrutiny of FDI transactions, "non-EU," "non-NATO," "non-Five Eyes," and similar designations may be ineffective labels, as foreign firms can make investments using Western-based subsidiaries.

The Swedish microchip firm Silex, in turn, was acquired "through a chain of investment holding companies [that] involved Chinese state-controlled funds. The new plant is located in a state-run industrial park, and has been backed by a state-run semiconductors fund, the Beijing Integrated Circuits fund," the *Financial Times* later established.[68] By treating a cutting-edge firm purely as a business, the Swedish government lost to China a key technology that would have benefited Sweden and its partners.

The case of Grindr, the gay dating app, demonstrates the growing intersection between seemingly ordinary companies and national security. In 2019, the Committee on Foreign Investment in the United States (CFIUS), the US regulator charged with scrutinizing foreign investments on national security grounds, forced a reversal of the acquisition of US-based Grindr.[69] The acquisition, by Chinese media company Beijing Kunlun Tech, had been finalized the previous year and not been blocked by CFIUS, perhaps logically so, as a dating app may ordinarily not trigger national security concerns. (Incidentally, Kunlun's initial stake, a 60 percent share of the company bought in 2016 for $93 million, is another example of the modest sums paid by Chinese firms, reflecting the often relatively small size of the acquired firms.)

After Kunlun's acquisition of Grindr, however, CFIUS became concerned when it was discovered that Kunlun engineers based in Beijing had been working on Grindr's database; Kunlun had shifted most of Grindr's operations there, away from Grindr's California home.[70] This raised the concern that Grindr users' data—such as private messages and HIV status—could become available to Chinese authorities and used to blackmail users in sensitive positions.[71] Grindr, in other words, had importance far beyond the $93 million stake. CFIUS forced Kunlun to divest Grindr.

The case also illustrates the lack of clarity regarding buyers' identities. Following Kunlun's forced divestment of Grindr, CFIUS approved a new buyer for the dating app. Following that acquisition, however, it was discovered that the new buyer—a newly formed US-based entity—was closely linked to Kunlun.[72] Prospective "know your buyer" rules akin to today's "know your customer" ones clearly involve more administrative effort by businesses and governments, but, if a business is important to national security, that additional step is warranted.

In the case of Linxens, the transaction raises the prospect that French authorities were unaware that Ziguang Liansheng served as a vehicle for Tsinghua University. In addition, precisely because many firms that have been acquired or received majority Chinese investments in recent years are relatively small and not household names, the transactions have received scant news coverage. The Chinese acquisitions of Imego, Norstel, and Silex[73] received virtually no attention in Sweden even though the Swedish firms produce cutting-edge technology.

In December 2020, China and the EU finalized their Comprehensive Agreement on Investment (CAI). European Commission President Ursula von der Leyen explained that the CAI

> will provide unprecedented access to the Chinese market for European investors, enabling our businesses to grow and create jobs. It will also commit China to ambitious principles on sustainability, transparency and non-discrimination. The agreement will rebalance our economic relationship with China.[74]

The CAI, however, provides no solutions to Chinese gray-zone practices including concerted takeovers and IP theft.[75] Furthermore, considering that China has violated previous treaty obligations including the Sino-British joint declaration on Hong Kong,[76] it is not clear that China will adhere to its CAI treaty obligations.

China's Military-Civil Fusion Strategy as Part of Subversive Economics

China's Military-Civil Fusion (MCF) strategy—which "leverag[es] the civilian sector to maximise military power"[77]—aims to establish China's armed forces as a world-class military by 2049, the same year Made in China 2025 aims to have established China as a high-tech manufacturing superpower. As Elsa Kania and Lorand Laskai observe, fusion

> is not yet a true reflection of realities on the ground in China. Over the past 30 years, China's defense sector has been primarily dominated by sclerotic state-owned enterprises that remain walled off from the country's dynamic commercial economy. At its core, MCF is intended as a remedy to this problem.[78]

Fusing military and civil innovation is a long-standing Chinese government ambition, albeit one that haltingly progressed under previous presidents. Until Xi came to power, China struggled to approach anything close to the United States' civil-military cooperation, in which the government has successfully incentivized private-sector research and development that could benefit the US armed forces. (GPS is an often-mentioned success story.) During Xi's tenure, however, MCF

> has been part of nearly every major strategic initiative, including Made in China 2025 and Next Generation Artificial Intelligence Plan. The goal is to bolster the country's innovation system for dual-use technologies in various key industries like aviation, aerospace, automation, and information technology through "integrated development."[79]

As a sign of the importance Xi affords MCF, in 2017 he launched the Central Commission for Integrated Military and Civilian Development, a new agency that coordinates MCF activities. He appointed Vice-Premier Zhang Gaoli to lead the commission's daily affairs, a role that ordinarily a less senior official would take on.[80]

The Ministry of Industry and Information Technology, meanwhile, oversees MCF's implementation, assigning "MCF mandates and funding to research institutions, pools of capital, companies, S&T [science and technology] projects, industry zones, and human capital programs."[81] The US government has expressed strong concern regarding MCF's impact on US industries and US companies' inadvertent role in it. In the May 2020 report "United States Strategic Approach to the People's Republic of China," the White House noted that MCF

> strategy gives the PLA [People's Liberation Army] unfettered access into civil entities developing and acquiring advanced technologies, including state-owned and private firms, universities, and research programs. Through non-transparent MCF linkages, United States and other foreign companies are unwittingly feeding dual-use technologies into PRC [People's Republic of China] military research and development programs,

strengthening the CCP's coercive ability to suppress domestic opposition and threaten foreign countries, including United States allies and partners.[82]

This concern is unlikely to subside under the Joe Biden administration.

Made in China 2025, MCF, and the strategy for Chinese great-power status can proceed at pace because China has the intent and capability to take advantage of Western industries. Western countries, in turn, inadvertently provide the opportunity for it to do so. Yet while no Western country would say it wanted to aid China's advance at its own expense, investments in and acquisitions of Western firms do precisely that. Although rules govern international trade, no international rules govern how private firms do business as long as they do not violate national laws. This, again, is the attractiveness of subversive economics: Another country can base a strategy for increased global power on tapping competitors' resources.

While China is the leading practitioner of subversive economics, the area is clearly not an inherently Chinese domain. On the contrary, the field is open to any country with intent and capability. Russian oligarchs and Middle Eastern royals have bought a string of elite Western sports clubs.[83] Russia's elite Kontinental Hockey League—sponsored partly by the country's energy giant Gazprom—has rekindled the Cold War rivalry between Soviet and US hockey by attracting Western hockey stars and even a couple teams to the league,[84] though North America's National Hockey League recruits far more Russian players than vice versa. North Korea for years operated a hostel on its embassy grounds in Berlin to raise hard currency, until a court forced the hostel to close in 2020.[85]

These transactions remain vastly more limited than China's and pose a decidedly smaller threat of subversion to Western economies. Nevertheless, when corporate transactions serve geopolitical purposes, can they still be considered pure business?

Property Purchases in Subversive Economics

Property purchases are also part of subversive economics, usually for logistical rather than commercial purposes.

Finland has, in the past decade, seen a significant rise in purchases by Russian nationals of properties located close to sensitive installations. To counter this development, in 2015 Defence Minister Jussi Niinistö introduced a government right of first refusal for property purchases near strategic installations.[86] Then, in September 2018, Finnish authorities conducted a massive raid on a property on the small island of Sakkiluoto in the Finnish archipelago. The holiday cottage had been outfitted with security cameras, motion detectors, satellite dishes, piers, a helipad, and sophisticated communications equipment.[87]

As with FDI, most Western countries have long maintained an open door for foreign property buyers and been less judicious than Finland has been. Such property purchases can range from cottages near sensitive installations to expensive London mansions that may be used for money laundering. In its 2020 report on Russia, the UK Parliament's Intelligence and Security Committee noted that

> whilst the Russian elite have developed ties with a number of countries in recent years, it would appear that the UK has been viewed as a particularly favourable destination for Russian oligarchs and their money. It is widely recognised that the key to London's appeal was the exploitation of the UK's investor visa scheme, introduced in 1994, followed by the promotion of a light and limited touch to regulation, with London's strong capital and housing markets offering sound investment opportunities. . . . The UK welcomed Russian money, and few questions—if any—were asked about the provenance of this considerable wealth.[88]

Acquisitions of ports are a related concern because they form vital nodes in global shipping, which transports 80 percent of world trade in goods.[89] In 2016, the Chinese logistics giant COSCO Shipping acquired a majority stake in Greece's Port of Piraeus, Europe's seventh-largest port, with which it already had a concession agreement. The 35-year concession agreement, signed in 2009, allowed COSCO to upgrade and run cargo piers.[90] In 2018, Greece endorsed China's Belt and Road Initiative, and in 2019, Greece's Deputy Foreign Minister Kostas Fragogiannis explained that "the objective is to transform [the Port of Piraeus] into the biggest transit hub between Europe and Asia and, potentially, the biggest port in Europe."[91] Such a development would increase European dependence on China and, as a result, China's opportunities for coercion.

Fears further increased when, also in 2019, Italy's Port of Trieste signed a memorandum of understanding with the China Communications Construction Company.[92] In late 2020, however, the Port of Trieste instead received a German majority owner when Hamburger Hafen und Logistik bought 50.1 percent of the shares.[93] However, as Charlie Lyons Jones and Raphael Veit note, "Chinese port holdings now span the globe and include investments in Greece, Myanmar, Israel, Djibouti, Morocco, Spain, Italy, Belgium, Côte d'Ivoire and Egypt, among others."[94]

As in other sectors, some investments have involved government-supported payments above market rate. COSCO, for example, in 2009 received a €215 million loan from the government-owned China Development Bank to invest in Greece's Port of Piraeus, and it subsequently received another €120 million loan from the bank for the same port.[95] Like other investments with links to a rival government, China's port investments illustrate the thin line between traditional commercial activities and legal activities in the gray zone. While German ownership of other European ports is unlikely to raise red flags, Chinese ownership does because of how the owner or the Chinese government may decide to use such a strategic asset.

A Political Juncture

China's "16+1" (later "17+1") platform with central and eastern European countries has long been a flagship format in its efforts to convince European governments of the benefits of closer economic cooperation. European participants' waning enthusiasm in the late 2010s, however, was a clear indication that these governments were growing concerned. Latvian Member of Parliament Ojārs Kalniņš commented on his country, observing that

> a positive thing is that we've managed to avoid an influx of Chinese capital. A couple of years ago we hosted the 16+1 meeting

[involving China and central and eastern European countries] here in Latvia. The prime minister of China participated. But we were careful and nothing materialised. At one point the Chinese offered to build RailBaltic, using Chinese firms of course. But RailBaltic is also about military mobility. We can't give such a contract to Chinese companies. Now we're building it using Baltic firms, and with significant financing from the EU.[96]

At a 17+1 virtual summit in February 2021, Estonia and Lithuania openly distanced themselves by sending lower-ranking officials than is customary.[97] In May, Lithuania left the group.[98]

Around 2020, Western governments' and parliaments' attitudes shifted substantially regarding investments by China. This is a significant development, considering that many countries had been highly reluctant to take action lest it harm their position as an attractive destination for Chinese investments. Western governments' growing concern is articulated by, for example, the US State Department, which warned that "the CCP is systematically reorganizing the Chinese science and technology enterprise to ensure that new innovations simultaneously advance economic and military development."[99] In November 2020, President Trump issued an executive order banning US companies and entities such as pension funds from investing in key companies that are part of MCF.[100]

Through legislation and other initiatives that same year, the EU, individual EU member states, and other Western countries also strengthened FDI scrutiny. In October 2020, the EU's foreign investment screening mechanism became fully operational.[101] Sweden strengthened its regulation that fall[102] (from a highly permissive basis), as did Australia, France, Italy, Poland, Spain, and the UK, among others.[103] The Czech Republic and other countries followed in spring 2021.[104] The UK legislation, for example, significantly expands the areas requiring government approval, including AI, autonomous robotics, cryptographic authentication, and engineering biology.[105]

These legislative steps followed the United States' long-standing screening by CFIUS, which the Foreign Investment Risk Review Modernization Act of 2018 (FIRRMA) strengthened.[106] In 2018, Germany quietly also strengthened investment regulations, stipulating that investments above 10 percent (down from 25 percent) in sensitive areas would require government approval.[107]

By 2022, the vast majority of Western countries will likely have strengthened their FDI regulations. This will at the very least create better insight into which foreign entities are investing in which firms, and it may lead to many more rejected transactions involving sensitive firms. The step, however, raises the question of who will acquire firms if certain foreign buyers are blocked. In cases ranging from Norwegian Air Shuttle to KUKA to Grindr, companies may want or even need to be acquired and may not be permitted to accept the most advantageous, or even the only, offer.

Maj. Gen. Pekka Toveri (ret.), at the time of the interview the Finnish Defence Forces' chief of intelligence, described the situation.

> What can a government do when a small municipality gets a very lucrative offer from a foreign company to do business—for example, to buy a major building or property—and you think it's bad for national security? The buyer offers a good price, too good even. The government could force the municipality to forgo the offer, but it's not necessarily in a position to reimburse the municipality for the lost income, which is a lot of money for a city council. So the city council might go for the deal. That leads to issues especially if you don't even know who the real owner is. At least Finland has a new law that requires preapproval for buyers that are not EU citizens. It will have some deterrent effect.[108]

VC Funding

Like all forms of gray-zone aggression, subversive economics is limited only by the aggressor's imagination. While Western governments and parliaments are introducing stricter rules on investments and acquisitions, their strategic rivals can shift their focus to another completely legal form of participation: VC startup funding.

VC is not inherently dangerous; on the contrary, it is the lifeblood of startups. With technological innovation becoming ever more important, startups must have access to capital that can sustain their operations until they start generating a steady revenue stream. While many governments issue grants to startups and the United States has outfits—most notably the Defense Advanced Research Projects Agency[109] and In-Q-Tel[110]—that fund or invest in innovation benefiting the US government, most startups rely on purely commercial VC funding.

Through VC investments, however, funders linked to foreign governments can also access other countries' best innovation at an early stage. It is thus hardly surprising that, as Chinese investment activity has grown, so has Chinese VC funding of cutting-edge Western startups. Such activity takes place through Chinese VC firms operating in Western innovation hubs, such as Silicon Valley in the US and Oxford and Cambridge in the UK. Like all VC firms, Chinese VCs active in such research hubs constantly monitor university innovation, spin-offs, and early-stage startups in which they can invest. In Silicon Valley, Chinese VC firm DHVC has several dozen early-stage startups—primarily in AI, biotech, and fintech—in its portfolio.[111] As Reuters reported in 2018, the firm was established and funded with help from the Chinese government.[112]

An Office of the US Trade Representative report found that, by November 15, 2018, 151 VC investments into US startups featured at least one Chinese investor, up from fewer than 20 in 2010. Los Altos–based TSVC, formerly TEEC Angel Fund, was jointly launched by the Shenzhen municipal government and Tsinghua University and has invested in nearly 200 tech startups.[113]

In Cambridge, Chinese VCs such as TusPark UK[114] (part of Tsinghua University) and Puhua Capital[115] continuously meet with startups and participate in sessions in which startups pitch potential investors. In spring 2020, Puhua participated (with European investors) in a funding round for the Oxford-based medical software startup Perspectum[116] and funded another medical technology startup, Cambridge-based Inotec AMD.[117] In November 2020, the Chinese tech giant Tencent invested in the Series C funding round for the Cambridge-based genomics startup Congenica.[118]

In the United States, the 2018 FIRRMA legislation tried to remedy the situation by making it more difficult for foreign VC firms to invest in cutting-edge tech. Other Western countries, however, have not passed similar legislation. In addition, FIRRMA does not apply to VC firms' limited partners. As the name suggests, limited partners have small involvement in the startups they fund; their funding is supposed to be passive capital, and they receive only basic information about the technology and financials of the startups they invest in. Limited partnerships are, however, a gray-zone area, as a limited partner may provide all the capital invested in a startup. This gives the limited partner considerable opportunity to informally steer the startup's strategy, including expanding or shifting focus to a particular country. Limited partners can also try to access confidential information about the funded startup's technology through, for example, conversations with staff. Even though limited partners are not entitled to such information, this rule is difficult to police.

Considering that startups are creating cutting-edge innovation, limited partnerships are a highly attractive proposition. VC firms are, however, not obliged to disclose the names of their limited partners. Some limited partners active in the West are known to be connected to the Chinese government. According to a 2018 Reuters investigation, no fewer than 20 Silicon Valley VC firms have Chinese limited partners linked to Chinese government entities.[119] Sabrina Yuan and Art Dicker note that, in the United States, the best option for Chinese-backed funds

> is to essentially not be Chinese. Under FIRRMA, even if 100% of the limited partner investors in a fund are Chinese, if the general partners of the fund are US citizens and fully empowered with discretion to make all investment decisions on their own, the fund is considered a US fund.[120]

Even under US legislation, which is stricter than other Western countries', it is thus easy for entities affiliated with strategic rivals to invest in promising startups. That early funding, in turn, can give them access to key innovation long before a firm is ready to be acquired. Equally troublingly, it is impossible to know how many Western startups have received VC funding from limited partners connected to governments that are engaged in gray-zone aggression against the West. It is, of course, also not possible to know which startups have received such funding.[121]

VC funding is also important because Chinese investors'—and the Chinese government's—objective may not be to acquire a company and take full control of it. Instead, getting access to pioneering innovation at an early stage often appears to be a strategy. Equipped with this knowledge, Chinese investors can encourage China-based companies to pursue the same innovation, and these firms can in turn strengthen their country's position in a global economy in which innovation is a fundamental asset.

Corporate Appointments

During the Cold War, countless Westerners knowingly or unwittingly served as Warsaw Pact agents of influence.[122] Indeed, in strategic competition among countries, each side typically tries to recruit locals of some prominence to speak on its behalf in their home countries. During the Cold War, however, there were decidedly few opportunities for influence activities in the business world because few businesses straddled NATO countries and the Warsaw Pact.

Since the end of the Cold War, commercial interaction among countries has skyrocketed. Western countries in particular have given foreign citizens and businesses largely unfettered access to their markets and indeed their societies. The same, however, is not true for many other countries. The EU-China CAI, for example, allows Chinese companies to buy EU-based broadcasters, cinemas, and other entertainment ventures, while China provides no such access in return.[123]

This has triggered considerable innovation in engaging locally prominent individuals for strategic advantages, a practice sometimes referred to as "elite capture." This term originates from the field of international development, referring to the capture of resources *by* the elite.[124] Today, however, it has an additional meaning: capture *of* the elite.

This capture can include appointments to various bodies and organizations and is thus a much wider concept than agents of influence is. The "captured elite" does not have to perform any functions for the other country apart from turning a friendly ear to it. In July 2020, for example, a dossier assembled by a British former intelligence officer documented alleged Chinese elite capture in the UK.[125]

Corporate appointments are a particularly problematic aspect of elite capture. During the Cold War, the few Warsaw Pact–based companies active in the West were hardly in the position to offer jobs or board appointments to retired politicians and other notable members of society.[126] Today, such opportunities are plentiful. In the first half of 2020, for example, the UK board of Huawei featured four members of the British political and business establishment—three with knighthoods and one a member of the House of Lords.[127] One of them, former BP CEO John Browne, served as chairman and is credited with having improved Huawei's image in the UK. Huawei's strategy appeared to have borne fruit when the UK government in early 2020 decided to include Huawei in the country's 5G network. When the government subsequently reversed its decision, Browne resigned.[128] Hong Kong–based HSBC, in turn, employs as its UK head of public affairs a former British ambassador.[129]

Germany's former Chancellor Gerhard Schröder chairs the shareholders' committee of Nord Stream,[130] the pipeline that transports gas from Russia to Europe. While Nord Stream is partly owned by western European energy firms,[131] it is majority-owned by Gazprom. Because of this link, Schröder has received enormous criticism for his role on Nord Stream's board. Former Austrian Foreign Minister Karin Kneissl serves on the board of Rosneft Oil Company, another energy giant controlled by the Russian government, as does Schröder,[132] while former Swedish Prime Minister Fredrik Reinfeldt serves on the board of a Hong Kong–based firm whose ultimate majority owner is the Chinese government.[133]

These appointments are not illegal. In most Western countries, politicians and senior officials leaving office are obliged to abide by a cooling-off period during which they must not accept private-sector appointments. Following that period, however, they are free to accept appointments, including with foreign firms. Members of parliaments such as the UK House of Lords and House of Commons are also free to hold concurrent private-sector appointments.[134] "It is notable that a number of Members of the House of Lords have business interests linked to Russia, or work directly for major Russian companies linked to the Russian state," the UK Parliament's Intelligence and Security Committee noted in its 2020 report on Russia.[135]

In itself, holding such appointments does not pose a risk to the individuals' home countries: Every multinational company today has a main board of directors comprising many nationalities, and regional or national boards in different parts of the world are composed of people with relevant expertise, contacts, and public standing. Companies need exactly that kind of expertise. It is, however, more problematic when firms representing countries that engage in gray-zone aggression appoint prominent personalities in countries against which their home governments engage in unfair competition. If those firms also do their governments' bidding, or are unfairly supported by their governments at the expense of Western competitors, their use of locally prominent figures is another iteration of subversive economics.

In 2020, the China Research Group—British members of Parliament who advocate for more caution in the UK's relationship with China—released a report that highlighted the risks posed by corporate appointments.[136] Tom Tugendhat, a Conservative member of Parliament who chairs the group, told the *Financial Times* that it is "unacceptable" that UK former politicians and senior officials "go on to leverage that knowledge to the advantage of our rivals and not our citizens."[137] However, while there are boards examining exiting politicians' and senior officials' corporate appointments to ensure compliance with lobbying rules, there is no CFIUS-like regulator that scrutinizes corporate appointments on national security grounds in the same manner as for acquisitions.

Subversive Economics' Core Threat to National Security

Investments and acquisitions by private firms from other countries are not a development simply to tolerate; on the contrary, industrialized countries depend on foreign investments. Today, however, Western countries are finding that what is good for their economies in the short term is not good for their countries in the long term. This, too, highlights the defender's dilemma.

The genius of subversive economics is it exploits globalization in a legal and barely noticeable way. Addressing this exploitation of globalization without damaging the fabric of the globalized economy also poses a seemingly intractable dilemma for targeted countries. Subversive economics may, in fact, constitute the most poisonous form of gray-zone aggression facing liberal democracies today because, at a superficial level, business opportunities involving foreign entities are an asset. Through no fault of their own, businesses are finding themselves on the front line of a geopolitical confrontation for which they are ill-prepared and that goes against the nature of the globalized market. As Henry Farrell and Abraham Newman point out, "Once it was the places that globalization hadn't yet reached that were politically dangerous. Now new political risks are found right at the heart of the global economy."[138]

VI

Coercion, Bullying, and Subversion of Civil Society

In January 2021, China's President Xi Jinping told the World Economic Forum that "the strong should not bully the weak. Decision [*sic*] should not be made by simply showing off strong muscles or waving a big fist."[1] In reality, China engages in bullying vis-à-vis countries and foreign companies as a foreign policy tool. Even in 1966, Fidel Castro complained about such practices by Beijing, accusing China of committing "a criminal act of economic aggression against [Cuba]."[2] He added that China's actions "can be explained only as a display of absolute contempt toward our country" and asked "whether in the world of tomorrow powerful nations can assume the right to blackmail, extort, pressure, attack, and strangle small peoples."[3]

In 1966, only a few countries were vulnerable to such coercion by China; today, most of the world is. And China is not the only perpetrator. Coercion, bullying, and subversion of civil society are expedient forms of gray-zone aggression, particularly for regimes that are not concerned about a tattered image. This chapter analyzes selected forms of coercion, bullying, and subversion of civil society.

Coercion Through Diplomacy

In October 2020, China's ambassador to Canada reacted to reports that Canada might accept asylum applications by Hong Kong democracy activists. Amb. Cong Peiwu told a news conference,

> If the Canadian side really cares about the stability and prosperity in Hong Kong, and really cares about the good health and safety of those 300,000 Canadian passport holders in Hong

Kong, and a large number of Canadian companies operating in Hong Kong, you should support those efforts to fight violent crimes.[4]

There is nothing illegal or indeed objectionable about saying a country should support another country's efforts to fight violent crime. However, what Amb. Cong expressed was a threat against Canada. In recent years, Chinese diplomats have frequently issued such veiled threats to Western countries over developments Beijing disliked. In summer 2020, after the UK government had reversed its decision to include Huawei in its 5G network, China's ambassador to the UK, Liu Xiaoming, voiced pointed criticism: "The way you are treating Huawei is being followed very closely by other Chinese businesses, and it will be very difficult for other businesses to have the confidence to have more investment."[5]

Such threats are not empty words. For example, starting in 2010, China suspended imports of goods such as salmon to punish Norway for the Norwegian Nobel Committee's decision to award that year's Nobel Peace Prize to Chinese dissident Liu Xiaobo.[6] Amb. Liu's suggestion that the UK's decision to exclude Huawei would prompt an exodus of Chinese investment from the UK was, in other words, clearly intended as a threat. Beijing has, as we have seen, also threatened the UK with retaliation over the UK government's decision to grant a path to citizenship for residents of Hong Kong, a former British crown colony.[7] In January 2021, China announced that it would no longer recognize the so-called overseas passports granted by the UK to Hong Kong residents who registered as British overseas nationals before the UK handed over Hong Kong to China in 1997.[8] The move could prevent British overseas nationals from leaving Hong Kong.

In September 2020, China's Foreign Minister Wang Yi weighed in against another country, announcing that the speaker of the Czech parliament's upper chamber, Miloš Vystrčil, would "pay a heavy price" for leading a senate delegation on a visit to Taiwan.[9] Earlier in the year, China's embassy in the Czech Republic had sent a letter to Vystrčil's predecessor, Jaroslav Kubera, warning that, if he proceeded with the trip, "Czech companies who have economic interests in China will have to pay for the visit to Taiwan by Chairman Kubera."[10] It added, "China is the largest foreign market for many Czech companies like Skoda Auto, Home Credit Group,

Klaviry Petrof and others."[11] Kubera died of a heart attack a week after receiving the letter, without having managed to visit Taiwan.

Sweden is, in turn, a regular recipient of coercive statements by China's ambassador in Stockholm, and not just over matters relating to Huawei. Amb. Gui Congyou, who has held the post since 2018, has sent numerous letters to news organizations whose coverage of China he considers too critical; several of the organizations described the letters as aggressive and threatening. In a 2020 interview with Sveriges Television, Amb. Gui continued the theme, describing Sweden as a "48-kilogram lightweight boxer who provokes a feud with an 86-kilogram heavyweight boxer."[12]

Worldwide, the picture has been similar over the past decade. Charles Parton notes that "behaviour deemed inimical to CCP [Chinese Communist Party] interests can be punished by downgrading relations and harming economic interests."[13] He lists selected cases in recent years, including the punishment of Norway over the 2010 Nobel Peace Prize and a ban on South Korean package-holiday sales by Chinese travel agencies after South Korea agreed to host US Terminal High-Altitude Area Defense (THAAD) missiles.[14] In addition, Beijing has threatened repercussions for any country whose officials meet with the Dalai Lama. This has led to many Western governments no longer meeting with the Tibetan religious leader.[15]

Coercive diplomacy has, in other words, already forced Western governments to change their behavior. Erik Reichborn-Kjennerud and Patrick Cullen liken intimidation to not just gray-zone aggression but war: "War is also an act of force to compel our enemy to do our will."[16] It works. As Ivar Kolstad documents, "Immediately following the peace prize, Norwegian agreement with Chinese voting in the United Nations on human rights resolutions increased."[17]

Russian top officials have at various times also issued ominous warnings to Western countries, usually relating to NATO membership. In July 2018, for example, Russian Defence Minister Sergei Shoigu criticized a recent cooperation agreement signed by Finland, Sweden, and the United States.

> The deal signed in May allows these countries to participate fully in NATO exercises and to use NATO forces. In turn NATO has been granted full, unobstructed access to these countries' airspace and territorial waters.

> I emphasize that these kind [*sic*] of steps by our western colleagues lead to the destruction of the current security system, increase mistrust and force us to take counter-measures.[18]

Generally, however, Russia appears to use coercion vis-à-vis NATO, EU, G7, and Five Eyes countries less frequently than China does. As Stanislav Tkachenko and Antongiulio de' Robertis pointed out in 2016, Russia's use of coercive diplomacy around that time was mostly against Ukraine and Syria.[19] This relative absence of coercion directed against the West may not reflect a lack of intent but rather a lack of capability and opportunity: Because it is not a major economic partner and certainly does not play the same role that China does in Western economies, Russia has fewer coercive levers at its disposal. Indeed, the levers it does have—primarily gas exports to Europe—could harm Russia more than the targeted countries, as threats to cut off gas deliveries would convince many European decision makers to turn to other energy sources.

Some Western governments are, of course, no strangers to coercive diplomacy. In pursuing its Clean Network agenda for 5G equipment free of Chinese participation, the Donald Trump administration pressured allies to join it by, for example, requiring all traffic entering and exiting US diplomatic facilities to have a "clean path"—that is, no involvement by Huawei or fellow Chinese firm ZTE.[20] Coercive US diplomacy, though, precedes Trump. Writing in 2020, Elizabeth Rosenberg et al. observed that

> the last decade has seen an explosive growth in U.S. coercive economic tools. . . . [The George W. Bush and Barack Obama] administrations expanded sanctions on Iran in unprecedented ways, invented new types of financial restrictions on Russia, and targeted a growing array of transnational threats. Under Donald Trump's administration, America has not only continued to expand its use of sanctions, it has also renewed and expanded other parts of America's coercive economic toolkit.[21]

While the US government may consider this a matter of creating global order, its use of coercive economics provides an excuse for other countries to use coercion in less-palatable ways.

Indeed, threats as a diplomatic tool are not new. Cato the Censor (also known as Cato the Elder and Cato the Wise) may have used his regularly repeated calls for the destruction of Carthage ("*Carthago delenda est*")[22] to convince Romans of the idea, but Carthaginians certainly also perceived them as a threat. In more recent years, sundry leaders have threatened retaliation—sometimes not compliant with international law—if another country fails to comply with demands. In March 2003, President Bush issued a 48-hour ultimatum to Iraq before the United States invaded it.[23] During the Vietnam War, President Richard Nixon contemplated starting a rumor that he might have lost his mind and would be willing to completely destroy Vietnam; Nixon referred to it as his "madman theory."[24] Its obvious purpose was to bully the North Vietnamese into concessions they had been unwilling to make.

China's threats and use of coercion, leveraging the interconnected nature of global business, are of a different character than are Russia's threats of war or bullying. While threats relating to war and issues such as NATO membership can be used only infrequently, coercion using globalized business or individuals can be used at will, targeting any country, sector, company, or person. Such coercion hits the essence of today's liberal democracies. While decoupling or retreating from globalization to shield society from coercion may seem desirable, it is hardly feasible.

Coercion of Companies

In October 2020, after Sweden announced that its 5G network would not include Huawei or ZTE, the Chinese Ministry of Foreign Affairs' spokesman issued another veiled threat: Sweden should "correct its wrong decision, to avoid bringing a negative impact to China-Sweden economic and trade cooperation and the operations of Swedish enterprises in China," Zhao Lijian told a news conference.[25] The following month, Ericsson CEO Börje Ekholm surprised the world by telling several media outlets that Sweden should reverse its ban on Huawei equipment in the 5G network.

Considering that his firm stood to benefit from countries' bans of Huawei, his stance seemed odd. Then he went further, repeatedly messaging Sweden's trade minister asking her to reverse the ban (decided by the Post and Telecom Authority, an independent government agency).[26] It transpired that Ekholm had been pressured by the Chinese government.[27] That forced him to consider whether keeping Ericsson in Sweden—where it generates 1 percent of its revenue—was tenable, considering it might cost the firm access to China, where it has parts of its supply chain and generates about 10 percent of its revenue. "At the moment Sweden is a really bad country for Ericsson," Ekholm told the minister.[28]

Sweden faced losing one of its most important companies because it made a decision that, while defensive in nature, angered another country. In May 2021, the *Global Times*—a newspaper owned by the Chinese government—reported that Beijing would give Sweden one "last chance" to reverse its 5G decision.[29] Sweden did not. The results were not slow in coming. On July 16, Ericsson presented its report for the second quarter of 2021. It showed growing worldwide sales—but a drop in China.[30] Around the same time, China Mobile—the country's largest mobile network operator—announced its latest 5G contracts.[31] It awarded Huawei 60 percent, ZTE 30 percent, and Ericsson only 2 percent, down from 11 percent in the previous round of China Mobile contracts.[32]

Other global brands have also been punished in China. Although the punishment has, as is the case with Ericsson, ostensibly been meted out not by the government but by other companies or the public, it nonetheless appears to be a coordinated action against the targeted companies' home countries. In March 2021, days after Canada, the EU, the UK, and the US sanctioned China over its treatment of the Uyghur minority, H&M (based in EU member state Sweden), Burberry (based in the UK), and US-based Nike were hit by Chinese consumer boycotts. In H&M's case, Chinese state-run media led the boycott campaign.[33] E-commerce websites, social media platforms, online maps, and even landlords removed the brands, allegedly over pro-Uyghur statements the brands had made.[34] Not long afterward, Nike CEO John Donahoe declared that Nike "is a brand ... of China and for China."[35] FC Barcelona, meanwhile, canceled sponsorship negotiations with H&M, citing H&M's problems in China.[36] This is a secondary effect of China bullying Sweden.

Coercion through the private sector, practiced primarily by China but available to any government with intent and capability, poses a serious risk to targeted countries. This is because, as discussed in previous chapters, today businesses large and small operate globally. When Chinese Foreign Ministry spokesman Zhao demanded that Sweden "correct its wrong [5G] decision, to avoid bringing a negative impact to China-Sweden economic and trade cooperation and the operations of Swedish enterprises in China," Swedish companies knew this could cause severe problems for their operations and balance sheets.

The Australian government has adopted a self-assured approach vis-à-vis China, and consequently, its private sector has suffered, especially businesses that export heavily to China. In fall 2020, the Chinese government banned imports of timber from the Queensland region, stating that it had found a beetle infestation in a shipment. Before that, Chinese officials had instructed China's steel mills and power plants to stop importing Australian coal.[37] Then China imposed a mix of tariffs and import suspensions on many Australian goods including barley, cotton, and red meat, de facto cutting off many Australian exporters from their main export market.[38] Australia may lose another $28 billion if Chinese tourism in the country dries up, which was certainly a factor when Beijing in 2020 publicly warned its population of prospective racist attacks in Australia.[39]

The import restrictions were a clear attack on Australia's industry by the country's largest trading partner. They appear to be a retaliation against the Australian government's independent stance vis-à-vis China, and Beijing has kept using the tool. "This virus has inflicted a calamity on our world and its peoples. We must do all we can to understand what happened for no other purpose than to prevent it from happening again," Prime Minister Scott Morrison told the United Nations in September 2020.[40] In apparent retaliation, China—alleging Australian "wine dumping" on the Chinese market, an unproven accusation—responded with punitive tariffs on Australian wine. The tariffs of up to 212 percent meant Australian winemakers were barred from their largest export market.[41] In February 2021, Beijing suspended imports of Taiwanese pineapples, claiming to have found "harmful creatures" in them, though the move was more likely retaliation for Taiwan's decision not to import a Chinese-made COVID-19 vaccine.[42]

Joel Fitzgibbon, the agriculture and resources spokesman for the opposition Australian Labor Party, reacted to the suspensions of Australian goods.

> How much more harm must our economy suffer before Scott Morrison admits to his mistakes, swallows his pride, and puts an appropriate level of energy into fixing our relationship with our biggest trading partner?[43]

Norway met the same fate after the Norwegian Nobel Committee—a body independent of the government—awarded the Nobel Peace Prize to Liu. Kolstad notes that

> overt Chinese sanctions against Norwegian exports to China would have been in conflict with WTO [World Trade Organization] rules. There can nevertheless be little doubt that non-tariff barriers to Norwegian exports were introduced following the Nobel peace prize. . . . Norwegian exports of salmon were subjected to more stringent and time-consuming sanitation and veterinary controls at the border, and importers were unable to get licences for larger quantities of Norwegian salmon.[44]

Between 2011 and 2013 alone, this led to losses of up to $176 million for Norwegian fish exporters.[45] In late 2011, the British daily *Independent* reported that the Norwegian Foreign Ministry "said overall trade with China had grown by 46 per cent over the past six months. But sales of fresh salmon, meanwhile, have collapsed 61.8 per cent."[46]

Fitzgibbon's comment highlights the dilemma of liberal democracies that are coerced through punishment of their businesses. If a country suspends imports only unofficially, blaming procedural issues such as sanitation needs or slowing demand (or, as in Ericsson's case, ostensibly private companies based in that country cutting business with companies based in the to-be-punished country), the affected country will struggle to prove the move is hidden punishment. This also means the WTO cannot intervene.[47] If a government warns citizens from visiting another country due to racist attacks, the targeted country can claim only that there is little risk of racist attacks; it cannot appeal to a global body. If a government warns of harm to another country's businesses should it make a particular decision, it again can do little to respond.

In early 2021, it emerged that China's near ban on importing certain Australian items had, in fact, cost Australia only around $3 billion. During the first 11 months of 2020, Australian exports amounted to $257 billion.[48] Even though the punitive measures arrived at the end of the year, the loss was relatively small and may suggest to other countries that standing their ground may be worth the effort, despite the harm to specific companies or sectors.

Using Private Citizens for Coercion

Just as international businesses can be tools of coercion in a globalized world, so can ordinary citizens living in or visiting another country. While wrongful detention of foreign citizens is not new, today it should be considered part of gray-zone warfare when used to coerce other countries, especially countries that would not countenance imprisoning adversaries' citizens to achieve diplomatic gains.

At the time of writing, several citizens of Western countries are being held on spurious charges in what appears to be an effort to punish or coerce their home countries. In December 2018, shortly after Canadian authorities acting on a US warrant had arrested Huawei executive Meng Wanzhou on suspicion of trading with Iran in breach of sanctions, Chinese authorities detained two Canadian citizens—think tank employee Michael Kovrig and businessman Michael Spavor—and accused them of espionage. In March 2021, after having been detained for more than two years,[49] the two men stood trial (separately). In a breach of diplomatic protocols, neither Canadian nor any other Western diplomats were allowed to attend.[50] In August 2021, Spavor was sentenced to 11 years in prison, in a court session from which Western diplomats were again banned.[51] The Chinese government, meanwhile, demands that Canada free Meng.[52]

Iran, in turn, is holding dual British-Iranian national Nazanin Zaghari-Ratcliffe after giving her a one-year prison sentence for having spread "propaganda against the Islamic Republic."[53] That sentence immediately followed a five-year prison sentence relating to alleged espionage against Iran.[54] Although the Iranian government has not connected Zaghari-Ratcliffe with any other dispute, there has been speculation that she is being held to pressure the UK government to refund a £400 million payment made by the shah of Iran for UK military equipment. Delivery of the equipment was canceled after the Iranian Revolution, which means Iran is owed a refund. However, the UK Ministry of Defence has refused to release it over fears that Iran will use the funds in the conflicts in Yemen and Syria.[55] Several other Britons and Americans are also being held in Iranian prisons; their families suspect Iran of using them for potential prisoner swaps with Iranian officials and businessmen arrested in the West.[56] (Only acts by governments are considered in this chapter, not regular banditry or acts during armed conflicts.)

In 2015, US college student Otto Warmbier was seized by North Korean authorities, who accused him of espionage. After being detained for 17 months, Warmbier was returned to the United States; by then he was in a coma, and he died shortly afterward.[57] While it is hard to prove that North Korea planned to use Warmbier to pressure the United States for money or other concessions, what is indisputably established is that he was released only after a US representative agreed that the US government would pay North Korea $2 million for the medical care Warmbier allegedly received in North Korea.[58] North Korea is known to use criminal means to access hard currency.

Questionable detainment of foreign citizens has long been a tool used in peacetime by authoritarian regimes.[59] During the Cold War, the Soviet Union and other Warsaw Pact states detained Western citizens, whose imprisonment could last for years. Walter Ciszek, an American Catholic priest originally detained by the Soviet Union on charges of spying for the Vatican, was held in Soviet prisons and labor camps for 25 years before being exchanged for a Soviet spy held by the United States. During the Cold War, hundreds of other Americans—most of whom had moved to the Soviet Union for ideological reasons—are thought to have been imprisoned by Soviet authorities.[60]

Similar to how the risk of coercion using businesses has grown because of globalization, today the potential for coercion through individuals is growing as individuals also become more globalized. Today, many more people—including people born in industrialized countries—live outside their countries of birth than was the case in 1990.[61] International travel, including to risky countries and regions, has likewise increased. For the governments of liberal democracies, it is virtually impossible to prevent citizens from visiting or living in dangerous countries. Yet, since such individuals can be used for diplomatic coercion, their personal choices become tools of gray-zone aggression.

The opportunities afforded to hostile governments by Western citizens in these hostile countries are obvious: Just as hostile countries can punish other countries by unofficially suspending imports, they can also punish them by detaining individuals on charges that are almost impossible for outside organizations or governments to contest. As with all forms of gray-zone aggression, a country that does not operate with the standards of a liberal democracy has more options. A liberal democracy would not arbitrarily detain a Chinese citizen to avenge a lawful arrest of one of its own citizens in China.

Sanctions

Sanctions are a legal tool that countries, including liberal democracies, deploy to pressure another country to stop unacceptable behavior. However, when Western countries use sanctions on less-solid legal grounds, it presents an opportunity for adversaries to retaliate similarly.

Sanctions can be used to nudge—not to say pressure—countries toward more just and peaceful behavior. In the 1980s, many countries used sanctions to pressure South Africa over apartheid. Additionally, a large number of Russian officials and businesses are under Western sanctions because of Russia's annexation of Crimea. Since 1979, the international community, led by the United States, has imposed various sanctions on Iran. Unlike the sanctions imposed on Russia after the annexation of Crimea, these have primarily been general sanctions that have hit businesses and the population hard. Sanctions between 2011 and 2015 seem to have convinced Iran to join the Joint Comprehensive Plan of Action (JCPOA, or the "Iran nuclear deal"), upon which some of the sanctions were lifted by the EU, UN, and US.

The United States has, however, also imposed unilateral sanctions on a weaker legal basis. In 1982, the Ronald Reagan administration imposed such sanctions on US and international companies that were building a Soviet gas pipeline to West Germany,[62] handing the Soviet Union a propaganda opportunity. Had the Soviet Union been more connected to Western industry and in a position to punish US firms without harming itself, Reagan's sanctions would also have given the Soviets an excuse to similarly target Western business undertakings it disliked. President Reagan, perhaps realizing the harm unilateral sanctions can cause the global order, lifted the sanctions several months later.

In May 2018, the Trump administration ended US participation in the JCPOA and reimposed US sanctions "with the stated purpose of compelling Iran to negotiate a revised JCPOA that takes into account U.S. concerns beyond Iran's nuclear program," causing "Iran's economy to fall into significant recession."[63] Under Trump, the United States also imposed unilateral sanctions against companies involved with the Nord Stream 2 pipeline between Russia and Germany.[64] While governments imposing such unilateral sanctions will clearly argue the measures are justified, such use weakens the case for sanctions against serious violations of international rules. Perhaps even more importantly, it gives gray-zone adversaries an excuse to sanction firms based in the United States or allied countries.[65] This may have been one of the reasons behind Joe Biden's decision, in July 2021, to end US opposition to Nord Stream 2.[66]

Supply Disruption

If Australia did not export so much to China, it would not risk Chinese coercion. The same holds true for all Western countries. China is the European Union's second-largest trading partner for imports and exports.[67] While trade disputes are not a new aspect of international coexistence, numerous liberal democracies are discovering that commercial links can also be used as tools of gray-zone aggression. These tools can include not just surreptitious import bans but also supply disruptions.

Indeed, in their efforts to globalize and thus make all economies more efficient, Western countries have unwittingly exposed themselves to more potential coercion. Global supply chains have "created vulnerability for disruptions or halts to deliveries as inventories quickly empty out if new goods do not arrive on time. That vulnerability can, in turn, be used for coercion . . . or to create anxiety in society."[68] China's mysterious suspension of imports from various countries illustrates the latter. It is also a reminder that the only limit to gray-zone aggression is the attacker's imagination.

Hostile states can, in fact, make gray-zone activities even more effective by learning from product shortages resulting from others' mistakes or misfortunes. The first weeks of the COVID-19 pandemic demonstrated the extreme importance of personal protective equipment for daily life to function. The devastating natural disasters and subsequent nuclear reactor accident that hit the Japanese region of Fukushima in 2011 forced local companies to close. Because major automakers depended on Fukushima-based companies for a specialty paint pigment, this local disaster caused global car production to stall.[69]

Even though companies have since tried to limit using single-source suppliers, many components in supply chains are highly specialized, which makes manufacturers vulnerable to disruption. As with other forms of gray-zone aggression, a temporary halt of crucial supplies would not have to be presented as a geopolitical act or announced at all; supplies could simply be delayed. In the just-in-time model still used by most companies, any delay causes disruption and financial losses for the recipient and, especially, the producer. This is, of course, what happened when China suddenly suspended imports of Norwegian fish, Taiwanese pineapples, and many Australian goods.

Medications are among the goods most vulnerable to supply-chain disruptions, especially because their production, too, involves many different components and thus transportation of components across different locations and countries. China is the world's leading source of the components used for medications, while India has emerged as the leading medication manufacturer and a leading exporter to Europe, North America, and other parts of Asia.[70] It is conceivable that China could disrupt supplies of these crucial components to coerce or punish countries of its choosing.

Rare earth minerals—a small but vital component in electronic devices, electric-car batteries, and renewable energy production—form another area of concern. In 2020, the European Commission warned that the EU is now so reliant on imported rare earth minerals that it is vulnerable to punitive measures by exporters.[71] The United States imports 74 percent of its rare earth mineral needs from China,[72] which in 2020 accounted for 60 percent of global production of rare earth minerals.[73] Companies based in the West have never been major players in rare earth mineral production, which involves highly time-consuming and thus expensive processing. With demand for rare earth minerals set to increase further in the near future, the West is thus dependent on a country that may decide to limit or completely suspend exports to coerce another country. China also appears to be pursuing a strategy to protect itself against rare earth mineral disruption. In 2014, China's State Reserve Bureau began stockpiling rare earth minerals in facilities that can store more than 40,000 tons. It has already acquired thousands of tons of rare earths including dysprosium and yttrium.[74]

Rare earth mineral coercion by China is already taking place. In early 2021, it emerged that China's Ministry of Industry and Information Technology was planning to cap production and export of 17 rare earth minerals in China. Such a move could severely affect production of weaponry such as the F-35 fighter jet used by the United States and many of its allies.[75]

An early case of rare earth mineral coercion occurred in 2010: After Japan arrested a Chinese fishing-boat captain near the disputed East China Sea islands, China suspended rare earth mineral exports to Japan.[76] In this instance, too, there was no official Chinese announcement; the deliveries simply stopped. As with all coercion, China's plan was to get Japan to comply with its wishes.

Japan, however, stood firm. The government began organizing alternative sources of rare earth minerals, including production in Japan. Then, in 2020, it introduced a plan in which companies wanting to buy existing rare earth mineral refineries, build their own facilities, or invest in mining operations overseas can obtain government-backed loans.[77] The Japanese government is also working with the United States and Australian governments to create viable rare earth processing facilities capable of competing with Chinese ones.

Civic Financing

Civic financing is not by definition used for gray-zone aggression. Western governments, nongovernmental organizations (NGOs), and private donors finance organizations and initiatives in other countries without considering it subversive. This includes funding for democracy promotion, news organizations, civic initiatives, and politician training, and it often includes Western experts. Although this is, from the Western perspective, done with the honorable objective of promoting freedom and democracy, one could argue that it violates the principle of noninterference in other countries' domestic affairs, a pillar of international relations since the Treaty of Westphalia.

The United States, fueled partly by its long-standing self-perception as a promoter of democracy as a global good, has a long history of trying to influence countries it considers poorly governed. In some cases, this is a noble effort, although regime-change undertakings ranging from Chile to Iraq have indisputably harmed the United States' global image. In most cases, countries that are subject to Western interference—even of a well-intended kind—cannot prevent the involvement, and sometimes they even invite it. Strategic rivals act differently. In China, activities that could be described as Western interference—including democracy promotion—are de facto not possible. In 2012, Russia's State Duma, responding to what it considered foreign interference in Russian affairs, passed the "foreign agents" law, which requires organizations engaging in political activity and receiving foreign funding to register as foreign agents.[78]

Even as they seek to limit Western influence in their own countries, China and Russia directly or indirectly finance Western parties, organizations, and universities in ways that were not possible during the Cold War and previous eras. While this does not have to be part of gray-zone aggression, it offers considerable opportunities for interference. Citizens and entities from countries seeking to undermine the West also use financing of Western organizations in a way that could harm the functioning of democracy in targeted countries. Charitable donations are a form of influence creation.

In most Western countries, it is legal for foreign citizens to donate to museums, universities, NGOs, and other charitable organizations. Indeed, in many cases, such organizations would struggle to survive without foreigners' generous donations. In the EU, some countries even permit donations by foreigners to political parties. In 2019, 20 of the EU's 28 countries prohibited donations from foreign sources to political parties, while 18 of 28 prohibited foreign donations to individual candidates.[79]

Of course, a foreigner can take EU nationality and donate money. In the UK, Lubov Chernukhin—the wife of a Russian oligarch who is a former deputy finance minister under Vladimir Putin—has given £1.7 million to the Conservative Party, which makes her one of the party's top donors. UK media have reported concerns that the funds originate with Suleyman Kerimov, a billionaire member of Russia's parliament, the State Duma. Because Chernukhin and her husband have taken British citizenship, officially there is nothing untoward about the donations.[80]

Rules regarding foreign donations to other causes are much less stringent than those governing donations to political parties are. The UK Parliament's Intelligence and Security Committee noted in its 2020 report on Russia,

> Several members of the Russian elite who are closely linked to Putin are identified as being involved with charitable and/or political organisations in the UK, having donated to political parties, with a public profile which positions them to assist Russian influence operations. It is notable that a number of Members of the House of Lords have business interests linked to Russia, or work directly for major Russian companies linked to the Russian state—these relationships should be carefully scrutinised, given the potential for the Russian state to exploit them.[81]

The potential for subversion through higher education is perhaps even more significant. In 2020, the US Department of Education announced that Yale and Harvard Universities had failed to declare several hundred million dollars in foreign donations from countries including China.[82] Also in 2020, prominent Harvard nanoscience professor Charles Lieber was arrested following discoveries that he had been receiving funding from China and working with Chinese scientists on sensitive projects that the US Department of Defense was also funding.[83] A US Senate investigation found that between January 2012 and June 2018, 15 US universities reported donations of $15 million from China's Center for Language Education and Cooperation (formerly "Hanban"), but when the Senate Permanent Subcommittee on Investigations requested financial records from 100 universities, it found Hanban had donated an estimated $113 million.[84]

Dmitry Firtash, a Russian-Ukrainian oligarch indicted for money laundering in Spain and bribery in the United States, has donated money to numerous organizations, including £6 million to the University of Cambridge.[85] In February 2021, British media reported that Oxford University will, after receiving a £700,000 donation from Tencent, rename its Wykeham chair of physics the Tencent-Wykeham chair.[86] Cambridge University has, in turn, received funding from Tencent for a postdoctoral research fellowship in quantum technology.[87] China and Western countries including the UK are in a close race to claim quantum supremacy.[88]

US think tanks also receive significant sums from foreign governments. According to a 2020 report by the Center for International Policy, the United States' top 50 think tanks received funding of more than $174 million between 2014 and 2018, with nearly 900 different foreign donations given. The funding came from more than 80 different countries and international organizations. Norway, the United Arab Emirates, and the United Kingdom were the top donors; China, Qatar, and Saudi Arabia were likewise generous donors.[89]

In October 2020, a new database compiled by the Anti-Corruption Data Collective revealed that seven post-Soviet oligarchs connected to interference efforts in the United States had donated between $372 million and $435 million to more than 200 leading US nonprofit organizations including top think tanks, Harvard University, the Museum of Modern Art in New York, and the Kennedy Center in Washington, DC.[90] Receiving donations clearly does not indicate that recipients function as donor mouthpieces. Nevertheless, the association of hostile governments with institutions in liberal democracies is yet another way liberal democracies' rivals exploit openness and can engage in reputation laundering.[91]

Public Humiliation

In November 2020, Canadian Prime Minister Justin Trudeau received a phone call from the climate activist Greta Thunberg, who encouraged Canada to leave NATO and enticed Trudeau to criticize Trump. After a while, Trudeau established that the caller was an impersonator, but the damage was already done. It was later found that Russian pranksters Vladimir Kuznetsov and Alexey Stolyarov organized the call.[92] The pair have pranked other leaders and famous personalities including Prince Harry, Sen. Lindsey Graham (R-SC), and the UK's then–Foreign Secretary Boris Johnson.

Prince Harry was enticed by the pranksters to say Trump had "blood on his hands,"[93] which could have caused a diplomatic incident between the United States and the UK. In their call with Sen. Graham, in which the pranksters posed as Turkey's defense minister, the senator called the Kurds a threat, a position that contradicted his often-stated support of them.[94] (The Turkish government considers the Kurds dangerous separatists.) In the call with Johnson, in which the pranksters pretended to be the prime minister of Armenia, Johnson lamented the poor state of UK-Russian relations.[95] Impersonating Belarusian opposition leader Sviatlana Tsikhanouskaya, the pair managed to speak with the Danish parliament's defense committee in a confidential video meeting lasting 40 minutes.[96]

Kuznetsov and Stolyarov's choice of targets might be completely random, or it may be based on entertainment value. However, the strong focus on Western leaders raises suspicion that the pair cooperates with Russian security services[97] and that their goal is to embarrass Western leaders as part of Russian coercive diplomacy efforts. Paolo Alli, formerly a center-right Italian member of parliament and president of the NATO Parliamentary Assembly, is certain the pair has political motives.

> When I was president of the NATO Parliamentary Assembly [PA], I got a call from the two pranksters, who were impersonating Andriy Parubiy [speaker of the Ukrainian parliament]. I was sure it was real; everything was perfect. They tried to get me to say negative things about Putin. The only thing that was strange was the reason for their call; Parubiy wouldn't call me out of the blue. But they had all my information and knew all

internal NATO PA correspondence. They had clearly invested a lot of effort in this phone call.[98]

To date, only Kuznetsov and Stolyarov appear to have systematically used public humiliation, and it remains unclear what their objective is beyond poking fun at mighty Westerners. Considering, however, their apparent preference for politically affiliated heavyweights—as opposed to pure celebrities—it stands to reason that they have used prank calls as a way of stoking division within the West.

Mass sharing of confidential comments is a related practice, though it is more earnest in nature than the Russian duo's prank calls are. WikiLeaks, for example, published confidential information, arguing it did so as a journalistic organization. The US Senate's investigation on Russia's inference in the 2016 elections, however, found that WikiLeaks had cooperated with Russia's Main Intelligence Directorate (GRU) in releasing hacked documents.[99]

Another avenue for public humiliation may also emerge. In 2020 and 2021, ransomware attacks grew in frequency and sophistication. The nature of ransomware attacks is to force victims to pay to have their blocked data returned, and many do. The day after it was crippled by a ransomware attack by a Russia-based gang, Colonial Pipeline paid the attackers a $5 million ransom.[100] When meat processor JBS was attacked shortly thereafter, it quickly paid the $11 million ransom.[101] North Korea engages in ransomware to raise hard currency and is thought to have stolen around $2 billion in this fashion.[102]

As noted in Chapter VII, organizations are becoming aware of the ransomware threat and are increasingly backing up their files to prevent extortion, though it is unclear how effective this strategy is. Either way, the potential for public shaming using confidential information gives ransomware hackers—including government-affiliated ones—the opportunity to attack and threaten to release all data unless they receive payment. Such data publication would put organizations under extreme pressure and make them inclined to pay. At the very least, since North Korea's hack of Sony Pictures and release of emails and other confidential information in 2014, companies are painfully aware of the reputational damage a hack and release could cause. This is a form of gray-zone aggression that primarily poorer countries could engage in.

While prank phone calls to Western leaders may simply be mischief for entertainment's sake, they could equally be part of a hostile-government effort to humiliate Western leaders or get them to reveal secrets. Funding of arts organizations, universities, and other institutions can be benign, but it may also be used for gray-zone aggression. Coercion using Western companies and citizens is clearly an act of aggression, as is punishing them through import suspensions. Once again, the West faces the defender's dilemma in determining how much interference has to be accepted as the cost of living in an open society and which tools can be used to dissuade other practices.

Influencing and Coercing Pop Culture

Cultural exchange among rival countries can help defuse tension, which is why, during the Cold War, artists were allowed to regularly cross the Iron Curtain.[103] Culture is, however, also a long-standing area of influence peddling used by rival governments. Today, how to influence and coerce pop culture is emerging as a new area of gray-zone aggression, practiced primarily by China.

In 2015, the Metropolitan Museum of Art in New York hosted its annual Met Gala, with China as its subject. China has in recent years become one of the most important markets in the global luxury and fashion industries, as a driver of sales and a manufacturing hub. The *Financial Times* reported that, in 2019, Chinese consumers accounted for approximately 40 percent of the €281 billion (approximately $335.5 billion) spent on luxury goods globally.[104]

The Chinese government, however, has a history of using China's position as a leading market for luxury goods to enforce key geopolitical points. In 2019, Christian Dior was forced to issue a statement saying it supported China's "sovereignty and territorial integrity," after a retail presentation in which Dior presented a map of China that did not include Taiwan as Chinese territory.[105] Earlier that year, fashion houses Versace, Coach, and Givenchy had been forced to apologize to China after selling products that implied Hong Kong, Macau, and Taiwan were independent of China.[106] Despite the brands' efforts to mend the rift, high-profile

Chinese ambassadors cut ties to them, denting the brands' standings in the Chinese domestic economy. In an interview with *Forbes*, Sarah Willersdorf—head of Boston Consulting Group's luxury, fashion, and beauty practice—explained why the loss of influencers was so harmful.

> Today, with the power of social media and influencers, one small misstep can rapidly reverberate to have massive implications for companies very quickly. This is especially true in China, where social media and influencers are the number one driver of luxury purchases.[107]

As with global haute couture, Beijing's pressure also influences the film industry. Governments influencing filmmaking is nothing new, including in the West. Hollywood has, despite its frequent criticism of the US government, also been an instrument of US soft power. As a storytelling medium, film can spread American ideas to foreign audiences, albeit not always how Washington would prefer. Beijing, by contrast, uses Hollywood's desire to reach China's market of 1.4 billion people as an opportunity to positively present China to global audiences. Global audiences, however, watch the films not knowing that is the case.

In a 2020 report, PEN America details how the publicity department of the CCP, known as the Central Propaganda Department, uses foreign film—particularly Hollywood productions—to "tell China's story well."[108] The Central Propaganda Department is in charge of ideology-related work and China's information dissemination system. Its major responsibilities include supervising national ideological and political education curricula; governing the publication, news, and film industries; and managing the leading state broadcaster, China Central Television (CCTV).[109] James Tager, the report's author and PEN America's deputy director of free-expression research and policy, notes that "Beijing recognizes that Hollywood—still the world's most significant center for storytelling through film—shapes the opinions and ideas of the world, and it seeks to ensure that power is used in ways consistent with its own interests."[110]

The Chinese government allows only a small number of foreign productions to be shown in China: typically 34 annually. Since 2016, every film released in China must be vetted[111] by the Central Propaganda Department and either the Ministry of State Security, State Ethnic Affairs Commission, Ministry of Public Security, State Administration for Religious Affairs, Ministry of Education, Ministry of Justice, or Ministry of Foreign Affairs.[112] Unsurprisingly, foreign studios thus face choosing between complying with the censors' demands to have a chance of getting their films released on the Chinese market or risking a loss by refusing. Beijing also incentivizes positive narratives about China through, for example, preferential release dates and advertising packages.

The power of the Central Propaganda Department vis-à-vis Western studios is strengthened by not only the fierce competition among studios to get their movies released but also the fact that foreign productions often receive financing from Chinese investors. Tager notes that "such companies appear to operate as go-betweens, extracting concessions from both the government and from their Hollywood partners—with Hollywood's concessions often coming in the form of film content that the CCP will view favourably."[113]

Foreign studios' interest in China is based on the fact that China already is the world's second-largest movie market. Indeed, before the COVID-19 pandemic, Hollywood studios' revenues in China sometimes exceeded their revenues from the US market. In 2019, three American blockbuster films—*Avengers: Endgame*, *Spider-Man: Far from Home*, and *Fast & Furious Presents: Hobbs and Shaw*—together made more than $2.6 billion in China.[114] "No other nation's box office is so integral to Hollywood's financial fortunes," Tager observes.[115]

Chinese officials are sometimes even invited on set during production. This setup is part of a joint production model involving a foreign and a Chinese studio, meaning government censors can act as production partners.[116] Perhaps the best example of how the Central Propaganda Department can embed its political messaging in joint productions, overtly and covertly, is Paramount Pictures' *Transformers: Age of Extinction*. *Variety*'s David S. Cohen described the film as "very patriotic. . . . It's just Chinese patriotism on the screen, not American."[117] The film received a major infusion of Chinese financing; was shot in Beijing, Guangzhou, and Hong Kong; and features Chinese stars Li Bingbing and Han Geng.[118]

All these factors have created a situation in which Hollywood increasingly makes crucial decisions about a film's content, casting, dialogue, settings, and plot based on censors' requirements. Indeed, to increase the chances of their films being admitted for release in China, Hollywood studios even try to anticipate censor requirements. In July 2020, former US Attorney General William Barr criticized US companies for becoming "pawns of Chinese influence."[119] Although he directed plenty of criticism at American tech companies, Barr also took aim at Hollywood studios for their self-censorship and "kowtow[ing]" to Chinese censorship demands. "Many more scripts never see the light of day because writers and producers know not to test the limits. Chinese government censors don't need to say a word because Hollywood is doing their work for them," Barr said.[120]

US productions that have been changed to please Chinese censors include *Red Dawn*, which depicted Chinese enemies invading an American town. This plotline changed when the motion picture's script was leaked and Beijing reacted with outrage.[121] In response, MGM Studios digitally replaced all Chinese flags, insignia, and other symbols with North Korean ones.[122] The same strategy was used in the *Top Gun* remake, *Top Gun: Maverick*, wherein Taiwan's flag was removed from Tom Cruise's bomber jacket.[123] Marvel Comics invited Chinese censors to its studios during the filming of *Iron Man 3*.[124] In 2016, Marvel released *Doctor Strange*, which was supposed to include a character known as the Ancient One, a Tibetan monk.[125] In the film adaptation, however, the studio recast the character as a Celtic druid-like figure over fears of offending the Chinese government by drawing attention to Tibet.[126]

Chinese influence on international film extends beyond censorship. The 1997 movie *Seven Years in Tibet*, featuring Brad Pitt, drew criticism from the CCP for negatively portraying Chinese military officers while positively depicting the 14th Dalai Lama.[127] Brad Pitt, his costar David Thewlis, and Jean-Jacques Annaud, the director, were promptly banned from entering China.

Around the same time, director Martin Scorsese was also banned from China following the release of his Disney-backed biopic of the Dalai Lama, *Kundun*. Chinese authorities found the film objectionable "on political grounds, given their official stance that the Tibetan spiritual leader is a dangerous separatist."[128] Disney CEO Michael Eisner promptly apologized to Chinese Prime Minister Zhu Rongji, explaining that "the bad news is that the film was made; the good news is that nobody watched it. . . . In the future we should prevent this sort of thing, which insults our friends, from happening."[129] After calling Taiwan a country in an interview with a Taiwanese news outlet in May 2021, *Fast & Furious* star John Cena posted a profuse apology on his Weibo account, saying, "I'm very sorry for my mistakes. Sorry. Sorry. I'm really sorry. You have to understand that I love and respect China and Chinese people."[130]

Richard Gere is one of few Hollywood celebrities not to bow to Chinese pressure. He remains banned from China and is also reported to have been blacklisted for roles in Hollywood productions. In an interview with the *Hollywood Reporter*, Gere said that there "are definitely movies that I can't be in because the Chinese will say, 'Not with him.' I recently had an episode where someone said they could not finance a film with me because it would upset the Chinese."[131]

Most countries worldwide exert some government-run system of approval for circulation, usually called a film classification board. As in China, such bodies approve every domestic and foreign film before it can be released in cinemas, typically judging the productions on suitability for children and teenagers. Although such bodies have been in place for about a century,[132] never before has a market with heavy censorship been among the world's most lucrative. PEN America states that the main reasons for Beijing's power over Hollywood are the Chinese market's size, which makes it key to a film's financial success; China's comprehensive censorship system, which allows government authorities to regulate all access to the market; and Beijing's clear message to filmmakers worldwide that criticism will be punished, while those who "play ball" will be rewarded.[133]

China also exerts pressure on the West through elite sports. As the most popular sports league in China (ahead of the Champions and Premier Leagues),[134] the NBA has been affected by such coercion. Basketball is an extremely popular sport in China: Over 300 million people play recreational basketball, and in 2018, about half a billion watched at least one NBA game.[135] In 2019 alone, this brought the NBA annual revenues of more than $4 billion.[136]

Given basketball's popularity, the NBA is the most strongly positioned sports organization to push back against Chinese government pressure. The *Wall Street Journal* notes that "China is a huge market for any enterprise, but there's only one NBA. There are other hotels, airlines and clothing brands. NBA basketball is irreplaceable."[137] Yet, despite its uncontested market share, the NBA has bowed to Chinese pressure even outside China. On October 4, 2019, Daryl Morey, the general manager of the Houston Rockets, tweeted on his personal account, "Fight for freedom, stand with Hong Kong."[138] The Chinese Basketball Association immediately suspended its relationship with the Rockets. Tencent—whose streaming deal with the NBA is worth $1.5 billion—said it would not be showing Rockets games, as did Chinese state television.[139]

Within days, the NBA issued a statement acknowledging that Morey's tweet "deeply offended many . . . friends and fans in China, which is regrettable," and China's consulate in Houston issued a public statement urging for "immediate concrete measures to eliminate the adverse impact."[140] Morey quickly deleted his tweet and subsequently issued a statement expressing contrition.[141] The Rockets owner, Tilman Fertitta, in turn tweeted to distance the team from Morey: "@dmorey does NOT speak for the @HoustonRockets."[142]

Like haute couture, films, and elite sports, the global music industry is vulnerable to coercion. Again, the main practitioner of such coercion is China, which seeks to change not only its global image but also its power to coerce, thanks to the size of its consumer market. Beijing has increasingly pressured the South Korean K-pop industry in particular. The health of South Korea's economy is based on the continued exportation of semiconductors, smartphone chips, petrochemicals, and K-pop to China and the United States.[143] Exports of the K-pop boy band BTS alone generate an estimated $5 billion annually for South Korea's economy.[144]

However, K-pop's popularity in China fell drastically in 2016 when South Korea agreed to cooperate with the United States to build a THAAD missile defense battery to protect South Korea from North Korean attacks.[145] Developed by the United States, the defense shield is designed to defend South Korea by intercepting North Korean missiles.[146] Beijing, however, viewed the THAAD system as an offensive, not defensive, act and issued a public statement condemning it.[147] China retaliated against South Korea by imposing a ban on all South Korean cultural imports for two years, with music and Korean television programs blocked on all streaming services.[148] At the time of writing, no major K-pop group has toured China since 2016.

As with foreign films, Beijing also seeks to censor the content of K-pop stars' public statements and songs. In 2015, Chou Tzuyu, a Taiwanese member of the K-pop band Twice, was forced to publicly apologize to Beijing after waving a Taiwanese flag during a reality television show.[149] In September 2020, Chinese internet users accused South Korean singer Lee Hyo-ri of "being disrespectful" of the late Mao Zedong after she suggested using "Mao" as her stage name during a television show.[150] A month later, BTS faced massive backlash in China over comments that band leader Kim Nam-Joon, known as RM, made about the Korean War.[151] In the acceptance speech for the Korea Society's James A. Van Fleet Award,[152] a recognition of the group's efforts to develop good relations between the United States and South Korea, RM mentioned the two nations' shared "history of pain" as they fought together against Beijing-backed North Korea: "We will always remember the history of pain that our two nations shared together and the sacrifices of countless men and women."[153] Advertisers quickly withdrew content featuring BTS from Chinese websites and social media platforms.

Fans and advertisers reacting against perceived snubs of their countries manifestly does not constitute gray-zone aggression. When governments, however, punish artists and encourage fans to protest against perceived or real slights—and when this is done to create a situation in which global celebrities are pressured to voice positive opinions about a country and suppress negative ones—it certainly constitutes influence peddling in the gray zone. Today's entertainment audiences also have no way of knowing how Chinese authorities influence the content they consume. That, too, constitutes subversive influence.

This does not mean countries should spread paranoia regarding hostile influences on entertainment; the US House Committee on Un-American Activities' hearings on alleged Hollywood Communists in the 1940s demonstrate where this can lead. Yet Western governments have struggled to identify any response to today's practices. This is partly because artists, studios, and fashion houses targeted by coercion operate independently of Western governments and partly because exploiting pop culture—like many other forms of gray-zone aggression—uses legal means.

VII

Gradual Border Alterations and Surreptitious Fishing: Use of Illicit Means

The illicit leg of gray-zone aggression comprises many hostile activities that even most ordinary citizens would recognize as unlawful. Because these activities, however, straddle the concepts of legality and war—and international law, international norms and conventions, and criminal law—they impede a nation's ability to muster an effective response.

This chapter examines selected forms of illicit aggression including theft of intellectual property (IP), physical harm to other countries' diplomats, and maritime and aerial harassment. They are not acts of armed conflict—which involves sustained use of force—but they violate international norms while leaving the targeted countries struggling to identify an appropriate response. They also capitalize on the combination of intent, capability, and opportunity, because international law governs war and the relations among countries, while nations' criminal laws cover the actions of individuals in that country. Because international law depends on universal acceptance, it is far less comprehensive than most countries' domestic laws are. It is also slow to adapt to new technologies and difficult to enforce.[1]

Perhaps paradoxically, international law is clearer in war than in peace because the norms are well established and simpler to enforce. Many illicit gray-zone actions perpetrated or supported by a state would ordinarily fall under criminal law. Targeted counties, however, face the challenges of not just bringing individual perpetrators to justice but also how to punish the state sponsors and deter further hostile acts.

Cyber Aggression

"I'll never forget. It was the 27th of June when I was woken up at four o'clock in the morning. A call came from the office that we had suffered a cyberattack," said Jim Hagemann Snabe, the chairman of A.P. Moller-Maersk, at a World Economic Forum event in January 2018.[2] Maersk is the world's largest container shipping company.[3] It transports 20 percent of the world's trade,[4] 12 million containers of goods annually, which Maersk's cargo ships bring to more than 300 ports worldwide.[5]

Maersk's computers went dark. Its chief technology and information officer at the time, Adam Banks, told an industry publication two years later,

> All end-user devices, including 49,000 laptops and print capability, were destroyed. All of our 1,200 applications were inaccessible and approximately 1,000 were destroyed. Data was preserved on back-ups but the applications themselves couldn't be restored from those as they would immediately have been re-infected. Around 3,500 of our 6,200 servers were destroyed—and again they couldn't be reinstalled.[6]

The globe-spanning firm's employees could not even phone one another or the company's customers: The network damage had rendered all Maersk landlines inoperable, and all contacts had been wiped from employees' cell phones. Fortunately for Maersk, a power outage in Ghana had knocked a company computer there off the network before the attack. With this single computer, Maersk managed to resume some of its operations, but even though its IT engineers worked quickly, it took several days for the company to return to some degree of normal service.[7]

Maersk's misfortune received much media attention, which was hardly surprising since the attack caused the company losses of up to $300 million.[8] Maersk had been hit by a computer virus that became known as NotPetya. So, it emerged, had numerous other pillars of the global economy. Pharmaceutical giant Merck could not fulfil orders for GARDASIL 9, the leading vaccine against the human papillomavirus and, as Bloomberg reported, "had to borrow 1.8 million doses—the entire U.S. emergency supply—from the Pediatric National Stockpile."⁹ In total, NotPetya cost Merck $870 million. FedEx's European subsidiary TNT Express was also hit, as were French construction company Saint-Gobain, American snack giant Mondelēz International (maker of, among other things, Oreo cookies and Nabisco chips), and the manufacturer Reckitt Benckiser Group (maker of Dettol, Durex, and other household items). All suffered major losses.

The international conglomerates were apparently accidental targets, "collateral damage of probably a state attack," as Snabe put it at the World Economic Forum event.[10] Indeed, NotPetya's intended target was Ukraine, where the virus hit hospitals, banks, power companies, card payment systems, airports, and government agencies, among other targets.[11] Ukrainians were left without power, access to their bank accounts, and the ability to pay for anything. The government struggled to operate, and air travel was disrupted. Although the harm was equivalent to that of a military attack, the risk of escalation meant Ukraine would have been ill-advised to respond with its full range of kinetic capabilities, and indeed it did not do so.[12]

Months after the attack, Western governments, including the United States, declared that NotPetya had been launched by a hacker group working for Russia's Main Intelligence Directorate (GRU). The White House press secretary declared in a statement on February 15, 2018,

> In June 2017, the Russian military launched the most destructive and costly cyber-attack in history.
>
> The attack, dubbed "NotPetya," quickly spread worldwide, causing billions of dollars in damage across Europe, Asia, and the Americas.[13]

On the same day, the UK Foreign and Commonwealth Office's Minister for Cyber Security Tariq Ahmad said that

> the UK Government judges that the Russian Government, specifically the Russian military, was responsible for the destructive NotPetya cyber-attack of June 2017.
>
> The attack showed a continued disregard for Ukrainian sovereignty. Its reckless release disrupted organisations across Europe costing hundreds of millions of pounds.[14]

In October 2020, the US government went one step further, charging GRU officers with the attack and, inter alia, with cyberattacks on the republic of Georgia, Emmanuel Macron's 2017 presidential campaign, and the 2018 Pyeongchang Winter Olympics.[15]

APT28—the group most often mentioned in connection with NotPetya—is well-known to Western governments. Its sister group APT29, which is thought to be affiliated with Russia's Foreign Intelligence Service, has been accused of hacking the Democratic National Committee in 2016[16] and institutions developing a COVID-19 vaccine.[17] Chris Inglis, former deputy director of the US National Security Agency and a commissioner of the Cyberspace Solarium Commission, pointed out that

> in 2012, 2013, [and] 2014, hostile states began to use aggression just below the kinetic threshold more frequently. While the US had launched a cyber command, it declared that it would only rarely use its offensive capabilities, because it knew that using the offensive capabilities would be escalatory. Then, in 2017 and 2018, North Korea and Russia committed the WannaCry and NotPetya attacks.[18]

The WannaCry attack affected computers in some 150 countries; the US government subsequently attributed it to North Korea.[19]

In Sweden, Erik Brandsma, CEO of the regional utility Jämtkraft at the time of the interview, noted that

> there have also been cyberattacks that we believe originated with foreign powers. They include a successful cyberattack on the social security system, a blackout at Arlanda [Stockholm's main airport], cyberattacks against news media. In addition, telecommunications masts have been sabotaged. Cyber intrusions into government agencies have increased in recent years. These attacks add up, and their increasing number gives Sweden cause for concern. Unfortunately, most of them are difficult to attribute.[20]

Inglis concluded that "deterrence in cyberspace has failed."[21]

He was proved right in 2020 and 2021, when numerous groups thought to be linked to hostile governments perpetrated a series of extraordinary attacks and intrusions on Western companies and governments. At the end of 2020, an intrusion subsequently attributed to APT29 that had gone undetected for months was discovered at the cybersecurity firm SolarWinds. But the intrusion did not end there. With SolarWinds as its springboard, APT29 had digitally invaded the US Departments of State, Homeland Security, the Treasury, Energy, and Commerce and US government agencies such as the Federal Energy Regulatory Commission—which regulates the sale and transmission of electricity and energy. The hack also struck foreign entities and scores of private companies. The SolarWinds hack was deemed the most devastating hack to date on the United States.[22]

Victims of previous APT29 intrusions "have included government, consulting, technology, telecom, and oil and gas companies in North America, Europe, Asia and the Middle East, according to FireEye, a cyber firm that itself was breached," the *Washington Post* reported.[23] In January and February 2021, Microsoft and some 30,000 of its clients were breached in a similar supply-chain attack.[24] In June, the US and other Western governments collectively attributed a slew of recent intrusions, including the Microsoft hack, to individuals affiliated with the Chinese government.[25]

Other cyber incidents in 2020 and 2021 included the previously discussed ransomware attacks against Colonial Pipeline, JBS, and the Irish national health service; North Korean hacks of companies developing COVID-19 vaccines[26]; and a suspected Chinese penetration of Australian companies and government agencies.[27] The French government revealed that it, too, had suffered a SolarWinds-like supply-chain intrusion. Even though French authorities rarely attribute cyberattacks to foreign states, in this case they attributed the intrusion to Russia.[28] The Norwegian government, in turn, attributed a March 2021 cyberattack on the Norwegian parliament to "actors operating out of China."[29] An even more serious incident occurred in October 2020: While Chinese and Indian troops were clashing in the Galwan Valley, Mumbai—a commercial hub home to some 20 million people—suffered a crippling power outage that affected hospitals, public transport, and other infrastructure.[30]

APT29's intrusions seem to have been intended for espionage, not disruption. Even espionage cyber intrusions, though, cause damage, and not just to the organizations affected but to their supply chains, as penetration of one link can harm other links too. In the SolarWinds attack, SolarWinds was not the target but merely the third party through which the attackers reached their targets, US government agencies. Even well-protected organizations can, as a result, be successfully penetrated through weak links in their supply chains. In addition, the line between espionage and destruction in cyberspace is razor-thin. An attack may begin as an espionage intrusion but spill over into destruction. Western governments, too, engage in cyberespionage, and some have the ability to cause destruction.

After the SolarWinds intrusion, the North American Electric Reliability Corporation—the joint US-Canada utility regulator—instructed utilities to assess their exposure to SolarWinds, warning that the intrusion "poses a potential threat" to parts of the power sector.[31]

The incidents also illustrate that, in gray-zone aggression, the traditional divide between national security and civil society in peacetime no longer exists. Inglis noted that

> we have to use all the instruments at our disposal by involving all parts of society. The current situation in the US, where we have a profound split between Republicans and Democrats and between the government and the private sector, is a golden opportunity for our adversaries.[32]

Chinese state-sponsored intrusion likewise mixes espionage and disruption—as was the case with the Microsoft hack attributed to Chinese operators—and features a heavy dose of IP theft. In a joint report released in February 2021, the Netherlands' intelligence, counterintelligence, and counterterrorism agencies noted that, regarding offensive cyber operations,

> China mainly focuses on espionage campaigns. These campaigns are aimed at obtaining high-quality knowledge and technology for their own economic development and the development of the armed forces. It follows from this that Dutch top sectors,

the Dutch defense industry and Dutch scientific and knowledge institutions run a high risk of Chinese (digital) espionage.[33]

In 2020, RedDelta—a Chinese state-sponsored hacker group—targeted the Vatican, apparently to gain insights into its negotiating position before the renewal of the 2018 China-Vatican provisional agreement,[34] and in 2019 another state-backed group targeted German industrial giants including Siemens, most likely to steal IP.[35] The state-sponsored group APT41 specializes in a combination of espionage and IP theft.[36]

North Korea appears to conduct a mix of espionage attacks, IP theft, and hacks to steal money. Iran seems to favor a mix of disruptive cyberattacks against regional rivals (primarily Israel), cyberespionage, and revenue-raising attacks.[37] A February 2021 indictment by the US Department of Justice (DOJ) illustrates the highly belligerent and innovative nature of North Korean cyber aggression. The DOJ charged three North Koreans, explaining that they had participated

> in a wide-ranging criminal conspiracy to conduct a series of destructive cyberattacks, to steal and extort more than $1.3 billion of money and cryptocurrency from financial institutions and companies, to create and deploy multiple malicious cryptocurrency applications, and to develop and fraudulently market a blockchain platform.[38]

A Canadian-American dual citizen also pleaded guilty to "being a high-level money launderer for multiple criminal schemes, including ATM 'cash-out' operations and a cyber-enabled bank heist orchestrated by North Korean hackers."[39]

These cases highlight how cyber aggression continues to evolve, becoming more sophisticated and targeted. David Omand refers to such aggression as "CESSPIT": crime, espionage, sabotage, and subversion perverting internet technology.[40] In the 2020 edition of its annual cyber-readiness report—based on surveys with companies in major economies including the United States, the UK, Germany, and France—the insurer Hiscox reported that the share of businesses affected by cyberattacks dropped between 2019 and 2020, from 61 percent to 39 percent, though it rose in some countries.[41] Because many regular criminals seem not to have kept up with the improving cyber defense, fewer organizations currently suffer serious harm. However, the median cost of incidents and breaches has increased significantly. Samu Konttinen, who was at the time of the interview CEO of the Finnish cyberspace security company F-Secure Corporation,[42] pointed out that globally "the volume of cyberattacks is not going up, but not down either. What's changing is that cyberattacks have become more sophisticated, and they're being directed against specific targets."[43]

Notwithstanding cyber-governance efforts such as the *Tallinn Manual on the International Law Applicable to Cyber Warfare*, state-sponsored cyber intrusion thus resides in a legal no-man's-land. Even though countries' criminal laws ban cyberattacks, it is unclear if even the most-sophisticated state-sponsored attacks—with damage equal to that of traditional military attacks—also violate international law. As Harriet Moynihan notes,

> Cyber operations that cause injury or death to persons or damage or destruction of objects could amount to a use of force or armed attack under the UN Charter (although the threshold for what constitutes a use of force is itself an area of controversy). But in practice, the vast majority of cyber operations by states take place below the threshold of use of force, instead consisting of persistent, low-level intrusions that cause harm in the victim state but often without discernible physical effects.[44]

Referring to Russia, Maj. Gen. Pekka Toveri (ret.), at the time of the interview the Finnish Defence Forces' chief of intelligence, observed that "they break international rules. What can we do about it? Naming and shaming doesn't seem to work."[45] Indeed, this is a constant challenge with illicit forms of gray-zone aggression. Naming and shaming is ineffective, and retaliation in-kind is inadvisable due to the risk of escalation or because it would violate liberal democracies' ethical norms.[46]

Insurance is another legal consideration regarding state-sponsored cyberattacks. Most insurance policies have a war clause that waives insurance payouts in case of armed conflict. War exemptions have long been standard in the insurance industry and reflect the far more significant damage caused during an armed conflict than in peacetime. If a cyberattack is attributed to a government, one could argue it should count as an act of war. That means the insurance war exemption could apply.

Indeed, following the NotPetya attack, Mondelēz sued its insurer, Zurich American Insurance, over its refusal to pay out Mondelēz's cyber-insurance policy. Zurich, in turn, argued that, as NotPetya was a state-attributed attack, it counted as an act of war and that Zurich was thus exempt from Mondelēz's cyber-insurance policy. At the time of writing, the case is being heard at the Circuit Court of Cook County in Illinois, where Mondelēz is based.[47] Whatever the court's decision, it will have significant implications, especially in light of the trends toward more-sophisticated attacks often sponsored by a government. Considering the documentation involved in insurance claims, gray-zone attacks could also create situations in which a government will need to present evidence to support its attribution of an attack to a hostile state.

As Gary Brown observes, the lack of state consensus on norms in cyberspace has led to an expansion of cyber operations

> into new and creative areas. . . . Many of these new areas of operations particularly affect civilian populations and are often conducted outside the context of armed conflict. This puts these operations beyond the reach of the heavy restrictions that international humanitarian law . . . imposes on state activities affecting civilians during armed conflict.[48]

Regardless of their status under international law, cyber offenses can be treated as violations of criminal law. Indeed, this is the basis on which the US government has indicted individual perpetrators of state-sponsored cyberattacks against the United States and its allies. Because criminal law involves charging individuals, as opposed to groups or countries, it is an extremely time-consuming avenue. The US government also conducts the investigations into individual perpetrators based in hostile countries, and announces the indictments against them, in the full knowledge that they are highly unlikely ever to be apprehended.

This quality—illegal but with the sponsoring government's legal responsibility unclear, all while indisputably damaging the targeted country—has made cyber aggression a popular form of gray-zone aggression. When asked to describe the reality of companies in the line of cyber fire, a senior executive with a leading European telecoms provider explained in an interview in spring 2020,

> We're seeing two types of attacks: those targeted specifically at our company and those where the attackers go after the easiest target. The latter is a risk for us through our supply chain. We try to make sure our suppliers are protected, but there's really no complete protection. Attacks are changing. Today on the dark web, if you have enough money you can buy what's essentially a 24-7 call center for DDOS [distributed denial-of-service] attacks.
>
> Ransomware attacks have become more frequent, so more people have begun using backups. In response, attackers have begun changing their tactics. Many no longer block access to data because organizations now have backups. Instead they threaten to publish sensitive information. As the saying goes, the attacker only has to be successful 1 percent of the time, but the defender has to be successful 100 percent of the time.[49]

The increase in sophisticated ransomware attacks noticed by the executive has since grown dramatically. The cybersecurity firm Check Point reports that ransomware attacks in the third quarter of 2020 increased by 50 percent compared to the first half of 2020.[50] That targeted entities often feel they have no choice but to pay the ransom or have their insurers do so further fuels the growth in ransomware attacks.[51] While ransomware is primarily the domain of criminal enterprises, the series of highly sophisticated attacks by Russian gangs in 2021 suggests the Kremlin at least tolerates the activity. In June 2021, Joe Biden said he had told Vladimir Putin that "we expect them to act [on the attacks] if we give them enough information to act on who that is."[52]

In a 2020 interview, Maj. Gen. Ed Wilson (ret.) of the US Air Force, who served as deputy assistant secretary of defense for cyber policy in the Donald Trump administration, presciently stressed that attacks on our CNI [critical national infrastructure] are a concern. The attacks are almost always linked to state actors. We also need to think about ransomware. It's being used against different institutions such as cities and hospitals. What if it moves to CNI?[53]

Since the interview, Colonial Pipeline and the Irish health service have been crippled. So have Vancouver's public transportation system,[54] a series of municipalities and hospitals,[55] and a Dutch logistics and warehousing company, the last causing a cheese shortage in the Netherlands.[56] Ransomware attacks on other parts of CNI such as energy or the internet would cause more harm still.

Attacks on cities including Baltimore[57] and Atlanta[58] illustrate a dilemma now facing liberal democracies: Increasing digitalization increases individual and collective convenience but gives attackers a bigger attack surface. In addition, the public's dependence on this convenience, coupled with the fact that most people have no training in how to conduct their lives during an interruption of vital services, means that even a brief interruption is likely to cause chaos. This, in turn, combines with anger directed at authorities that a hostile state can amplify through social media. I refer to this as the convenience trap. Thanks to better cyber defense, today cyberattacks such as the one directed against Estonia in 2007 pose a smaller risk, but targeted attacks could cause serious harm because the convenience trap is making the public more dependent on digitally powered services. But, said Konttinen,

> Our weak link is not the technology itself. To efficiently protect a company from cyberattacks, technology, people, and processes need to be aligned. The problem is that IT security is often treated as an afterthought, something that IT guys will look after but not a priority.[59]

Along with the declining utility of run-of-the-mill illicit cyber activity, attackers' strategies and indeed identities also seem to be changing. Konttinen illustrated how their strategies are changing from those of common crime to those of military operations.

> Opportunist attackers, the sort of attackers who used to dominate, don't care who the target is. They just want the money. Armed forces are not opportunistic. They want to attack a particular country, not just any country. This is the direction in which cyberattacks are developing. They're becoming so sophisticated that you can't stop them.
>
> Five years ago, the idea was that you could stop nearly all cyberattacks. That's no longer possible. In most cases, the best you can do is to detect the attack. Today it can take 100 days for a company to realize it has been attacked. That's clearly very dangerous because in that time a lot of damage can be done. But you can and should detect attacks. It's like burglars: You can't prevent burglars from attacking your house, but you can make sure they don't get very far.[60]

The SolarWinds attack demonstrated precisely this development, having gone undetected for months.[61]

Konttinen described the shift in cyber aggression from run-of-the-mill criminals toward more state-sponsored, targeted activity.

> In many cases, nation-states are behind these sophisticated cyberattacks. They have large budgets that they can clearly use. These targeting attackers go after specific organizations. There are hacktivists as well, who're a category to themselves somewhere between criminals and state actors.[62]

Hacktivists could, of course, be enlisted to hack on a hostile government's behalf.

Kevin Brown, managing director of BT Security, explained that

> three years ago, I would have said that hacktivism was the main threat, along with terrorism, criminals, and state-sponsored aggression. But that has all come together in the past two—three years. It's very hard to tell what's what in the attacks. Every day there's an average of 4,000 cyberattacks on BT. But the attacks are not necessarily aimed at us because of who we

are. We have a large attack surface because of what the UK is: a large economy, a vibrant economy, and we're members of Five Eyes.[63]

BT is not primarily targeted because attackers wish to harm the company; they instead target it because it forms a vital part of British and Western society. As with all forms of gray-zone aggression using licit or illicit means, it is important to bear in mind that, while China, Iran, North Korea, and Russia are the top practitioners of cyber aggression—because they have not just intent but also capability—other countries and sub-state groups could also seize the opportunity as long as there is no effective deterrence.

Brown's observation regarding attackers' blending nature illustrates another troubling reality. Even though attacks are becoming more sophisticated and targeted and are increasingly perpetrated by skilled groups, it is often difficult to conclusively pinpoint their provenance. Western governments typically want near-complete certainty before attributing an attack to a hostile state, which slows the attribution process and may even make attribution impossible. This is not just a result of the well-known challenge in linking the attacker to a sponsoring institution, but because new forms of cooperation between hostile states and proxies are emerging. Writing after the SolarWinds hack in December 2020, Microsoft President Brad Smith highlighted

> the growing privatization of cybersecurity attacks through a new generation of private companies, akin to 21st-century mercenaries. This phenomenon has reached the point where it has acquired its own acronym—PSOAs, for private sector offensive actors. Unfortunately, this is not an acronym that will make the world a better place.[64]

As an example of this growing category, Smith mentioned the NSO Group, an Israeli firm.

> NSO created and sold to governments an app called Pegasus, which could be installed on a device simply by calling the device

via WhatsApp; the device's owner did not even have to answer. According to WhatsApp, NSO used Pegasus to access more than 1,400 mobile devices, including those belonging to journalists and human rights activists.[65]

In July 2021, a leak revealed that less-than-democratic governments have tapped the phones of tens of thousands of politicians (including Macron), journalists, and activists using Pegasus.[66]

The mercenary arrangement, in which nation-states increasingly rely on a network of proxies including freelancers and mercenary-like companies, benefits the sponsoring state because it can obfuscate the link between itself and an attack, a reality that has, to date, made attribution and retaliation distinctly challenging. It is also an extremely dangerous trend, as the involvement of outside groups and individuals in nation-state aggression risks the tools proliferating. Konttinen pointed out that this is already happening: "Sometimes the technology leaks to criminals. It's like nuclear weapons ending up in the hands of criminals. It's very alarming."[67]

Nuclear proliferation has helped countries outside the group of official nuclear-weapons states acquire nuclear arsenals. Cyber weapons may be less dangerous than atomic ones are, but they are also far easier to spread. Ciaran Martin, the inaugural CEO of the UK's National Cyber Security Centre, points out that

> the proliferation of dangerous cyber weapons is a serious risk that doesn't get enough attention. . . . Some companies can already sell quite dangerous services quite legally to anyone willing to pay. And state [cyber] capabilities can be leaked, lost, sold or stolen more easily than most physical weapons.[68]

This development emphasizes the need for targeted countries to not just increase resilience to attacks but also improve deterrence by punishment, building on existing initiatives such as the United States' Defend Forward model. But eye-for-eye retaliation, which is regularly proposed following incidents such as SolarWinds, is not a viable deterrence strategy: It has a limited effect on groups of actors whose affiliations with a hostile government may be unclear, it needlessly exposes the defending state's cyber tools, and it risks dangerous escalation. Constant retaliation would, in fact, undermine deterrence.[69]

IP Theft

In addition to causing disruption or accessing government secrets, the objective of cyberattacks is often to steal IP as part of a national effort to catch up with, and even overtake, liberal democracies' industries. IP theft through cyber intrusion and other means is a long-standing form of gray-zone aggression to which targeted countries have struggled to establish effective deterrence. As with most forms of gray-zone aggression, the challenge is that individual cases of IP theft may appear negligible, but collectively they can significantly harm the West. If Western firms do not get the expected competitive advantage from investment into research and development (R&D) because IP is stolen by competitors that then undersell the firms, high-tech innovation in the West will suffer. Since innovation is key to economic growth, a decline could trigger a long-term economic downturn.

In its December 2020 report *The Elements of the China Challenge*, the US State Department summarized Chinese IP theft.

> The [People's Republic of China] has perpetrated the greatest illegitimate transfer of wealth in human history, stealing technological innovation and trade secrets from companies, universities, and the defense sectors of the United States and other nations. According to research cited by the Office of the United States Trade Representative, China's efforts—including forced technology transfer, cyberattacks, and a whole-of-nation approach to economic and industrial espionage—cost the U.S. economy as much as $600 billion annually. This staggering sum approaches the Pentagon's annual national defense budget and exceeds the total profits of the Fortune 500's top 50 companies.[70]

Referring to cyber intrusion in their company, a senior executive in the Finnish CNI sector said, "It's not just Russia but other countries as well.

Some engage in industrial espionage. This is absolutely nothing new, but digital tools make it different. There are efforts to penetrate my company every day."[71]

Chinese IP theft has been pervasive for years. Already in 2006, the state of affairs prompted Sen. Chuck Schumer (D-NY) to warn that "China's refusal to play by international economic rules cripples our ability to compete on a level playing field."[72] In 2013, the US Commission on the Theft of American Intellectual Property named China as the world's largest source of IP theft.[73] The commission estimated China's share of IP theft from US companies at 50 to 80 percent, writing,

> A core component of China's successful growth strategy is acquiring science and technology. It does this in part by legal means—imports, foreign domestic investment, licensing, and joint ventures—but also by means that are illegal. National industrial policy goals in China encourage IP theft, and an extraordinary number of Chinese in business and government entities are engaged in this practice.[74]

It estimated IP losses to reach $300 billion annually, an amount comparable to the United States' combined exports to Asia.[75]

The problem has persisted in other advanced economies too. Wilson pointed out that

> anything that's in [China's] five- or 10-year plan they're likely to try to achieve through IP theft. And they don't differentiate between what they need for their national security and what they need for their economy.[76]

Norway's head of counterintelligence, Hanne Blomberg, painted a similar picture: "For some countries, research and development in other countries is a subject of espionage. This activity is targeted especially at R&D within technology, and it includes stealing technology," she told Norwegian media in February 2021.[77]

Targeted nations thus face the dilemma of when to respond. A muscular response to a single theft would appear disproportional and escalatory, but it is also difficult to determine an appropriate time to react to aggression that damages national security only in aggregation. The Barack Obama administration attempted to stem at least the cyber-enabled part of IP theft via a 2015 agreement with China. In the agreement, which was followed by similar agreements between China and countries including Australia, Germany, and the UK, the US and China promised not to "conduct or knowingly support cyber-enabled theft of intellectual property, including trade secrets or other confidential business information, with the intent of providing competitive advantages to companies or commercial sectors."[78] Also in 2015, G20 countries including Russia accepted the norm against cyber-enabled IP theft.[79] Initially, cyber-enabled IP theft appeared to decrease, but it is unclear whether this was a result of the treaty or an already initiated reorganization of departments within the Chinese armed forces.

Either way, within a couple years, Chinese cyber-enabled IP theft was rising again.[80] China's intentions to eliminate cyber-enabled IP theft also appear insincere considering that, between 2014 and 2017, attackers who were subsequently identified as members of APT10 (which is linked to the Chinese Ministry of State Security) perpetrated a string of cyberattacks against technology-heavy Western firms. Huawei's rival Ericsson was a key target of the attacks, which were collectively labeled Cloud Hopper. "This was the theft of industrial or commercial secrets for the purpose of advancing an economy, the lifeblood of a company," former Australian National Cyber Security Adviser Alastair MacGibbon told Reuters.[81]

IP theft is also pervasive outside cyberspace. A good example of this is ASML Holding, a Dutch maker of computational lithography that lost vital IP to XTAL, a subsidiary of the China-based company Dongfang Jingyuan, which in turn has ties to the Chinese Ministry of Science and Technology.[82] The Chinese firm promptly used the IP and proceeded to snag ASML customers.[83]

Indeed, IP theft predates the digital era. Two centuries ago, the United States was a master practitioner of the trade, with Treasury Secretary Alexander Hamilton declaring in 1791 that the country needed "to procure all such machines as are known in any part of Europe."[84] That same year, he authorized his department to pay $48 "to subsidize the living expenses of an English weaver who pledged to deliver to the U.S. a copycat version of a British spinning machine."[85] IP theft, too, illustrates how an aggressor's intent and capability can form a powerful combination of opportunity (whether that is the pecuniary weakness of an 18th-century English weaver or the IT networks of a globalized 21st-century US technology firm).

In 2012, Huawei wanted a certain US-based robot as badly as 18th-century America had wanted a British spinning machine. In a January 2019 indictment, the DOJ charged Huawei with concerted and successful efforts to steal technical details of this cutting-edge robot. The robot, developed and owned by T-Mobile and nicknamed Tappy, tested T-Mobile handsets before market release. Although Huawei had developed a similar robot, it was far less successful. Huawei asked T-Mobile whether it would sell or license Tappy, but T-Mobile turned down the proposition.

Huawei staff in the United States then proceeded to scrutinize and take pictures of Tappy, which raised suspicions among T-Mobile staff and ultimately restricted the Huawei engineers' access.[86] Huawei's China-based robot team then dispatched one of its engineers to T-Mobile's lab. The DOJ indictment describes the events on a decisive day.

> Later on May 29, 2013, A.X. used his badge to access the T-Mobile Tappy laboratory. As he was preparing to leave the laboratory, A.X. surreptitiously placed one of the Tappy robot arms into his laptop bag and secretly removed it from the laboratory. T-Mobile employees discovered the theft later that day, and contacted A.X. A.X. initially falsely denied taking the robot arm, but then later claimed he had found it in his bag.[87]

Even though T-Mobile spotted the theft and the preceding visits, the damage was done. Huawei had illegally acquired crucial parts of T-Mobile's IP.

Theft of highly sophisticated technology such as Tappy is an even more pressing problem because it can mean the loss of not just sales volume but also sometimes even the IP owner's viability as a company. IP theft "to me really stands out as the greatest long-term threat to our nation's information and intellectual property, and to our economic vitality," FBI Director Christopher Wray said at a conference in 2020, adding that "the FBI has about a thousand investigations involving China's attempted theft of U.S.-based technology in all 56 of our field offices and spanning just about every industry and sector."[88] The sectors include highly sensitive weapons research.

China's Thousand Talents program recruits scientists and encourages participants to send Chinese institutions knowledge gained abroad. By 2017, the program was estimated to have enlisted more than 7,000 top scientists, including several Nobel laureates. While the program is not illegal, it exploits Western openness by draining top Western institutions of expertise for China's benefit in a way that can include illegal elements. "In recent years, federal agencies have discovered talent recruitment plan members who downloaded sensitive electronic research files before leaving to return to China," a US Senate subcommittee noted in a 2019 report.[89] In 2021, the Netherlands' Military Intelligence and Security Service reported that "dozens of Chinese students at Dutch universities are obtaining a PhD in military-relevant technology" and that these students are "directly linked to the Chinese armed forces or the Chinese defense industry."[90]

IP theft has also long plagued less technology-intensive areas. Luxury brands have for years faced a seemingly unstoppable production of counterfeit goods made in China and other countries. In a 2021 report, the European Commission notes that IP-intensive industries account for 45 percent of the EU's gross domestic product and 38.9 percent of its jobs[91] but that counterfeit goods account for 6.8 percent of EU imports from non-EU countries.[92] This means manufacturers in other countries steal EU firms' IP and then sell their—cheaper—counterfeit goods back to the EU. Between 2013 and 2017, counterfeit goods annually cost the EU an average of nearly 400,000 jobs in the clothing, footwear, and accessories sector; an average of more than 160,000 jobs in the cosmetics industry; and nearly 50,000 jobs in the pharmaceuticals industry.[93]

Even the theft of relatively basic IP thus significantly damages the targeted country. While such counterfeit production and export is not directed by hostile governments, the problem's persistence suggests it is tolerated by them. The European Commission identified China as the main source of counterfeit goods arriving in the EU.[94]

In addition to trying to ensure compliance through treaties, the US government has again turned to the criminal justice system. The Trump administration made a particular push in this area. In 2018, the DOJ created the China Initiative to prosecute those involved in IP theft. That year, the DOJ indicted 10 Chinese nationals over IP hacking and espionage against many Western aerospace companies.[95] This activity, which occurred over several years, contributed to the development of the C919, an airliner by the Commercial Aircraft Corporation of China that will become a rival of Boeing and Airbus aircraft.[96]

In 2020, the DOJ indicted two Chinese nationals over a wide range of IP-theft hacks, stating that they

> conducted a hacking campaign lasting more than ten years to the present, targeting companies in countries with high technology industries, including the United States, Australia, Belgium, Germany, Japan, Lithuania, the Netherlands, Spain, South Korea, Sweden, and the United Kingdom. Targeted industries included, among others, high tech manufacturing; medical device, civil, and industrial engineering; business, educational, and gaming software; solar energy; pharmaceuticals; defense.[97]

These are some of the core sectors of China's industrial strategy. Other individuals recently indicted include Li Chen, a researcher in pediatric diseases who was participating in US government-funded research at Nationwide Children's Hospital in Ohio while being funded by the Chinese government. In 2020, she pleaded guilty to stealing IP from the hospital.[98] The fact that IP theft covers every iteration of every sector—including airliners, advanced technology, and medical research—makes it even harder to police.

The dilemma of how to punish—and ideally deter—lawbreakers operating on behalf of a foreign government is not new. In 1839, Lin Zexu, China's imperial commissioner charged with combating British merchants' opium smuggling into China, took swift action by throwing 1,200 tons of the drug into the Pearl River. Britain retaliated by ordering all foreign merchants to leave the trading hub of Guangzhou. Even so, Lin did not acquiesce. "Suppose the subject of another country were to come to England to trade. He would certainly be required to comply with the laws of England," Lin wrote to Queen Victoria.[99]

GRADUAL BORDER ALTERATIONS AND SURREPTITIOUS FISHING 129

Today, subversive measures including IP theft that may violate criminal laws but not international law are equally challenging to address in a manner that convinces the rival nation to stop organizing or condoning the practice. While the criminal justice system can clean up selected cases, it certainly is not a deterrent. Even though Beijing has promised Western governments it will better police IP theft, there has been only limited improvement. As Daniel Rechtschaffen observes, in 2019 China "created an IP tribunal that allows plaintiffs to appeal local judgments up to the Supreme People's Court. But interference is almost guaranteed if the defendant is a politically influential company."[100]

European countries have been less assertive than the United States has been. The European Commission's biannual IP report names and shames countries, the 2021 version noting that more than 80 percent of the counterfeit goods seized by EU authorities originate in China and Hong Kong. IP theft stemming from India, Russia, Turkey, and Ukraine also causes serious harm to EU-based businesses.[101] European governments, though, almost never take China to task over IP theft. Australian politicians have been somewhat more assertive. Former Prime Minister Malcolm Turnbull said in 2020,

> The issue with China has been that its targets have been commercial ones as well as traditional governmental ones. No one should be surprised if foreign countries are getting hold of the plans for the latest submarine or missile, but people are very disappointed if a state actor is rummaging through commercial firms' intellectual property. Of course, China has done that; their state agencies have done that.[102]

The fact that IP theft continues on a grand scale demonstrates the futility of naming and shaming as a strategy toward countries that are not bothered by a tarnished image.

IP theft can, like many other forms of gray-zone aggression that include violation of laws, be described as merely criminal activity. Yet its continuously large volume suggests it is not merely tolerated but also encouraged—to use the US IP commission's words—by the Chinese government to strengthen its global position at the West's expense. "Rules, once made, should be followed by all," Xi Jinping said in a video address to the 2021 World Economic Forum's Davos Agenda.[103] Considering China's continuous violations of international rules, including in cyberspace and the area of IP theft, Xi's statement seemed intended to taunt the West.

Coordinated IP theft compellingly illustrates the combination of different efforts a country can use to weaken a rival or strengthen its own position. While China is today's prime practitioner of this combined strategy, the West's openness means other rivals and would-be rivals can decide to pursue the same strategy. This reality, again, highlights the defender's dilemma: There is only a thin line between illegal gray-zone activities that liberal democracies cannot reasonably combat if they want to remain open societies and illegal gray-zone activities that are so destabilizing that the offenses must be forcefully tackled. Indeed, one form simply might need to be considered common crime because it does not warrant deterrent action beyond criminal justice, while another should be treated as hostile-state activity warranting government-led deterrence.

Even though all IP theft is highly damaging to the affected companies, from a national security perspective there is clearly a difference between IP theft in the apparel and semiconductor industries. This dilemma is compounded by the fact that, individually, illegal acts such as IP theft are usually too small for retaliatory response. But without retaliation and improved defense, the illicit activities will continue to increase. IP theft not only weakens Western economies but is also used with other forms of gray-zone aggression to form a cocktail of aggressive means that cause lasting harm to Western countries.

Assassinations and Physical Harm

While state-sponsored assassinations on foreign soil are primarily directed against specific individuals, they also count as gray-zone aggression because they destabilize the country in which the criminal act takes place and, in the case of intelligence assets, signal that cooperating with that country is dangerous. Perhaps the best-known recent example is the 2018 assassination attempt of the former Russian spy Sergei Skripal and his daughter Yulia in Salisbury, England. Because the assassination attempt was linked to a foreign government and involved the nerve agent Novichok, the UK government considered it not merely a criminal act but a gray-zone attack on the UK. The "Russian State was culpable," then–Prime Minister Theresa May informed Parliament.[104]

Western governments do not have an entirely clean record for violent interference in other countries. In 2020, the United States assassinated the commander of the Islamic Revolutionary Guards Corps' Quds Force, Maj. Gen. Qassem Soleimani, in a targeted drone strike.[105] The CIA was involved in plotting the assassination of Patrice Lumumba, the first prime minister of the Democratic Republic of the Congo, in 1961.[106] Even if a liberal democracy argues that an assassination is justified—as the Trump administration did with Soleimani—carrying out assassinations in other countries removes the high ground from which liberal democracies can avenge assassinations in their own countries.

In 2017, a mysterious brain illness, subsequently labeled Havana syndrome, began afflicting US diplomats in Cuba and China.[107] Around the same time, Canadian diplomats posted in Cuba reported experiencing similar symptoms, a combination of dizziness, intense headaches, vertigo, and ear pain. A subsequent US National Academies of Sciences, Engineering, and Medicine investigation established that the diplomats' symptoms were "consistent with the effects of directed, pulsed radio frequency . . . energy."[108] While it noted that the Soviet Union had conducted research into the effects of pulsed radio frequency energy, the investigation was unsurprisingly unable to identify the attacker or any sponsoring nation.

In spring 2021, several US government workers based in Miami, Florida, also reported suddenly experiencing the symptoms, as did two US National Security Council (NSC) officials in Washington, DC.[109] The NSC is in charge of coordinating the US government's investigation into the incidents. A dozen CIA officers serving abroad, meanwhile, had to return to the US in 2021 after they, too, reported similar symptoms.[110] Then, in July 2021, it emerged that, as of January 2021, more than 20 staff members at the US embassy in Vienna, Austria, have reported experiencing the same symptoms.[111]

Harming a country's diplomats and officials violates domestic laws, the Vienna Convention on Diplomatic Relations, or both. But the harm extends beyond the individuals suffering symptoms, as other diplomats, CIA officers, and officials will hesitate to take positions that could expose them to such an affliction. Yet ambiguity regarding the exact nature of the sponsor of an attack makes it impossible for the targeted country to respond in any fashion. The attacks are extremely cunning gaslighting in the gray zone. Clearly, in-kind retaliation for such attacks on embassy personnel is diplomatically unpalatable, not to mention a violation of the Vienna Convention.

Territorial Violations and Harassment

China illegally constructing artificial islands in the South China Sea is a prime example of another form of illicit gray-zone aggression: subversive border alterations. As part of gray-zone aggression, countries can use other means to achieve territorial changes, denying adversaries an obvious opportunity to intervene. As Tara Davenport notes,

> China's massive island-building project, which began after the Philippines' initiation of Annex VII arbitral proceedings against China in January 2013, created more than 12.8 million square metres of new land in less than three years.[112]

The construction involved the multiyear, step-by-step addition of mass and infrastructure to reefs and tiny, previously uninhabitable islets in strategic waters claimed by several countries. A 2014 US-China Economic and Security Review Commission report summarized the then-current state of construction.

> In addition to dredging sand to make islands out of these reefs, China appears to be expanding and upgrading military and civilian infrastructure—including radars, satellite communication equipment, antiaircraft and naval guns, helipads, and docks—on some of the manmade islands.[113]

In 2020, the BBC reported that

> in the six years since China began reclamation of several reefs and atolls in the Spratlys, satellite and air surveillance has revealed one of the world's greatest feats in maritime engineering and military construction.
>
> In addition to the military facilities on the islands—including 3,000m runways, naval berths, hangars, reinforced ammunition bunkers, missile silos and radar sites—images show neatly arranged accommodation blocks, administrative buildings roofed with blue ceramic tiles, hospitals, and even sports complexes on the reclaimed islands, which have become visibly greener.[114]

While China, Malaysia, the Philippines, and Vietnam had all conducted limited construction in the disputed area,[115] the activity radically increased with China's construction of artificial islands: "As observed by the Tribunal in the South China Sea Arbitration, '[w]hatever the other States have done within the South China Sea, it pales in comparison to China's recent construction.'"[116] The Philippines had challenged the construction on the Johnson Reef, Cuarteron Reef, Fiery Cross Reef, and Gaven Reef (North)—which are also claimed by the Philippines, Taiwan, and Vietnam—at a United Nations Convention on the Law of the Sea (UNCLOS) tribunal. When the tribunal upheld the Philippines' case on whether China could claim an exclusive economic zone (EEZ) around its newly constructed islands, China dismissed the ruling as "nothing more than a piece of waste paper."[117]

Through gradual construction in contested waters, China succeeded in establishing territory in a location that is not just of immense geopolitical value but also situated among an abundance of natural resources. Indeed, even though the UNCLOS tribunal upheld the Philippines' claim, giving coastal states including the Philippines the rights to these resources, China disregarded the ruling. Writing in 2018, Bill Hayton observed that

> China is continuing to pressure those countries to give away their rights to the oil, gas and fish. Under the name of "joint

development" China is continuing to demand a share of those countries' resources even though the tribunal clearly ruled those demands illegitimate. In May 2017, President Rodrigo Duterte of the Philippines said publicly that his Chinese counterpart, Xi Jinping, had personally threatened him with war if the Philippines attempted to tap the large gas reserves in an area of the sea known as the Reed Bank.[118]

Rear Adm. Mark Montgomery (ret.) of the US Navy, who, during part of the island-construction period, served as director of operations at US Pacific Command and commander of Carrier Strike Group 5 embarked on the USS *George Washington* stationed in Japan, observed,

> In hindsight, it was an extremely long-term campaign by the Chinese to create conditions harmful to US interests. The process was extremely slow and cloaked in disinformation. The Chinese took advantage of the fact that in Southeast Asia we don't have strong alliance structures and a number of countries there are susceptible to Chinese economic and security pressure. The Chinese also took advantage of the fact that we were distracted in the Middle East. These new islands have an impact on the countries in the region and weakened the United States' standing as a credible ally among our allies and partners there.[119]

If China had claimed territory through an invasion or annexation, the violation of international law would have been obvious, and the act would have resulted in an immediate regional or international response. Indeed, the US and allied presence in the region most likely deterred China from using this avenue. Because it instead surreptitiously built artificial islands and because each step was relatively minor, the extent and true nature of its actions did not become clear until the islands were near completion.

As a result, at no point did the affected neighbors or the United States deem a muscular response or a signal of punishment suitable, and the construction continued. As Erik Reichborn-Kjennerud and Patrick Cullen note,

GRADUAL BORDER ALTERATIONS AND SURREPTITIOUS FISHING 135

> Ambiguity is used to complicate or undermine the decision-making processes of the opponent. It is tailored to make a military response—or even a political response—difficult. In military terms, it is designed to fall below the threshold of war and to delegitimize (or even render politically irrational) the ability to respond by military force.[120]

Ultimately, China created a fait accompli without having to pay a price for it—the precise objective of gray-zone aggression. The combination of (duplicitous) intent, capability, and opportunity was again used successfully.

Russia's annexation of Crimea is perhaps the best-known recent example of territorial violation in the gray zone. In the republic of Georgia, meanwhile, Russia has engaged in border manipulation—what Georgians refer to as "borderization"—between South Ossetia and Georgia. From Georgia's perspective, this de facto border alteration comprises two parts:

> The materialization of the previously theoretical boundary along the ground in the form of border markers, barbed wire, and the increased prevalence of border patrols, while the second is that this materialization frequently results in the advance of the Georgian-South Ossetian boundary line deeper into previously Georgian-held territory.[121]

China, in turn, has been constructing roads and military outposts in Bhutan.[122] In these cases, too, because the border alteration involves a string of smaller steps rather than armed conflict, the aggrieved party has precious few tools with which to signal punishment. Indeed, before the string of events is complete, it is difficult for the aggrieved party to signal precisely where its redline should be.

Illegal, unreported, and unregulated fishing likewise belongs in the category of territorial violations and harassment. Although it is primarily a criminal issue, it is now pervasive; around one-fifth of the world's fish are caught this way.[123] Indeed, the practice is so extensively used by Chinese fishing fleets that it can be described as exploitation in the gray zone rather than as criminal activity by individual fishermen. In 2020, for example, a Chinese fishing flotilla parked off the coasts of several Latin American countries, fishing their waters dry and violating environmental regulations.[124]

In late 2020, an armada of some 325 Chinese vessels had spent months by the Galápagos Islands off the Ecuadorian coast. When fishing in Ecuador's EEZ, the vessels sometimes turned off their responders, which violates seafaring norms and made their presence in the EEZ much harder to detect. Already that August, the Ecuadorian navy reported that 149 vessels had turned off their communications equipment and that some had also changed their names to avoid supervision.[125] In addition to violating seafaring safety regulations, the fishing armada violated rules on environmental protection and sustainable fishing, important matters in the ecologically sensitive Galápagos.[126]

In March 2021, nearly 200 vessels identified as belonging to China's maritime militia arrived in the Philippines' EEZ and stayed there; they were later joined by dozens more vessels.[127] When the Philippine government protested to the Chinese government about a week later, the Chinese government claimed the vessels were merely seeking shelter, which is permissible under maritime law. Philippine Secretary of National Defense Delfin Lorenzana correctly observed that "if it's true that they are sheltering from the elements, that area is open sea and not conducive for sheltering."[128] China's distant-water fishing fleet, thought to feature up to 17,000 vessels, has also engaged in similar exploitation off the coasts of West African countries.[129]

In July 2021, French President Macron announced the creation of a South Pacific coast guard network comprising France and South Pacific nations. It is tasked with countering predatory behavior, which is understood to mean Chinese predatory fishing.[130] While Indian, Iranian, and Pakistani fishermen, in turn, have been spotted illegally fishing off the coasts of Somalia and Yemen,[131] this appears to be opportunism by fishermen, not a concerted practice.

Chinese civilian vessels harass other countries too. The country's maritime militia, a fishing-vessel fleet designed to win without fighting, is a long-standing Chinese gray-zone tool. During the Vietnam War,

GRADUAL BORDER ALTERATIONS AND SURREPTITIOUS FISHING 137

> A key lesson learned for Beijing was that leveraging fishing militia forces was far less likely to trigger U.S. intervention . . . even when the threatened neighbor was a U.S. ally. It is fair to say that this was the genesis of Beijing's strategy to routinely employ irregular forces in gray zone operations in the East China Sea and South China Sea.[132]

Precisely because large-scale illegal behavior by commercial entities that ostensibly have no government links can trigger armed conflicts, the countries targeted by Chinese mass-scale fishing have mostly responded by raising awareness of the activities. Such rule-breaking behavior, however, not only harms the affected countries but also erodes international norms.[133]

Western countries have also used private traders for geopolitical purposes. In the 18th and 19th centuries, for example, British traders illegally sold so much opium in China that it caused widespread addiction, which led to social unrest and eventually caused the Chinese government to destroy large quantities of the drug. This eventually led to the Opium Wars. However, while Western countries should apologize for such transgressions committed by previous generations, the fact that the transgressions occurred should not silence Western governments over practices taking place today. Indeed, such "whataboutism" is a concerted strategy by the Chinese government whenever a foreign government addresses China's current violations of norms.[134]

Harassment in National Airspace and of Civilian Maritime Crews

Violations of other countries' airspace and territorial waters are a part of gray-zone aggression that is illegal and easily attributable to a government. On October 7, 2020, Taiwan's Defense Minister Yen De-fa reported that the Taiwanese air force (Republic of China air force) had so far that year scrambled 2,972 times against Chinese aircraft, at a cost of T$25.5 billion (USD 886.49 million).[135] On January 23, 2021, no fewer than eight nuclear-capable Chinese bombers and four fighter jets entered Taiwan's air defense identification zone. While an air defense identification zone is not the same as a country's airspace, the flights were nonetheless a clear provocation.[136]

The Russian air force engages in similar behavior. In 2020, NATO Baltic Air Policing (BAP) jets scrambled 150 times, compared to 170 times the previous year.[137] While the number of BAP scrambles fell somewhat compared to in 2019, there was an increase in Russian air activity over the Atlantic Ocean and the Black Sea. In 2020, NATO air forces scrambled more than 400 times across Europe; nearly 90 percent of the cases were responding to Russian military aircraft.[138] In scramble statistics, NATO counts the number of times its jets took to the skies; it does not count the number of Russian aircraft intercepted. One intercept mission can involve one or several Russian aircraft.

While near incursions are not illegal, flying near another country's airspace without communication violates international aviation standards. "Russian military aircraft often do not transmit a transponder code indicating their position and altitude, do not file a flight plan, or do not communicate with air traffic controllers," NATO stated.[139] In 2015, the Turkish air force shot down a Russian jet that was on a combat mission in Syria. Turkey claimed the aircraft was violating Turkish airspace, though Russia claimed it was in Syrian airspace.[140] While Turkey's response will deter Russian aircraft from straying near its airspace again, its response also risked significant escalation.

Gen. Riho Terras (ret.), Estonia's chief of defense from 2011 to 2018 and now a member of the European Parliament, described the situation.

> When I was chief of defense, the Russian pressure started. It wasn't completely absent before, but starting from the Georgian war, border violations by the Russians occurred in significantly higher numbers.
>
> The place where the violations occurred were under Saint Petersburg air traffic control. The route through Estonian airspace is a couple of minutes shorter than not flying through Estonian airspace. During Soviet times, the Soviet air force obviously used that route, but the Russians don't change their habits when world history changes. At the time, [NATO's] Baltic Air Policing was based in Lithuania, and it was too far from

the violations in our airspace. We gave the Russians notes of complaint, but nothing changed.

But after [the Ukraine conflict began], they started flying strategic bombers through our airspace. That never happened even during Soviet times. That's a show of force vis-à-vis NATO. And they weren't using responders. It's common practice that you should use responders, but it's not codified in law.

In addition, Estonia has problems with Russian ships that aren't warships but [are] in the service of the navy, for example ISTAR [intelligence, surveillance, target acquisition, and reconnaissance] and research vessels. According to international law, you should give safe haven to all ships during bad weather. After Ukraine, every now and then these ships would take refuge next to our islands during bad weather and stay for days. We only had minehunters, which are slow and couldn't get there quickly to establish a complete picture. Now we've built higher-speed boats.

Countries have to have units on alert for violations of airspace all the time, even if there are no violations. It's a question of air sovereignty.[141]

As Terras' account underlines, the maritime domain offers plenty of opportunities for gray-zone aggression because it is so easy to mask the activity's true intent. For much of 2020, large numbers of Chinese sand-dredging vessels extracted sand off the Matsu archipelago, which belongs to Taiwan. Although China needs sand for construction, the vessels' main purpose appears to be to wear Taiwan down by forcing it to respond. The vessels often dredge not only just outside Taiwanese waters but also inside them.[142] Either way, Taiwan's coast guard has to respond. In 2020, Taiwan expelled nearly 4,000 Chinese sand-dredging and sand-transporting vessels, a 560 percent increase from 2019.[143]

Maritime harassment of civilians is likewise a gray-zone feature. In 2015, for example, civilian crews lay the NordBalt energy cable linking Lithuania and Sweden through the Baltic Sea. At the time, both governments had noted a growing pattern of Russian provocations in the Baltic Sea. On April 30, 2015, a vessel from the Russian navy's Baltic Fleet entered

Lithuania's EEZ, traveling toward a NordBalt construction ship managed by the Swedish-Swiss engineering conglomerate ABB. Upon arrival, it tried to chase the construction ship away. "The ALCEDO vessel chartered by ABB was asked by the Russian Navy to leave its position in Lithuania's exclusive economic zone, where it had a legitimate right to be, according to international law," Swedish Foreign Ministry spokesman Gabriel Wernstedt told media at the time.[144]

In 2019, Iran's Islamic Revolutionary Guards Corps went further, seizing the Swedish-owned, UK-registered cargo ship *Stena Impero* in the Strait of Hormuz. The vessel had 23 crew members from India, Latvia, the Philippines, and Russia on board.[145] Although the *Stena Impero* was released after two months, the incident caused the UK to increase the Royal Navy's presence in the region and highlighted gray-zone threats in the maritime domain. Eighty percent of the world's trade is transported by sea,[146] and the increasingly globalized nature of supply chains now means that finished products sometimes travel among countries several times throughout their production.

In addition, the now extremely common mix of countries involved in merchant shipping causes challenges when deciding how to handle gray-zone incidents such as the *Stena Impero* seizure. Like the *Stena Impero*, today merchant marine vessels are often owned by a firm in one country, registered in a second country, and crewed by mariners from many other countries. Statistics from the International Chamber of Shipping show that globally, as of January 2021, there are an estimated 1,647,500 seafarers, with China, Indonesia, the Philippines, Russia, and Ukraine the major countries of origin.[147] Setting aside the related problem of piracy, Iran's seizure of the *Stena Impero* highlights obvious challenges to Western countries, especially how best to handle the seizure of a vessel owned by a Western country but registered in a flag-of-convenience country and often crewed by sailors from countries that engage in gray-zone aggression against the West.

Air incursions are a relatively straightforward gray-zone activity, albeit one that forces the targeted country to respond, draining its personnel and equipment resources. With maritime harassment and incursions, by contrast, targeted countries that are less powerful than the perpetrator is can do little to change the aggressive behavior. After the Russian harassment of the NordBalt crew, Lithuanian Foreign Minister Linas Linkevičius said that "if similar incidents happen again, the possibility of employing international legal instruments against the Russian Federation will be considered."[148] That is better than no response, but it is hardly a powerful deterrent. If the aggressor country is not bothered by a reputation as a rule breaker, it can proceed unimpeded.

While harassment of civilians and degradation of another country's habitat fall short of a military attack, they are illegal behavior targeted countries cannot afford to tolerate. The same is true for cyber aggression, IP theft, and the harm of individuals protected by law. All these forms of aggression are possible thanks to an aggressor's intent and capability and the opportunity unintentionally offered by the targeted country. That makes them quintessential to gray-zone aggression.

VIII

Producing Fear in the Enemy's Mind: Adapting Cold War Deterrence for Gray-Zone Aggression

> The reason Westminster Abbey has a hawk is not for it to eat pigeons that get into the abbey. The hawk is there to make the pigeons *think* it will eat them.[1]
>
> —Westminster Abbey choirboy

The person who has best described the essence of deterrence did so in one sentence—and he is a fictional character. "Deterrence is the art of producing in the mind of the enemy the fear to attack," Dr. Strangelove says in Stanley Kubrick's eponymous 1964 masterpiece.[2] The word stems from the Latin verb *deterrere*, which means to discourage from, avert, or frighten away. Deterrence, in other words, rests on psychology.

Forms of Deterrence

Dr. Strangelove has considerable nonfictional deterrence company. The US Department of Defense describes deterrence as "the prevention of action by the existence of a credible threat of unacceptable counteraction and/or belief that the cost of action outweighs the perceived benefits."[3] The UK Ministry of Defence's Development, Concepts and Doctrine Centre (DCDC), in turn, defines general deterrence as

> a function of grand or national strategy. It is a general reputation, generated over time by a posture (and visible actions) that portrays an image of credibility and resilience regarding any hostile intent. This reputation is built by how adversaries

interpret that posture. It is essential to understand that posture is not the same as reputation. Any actor may choose its posture, but cannot choose their reputation; that is for other actors to decide based upon their perception and interpretation of that posture.[4]

General deterrence comprises deterrence by denial and punishment, which a country can opt to use in different proportions when designing its deterrence posture. In practice, deterrence by denial consists of resilience and entanglement. It is vital to, in particular, understand the value of resilience, indisputably the less glamorous part of deterrence and one that has long been treated as an afterthought. Despite this neglected position, deterrence by resilience can significantly change the attacker's cost-benefit calculation.

In addition to general deterrence—the posture with which a country communicates its standing and national security approach to other countries—countries maintain tailored deterrence, characterized by DCDC as "the term used to describe specific deterrence messages and responses for specific audiences and adversaries."[5] Through tailored deterrence, countries can communicate differently to the respective recipients. During the Cold War, for example, the United States used different tailored deterrence for the Soviet Union and the Vietcong. The UK government displayed one form of tailored deterrence vis-à-vis the Warsaw Pact and another against the Irish Republican Army.

A third expression is immediate deterrence, the form perhaps most commonly discussed in the public debate. After the SolarWinds hack against the United States, which came to light in December 2020 and which the US government subsequently labeled a Russian intelligence operation, the public debate demanded the United States respond to "deter" the attacker, by which the discussants meant "retaliate."[6] Although deterrence takes place *before* an act of aggression, retaliation can be used to try to deter future attacks. The form of deterrence closest to such incident response is immediate deterrence, defined by DCDC as including

> actions to enhance denial capabilities, as well as making them more credible. In this type of deterrence activity,

> imposition-of-costs is the principal means of influence. Denial-of-benefits may also work, but their provisions will usually have to be in place already.[7]

Immediate deterrence, therefore, cannot be improvised in case of an attack and certainly cannot be successful without comprehensive general and tailored deterrence already in place. Unlike traditional displays of military strength, certain forms of retaliation lose clout as soon as they have been used. This is the case with cyber weapons, which begin figuratively rusting after first use. The originators—thought to be Israel and the United States—of Stuxnet, the computer virus that in 2010 destroyed uranium enrichment centrifuges at Natanz to stall Iran's nuclear program, paid such a price. Because the attack involved showing the weapon, Iran got a chance to examine it. The weapon became virtually useless. This often fleeting nature of newer tools of retaliation influences deterrence, as decision makers will hesitate to threaten their use—let alone use them for anything other than extremely serious incidents—lest the tools lose power.

DCDC describes extended deterrence as

> usually taken to mean a more capable actor conducting deterrence on the part of a (usually allied) actor who lacks capability or capacity. Extended deterrence is adversary focused, stating a commitment to punish the adversary for attacks on the ally. For example, NATO's operations and forward presence on its eastern periphery can be viewed as a policy of extended deterrence against external threats to the national integrity of the Baltic states.[8]

Extended deterrence in the nuclear age has meant that nearly all European countries' deterrence postures have at some point featured nuclear weapons even though most of them possessed none. West Germany, for example, had significant numbers of Bundeswehr soldiers stationed along the intra-German border and was backed up by allied troops stationed in West Germany, but its ultimate deterrent remained the US nuclear umbrella. It was therefore not surprising that, in the late 1970s, West German Chancellor Helmut Schmidt strongly advocated bringing US nuclear weapons to West Germany in response to the Soviet Union stationing SS-20 nuclear missiles in East Germany.

That makes extended deterrence the nation-state equivalent of the schoolyard conversation in which one child argues with another and then resorts to the argument that "my dad is stronger than yours," whereupon the second child counters with the same argument. Having failed to determine whose dad is stronger, the two retreat to their respective corners with neither having the courage to strike first lest they find out. By definition, extended deterrence is more vital to countries benefiting from the extension than to the countries providing it.

More importantly, the posture must convince the adversary, which means both the receiving and extending countries' populations have to support the deterrence. Gen. Riho Terras (ret.), who was until 2018 Estonia's chief of defense, explained that

> a British or German taxi driver, not to mention ordinary Americans, need to believe that Estonia is worth defending. That's very difficult. How can you make them believe it's important? If we don't have that support by the public, it affects deterrence. That's why Estonia sends soldiers to serve with the French in Mali.[9]

By providing troops to Mali and Afghanistan and for other international missions, Estonia demonstrates it is a valuable ally. That makes it easier for decision makers in the countries extending deterrence to commit troops and resources to Estonia. If, however, an adversary assumes the public will disapprove of major support for an ally during a crisis, extended posture is ineffective. "It's not absolutely necessary for us as NATO member states to believe in NATO's strength, but it's vital for Russia to do," Terras pointed out.[10]

Some countries, such as Sweden and Finland, maintained a Cold War policy of nonalignment and thus were not included under a nuclear umbrella.[11] Unsurprisingly, they instead pursued a concerted strategy of strengthening societal resilience. While societal resilience is indisputably a less menacing form of deterrence than is nuclear punishment, it can change a potential adversary's calculation regarding the outcome of an attack, thereby deterring the attack altogether. Sweden's and Finland's Cold War deterrence-by-denial postures offer lessons that are highly relevant in the context of gray-zone aggression.

The Psychology of Deterrence

Deterrence thinking existed before the nuclear age—and before the modern age. In *History of the Peloponnesian War*, Thucydides quotes Hermocrates of Syracuse, who observes that "the aggressor deems the advantage to be greater than the suffering; and the side which is attacked would sooner run any risk than suffer the smallest immediate loss"[12] and that "when there is mutual fear, men think twice before they make aggressions upon one another."[13] Long before the nuclear age, leaders followed Hermocrates' commonsense insight. No king, general, or other leader would state that they entered an armed conflict on their own volition even though doing so was certain to harm their side. Just as no burglar would enter a house if they knew a pack of bulldogs would thwart their work or harm them, no leader would attack a rival group or country if they were certain of defeat. This basic principle is referred to in deterrence theory as rational choice theory, a term borrowed from rational actor thinking in economics.

Not all actors, however, pursue what their adversaries and perhaps outside observers would consider the rational choice. Of the conflicts that occurred between 1816 and 1974, 22 percent involved weaker military powers invading stronger ones.[14] This may be because there is no guaranteed connection between deterrence input and outcome. Leaders may instead act in a manner that appears advantageous to them even though it seems foolish to their adversaries and outside observers. Japan's attack on Pearl Harbor certainly falls into this category. Despite being fully aware of the United States' superior strength, Japan attacked, believing that war was inevitable and that the United States' increasing strength meant it would be better for the war to happen sooner rather than later. Jeffrey Record notes,

> A month before Pearl Harbor, Army Chief of Staff Hajime Sugiyama warned that "the ratio of armament between Japan and

the United States will become more unfavorable to us as time passes; and particularly, the gap in air armament will enlarge rapidly." In 1941 the United States produced 1,400 combat aircraft to Japan's 3,200; 3 years later, the United States built 37,500 to Japan's 8,300.

Thus the [US] oil embargo drove the Japanese into the logic of preventive war: given war's inevitability and our declining military power relative to the enemy's, Japanese leaders reasoned, better war now than later.[15]

Lawrence Freedman observes that, as a strategy, deterrence involves

> deliberate, purposive threats. This concept developed prior to the Second World War in contemplation of strategic air raids. The presumption of civilian panic that had animated the first airpower theorists retained a powerful hold on official imaginations. The fear of the crowd led to musings on the likely anarchy that would follow sustained attacks.[16]

This thinking carried over and intensified with the advent of the nuclear age. The United States and the Soviet Union realized deterrence would be vital if they and their respective blocs were to coexist.

With nuclear arsenals taking on a decisive role in the countries that possessed them—and soon in the countries protected by extended deterrence—nuclear arsenals quickly became the central pillar in the rapidly growing field of deterrence theory. In 1946, Frederick Dunn argued,

> The atomic bomb is one of the most persuasive deterrents to adventures in atomic warfare that could be devised. It is peculiarly well adaped [sic] to the technique of retaliation. One must assume that, so long as bombs exist at all, the states possessing them will hold themselves in readiness at all times for instant retaliation on the fullest possible scale in the event of an atomic attack. The result would be that any potential violator of a limitation agreement would have the terrifying contemplation that not only would he lose his cities immediately on starting an

attack, but that his transportation and communication systems would doubtless be gone and his industrial capacity for producing the materials of war would be ruined.[17]

This reality fundamentally changed the nature of warfare, as the influential deterrence theorist Bernard Brodie observed in 1946.

> Thus, the first and most vital step in any American security program for the age of the atomic bombs is to take measures to guarantee to ourselves in case of attack the possibility of retaliation in kind. . . . Thus far the chief purpose of our military establishment has been to win wars. From now on its chief purpose must be to avert them.[18]

Thomas Schelling stressed the same point. As Freedman notes, for Schelling the value of nuclear-powered armed forces lay not in using them, "which would constitute a gross failure of strategy, but in what opponents might do to avoid it."[19] Or, as Gen. Kevin Chilton and Greg Weaver put it, "The avoidance of nuclear war—or, for that matter, conventional war on the scale of World War I or World War II—rather than its successful prosecution became the military's highest priority."[20] The advent of nuclear weapons meant every potential conflict involving NATO and the Warsaw Pact had them at the top of the pyramid. This type of pyramid inevitably dominated not just strategic planning relating to deterrence and war—including the Korean and Vietnam wars—but also countries' perceptions of their role in the world and how they could use it. Over the years, the position of nuclear weapons at the top of the deterrence pyramid has unsurprisingly prompted several countries outside the group of official nuclear-weapons states to try to develop nuclear weapons, in some cases successfully.

That is not to say nuclear weapons provided blanket deterrence of all Cold War aggression. The Soviet Union and its satellite states successfully employed what would today be called gray-zone aggression—for example, in the area of disinformation. These efforts included front publications and organizations and the infiltration of existing nongovernmental organizations such as the World Council of Churches, which it managed to steer in an anti-US direction.²¹ A false rumor linking HIV/AIDS to US Army medical experimentation at Fort Detrick in Maryland originated with a Soviet physician in East Germany and was disseminated by Warsaw Pact organs so successfully that it remains in circulation.²² Of course, the United States and its allies likewise engaged in gray-zone efforts to undermine Warsaw Pact regimes. Radio Free Europe and Radio Liberty, two radio stations broadcasting into Soviet satellite states and the Soviet Union respectively, were for years funded by the CIA and after that by the US Congress.²³

The "salami tactic" that China skillfully practiced when constructing artificial islands in a strategic and contested part of the South China Sea posed a similar dilemma during the Cold War, as illustrated in the British television series *Yes, Prime Minister*'s famous nuclear deterrence skit.

> UK government adviser: "Prime Minister, you do believe in the nuclear deterrent?"
> Prime Minister Jim Hacker: "Oh yes."
> . . .
> UK government adviser: "Whom does it deter?"
> Prime Minister Hacker: "The Russians . . . because they know that if they were to launch an attack I'd press the button . . . as the last resort."
> . . .
> UK government adviser: "What is the last resort? . . . If they try anything it will be . . . slice by slice, one small piece at a time. Will you press the button if they invade West Berlin? . . . Scenario I: Riots in West Berlin, buildings in flames, East German fire brigade crosses the border to help. Would you press the button?"
> Prime Minister Hacker: [Shakes head]
> UK government adviser: "The East German police come with them. The button?"
> Prime Minister Hacker: [Shakes head]²⁴

Nuclear weapons became the foremost tool in the general deterrence of the eventually five official nuclear-weapons states and featured heavily in the strategy of countries under the US or Soviet nuclear umbrella. Given the seriousness of the matter, and the implications if a nuclear-weapons state misinterpreted an adversary's actions, it is not surprising that a range of extraordinary thinkers tackled nuclear-based deterrence. Schelling, an economist, gained worldwide recognition as a deterrence theorist by applying game theory to the prospect of nuclear conflict. "[In 1958] I began to appreciate that the most immediate and important application of the kind of 'game theory' I was pursuing was in military foreign policy, especially nuclear weapons policy," he wrote in his biographical statement for the Nobel Memorial Prize in Economic Sciences, which he was awarded in 2005.[25]

His Nobel Memorial Prize, in fact, had little to do with economics. Instead, he was awarded the prestigious prize for his use of game theory in nation-state deterrence and thus "for having enhanced our understanding of conflict and cooperation through game-theory analysis," as the Nobel Prize committee described the prize motivation. The committee explained Schelling's contribution as

> a creative application of game theory to important social, political and economic problems. [He] showed that a party can strengthen its position by overtly worsening its own options, that the capability to retaliate can be more useful than the ability to resist an attack, and that uncertain retaliation is more credible and more efficient than certain retaliation. These insights have proven to be of great relevance for conflict resolution and efforts to avoid war.[26]

Freedman summarizes Schelling's approach similarly: "Under this proposition, strategy moved from considerations of conquest and resistance to deterrence, intimidation, blackmail, and threats."[27]

The Nobel Prize committee's observation that Schelling showed how "uncertain retaliation is more credible and more efficient than certain retaliation"[28] bears repeating, as it is also applicable to deterrence of gray-zone aggression. It illustrates that deterrence is fundamentally about psychology and that lessons from Cold War deterrence of conventional and nuclear threats can be applied to today's gray-zone aggression.

What Deters?

Just a few years before Schelling began applying game theory to nuclear conflict, a young Henry Kissinger first gained academic prominence with the publication of his doctoral thesis, *A World Restored: Metternich, Castlereagh and the Problems of Peace 1812–1822*,[29] which, despite focusing on diplomacy in 19th-century Europe, contained important lessons for the nuclear age. As Robert Kaplan notes, in *A World Restored* Kissinger implied that "the task of statesmen remained the same: to construct a balance of fear among great powers as part of the maintenance of an orderly international system."[30] This approach can be part of both a realist and an idealist foreign policy.

Cold War nuclear-based deterrence can be viewed as a pyramid similar to the food pyramid. As previously mentioned, the top layer features nuclear weapons, the middle layer features conventional military strength (personnel, training, and equipment), and the bottom layer features societal resilience, the bread and potatoes of deterrence. While resilience may not, on its own, instill fear in the prospective attacker, demonstration of capability—including the risk of entanglement it poses to the attacker—influences a prospective attacker's cost-benefit calculation. During the Cold War, it was relatively easy to understand which components should be part of the deterrence pyramid and how they should be arranged so that a country would establish in the adversary's mind an image of credibility and resilience.

This is less obvious today. Furthermore, deterrence must not be static. Instead, regardless of the tools used to deter, the element of surprise plays a central role. For Schelling, surprise (and the resulting fear on the adversary side) is decisive.[31] Similarly, Herman Kahn—a key deterrence theorist of the early nuclear age—ranked "frightening" as the most desirable characteristic of deterrence.[32] Because the objective of deterrence is to change the adversary's cost-benefit calculation, surprise elements increase the deterrent power as the adversary cannot prepare for them.

This makes the much-discussed nuclear no-first-use policies a less good idea for NATO's nuclear member states than they may seem. By cutting themselves off from the option of first use, these nuclear powers would voluntarily forgo an important surprise element of their deterrence. While no-first-use policies clearly have little effect on gray-zone aggression, they matter in deterrence of traditional military threats.

Even countries' actions during nonwar events such as terrorist incidents can add to, or subtract from, the image projected in general deterrence. During the 1980 Iranian embassy siege in London, for example, the UK government took decisive action, sending special forces into the building to liberate the hostages in an operation watched on television worldwide. The incident strengthened the UK's image as a hard-nosed actor and thus contributed to the "combined shield": the collection of capabilities that form the deterrence other countries evaluate when making decisions. The combined shield is even more relevant to gray-zone aggression than it is to nuclear and other forms of aggression.

Depending on the country, general deterrence aims to project an image of defense (deterrence by denial—that is, resilience and entanglement), offense (deterrence by punishment), or a combination of the two. During the Cold War, Sweden and Finland had no intent to attack the Soviet Union but were determined to use all means available to defend their territories. While it is highly likely that the Soviets would ultimately have prevailed, the cost in lives, time, and expense of such an operation may not have been worth the price. Similarly, one can speculate whether the Soviet Union would have invaded Afghanistan had the various rebel groups subsequently known as the mujahideen been in a position to signal their deterrence posture—which primarily featured entanglement—beforehand. The same goes for the US invasion of Afghanistan more than two decades later.

This, again, underlines the importance of general deterrence as not only a posture but also a reputation. To this day, Finland benefits from the resilience it displayed during World War II, which it has taken pains to demonstrate through its comprehensive system of whole-of-society engagement and training ever since. A country can decide its posture, but its reputation is the result of the adversary's evaluation. Leaders of Western countries would be well-advised to consider what effect their populations' internal divisions and increasing "snowflake" reputations have for adversaries' cost-benefit calculations.

It is, again, entirely possible that the Soviet Union never seriously contemplated annexing, invading, or otherwise attacking Sweden or Finland and that their resilience-focused deterrence made no difference. It is also possible, though less so, that NATO's deterrence by punishment made no difference to Soviet planning regarding West Germany and other NATO member states. John Mearsheimer notes that "generally when one side has an overwhelming advantage in forces, deterrence is very likely to fail—regardless of the chosen strategy."[33] When, however, does it succeed? Nobody knows for certain, precisely because deterrence is not a mechanistic task but a psychological one.

This poses a dilemma in designing deterrence. Even though NATO's Enhanced Forward Presence (EFP)—the alliance's four battle groups deployed on permanent rotation in the Baltic states and Poland—is set up to deter Russian military aggression, it is impossible to measure whether it is having an effect. EFP may have persuaded Russia that its cost-benefit calculation of territorial aggression against one or more of these countries would be negative and therefore inadvisable. Russia also may have in recent years never considered territorial aggression against the countries.

It is, however, also conceivable that EFP has made little difference to deterrence and that the countries' own efforts form the decisive deterrent. Terras observed,

> We have more than 60,000 Estonian, Latvian, and Lithuanian soldiers ready to die for the country. EFP just gives the reassurance that the alliance supports us. We have a plan for unconventional war. If someone takes a city, we'll go underground. We've made this public to everyone. It's like a modern Forest Brothers movement. The details are secret, of course, but the plan is even mentioned in our national security strategy, so our adversaries know about it. The point of deterrence is that you have to show that you will sell yourself as expensive as possible.[34]

The impossibility of proving a negative is, in fact, deterrence theory's fundamental challenge. Freedman notes that the best clues "come from the deterrer's own utterances. . . . Successful deterrence is a product of clear foreign policy, confirming what you care about and declaring and demonstrating vital interests."[35] Apart from such clues, however, without access to an adversary's reasoning, measuring the success of deterrence remains an extremely difficult if not impossible task. In lieu of a detailed understanding of an adversary's thought process and modus operandi, the United States and its allies often wargame scenarios in which they try to imagine how an adversary would react. That poses a problem because, as Adam Lowther notes,

> *the United States often does not understand its adversary.* . . . American decision makers often operate without understanding the culture, history, language, politics, and religion of an adversary. Mirror imaging frequently occurs.[36] (Emphasis in original.)

The Importance of Understanding the Adversary

Perspective linked to culture and circumstance matters because leaders—of democratic countries or authoritarian ones—do not make decisions in a vacuum. During the Cold War, the US undertook some attempts to better understand Soviet leaders' thinking. As Austin Long notes,

> RAND Kremlinologists . . . sought to probe the Soviet Union for "exceptions" to common expectations. . . . Philip Selznick's *The Organizational Weapon* and Nathan Leites' *The Operational Code of the Politburo* . . . sought to understand both the remarkable success of communist organization as well as its weaknesses.[37]

Other researchers attempted to categorize Soviet leaders. Long notes that "one model was heavily dependent on the particular constellation of Soviet leaders and their personality types; another was that of the 'doctrinaire Marxist-Leninist.'" There was also a bureaucratic-politics model.[38]

The efforts, however, never went much further, and Warsaw Pact leaders likewise struggled to understand Western leaders' thinking. This resulted in security dilemmas of misinterpreted signals such as NATO's 1983 Able Archer nuclear exercise. US intelligence records released in February 2021 show that Able Archer caused such concerns in Moscow that it ordered its nuclear forces in East Germany to be placed on "a 30-minute, around-the-clock readiness time and assign[ed] priority targets."[39] The

US government concluded that "Soviet military leaders may have been seriously concerned that the US would use Able Archer 83 as a cover for launching a real attack."[40]

Such near catastrophes illustrate that, to build successful deterrence, countries need to better understand their adversaries and try to view any given situation from the adversary's perspective. As Kissinger demonstrated in *A World Restored*, leaders are influenced by their countries' histories and power equilibriums, domestic considerations, and their own personal backgrounds. Austria's 19th-century Chancellor Klemens von Metternich successfully shored up his country's dwindling fortunes through a range of agreements with countries that today would be characterized as friends, frenemies, and enemies. He did so not by attempting to divine their intentions through calculations conducted from afar but based on direct interaction. Kissinger describes how, after having arranged for the daughter of Austria's emperor to marry Napoleon Bonaparte, Metternich—eager to better understand Napoleon's sometimes unpredictable decision-making—traveled to Paris "to help the new Empress acclimatize herself—and to divine Napoleon's next move."[41] Writing about *A World Restored*, Francis Fukuyama concludes that foreign policy cannot be deconstructed to an

> abstract, highly reductionist model. Kissinger never suffered from this kind of physics-envy; he (and [Hans] Morgenthau) were always conscious of the fact that foreign policy was made by statesmen who operated in a specific historical, cultural, and political context that shaped their goals and limited their options.[42]

This reality is as important to consider in today's geopolitical context as it was in early 19th-century Europe and 1957, when *A World Restored* was published. As Keith Payne noted in 2010, "Deterrence involves exploiting opponents' fears and sensitivities."[43] These may be fears and sensitivities completely linked to the deterrence, or they may be influenced by aspects unique to the country, leadership, or top decision maker. Intelligence services can, of course, provide some amount of detail regarding leaders' thinking, but unless the respective agents have supreme access, such intelligence is unlikely to paint a complete picture.⁴⁴ Indeed, because their mission is to gather specific information, intelligence services may not even be able to fully capture the nature of an adversary. As with any country, an adversary country is composed of leading personalities who may think, react, and operate differently and may disagree among themselves.

Western countries are not alone in mirror imaging. Over the past several years, President Vladimir Putin and his top aides have had only limited contact with Western leaders. Without regular conversations, the Russians have most likely built an erroneous picture of Western intentions. This unfortunate reality may explain some of Russia's actions in the gray zone and beyond.

Bluffing, Posturing, and Credible Deterrence

If mirror imaging is a psychological trick one or both sides may inadvertently play on themselves, bluffing is a deliberately used trick, albeit one that carries considerable risk. As Schelling notes, "A persuasive threat of war may deter an aggressor; the problem is to make it persuasive, to keep it from sounding like a bluff."⁴⁵ The most credible deterrence is the variety that gives the adversary no opportunity to suspect bluffing; as a result, an automatic and irrevocable nuclear response to a nuclear attack at times appeared attractive.

The obvious disadvantage of irrevocable and clearly communicated deterrence by punishment is that it locks the targeted country into an action that will also inflict self-harm. As Long notes,

> Schelling and Kahn both discussed this concept, and it is parodied in *Dr. Strangelove*, whose titular character notes, "because of the automated and irrevocable decision making process [that] rules out human meddling, the doomsday machine is terrifying. It's simple to understand. And completely credible and convincing."⁴⁶

The doomsday machine points to the role that artificial intelligence may come to play in deterrence.

Seeking to deter Iraq from invading Kuwait before what later became the first Gulf War, US Secretary of State James Baker delivered a stark missive to Iraqi Foreign Minister Tariq Aziz. In the letter, from President George H. W. Bush and addressed to President Saddam Hussein, Bush reminded the Iraqi leader that the United States had not only overwhelming conventional forces but also nuclear weapons. The letter failed to impress Aziz, who responded,

> Mr. Secretary, Iraq is a very ancient nation, we lived for six thousand years. I have no doubts that you are a very powerful nation, I have no doubts that you have a very strong military machine and you'll inflict on us heavy losses, but Iraq will survive and this leadership will decide the future of Iraq.[47]

Bush's letter, Baker later explained, spelled out that, if Iraq used chemical weapons against US forces, the American people would "demand vengeance and that we had the means to achieve it."[48] Aziz later recounted his meeting with Baker.

> I read [the letter] very carefully. And then when I ended reading it, I told him, "Look, Mr. Secretary, this is not the kind of correspondence between two heads of state. This is a letter of threat, and I cannot receive from you a letter of threat to my president," and I returned it to him.[49]

While Aziz may have considered the letter inappropriate, he most likely also assessed that the Bush administration would not risk a nuclear war over Kuwait.[50]

The United States failed in its deterrence because it engaged in mirror imaging and did not appreciate the unique aspects of Iraq, its history, and its leadership. Aziz and Saddam, in turn, failed to appreciate that the United States did not employ bluffing as a strategy in the same way they did; they appear, therefore, not to have taken Baker's threat of an invasion seriously.

Bluffing has, in fact, been attempted in various eras and contexts. Referring to the Far East during World War II, Edwin Layton observes that by "embarking on a deterrent policy before the military forces were installed in the Philippines to make it credible, Britain and the United States succeeded in making the concept of a preemptive strike an attractive option to the Japanese."[51] Japan perceived British and US deterrent messaging to be a bluff.

These failures in deterrence messaging again highlight the need for not just tailored deterrence but also a sophisticated understanding of the adversary. As Barry Schneider notes, Bush and Saddam "inherited a different set of world, regional, and domestic problems and pressures."[52] Such seemingly secondary considerations can, as Bush and his son George W. Bush were to discover, be fundamentally important in deterrence. Saddam's failed deterrence before the first Gulf War, in turn, was a mistake, but not a disastrous one. In 2003, however, he made the same mistake—bluffing about Iraqi capabilities and dismissing US posturing as bluffing—in trying to deter the United States. This time his bluff proved fatal. The West, though, engaged in mirror imaging and missed Saddam's bluff on weapons of mass destruction. With better knowledge and appreciation of the leaders' personalities and their cultural contexts, on both sides, deterrence may have worked.

The Significance of Leaders' Personalities

Leaders' personalities may matter as much in deterrence as they do in transnational cooperation. The importance of personalities in international cooperation was demonstrated in an unlikely manner by Kissinger himself in 2015, at a memorial ceremony for Schmidt. Kissinger, in an exceptionally rare speech in his mother tongue, praised his longtime friend.[53] Judging exclusively from external factors, such a friendship was highly unlikely to exist, yet it did. A former cabinet minister of a leading EU member state noted,

> Cynics underestimate the value of people-to-people understanding. I recall at the Prague Summit in 2002 watching [Jacques] Chirac working the room building a majority to get a French deal on the [EU common agricultural policy]. Never wasted an

opportunity, and it worked. The lack of contact between people at the working level is also a serious problem in dangerous times.[54]

Personal relationships can, of course, be taken too far. Leaders pursuing them to circumvent the need for deterrence are highly likely to fail, as was the case with Donald Trump and his engagement with Kim Jong Un.

During the Cold War, frank exchanges between NATO and Warsaw Pact leaders about their motivations and how they would respond to different deterrence moves were virtually nonexistent.[55] Invaluable lessons could, however, have been learned in the early years after the end of the Cold War. Warsaw Pact leaders and officials should have been comprehensively interviewed during that period, including on what deterred actions they may otherwise have taken. Such comprehensive interviewing never took place. As a result, a unique opportunity to learn about the effectiveness of various forms of deterrence—especially the actions that changed the leaders' cost-benefit calculations—was lost. Nearly every senior leader in power at the end of the 1980s is now deceased, though, crucially, Mikhail Gorbachev is still alive.[56]

Assessing Intent

Intent—or its misunderstanding by a potential adversary—also complicates the effectiveness of deterrence. Due to the mutual lack of knowledge about the other side's motivation and reasoning, the United States and Soviet Union struggled to understand each other's intentions during their closest nuclear encounter—the Cuban missile crisis.[57] This once again underlines the central point of understanding how deterrence signaling is received. While it may be delivered with one set of intentions, it may be received differently. While NATO's EFP in the Baltic states and Poland is of a defensive nature and intended as a deterrent, in a Kremlin cut off from regular exchanges with Western leaders, it may be perceived as a precursor of an attack on Russia. George Robertson, former NATO secretary-general and UK defense secretary, observed, "Unless we make it clear, repeatedly and regularly and believably, that we have no hostile intent but that one foot into Estonia would trigger massive retaliation, then we will continue to slide around building suspicion in the Kremlin."[58]

In fact, understanding what information leaders such as Putin receive is vital to discerning which, and how, deterrence messaging works. Authoritarian leaders frequently operate in a bubble in which subordinates provide only the information they think the leaders want to hear. Such leaders may, as a result, make national security decisions based on assessments unconnected to Western deterrence. Maj. Gen. Pekka Toveri (ret.), at the time of the interview the Finnish Defence Forces' chief of intelligence, observed, "That's why it is crucially important to know on what information Putin makes his decisions, so that we can bolster our deterrence the right way."[59]

Conversely, the West's internal convulsions—ranging from American culture wars to searing intra-EU debates about member states' burden sharing—can incorrectly signal weakness to hostile countries' leaders. Toveri pointed out that

> they see [the] West as weak, especially morally and spiritually. That is the story that they have fed to their people for over a decade now. The problem is that they start to believe their own story, which weakens the effectiveness of [the] West's deterrence.[60]

In addition, Western leaders' frequent appearances in the news and on social media give adversaries a comprehensive—but potentially highly flawed—understanding of the mood and thinking of such leaders.

The effectiveness is, of course, also harmed if a deterrent is used for wrong purposes. After President Trump's incitement of supporters to attack Congress caused a mob to storm the Capitol on January 6, 2021, Speaker Nancy Pelosi (D-CA) contacted Chairman of the Joint Chiefs of Staff Gen. Mark Milley. "This morning, I spoke to . . . Milley to discuss available precautions for preventing an unstable president from initiating military hostilities or accessing the launch codes and ordering a nuclear strike," Pelosi informed members of Congress.[61] While Pelosi's move undoubtedly served its domestic political purpose, it weakened the United States' nuclear deterrent by making the arsenal appear to be a domestic chess piece.

Understanding how a deterrence message is received—which may be different among intended and unintended recipients in general, tailored, extended, and immediate deterrence—is vital to ensuring deterrence's effectiveness. That the Cold War ended without a direct confrontation between the two blocs suggests that their respective deterrence was successful. Yet, not understanding the opponent's intent unnecessarily increased risk at crucial points throughout this era.

Applying Cold War Deterrence Lessons

Despite the near disasters due to a lack of understanding of the opponent's intent and thought process, after the Cold War, the tenor was that deterrence had worked. It was therefore perhaps logical that several years later, in 2005, Schelling received the Nobel Memorial Prize. But in his Nobel lecture, Schelling delivered a warning.

> There is much discussion these days of whether or not "deterrence" has had its day and no longer has much of a role in America's security. There is no Soviet Union to deter; the Russians are more worried about Chechnya than about the United States; the Chinese seem no more interested in military risks over Taiwan than [Nikita] Khrushchev really was over Berlin; and terrorists cannot be deterred anyway—we don't know what they value that we might threaten, or who or where it is.[62]

Sixteen years after Schelling's warning, the geopolitical scenario looks different, but his point is still valid. While nuclear-based deterrence has its place in the deterrence pyramid, it has little if any effect on gray-zone aggression. The reason for this is credibility: While it is proportionate and therefore credible to respond to a nuclear threat with nuclear-focused deterrence, it is wildly disproportionate and therefore not credible to seek to deter gray-zone aggression with the same means.

The nuclear threat, of course, remains, and with it the need for nuclear deterrence. That is the case despite the success of movements such as Global Zero and the International Campaign to Abolish Nuclear Weapons and even though President Barack Obama in his 2009 Prague speech promised "clearly and with conviction America's commitment to seek the peace and security of a world without nuclear weapons."[63] Nuclear deterrence also remains valid under the no-first-use policy maintained by four of the five official nuclear-weapons states. (Russia no longer has a no-first-use policy; the United States reserves the right to first use against Russia, China, and the unofficial nuclear-weapons state of North Korea, but not against signatories of the Treaty on the Non-Proliferation of Nuclear Weapons.[64]) As Chilton and Weaver argued in 2010,

> US nuclear forces cast a long shadow over the decision calculations of anyone who would contemplate taking actions that threaten the vital interest of the United States or its allies, making it clear that the ultimate consequences of doing so may be truly disastrous....
>
> As a result, US nuclear forces make an important contribution to deterring both symmetric and asymmetric forms of warfare in the twenty-first century.[65]

Yet, precisely because these weapons are so powerful, using them to signal punishment of acts of gray-zone aggression is not credible and therefore not effective. Unsurprisingly, France, NATO, and the United States have not communicated, to date, the intent to respond to hacks and other gray-zone attacks with nuclear means, precisely because adversaries are likely to assume they would never follow through on such threats. Against this background, it was all the more surprising that, in its March 2021 report *Global Britain in a Competitive Age: The Integrated Review of Security, Defence, Development and Foreign Policy*, the UK government announced potential nuclear retaliation against biological, chemical, and gray-zone aggression. The government stated that

> the UK will not use, or threaten to use, nuclear weapons against any non-nuclear weapon state party to the Treaty on the Non-Proliferation of Nuclear Weapons 1968.... This assurance does not apply to any state in material breach of those non-proliferation obligations. However, we reserve the right to

review this assurance if the future threat of weapons of mass destruction, such as chemical and biological capabilities, or emerging technologies that could have a comparable impact, makes it necessary.[66]

The current lack of effective deterrence against gray-zone threats illustrates a fundamental point: Deterrence must be dynamic. If a country does not build and constantly refine its general and tailored deterrence and does not communicate its intent, its deterrence becomes static. DCDC points out that "deterrence is no longer a defensive or semi-passive theory based on conveying intent and capability; it now has to involve active measures as part of a constant conflict below the traditional threshold of what used to be called war."[67] While the nuclear-focused deterrence pyramid works well for traditional aggression, it has little relevance and therefore little effect on gray-zone aggression.

The proof that more dynamic deterrence is needed is, of course, the increase of gray-zone aggression. Hostile governments coercing Western ones by detaining their citizens or threatening their businesses are not deterred by nuclear arsenals, nor are such governments' proxy hackers or businesses that exploit Western countries' openness to access their top innovation or steal intellectual property.

The challenge facing the West is therefore how to credibly deter forms of aggression that individually do not threaten the targeted country's vital interests but that collectively cause severe harm to the targeted country. Rear Adm. Mark Montgomery (ret.), previously director of operations at US Pacific Command and now executive director of the US Cyberspace Solarium Commission, said,

> We've been using the old model of nuclear deterrence, where deterrence by imposition of costs clearly works. The US and Russia/the Soviet Union—we both felt that way. But in cyberspace, you don't have that deterrence. The reason we know that deterrence in cyberspace isn't working is that we've had a reasonably robust Cyber Command with known offensive capabilities for five years now, and even so, we've observed the Chinese conduct a decade-long campaign of cyber aggression and

intellectual property theft to, for example, steal technological secrets. They conduct it below the level where we'd respond with a use of force, and they clearly know what that level is. And judging by their behavior, the Russians are not deterred by our offensive cyber capabilities either.

The North Koreans are even more brazen. They know our offensive capability and how it compares to their own capabilities, and they attack anyway. Iran's capabilities are much smaller than, say, China's, but it's much harder to assess their intent. And they seem more willing to take disproportionate risks.[68]

The undeniable advantage—from the aggressor's perspective—of these forms of aggression is precisely that the West's deterrence tools are not set up for threats and aggression below the threshold of war.

The threshold of war is blurry; NATO's Article V, for example, refers only to an "armed attack."[69] Although there is clearly wiggle room in the definition of "armed attack" that an adversary could exploit, the West's rivals would gain little from a war with the West. Even countries such as Taiwan that do not have formal security cooperation with the United States by means of a NATO-style mutual defense alliance could count on support from the United States and other friendly nations. Paradoxically, the success of traditional deterrence has forced the West's rivals to innovate. The result is gray-zone aggression, which involves relatively little cost but yields considerable benefit.

China, meanwhile, not only has accelerated its gray-zone aggression but is also strengthening its deterrence pillars; these include its nuclear forces, conventional forces, "information warfare forces; a flexible space force; and something it refers to as an 'innovative and developmental civilian deterrence force.'"[70] Andrew Krepinevich Jr. quotes the People's Liberation Army's description of the new Chinese deterrence.

> In particular, the emergence of new deterrence forces, based on new technology such as information, cyberspace, space, and new-material technologies, is revolutionarily changing the mechanism, method, and area of operation. It heralds a

completely new method of deterrence, symbolized by constructing [an] asymmetrical method of deterrence.[71]

As Krepinevich notes, the Chinese government has not elaborated, to date, on this new deterrence: "It would seem essential for them to communicate to those they seek to deter just how this 'new method' applies to them."[72] It is with deterrence as with a tree falling in the forest: If nobody is there to hear it fall, does it make a sound? If deterrence is not successfully communicated, it does not exist. This applies to Western deterrence of new threats as much as China's "asymmetrical" deterrence.

Making a related point, Krepinevich argues that

> the expansion of military competition in the relatively new domains of space, cyberspace, and the seabed finds a growing number of state and non-state rivals competing for advantage. In each domain, the competition favors the offense. This undermines deterrence through denial since, all other factors being equal, the costs associated with taking a proscribed action are less than those needed to block the action successfully.[73]

That reality also holds true for gray-zone aggression. Some countries have established efforts aimed at deterring gray-zone aggression. On the deterrence-by-denial side, countless companies and government agencies have improved their defenses against cyberattacks, though as the December 2020 discovery of the SolarWinds hack made clear, that defense has gaps. Also on the deterrence-by-denial side, the US armed forces have conducted cyber defense exercises such as Cyber Guard and Jack Voltaic in cooperation with the private sector. In January 2021, the Czech Republic conducted the world's first joint military-industry gray-zone exercise, based on a report of mine.[74] The exercise, which included several gray-zone scenarios, involved key Czech companies.[75] In addition to practicing gray-zone scenarios, such exercises strengthen deterrence by resilience by signaling to prospective attackers that their cost-benefit calculations will be unfavorable.

Latvia has introduced a comprehensive defense policy, which is modeled on the Swedish and Finnish total defense model and features regular crisis-preparedness cooperation between the government and private sector and a national security curriculum that is being rolled out at every secondary school in the country.[76] Lithuania, in turn, has reinstated national service (this time with a selective rather than universal model).[77] Yet, while such efforts have great value in signaling deterrence by denial, they cannot exist in isolation. Any deterrence posture needs a combination of denial and at least some punishment.

On the deterrence-by-punishment side, the United States has given its Cyber Command a Defend Forward framework that increases US deterrence by punishment in cyberspace. Among its other methods, the Cyber Command signals to would-be attackers that it has identified them. This constitutes what one might call a horse's-head-in-the-bed strategy,[78] or personalized deterrence.[79] In Francis Ford Coppola's film *The Godfather*, Jack Woltz wakes up to find the severed head of his horse in his bed. He gets the message without the Corleone family needing to inflict any violence on him. Like the US Cyber Command, the UK's new National Cyber Force engages in offensive cyber operations and thus deterrence by punishment.[80] Additionally, in the United States, 26 policy proposals put forward by the Cyberspace Solarium Commission were adopted by Congress as part of the 2021 National Defense Authorization Act; they include establishing a White House cybersecurity director position.[81]

These, though, are individual initiatives. The existence of gray zone aggression and a new comprehensive model of Chinese deterrence make it imperative for the West to build comprehensive gray-zone deterrence. Because deterrence rests on psychology—not specific tools—existing models of deterrence by denial and punishment discussed in this chapter can be adapted to gray-zone aggression.

The applicability of deterrence through resilience is obvious. With gray-zone aggression frequently directed against civil society, societal resilience possesses enormous potential. Deterrence by punishment can likewise be adapted to gray-zone aggression, featuring imposition of costs in areas that are valuable to adversaries' key decision makers. Should the West, however, manage to establish deterrence against existing forms of gray-zone aggression, it would raise another aspect of the defender's dilemma: how to avoid inadvertently creating a situation in which precisely that deterrence causes adversaries to innovate even more.

This is why a sophisticated understanding of the to-be-deterred rival—including culture, intent, political-military objectives, and economic motivations—is even more necessary today than during the era of nuclear-dominated deterrence. Given that the overarching threat of nuclear conflict has subsided in favor of persistent gray-zone aggression, dialogue with adversary countries' leaders that was virtually impossible during the Cold War—which could yield insights about which forms of deterrence work and which Western actions are perceived as provocations without being intended as such—has a greater chance of taking place today.

Today's slightly less immediate risk of nuclear war, combined with the increasing use of gray-zone aggression, also means that the deterrer can experiment somewhat in building dynamic deterrence. Failure to deter, or ill-conceived deterrence by punishment, would be less catastrophic than failed nuclear-based deterrence would be. It is, in fact, necessary to experiment to create gray-zone deterrence that is effective and dynamic.

Conversely, precisely because the new forms of aggression are, in isolation, often negligible and their aggressive intent is not immediately obvious and because the attackers often employ means that would be out of the question for liberal democracies, the challenge is to establish deterrence that does not lead to escalation. Although seemingly paradoxical, the body of deterrence knowledge accumulated during the Cold War offers a formidable basis on which to innovate and create new forms of deterrence.

IX

Cold War Swedish and Finnish Total Defense as Deterrence

In 1935, Erich Ludendorff, a military theorist and World War I general, summarized what he considered the reality of that war, which differentiated it from previous ones.

> The World War showed a completely different character than all wars of the past 150 years to date. Participating in it were not just the armed forces of the warring countries, which engaged in their mutual annihilation; the peoples themselves were put at the service of the warfare.... The total war, which is not just a matter for the armed forces but also directly touches the life and soul of every single member of the warring peoples, was born.[1]

If total war had already established itself, the way to win was clearly to perfect it. In *Der totale Krieg* (*The Total War*), Ludendorff outlined how Germany should do this.[2] The title of his book quickly established itself in the vernacular. *Der totale Krieg* was published when the totality concept was in vogue in Germany. Two years previously, soon after the Nazis' rise to power, the jurist Ernst Forsthoff argued in *Der totale Staat* (*The Total State*) that only a state that expanded its control to every element of society could assure the nation's survival.[3]

Nazi Germany, of course, went on to become a totalitarian state. As Lawrence Freedman points out,

> For the Nazis in Germany and the militarists in Japan, total war was not so much a matter of strategy as of world-view. The logic was totalitarian, not only in terms of the state controlling all aspects of the economy and social relationships but also in the presumption that all individuals must act in its service.[4]

That the totalitarian state of Nazi Germany engaged in total war is not just a matter of historical interest but also highly relevant today, when the West's authoritarian rivals use their governments' enormous reach and power as an exceedingly effective tool of aggression. Many aspects of gray-zone aggression directed against the West would not be possible in countries with limited government powers.

Nazi leaders enthusiastically adopted Ludendorff's concept.[5] Today, the wider public associates the concept of total war with Joseph Goebbels' "Sportpalast" speech in 1943. "Do you want the total war?" Goebbels shouted. "Yes!" the audience enthusiastically responded.[6]

In reality, Nazi Germany had begun employing total war before this speech. In March 1941, Adolf Hitler addressed some 200 Wehrmacht generals, preparing them for what would become Operation Barbarossa. Jan Willem Honig describes the reaction of Gen. Franz Halder, chief of staff of the Army High Command and subsequently a key Barbarossa commander. Halder described "a type of conflict that, with chilling deliberation, would develop into one of the most pitiless and deadly fought between two societies in history."[7]

In Sweden, political and military leaders were paying close attention. As Germany rearmed and eventually invaded not just continental European countries but also Sweden's immediate neighbors Denmark and Norway, the Swedish government rushed to improve national defense. Compulsory military service was dramatically expanded, and between 35,000 and 40,000 new recruits went through initial training each year (with the training period expanded to 360 days), resulting in a maximum mobilized strength of 320,000.[8] In addition, men older than age 47 and teenagers were invited to join the new Home Guard. Within months, 90,000 had done so, while another 300,000 citizens volunteered through other organizations.[9]

The Swedish government could also count on the country's volunteer defense organizations, which focused on skills the country might need in a war or other major crisis[10] and that, by the early 1900s, counted more than half a million members.[11] These organizations included Lottakåren (the Lotta Corps), a women's auxiliary support organization.[12] In 1940, the government estimated that, in addition to the mobilized military strength of 320,000, the country had an equal number of citizens involved in defense efforts through volunteer organizations.[13]

Yet a mobilized strength of 320,000 backed up by the Home Guard, Lottas, and other volunteer organizations was hardly going to dissuade Hitler from invading Sweden if he wished to, especially since Sweden had dramatically cut its defense capabilities during the late 1920s and early 1930s and had highly limited heavy weaponry.

Sweden could, however, make the prospect of occupying Sweden unattractive. The government set about changing Nazi Germany's cost-benefit calculation by increasing societal involvement to keep the country operating during an invasion. In this fashion, Sweden increased the time, effort, and expense conquering it would entail. The military service requirement for all able-bodied men was supplemented with a civil defense requirement, which obliged employers to contribute to the war effort by making key staff (regardless of seniority) available, among other requirements.[14] Like other countries, the government also conducted what would today be called strategic communication.

Other measures were also similar to those in other countries. A new agency, the Government Information Board (SIS), monitored public opinion and led public awareness campaigns to, for example, remind people to avoid loose talk. In a system that remained in place during the Cold War, the SIS also passed so-called gray slips of paper to journalists and editors, informing them which news should not be publicized.[15]

In 1943, the government added to the combined national effort *If War Comes*, a leaflet that described how citizens should act in potentially occupied and in free parts of the country. The key message of the leaflet, which was sent to households nationwide, was:

> Every attack on our country's freedom and independence shall be met with weapons. Total war requires total defense. All information to the effect that resistance is to cease is false. Sweden wants to defend itself, can defend itself, and will defend itself.[16]

Around the same time, Sweden achieved a level of self-sufficiency that would allow it to sustain itself for six months in case of a blockade.[17] Thus was born the policy of total defense.

In building resilience, Sweden drew on Finland's experience during the Winter War. In that war, which began with a Soviet air and land attack on

November 30, 1939, Soviet troops attacked Finland's far smaller armed forces. Although the Finns lacked tanks and artillery, they had a professional command and a motivated reserve officer corps. On that basis, and under the military leadership of the brilliant Field Marshal Carl Gustaf Mannerheim, Finland mounted a disciplined defense effort that bogged down the Red Army through exemplary use of resilience and entanglement. In practical terms, this involved Finnish soldiers, often equipped with just skis, rifles, and Molotov cocktails, halting Soviet infantry advances. While this could not halt advancing tanks, the cheap Molotov cocktails proved a surprisingly effective weapon against Soviet armored vehicles. Finland's civilian population, in turn, united in its support of the defense effort, which likewise surprised the Soviets as the Finns had lived through a bruising civil war just over two decades previously. A puppet government installed by the Soviets had such minimal support that, after initially refusing to negotiate with Finland's legitimate government, the Soviets eventually had to do so.

Even though the Finns had no choice but to cease resistance 105 days after the invasion, they had turned what the Soviets assumed would be an easy annexation into a prolonged nightmare that caused the Soviets significant loss of blood, treasure, and reputation. (Five years later, Finland once again outwitted the Soviets when Finnish military officers—acting on Finnish fears that the Red Army would occupy the country after World War II—managed to clandestinely bring the country's signals intelligence apparatus, including equipment and some 750 officers, to Sweden.[18]) For Finland, the successful resistance meant that, despite having to relinquish territory, the country avoided occupation and, crucially, could continue functioning as an independent nation.

Finland's Winter War effort demonstrated the feasibility of total defense and thus of the combination of deterrence by denial (in this case, resilience and entanglement) and the imposition of costs. While the Soviets had intent and capability, the Finns significantly reduced the Soviets' opportunity. The Finns' tenacious efforts likely changed the Soviets' cost-benefit calculation for any future attacks and proved that, even ahead of a David versus Goliath confrontation, the David side would have a chance of deterring the Goliath side if using all parts of its society.

Sweden's Cold War Total Defense

Sweden's massive efforts in building total defense during World War II alone did not change Hitler's mind regarding a potential invasion of the country. More likely, he directed his attention elsewhere for other reasons. Nevertheless, following the end of the war, the government realized it needed to increase its total defense efforts. It modernized the equipment and doctrine of all the services and put great effort into equipping the navy and air force.[19] The Swedish air force—featuring a fleet of largely Swedish-made aircraft—subsequently became one of the Cold War's largest.[20]

More importantly, the government began improving the country's whole-of-society resilience. It continued sending *If War Comes* leaflets to households, now with "total war must be met with total defense" as its key message.[21] The easy-to-read instructions with illustrations and bullet points covered how to leave the house in case of evacuation, what to bring, and how to treat exposure and biological weapons, among other matters. The leaflet's content was also included in the phone book. The government tested an alarm signal quarterly that was so much part of society that the population affectionately referred to it as Hesa Fredrik (Hoarse Fredrik).[22] The volunteer defense organizations—each specializing in skills such as facilitating radio communications, training dogs for the armed forces, and caring for farm animals during crises[23]—enhanced their activities and command-and-control structures as their nationwide memberships continued growing. Several organizations, such as the Red Cross, also received government funding to train the public in basic resilience skills.[24]

The country also developed the so-called civil defense duty—the military service's civilian twin—into a highly refined system. The country's military regions each had a corresponding civil defense structure, including a civilian commander (typically a county governor).[25] One of these commanders acted as civil defense commander in chief, reporting directly to the cabinet. Nationwide, the civil defense organization "built emergency shelters, procured gasmasks, extinguished fires, planned evacuations, transported civilians to hospitals, and provided first aid in case of air raids."[26]

By 1959, the country had managed to build a network of highly sophisticated shelters, many of them with space for several thousand people.

A certain category of shelters was to be used for the regular population; there were some 30,000 of these, primarily located in newly constructed neighborhoods and used on an everyday basis for bike and stroller storage, as event spaces, or for commercial warehousing. Other shelters, primarily located in central urban locations, were to house those involved with civil defense. Such shelters were built with a longer stay in mind, and they often featured theaters and car repair shops. On an everyday basis they were used for youth clubs and adult education and by assorted civil-society associations. The country's civil defense organization also had its own underground command centers around the country, equipped with sleeping quarters, canteens, independent water supplies, and backup generators. On an everyday basis, these shelters were used for training civil defense personnel.[27]

Indeed, civil defense involved large parts of the population, with all Swedes age 16–65 who were not part of the military defense effort obliged to make themselves available should they be needed. In peacetime, that meant an organization of 150,000–200,000 people, often men older than age 47 who were no longer eligible for service in the armed forces; an average of 30,000 women were also part of the peacetime organization.[28] The mobilized strength in case of war would have been significantly larger: In addition to around one million military members, it would have comprised some 2.2 million people involved in the civil defense effort, including in volunteer defense organizations.[29] More than three million Swedes engaged in total defense, including a mobilized military strength of one million, is an astonishing figure for a country whose Cold War population ranged from 7 to 8.5 million.

Civil defense also included so-called war placement. Through the war placement system, experts at all levels of seniority were assigned specific wartime roles. Engineers, executives at strategic companies, farmers, and even day care providers who were deemed essential to the resilience effort were assigned wartime roles by the government, sometimes in the government itself and sometimes in their regular places of work. The guiding idea in war placement, as in all total defense, was to demonstrate resilience and keep the country operating with as little disruption as possible in case of crisis. War placement also included professions such as journalism, which kept many news organizations going (sometimes in backup facilities);

some journalists had war placement in the government's wartime communications effort.

In addition to people, many private tractors and cars had war placement and could be assigned wartime roles by the government.[30] A more unusual aspect was the "web," an unofficial group of contacts maintained by Security Police officers nationwide to keep an alert eye on Soviet activities. Through the web, the Security Police—Sweden's agency in charge of counterintelligence—was, for example, able to establish how the Soviet Union used athletic encounters for espionage purposes.[31]

Sweden also built a system of so-called K companies, businesses whose operations were so central to the country in case of war that they would need to keep functioning with minimal disruption. The government constantly mapped and assessed the entirety of the country's private sector to keep its K-company list up-to-date; in 1995, when the Swedish government began winding down total defense, the list included some 11,000 businesses.[32] The businesses—which included not only Saab and Volvo but also select banks and the Stockholm Stock Exchange—were required to maintain supplies that would allow them to keep operating close to normal levels even if imports were disrupted. The government, cooperating with some 250 of the companies, maintained stockpiles of strategic imported components such as oil and coffee.[33] In some cases—such as with Saab, Volvo, and the arms manufacturer Bofors—government-industry construction of underground factories further aided continuity of operations in case of war.[34]

In total defense exercises organized by the government, the armed forces practiced defense with all levels of government, the private sector, and volunteer organizations. One component was, for example, coordinated ground-troop activation and civilian evacuation in areas hit by a Soviet ground assault; other common features included delivery of health care and fuel.[35] Like all military exercises, these were important not just for training but also to signal capability and intent to would-be attackers. In addition, the armed forces regularly conducted smaller-format exercises that also involved the Home Guard and volunteer defense organizations.[36]

Combined, these efforts created a system in which the government, private sector, and citizenry collaborated to an extraordinary extent. As Björn Körlof notes,

> Military service played an important role for societal cohesion, even though it only included men. The volunteer defense organizations [such as the Lottas], however, connected a large part of the population in activities that included volunteer training for duties in total defense.[37]

Almost as a side benefit, the national security effort aided social cohesion.

> Men and women of all societal classes . . . developed camaraderie, trust in one another and knowledge about the total defense system of which they were all part. . . . The majority of the population was prepared for its role and its contribution if war broke out.[38]

Naturally, Sweden's close call during World War II instilled among the population fear of another invasion and thus a corresponding will to be part of the defense effort, which unsurprisingly subsided somewhat as decades passed. Importantly, however, because the total defense structures and planning were maintained until the end of the Cold War, the total defense effort did not hinge merely on Swedes' individual motivations.

The exceptionally strong focus on involving the public in national security allowed Sweden to not only build a disproportionately strong combined shield but also do so at relatively little expense considering the size of its prospective attacker. Throughout the 1970s, Sweden spent around 3 percent of gross domestic product on military defense.[39]

Finland's Cold War Total Defense

Finland, too, proceeded to build national defense based on total defense, and it did so having experienced three wars during World War II. In the 1941–44 Continuation War to reclaim territory seized by the Soviet Union during the Winter War, Finland was supported by Germany's Wehrmacht. After being forced by the Soviet Union to sign an armistice in 1944, the Finns then fought to drive the Wehrmacht out of their country. It is no exaggeration to say that Finland was tested more than any other country its size was and that its efforts were innovative and heroic and its internal cohesion exemplary. "We were smart not to annex [Finland]. It would have been a festering wound. . . . People are stubborn there, very stubborn," Vyacheslav Molotov, the Soviet foreign minister during World War II, later concluded.[40]

These efforts, of course, allowed Finland to avoid the fate of every other small country invaded during World War II: occupation. After World War II, Finland remained nonaligned even as it maintained close ties with the Soviet Union. These ties may have been a bitter pill for large parts of the public to swallow, but they were one of the few ways Finland could increase its security, as Finnish leaders were aware that other countries would not come to Finland's aid if the Soviets decided to attack again. That prospect was real. In 1940, Molotov told a Lithuanian colleague,

> You must be realistic enough to understand that the fate of the small nations is to disappear. Your Lithuania, together with the rest of the Baltic nations, as well as Finland, will become part of the glorious family of Soviet nations.[41]

Finland's Defence Revision Committee, established as the war ended in 1945 and charged with developing the country's national security strategy, noted in a 1949 report, "It is perfectly clear that no country will guarantee our neutrality and territorial integrity without some benefit to itself, in other words without gaining advantages in one form or another."[42] This is an important reason Helsinki signed the Friendship, Cooperation, and Mutual Assistance (FCMA) treaty with Moscow in 1948, stipulating that Finland would defend itself by all means available against an attack by "Germany or any state allied with the latter" and that it would be assisted by the Soviet Union if necessary.[43]

Understandably, political leaders publicly played down fears of aggression by the Soviet Union itself.[44] The Defence Revision Committee "made every attempt to avoid naming any potential aggressor, contenting itself with mentioning that it would most probably be a question of Finland becoming embroiled in a conflict between the Western and Eastern blocks [sic]."[45] In reality, though, Finland's total defense focused on Soviet aggression. That the committee—comprising six members of parliament, primarily from leftist parties, and five military officers[46]—managed to reach a consensus even though the country was politically divided over how to handle relations with Moscow points to a profound national commitment to keeping the country safe.[47]

In large parts of Finnish society, there were, however, also concerns of takeover attempts by Finnish Communists, many of whom were deeply suspicious of strong defense. The takeover risk was real in a country still reeling from its 1918 civil war between socialist "Reds" and "White" liberal farmer bourgeois. In 1948, the fears became acute. Referring to President Juho Kusti Paasikivi, Pekka Visuri notes that

> the President's tough position [on keeping key installations safe] was influenced by the consideration that provocation by even a small group could quickly lead to a crisis to which the Soviet Union might choose to react. The Government was determined to maintain order within the country at all costs.[48]

Even in the early 1950s, however, many Finnish decision makers including Paasikivi suspected that the hostility against national defense voiced by many Finnish Communists was directed by Moscow. Such fears portend today's concerns in some Western countries of hostile governments exploiting domestic divisions. Today, as in 1950s Finland, the obvious challenge stemming from threats below the level of armed conflict is, of course, that they are often not obvious until it is too late to tackle them.

Finnish leaders also had to contend with the real risk of Soviet invasion. Paasikivi, a veteran of Finnish dealings with the Soviet Union who led negotiations with Moscow to end the Winter War, wrote in his diary that "we had to comply with the demands of the cooperation agreement but still be prepared for the Soviets breaking that agreement and invading by force."[49] How does one keep a country safe, especially from a nominal ally that might opt to use either conventional aggression or a hybrid mix and that is also attempting to weaken that country's society through gray-zone means such as political infiltration?

In addition to these highly delicate problems, Finland faced the prospect of being dragged into a conflict between NATO and the Warsaw Pact, as the Soviet Union might have extended its air defense systems over Finnish airspace, thereby triggering NATO bombing of Finland. The only workable solution was total defense with its focus on deterrence by resilience.

Finland maintained its system of general conscription for men, with which it would reach a wartime strength of 403,000,[50] and began building civil defense similar to Sweden's. In military and civil defense, however, Finland had to consider not just strong opposition from Finnish Communists but also its obligations under the FCMA treaty. Moscow forced Finland to ban what it labeled fascist volunteer defense organizations. In reality, this meant the Protection Corps—a crucial umbrella auxiliary defense organization—had to be disbanded. This was a heavy blow to Finland—among Lottas alone, 10,000 served in the war effort at any given time, and the Lotta Svärd organization comprised more than 170,000 women in 1943[51]—and of course meant that creating any new volunteer organization could trigger intervention by Moscow.

Finland therefore had to focus even more on pure societal resilience than Sweden did. Primarily, this meant strengthening the population's psychological resolve. In addition to maintaining standard preparedness measures such as strategic reserves, the Finnish government introduced an innovative concept known as *henkinen maanpuolustus* (HMP), adopted from Switzerland's *Geistige Landesverteidigung* (GLV), "mental national defense." During World War II, the Swiss government successfully established GLV, a nationwide educational and public awareness program, to turn democracy and neutrality into national core values.[52] Finland launched HMP with a similar objective. One might call HMP a national security inoculation to make the population resistant to foreign interference and more willing to band together to keep the country safe even under conditions de facto imposed by Moscow.

The board in charge of HMP was launched in 1963 and began educating citizens through public awareness campaigns and reading materials. It also conducted research, polling the population on matters of neutrality, democracy, and national defense.[53] Juhana Aunesluoma and Johanna Rainio-Niemi note that

> according to one description, the board was responsible for nearly all aspects of social and political opinion formation at

all layers of society, including state administration and political life, the media, the education system, and the many voluntary associations in Finnish society.[54]

The program succeeded. By the mid-1970s, HMP was considered so pervasive that large parts of Finnish society rebelled against it and the board was replaced by an organization with a smaller mandate.

Through HMP and its successor, successive Finnish governments helped instill among Finland's initially disjointed population a willingness to defend the country. To this day, Finns are annually asked the same question in a national poll: "If Finland is attacked, should the Finns—in your opinion—defend themselves with weapons in all situations, even if the result seems uncertain?"[55] In 1970, the first year the survey was carried out, a majority responded no, but by the early 1980s, around 70 percent responded yes. The figure remained at that level until the late 2010s, when it dropped to around 65 percent.[56] Finland's strong focus on strengthening the population's mental resilience to national security threats has obvious relevance to today's gray-zone threats. Indeed, the Finns' will to defend their country has remained strong even as threats have changed.

One aspect developed and perfected by Sweden and Finland that has remained a key component of Finnish total defense is the National Defence Course. The then-unique course was launched by the Swedish government in the early 1950s to educate leaders from all parts of society. Finland launched its National Defence Course in 1961, with a similar mission:

- Give civilian and military personnel in leading positions an overall view of the country's security and defense policy,
- Teach participants about the organization and preparedness of the different sectors of society involved in one or more aspects of total defense,
- Familiarize participants with the tasks of the different sectors of society and these sectors' roles in national security, and
- Promote cooperation and networking among key personnel in the different sectors of society involved in total defense.

The residential course lasts for 3.5 weeks; over time, supplemental courses have been added to update graduates and networks. Graduates can also opt to join the National Defence Course Association, which offers regular seminars and an annual overseas study trip. Participants—who are nominated and then selected from a highly competitive pool of applicants—include rising private-sector executives; members of parliament; leaders from media, labor unions, employer organizations, and nongovernmental organizations; academics, artists, and arts-sector managers; government officials; and (the smallest percentage) armed forces and border guard officials.

The course—whose board includes Finland's chief of defense, several state secretaries, the chair of the Central Organisation of Finnish Trade Unions, and the chairman of the Confederation of Finnish Industries, among others—quickly became so prestigious that participation became a badge of honor for rising leaders.[57] More importantly, the course not only established a basic level of national security knowledge among leaders across Finnish society but also created cohesion among them. If a crisis were to befall Finland, the country would have leaders in every sector who were not just conversant with total defense and their organizations' roles in it but also connected with other leaders across society. In addition to contributing to resilience during a potential war, that knowledge and cohesion among leaders signaled to prospective invaders unity of resolve.

Finland's National Defence Course remains in place, with exceptionally high participant interest and long waiting lists. In addition, participants can now attend regional defense courses. By autumn 2019, 229 3.5-week national courses had taken place, with more than 9,300 leaders participating—88 percent of them civilians.[58] In Finland's current parliament, which features numerous young members, 122 of 200 members have attended the National Defence Course, as have 15 of 18 ministers in the cabinet.[59]

While Soviet conditions on military activities forced Finland to innovate in societal resilience, its experience also provides valuable lessons for countries facing no such conditions. One reason is the cost-benefit calculation of societal resilience: At relatively little expense, resilience and thus deterrence can significantly increase. It is irrelevant whether Finland or another country has large armed forces with first-rate equipment if they are not supported by a resilient and united population.

Maj. Gen. Pekka Toveri (ret.), the Finnish Defence Forces' (FDF) former chief of intelligence, explained that the FDF

> have more or less accepted that we have to get along with quite small resources, because governments have used money more for social welfare, education, and so on. But it's easier to accept, because within FDF we think that it makes Finland [a] better place to live, and that makes people more willing to defend it. That willingness is a hugely important part of national deterrence. If you think that your country is terrible and there is nothing there for you, why would you [be] prepared to fight for it?[60]

Comparing Finland during World War II and the Cold War with the experiences of Georgia in 2008 and Ukraine in 2014, Gen. Riho Terras (ret.) noted that

> psychological defense is really important. That's what was missing in Georgia and Ukraine. You have to make sure that your own nation believes in itself, which is what the Finns did. In Georgia and Ukraine, people didn't believe in their government.[61]

Operating within this reality of budgetary constraints during the Cold War, the FDF also developed what later became known as systematic guerrilla warfare. Although the FDF had not, before the Winter War, prepared for guerrilla-like operations, during the war regular forces operated behind Soviet lines to reconnoiter, isolate the enemy, and cut Soviet lines of communication.[62] Photos of white-clad Finnish soldiers blending into snowy landscapes and bedeviling invaders became the war's lasting image. It is symptomatic that Finland formalized its systematic guerrilla warfare after World War II even though the Soviet Union was a nominal ally. Toveri said,

> Some units (we called them *sissi*, guerrilla units) were equipped and trained to operate behind the enemy lines as small units, squads, and platoons. These units were supposed to wear down the enemy by hitting their transportations and camps with

small scale ambushes, mortar attacks and mines. The idea was to use more hit-and-run tactics, and to use constant harassing to deny the enemy peace. Those activities should also make it easier to conduct operations towards the rear of enemy forces with conventional forces, as happened during the Winter War. The majority of the forces were supposed to fight as conventional forces, but every unit received rudimentary *sissi* training. The idea was that if the situation and the enemy's overwhelming forces didn't make it possible to continue fighting conventionally, the units should resort to guerrilla warfare. The motto was always, "never give up."[63]

Although the *sissi*'s existence was not kept secret from the Soviet Union, the operational planning and preparations aimed against incursion from the East were, unsurprisingly, confidential. Vesa Tynkkynen and Petteri Jouko observe that "operations directed against the Soviet Union were practiced only in a clandestine manner."[64] Soviet leaders acted with the knowledge that Finland would seek to entangle any future invader the same way it had done so during the Winter War.

Lessons from Swedish and Finnish Cold War Total Defense

Virtually no Swedish or Finnish decision maker, of course, harbored the illusion that total defense would triumph over total war. At least from the 1960s onward, Sweden relied on tacit support from the United States, which would have come to Sweden's aid in case of a Soviet attack.[65] The Soviet Union likely was aware of the arrangement, which in that case functioned as extended deterrence. Nevertheless, despite their exposed geographic locations, Sweden and Finland could almost uniquely count on the public to contribute to the national effort in case of war and indeed to the preparation that is so vital for not just a well-functioning war effort but also deterrence signaling to prospective attackers. After the Cold War, Finland maintained its total defense, while Sweden dramatically reduced it. Toveri summarized the nature of Swedish and Finnish total defense if maintained well.

The real strength of this model is that it makes it possible to fully utilize the intellectual know-how, skills, and resources of the nation for the defense. When an IT engineer comes up with an idea on how to better protect our critical infrastructure, he can benefit from his training as a reserve electronic warfare officer. Or an IT engineer can benefit from his civilian skills while serving as a signals officer in a brigade headquarters during an exercise. I've seen how a reserve officer who was also [a] Microsoft research engineer reconfigured his units [sic] C2 [command-and-control system] to better serve their needs during an exercise. Or the director of a regional hospital can come up with ideas for how to support other authorities during crises thanks to having participated in a regional defense course and getting to know all the regional players during the course.[66]

Other countries, too, developed civil defense during the Cold War. Home Guard–style organizations were launched and expanded; citizens were instructed in what to do in case of a nuclear attack. No country, however, used national resilience as a strategy of deterrence by denial as comprehensively as Sweden and Finland did. These countries had two advantages: a clear threat and a cohesive population willing to do its part. While totalitarian and authoritarian regimes can deploy the whole of society in aggressive pursuits, their totality-based efforts cannot last because civil society does not participate of its own free will.

As Sweden and Finland demonstrated, liberal democracies can build lasting resilience based on their citizens' dedication to their countries and their ways of life. This clearly does not happen automatically, and engagement of the kind the two countries enjoyed during the Cold War may not be possible in every country. Nevertheless, unlike authoritarian countries' browbeaten civil societies, citizens of liberal democracies may, if offered education and opportunities for engagement, discover they can play a role in keeping their countries safe.

Swedish and Finnish Cold War total defense is thus more than a historical case study. The two countries' Cold War efforts demonstrate that civil society can, through government-led initiatives and opportunities for involvement, play a key role in resilience and thus deterrence. If a country or a group can demonstrate that an adversary will encounter a quagmire that would alter the attacker's cost-benefit analysis, the defender will instill in the adversary's mind the fear to attack. If the Vietcong, for example, had signaled resilience, entanglement, and imposition of costs, the United States may have thought differently about how to execute its Southeast Asia containment strategy.

More than a decade ago, Estonia became arguably the first country to introduce Sweden's and Finland's Cold War total defense lessons in a post–Cold War setting. When Russia invaded Georgia in 2008, Terras—then the Estonian Defence Forces' deputy chief of staff for operations—traveled to Georgia to support the Georgian armed forces. He explained that the "biggest challenge the Georgians had was not military but making the government . . . work. Based on this, and based on our own experience with Russia's cyberattacks in 2007, I and others concluded that the military is not enough."[67]

Gradually, Estonia built a total defense system modeled on Finland's and Sweden's models. Building such a system in a highly advanced society such as Estonia—the world's most digitized country—involves decisions even more difficult than those made during the Cold War—for example, regarding what constitutes a vital service. "Some people consider television vital. But in reality the [only] three . . . services you really can't be without are power, food, and medical services," Terras said.[68]

Niklas Karlsson, vice chair of the Swedish parliament's defense committee, illustrates the complex reality facing today's national security decision makers.

> We know that we have to strengthen defense. But what do we need? In another five—six years' time, the world will likely be even more unsettled. At this point, we can only make an educated guess as to what we'll need.[69]

However, the psychology of total defense can be applied to gray-zone aggression. This is especially important as gray-zone aggression should be deterred in the gray zone and not be allowed to grow.

X

Building a Wall of Denial Against Gray-Zone Aggression

"In case of war, please ring [the bell] twice."[1] In 1939, Rudolf Minger was prepared. The Swiss defense minister's advantage was, of course, that he had a good idea of what sort of attack to expect, and so did his country's population. Defending a country against gray-zone aggression poses a much harder challenge because the targeted country cannot be sure what forms of gray-zone aggression will be used and who should mount the defense and deterrence.

Deterrence of gray-zone aggression is possible, though it requires a radical shift in liberal democracies' approach to national security, toward a system that involves not just the government but also the private sector and wider society. Collectively, the government and civil society can create a wall of resilience that denies opportunities to aggressors. Together, liberal democracies' governments can also develop deterrence by punishment by playing to their strengths: that they have allies, that their citizens and private sectors can choose to play a part in national security if offered the opportunity, and that their countries have assets foreign governments and leaders desire.

In addition to deterrence, scholars of the field often discuss dissuasion, which denotes deterrence by denial before any action occurs. For the sake of simplicity, this chapter combines dissuasion and deterrence under the label of deterrence, which it divides into two parts: deterrence by denial and deterrence by punishment. This chapter outlines a whole-of-society model for deterrence by denial.

Civil Society, a Resource

NATO's Article III, known as its resilience article, reads: "In order more effectively to achieve the objectives of this Treaty, the Parties, separately and jointly, by means of continuous and effective self-help and mutual aid, will maintain and develop their individual and collective capacity to resist armed attack."[2] Even though the North Atlantic Treaty was signed in 1949, NATO never treated resilience as a priority, partly because its member states could rely on the alliance's powerful deterrence by punishment. By contrast, as we have seen, during the Cold War, Sweden and Finland made exemplary use of resilience, creating a wall of denial that signaled to the Soviet Union that an invasion would involve an unpalatable cost-benefit calculation.[3]

NATO did increase its focus on Article III at its 2016 Warsaw Summit, when it adopted the so-called seven baseline requirements for civil preparedness.

1. Assured continuity of government and critical government services;

2. Resilient energy supplies;

3. Ability to deal effectively with uncontrolled movement of people;

4. Resilient food and water resources;

5. Ability to deal with mass casualties;

6. Resilient civil communications systems;

7. Resilient civil transportation systems.[4]

As NATO officials Wolf-Diether Roepke and Hasit Thankey note, "Resilient societies... have a greater propensity to bounce back after crises: they tend to recover more rapidly and are able to return to pre-crisis functional levels with greater ease than less resilient societies."[5]

With whole-of-society gray-zone threats targeting them, liberal democracies must similarly create a whole-of-society wall of denial as the bottom of their deterrence pyramid, to form part of countries' general deterrence. (As discussed in American Enterprise Institute reports of mine, deterrence by punishment is more useful in tailored deterrence, in which a country shapes its messaging to other countries, groups, and prospective acts of aggression.)[6]

A whole-of-society wall of denial is a radically different approach from the one most governments currently maintain. Except for papers about Sweden's and Finland's Cold War total defense, the concept has also not been comprehensively explored in academic papers. In their excellent gray-zone report, Lyle Morris et al. propose "a whole-of-government approach" with a range of government initiatives to dissuade rivals from engaging in gray-zone aggression. The proposed initiatives include

> continu[ing] to reaffirm, through regular senior leader statements and official policy documents, the U.S. commitment to formal allies in Europe and Asia and back[ing] these statements with enhanced participation in bilateral and multilateral forums to deal specifically with such gray zone tactics as cyberattacks and disinformation....
>
> The United States could undertake a major diplomatic initiative, coordinated through the State Department and U.S. embassies, to reinforce the international legal implications of gray zone aggression.[7]

The UK government's Fusion Doctrine from 2018 also foresees an effort exclusively undertaken by the government.

> This approach will ensure that in defending our national security we make better use of all of our capabilities: from economic levers, through cutting-edge military resources to our wider diplomatic and cultural influence on the world's stage. Every part of our government and every one of our agencies has its part to play.[8]

In its *National Security Capability Review* from 2018, the UK government also addressed gray-zone aggression, explaining that

> many adversaries seek to do us harm or subvert us in less destructive ways, calculated to avoid provoking an armed response. We will seek to raise the cost of their malign behaviour, restrict and reduce it using the full range of capabilities available

to us. Some of the many capabilities enhanced as a result of SDSR [the Strategic Defence and Security Review] 2015 include the new powers in the Criminal Finances Act 2017 to recover criminal assets and our offensive cyber capabilities to detect, trace and retaliate in kind.[9]

The UK government labeled this innovative approach "modern deterrence."

Multilateral contacts certainly ought to be strengthened. As Niklas Karlsson—a Social Democratic member of the Swedish parliament and vice chair of its defense committee—pointed out, Western governments should "make sure that foreign policy is the first line of defense." He also noted that "the UN and the Council of Europe have been languishing for some time. In the '90s, institutions like these were essentially demoted to a secondary role. Now they need an upgrade again."[10] Furthermore, it is in the interest of leaders of Western countries and their adversaries to maintain a constant dialogue, although this is currently not taking place. Such dialogue would not only help the countries build cooperation wherever possible but also help reduce the risk of misunderstandings and resulting security dilemmas.

But until recently, Western governments in the 21st century have shown little interest in involving wider society in resilience and thus deterrence. Indeed, most Western governments have appeared not to consider civil society's potential even though most of them had some form of civil defense during World War II and in the early Cold War years. In World War II Britain, for example, citizens participated in the war effort in a plethora of roles, such as bike messenger, fire watcher, rest center operator, first aid helper, search-and-rescue member, and air raid warden. This system continued after World War II, somewhat modified as the Civil Defence Corps. Although the corps was led by the government and designed for wartime use, its members naturally used their skills during everyday contingencies. The Civil Defence Corps was disbanded in 1968.[11]

Today, civil society could play an even more pivotal role, precisely because current aggression is so often directed against civil society. When trying to improve defense and deterrence while leaving society out, governments practically guarantee they will be overstretched while leaving civil society—individuals, businesses, and other organizations—as passive observers of their own fates. Even if a government of a liberal democracy wanted to extend itself to form an omnipresent wall of denial while signaling punishment to would-be aggressors, the costs would be prohibitive, and the effort would be ineffective. This is one reason no government has tried to extend a cyber-protection umbrella over its entire society.

Indeed, because defense should also aim to deter, a whole-of-government approach signals that a vital part of society does not wish to be involved or is considered a liability by its own government. This not only indicates weakness but also practically invites adversaries to target civil society. If the private sector is not involved in government-coordinated resilience, its absence signals to a country's adversaries that they can target businesses. The same is true for the citizenry.

Hostile states monitor involvement in resilience efforts—and lack thereof. Precisely because the West's adversaries are adept at spotting and exploiting weaknesses, those with both capability and intent will use the opportunities offered to them. The existing results illustrate the damage: cutting-edge businesses lost, others coerced, academic integrity in doubt, and citizens who have lost faith in their countries' institutions.

Governments may not even be best placed to defend countries against all forms of gray-zone aggression. While governments—with their monopoly on violence—should defend their countries against attacks involving sustained use of force, it is unclear how they alone could convincingly defend their countries against subversive investments, coercion of businesses, or interference through academia and popular culture. Ole Wæver et al. define societal security as "the ability of a society to persist in its essential character under changing conditions and perceived or actual threats."[12] This is clearly the baseline that liberal democracies' governments and civil societies must jointly be able to muster. Governments, meanwhile, must lead in deterring illicit forms of gray-zone aggression such as "borderization" and intellectual property (IP) theft.

In a fundamental shift from its previous policy, in its 2021 Integrated Review, the UK government embraced the whole-of-society concept. In his foreword to the review, Prime Minister Boris Johnson writes that "COVID-19 has reminded us that security threats and tests of national resilience can take many forms,"[13] and the review lists as a priority action to establish a "whole-of-society" approach to resilience, so that individuals, businesses and organisations all play a part in building resilience across the UK. We will seek to develop an integrated approach, bringing together all levels of government, CNI [critical national infrastructure] operators, the wider private sector, civil society and the public.[14]

A highly innovative step as part of this whole-of-society approach is the UK government's intention to create a civilian reserve.[15]

This is precisely the right approach to take. By involving all parts of society, targeted countries can minimize the opportunity for gray-zone aggression. The collective resilience can signal to adversaries that the cost of aggression will outweigh the benefit. Such signaling is a continuation of Sweden's and Finland's Cold War deterrence by denial and would signal that, while targeted countries might be easy to attack, they will significantly reduce the winner's spoils and make sure aggression involves more effort than the attacker wants to expend. The same collective resilience will, of course, also reduce the effect of gray-zone aggression should the deterrence signaling fail.

The point of departure must be to treat the citizenry as a resource rather than a fragile entity whose only attribute is the need for protection. As Carl Rådestad and Oscar Larsson observe, "Activated citizens are not necessarily silent recipients of services, but may also become activists and create pockets of resistance and shift the burden of responsibility away from themselves during and after emergency situations."[16]

By empowering the population, governments can achieve two goals. The public—both the private sector and the citizenry—assumes some of the duties the government would otherwise have to execute, which frees up the government to focus on duties it alone can perform. In addition, civil society becomes an integral part of national security, thereby reducing gaps adversaries would otherwise seek to exploit. This approach also turns civilian experts into a society-wide resource, increases governments' freedom of action, and provides resource strategies the government may wish to pursue. This way, governments and their societies form a combined shield to deny adversaries the benefits they seek and negatively influence adversaries' cost-benefit calculations.

Such an approach clearly involves a major shift in policy and practice. While most armed conflicts are whole-of-society efforts, whether or not the public has chosen to participate, in peacetime, liberal democracies' civil societies are rarely asked to participate in national security. Except for a small number of countries such as Finland, governments have formed a shield over their civil societies instead of building a combined shield integrating their civil societies. Western governments' challenge today is to engage citizens and organizations that have had minimal interaction with national security, thus creating a credible bottom layer of the deterrence pyramid.

Before the UK government's significant shift with its 2021 Integrated Review, some other larger countries had floated more-modest ideas. For example, Germany's 2016 national security white paper called for

> whole-of-society resilience and thus comprehensive defence capabilities. . . .
> This includes better protection of critical infrastructure, reduced vulnerabilities in the energy sector, civil defence and disaster control issues. . . . Politicians, the media and society must all help when it comes to exposing propaganda and countering it with facts.[17]

Yet such calls were mostly not followed by deeds. In fact, while the World War II generation is habitually lauded as "the greatest generation," since the end of the Cold War most Western governments have been wary of asking their citizens for even the most rudimentary contributions to national security.

This reluctance was certainly influenced by the early 21st century's prevailing neoliberal mood, in which citizens increasingly saw—and were encouraged to see—national security as a service provided by the government in exchange for their taxes, not a collective undertaking. In addition, the 21st century's largely peaceful decades in the homeland did not require much societal involvement in national security. Yet governments may also have lacked confidence in citizenries' abilities. Rådestad and Larsson note that

> social constructions regarding how individuals behave in a crisis are now often based upon the assumption that people panic and desperately need the support of public authorities. . . . One common assumption is that crisis situations are typically accompanied by outbreaks of lawlessness and social chaos due to the irrational behavior of helpless individuals, who almost immediately return to a Hobbesian state of nature.[18]

The combination of citizens largely left to pursue their individual happiness and being enticed to conduct an increasing number of tasks (from airport self-check-ins to supermarket self-checkouts) while not being entrusted to participate in or even understand matters of their country's security is paradoxical and baffling. Indeed, it stands to reason that governments can incentivize personal responsibility in matters of national security just as companies do in their respective areas. Indeed, it is highly likely that, if given the opportunity to be part of national security in the widest sense—that is, helping keep their families, communities, and the country safe—the majority of citizens would prefer feeling empowered rather than helpless during crises big and small.

During the Cold War, virtually all European countries had mandatory national service for men, but this was mostly phased out after the Cold War ended. Sweden also dismantled its impressive total defense system and thus jettisoned not just the involvement of citizen volunteers but also the private sector. Since then, Sweden has introduced highly selective military service for men and women, Norway has expanded its highly selective military service to women, and Lithuania has introduced a less selective model.[19] Although these models have considerable benefits, as do related models in other countries such as Denmark and mandatory military service in Finland and Estonia, they clearly do not constitute comprehensive citizen participation in gray-zone defense and deterrence.

Because it did not dismantle its Cold War total defense, Finland remains the Western country best set up for gray-zone defense. Yet not even its combination of reserves comprising all former conscripts and therefore a cross section of society, newer initiatives such as disinformation literacy training in schools,[20] a national defense course, and government's first right to buy properties in sensitive locations provides sufficient deterrence of gray-zone aggression in its various incarnations.

Creating Societal Resilience to Form Deterrence by Denial

Perhaps unsurprisingly, the Nordic countries remain ahead of the curve in making civil society part of national resilience and thus deterrence by denial. In its 2018 *Security Strategy for Society* report, the Finnish government explains that the country's "preparedness is based on the principle of comprehensive security in which the vital functions of society are jointly safeguarded by the authorities, *business operators, organisations and citizens*."[21] (Emphasis added.) Finland also recognizes the growing importance of the private sector even compared to during the Cold War, a result of privatizing CNI: "Business operators are playing an increasingly important role in the preparedness process. In particular, companies will continue to play a key role in the process of ensuring the functioning of the economy and the infrastructure."[22]

Sweden is (partially) rebuilding its total defense: The all-hazards Swedish Civil Contingencies Agency (MSB) is a global leader in public education and crisis coordination, and in March 2021, the government announced it will create a new agency for psychological defense.[23] Sweden has also updated its Cold War total defense exercises that involved the armed forces, the MSB's predecessor, all levels of government, auxiliary defense organizations, and businesses linked to the national defense effort. The last such exercise took place in 1987, but in 2019, Sweden resurrected the concept with a new exercise, Total Defense Exercise 2020.[24] The focus of the total defense exercises, however, remains conventional, armed forces–led aggression.

Denmark, in turn, explains in *Foreign and Security Policy Strategy, 2017–18*, that the government intends to "reach out and strengthen Denmark in collaboration with civil society organisations, the business community, universities and think tanks. Denmark is at its strongest when we stand together."[25]

The Nordics are joined by their Baltic neighbors. In its *National Security Concept 2017* report, the Estonian government states it aims to "increase peoples' [sic] perception of security and enhance their ability to evaluate various threats and factors that influence security, as well as their ability and readiness to counter such threats."[26] While not as all-encompassing as Sweden's Cold War total defense was, Estonia's whole-of-society model includes, among other things, a cyber defense unit, in which civilian IT experts volunteer their time defending the country against cyber threats.[27] Latvia's comprehensive national defense, initiated in 2018, similarly highlights the role of civil society. In 2020, for example, the country published *72 Hours*, a leaflet similar to Sweden's *If War Comes*, which Sweden itself updated and reissued as *If Crisis or War Comes* in 2018.[28]

Soon after the leaflet's launch, Latvian Minister for Defence Artis Pabriks wrote,

> Covering a broad range of crises, "72 hours" therefore prepares society for catastrophes we cannot specifically predict, like the coronavirus pandemic that the world is facing right now, and includes instructions on actions to take, details on the civil defence warning system and information channels, as well as information on water and food reserves and primary health care. It has to be emphasised though, that preparedness cannot avert crises; what it can do is reduce the extent of possible negative consequences.[29]

"Catastrophes we cannot specifically predict" and "reduce the extent of possible negative consequences"[30] are precisely what every country targeted by gray-zone aggression should strive for by using every lever at its disposal to build the bottom layer of the deterrence pyramid. Indeed, because gray-zone aggression—unlike traditional military aggression—targets countries regardless of their geography, it is a wake-up call for countries located far from potential military aggressors. Such countries, including the United States, have in recent decades had the luxury of treating national security as a concern that can be addressed almost exclusively by the armed forces and other parts of the government. It points to a changing mindset that in 2020 the US Cyberspace Solarium Commission proposed that Congress "codify the concept of 'systemically important critical infrastructure,'" which would guarantee operators US government support—and create and fund a joint collaborative environment for the sharing and fusing of threat information.[31] The 2021 ransomware attack that crippled Colonial Pipeline was a clear wake-up call for parts of the US public.

In other countries that have traditionally been less inclined toward whole-of-society efforts, the direction is also changing somewhat. In 2019, France launched a new form of national service, initially on a pilot basis. During the monthlong program, 16-year-olds are taught skills such as map reading and spend time doing community service. "What's missing is a moment of cohesion . . . of youth coming together from different parts of France, from different social backgrounds, sharing their experiences and their commitments for society and the country," Junior Education Minister Gabriel Attal explained when the initiative was launched.[32] While the training thus primarily has a social objective, it could help contribute to resilience. So could Germany's small Your Year for Germany program, launched in 2020, in which young Germans can spend six months training with the armed forces and six months assisting in homeland protection in their home regions.[33]

Such initiatives alone, however, do not create deterrence, and this is not the intention. A more focused effort is Latvia's Comprehensive Defense Approach. As part of this strategy, in 2019 the Latvian government invited more than 90 key companies and nongovernmental organizations (NGOs) to its annual whole-of-government crisis management exercise. The policy also features a national security curriculum for 16- and 17-year-olds. As part of the curriculum, introduced in 2019 and gradually rolled out since then, teenagers spend one hour each month learning practical skills such as map reading, basic military skills, and the foundations of Latvian national security and the threats facing it. They can also participate in voluntary summer camps.[34]

Involving Citizens

How, then, can countries better populate the bottom layer of the deterrence pyramid to help form a wall of denial that can change a gray-zone aggressor's cost-benefit calculation? Like the bottom layer in the food pyramid with its bread and potatoes, the bottom layer in the deterrence pyramid are the functions that may seem trivial but are nonetheless central to the organism's functioning.

Unlike military aggression, which most citizens of liberal democracies have not experienced and are unlikely ever to experience, gray-zone aggression is very real. Americans and others are now aware that disinformation and ransomware attacks condoned or even instigated by foreign governments harm their democracies. Citizens everywhere have seen a pandemic dramatically disrupt their lives and realized that such disruption can happen again, caused again by Mother Nature—or a hostile state. They know that an internet or electricity outage will immediately affect their daily lives. At the very least, since spring 2020, when COVID-19 created shortages of personal protective equipment and stockpiling led to empty shelves in supermarkets, they are familiar with the fragility of supply chains. Indeed, liberal democracies' openness combined with the convenience trap—Western societies' enormous and growing dependence on digitally powered conveniences, which increases their vulnerability—means ordinary citizens today are exposed to national security threats in a way they have not been during previous nonwar periods.

Precisely because gray-zone aggression affects ordinary citizens, it is in their interest to limit its effect. This is also true for citizens who may have no interest in national security or who may be uneasy about military activities. But for citizens to want to do their part, governments must be transparent about the threats and aggression facing the country. This involves sharing and articulating information in a way that most governments are unaccustomed to. If they do not, many citizens are likely to suspect that the asked-for involvement is driven by special interests, not genuine needs. If a majority of Swedish citizens during the Cold War had mistrusted government information about threats facing the country, hundreds of thousands of them would not have joined auxiliary defense organizations, and it is unlikely that one of them would have spotted and reported the Soviet U-137 submarine that, in 1981, ran aground off the coast of Sweden.[35]

Public Awareness Campaigns. Governments can build on this close link between citizens and new national security threats by offering training to different groups of citizens. The first step by any country targeted by gray-zone aggression must certainly be to educate its public about it in the same vein as Sweden's Cold War *If War Comes* and today's *If Crisis or War Comes*, Latvia's *72 Hours*, and earthquake zones' public awareness campaigns. While citizens may have heard of disinformation disasters such as the January 6 assault on the US Capitol or may have seen supermarket shelves empty during the first weeks of COVID-19 or gasless gas stations during the Colonial Pipeline ransomware attack, this does not mean they understand national security threats, their potential role in minimizing the effect of these threats, or how to stave them off altogether.

Sweden and Finland made virtually every resident a participant in their Cold War efforts to deny the adversary advantages. This began at the most rudimentary level: knowing how to identify a national security contingency, prepare for it, and respond. *If War Comes* was that most basic part of resilience.

Current governments can use this model, adapting the information to match what they consider their most critical national security threats. Such information is necessary even though many citizens of advanced societies consider themselves well educated. While they may indeed be well educated, it does not mean they understand contemporary risks to their societies. Regarding information and disinformation, Ojārs Kalniņš, a Latvian member of parliament for the New Unity party and vice chair of the foreign affairs committee, observed,

> People need to be educated about what our adversaries' efforts are. This also creates a dilemma: How do you maintain free speech when people spread lies online? I recently got into a bit of an argument with an American friend of mine, who complained that things he writes on Facebook are being taken down. There's no right to have everything you say published! Many years ago, I used to write letters to the editor. Sometimes they'd get published, sometimes not. You didn't have the right then to get anything you wanted published, and you shouldn't have any such right now either! I'm also concerned about young

people's tech skills. They're very savvy about the technology but not about the content.³⁶

In Lithuania, the country's public-service broadcaster, Lithuanian National Radio and Television (LRT), now educates the public through national security–related programming. Monika Garbačiauskaitė-Budrienė, LRT's CEO, explained that

> together with the Journalism Development Network [a global network of investigative journalists], LRT has launched the fact-checking project Facts on its web portal, which address[es] cases of news manipulation and educates people in how to recognize cases of misleading or manipulative information.³⁷

She also highlighted the show *Battlefield*, which is "dedicated to security and defense topics and among them regularly covers issues of information security examining cases of information influence and manipulation."³⁸

News organizations could, in fact, play a crucial role in educating the public—beyond their current role providing news—while helping increase trust in vetted news and societal institutions. Just as elected politicians regularly meet with constituents in their constituency offices, thereby maintaining and strengthening a vital link, news organizations could launch similar open houses in cities where they are based or have offices, on a pop-up basis, in other cities and towns. Such encounters with journalists, in which the guests could also participate in news meetings during which the next bulletin or newspaper edition are planned, would allow ordinary citizens to learn how news is made and could help dispel concerns that journalists collectively provide slanted or inaccurate coverage.

Indeed, because distance and lack of exposure breeds fear, such encounters would help many ordinary citizens (and by extension their friends and social media contacts) realize that news media are not inherently nefarious. Increased trust in professional news organizations would, of course, reduce the opportunities for disinformation to spread.³⁹ Conversely, the interaction would help journalists better understand ordinary citizens' concerns.

Considering that lack of access to quality journalism also increases the gray-zone attack surface provided by social media, governments—working with news organizations—could also launch voucher schemes that would give residents free access to a news outlet of their choice for a certain period.

While learning about national security threats is never enjoyable, doing so while having a chance to prepare is certainly preferable to learning about them when they have already struck. Indeed, judging from real estate prices in earthquake zones with frequent public awareness campaigns such as Tokyo[40] and San Francisco,[41] keeping citizens informed about risks does not cause panic.

Societal Stress Testing. Governments could also introduce societal stress testing. After the 2008 financial crisis, governments introduced stricter stress tests for banks.[42] Thanks to this comprehensive stress-testing regime, governments, borrowers, and the wider public can be certain that the global financial system will survive any future financial crises relatively intact. This creates confidence in the banking system.

The same model could be used for the population to test and improve resilience for, say, outages of internet, water, or electricity or the spread of dangerous viruses. If local authorities, working with the relevant providers and retailers, shut off water, electricity, certain food items, or the internet on apparently random dates throughout the year, residents would learn to prepare for such situations and would know what to do while it was happening. Regular stress testing would help citizens gain enough preparedness skills that they would not panic in case of a real crisis.

This is important because citizen panic can severely exacerbate a crisis. During the Colonial Pipeline incident, the original gas shortage was relatively moderate, but panicked consumers hoarding gas made it far more severe.[43] At one point, for example, 86 percent of gas stations in the District of Columbia reported outages.[44] Indeed, citizens could regularly stress test themselves for various disruptions to daily life. Authorities could highlight such crisis proficiency, both to reassure the country (as is done with bank stress testing) and change a prospective attacker's cost-benefit calculation.

In 2019, Fort Bragg US Army base in Georgia conducted precisely such a stress test; the commander turned off the power and instructed the base's

50,000-some soldiers and officers to continue their daily work without providing further details.[45] While stress testing for gray-zone aggression is a new concept, earthquake zones have long practiced earthquake drills.[46] Texas residents, meanwhile, would certainly have had a less disastrous encounter with power outages during the 2021 winter storm[47] had local authorities conducted stress testing for such a contingency.

Resilience Training Courses. More comprehensive training could be provided through government-supported resilience training courses. One model would be to offer such courses to teenagers during school breaks, either in one chunk of three to four weeks during the summer or as one-week segments during other school holidays. The training—offered in a residential setting on, for example, university campuses during university breaks—would be voluntary and feature basic resilience skills including information literacy, crisis preparedness, and responses to crises ranging from pandemics to supply-chain disruptions.

While the government would fund the courses and set the curriculum, the training could be delivered by NGOs such as the Red Cross, high school teachers with specialized skills, and military personnel on secondment and thus teaching in a civilian capacity. Upon completion of the course, participants could receive—depending on the respective country's system—university application points or other credit for university applications or tax credits for those planning to enter the labor market immediately after completing secondary education. The course certificate awarded upon completion could be kept current through refresher courses. Participants keeping their certificates current could also receive tax credits. Because the curriculum would reflect current gray-zone threats, the curriculum of the initial course and refresher courses could be continuously updated to reflect evolving gray-zone forms of aggression.

In addition to offering a meaningful activity to late teens during their school breaks, the courses would be an opportunity for teenagers from different backgrounds to interact based on a crucial and highly relevant subject. While teenagers from different backgrounds also meet in school, schools remain an insufficient tool of societal integration. Resilience courses—much like past generations' national service—would increase the opportunities for interaction across societal groups and thus for societal cohesion. This is especially important because liberal democracies' adversaries are adept at identifying and exploiting gaps in societal cohesion. During the 2016 US election campaign, Russia's social media interference campaign especially targeted Black voters.[48]

Graduates of the training would be entered into a central database and would be available to assist emergency services and crisis agencies, assisting rather than displacing firefighters, ambulance crews, Red Cross workers, and other responders. By virtue of being registered in the database along with their addresses, they would be able to attend follow-up training in their local areas and thus keep their status as resilience aiders current. In addition, just as they have introduced apps for COVID-19 tracing, government authorities could launch "citizen-aider" apps in which trained citizens would receive requests for responders in their local areas and could indicate their availability to assist.

The devastating floods in July 2021 that killed hundreds of people in Germany and Belgium illustrate the need for citizens trained in basic emergency preparedness and emergency response, because, in a crisis, first responders may not be able to immediately reach local communities. Another example is the July 2021 crisis in the UK that led to empty supermarket shelves. The crisis was caused by fast-rising COVID-19 infection numbers. The growing numbers led to an explosion of notifications via a national app that alerts people who have been in close contact with an infected person, meaning they have to self-isolate for 10 days. During one week, some 620,000 people were pinged, including health care and retail workers.[49] This led to supermarket product shortages and a request for the armed forces to be called in to stock shelves.[50] With resilience training in place, the government would have been able to help retailers provide an essential service by calling up graduates of the resilience training.

Resilience training would not have to be limited to teenagers. While 17- and 18-year-olds are physically stronger than most other citizens are and an easier group to bring together, citizens' impromptu willingness to help during COVID-19 and various other crises, from hurricanes to forest fires, demonstrates enormous potential for communal efforts—but such efforts have to be organized *before* a crisis. Indeed, resilience training could be a way to harness and build on the skills of not just 17- and 18-year-olds but also other groups, including retirees, people on nontraditional career paths who may be working part-time or freelance, people who are between jobs, or even people in full-time employment. Certain groups often feel marginalized, having (perhaps temporarily) left the labor market. The UK's planned civilian reserve, which would comprise experts in relevant fields as opposed to citizens trained in basic resilience skills, is another highly productive way of involving members of civil society.

Resilience training would benefit not just them and the social fabric of society but also contingency management and therefore deterrence by denial. The rapid spread of the QAnon conspiracy theory[51] is fueled by many citizens feeling left out of a society that seems to be mysteriously run by an inner circle, with ordinary citizens left to be observers of their own lives. Opportunities to play a constructive role in the community, alongside fellow citizens, could counteract that.

In addition, every societal group would benefit—in skills acquired and social connections established—from participating in resilience training, and society would benefit as a result. In the case of people in full-time employment, training would best be delivered during weekends, as is already the case with armed forces reserves. All groups should be invited to attend refresher courses to keep their resilience status (and thus tax credit and eligibility for crisis responder duty) active.

This would also aid crisis response, as services needing assistance could quickly reach local graduates of the training; that is, there would be an advantage of not just speed but also expertise in the local area. This can be contrasted with existing crisis response efforts, in which the armed forces frequently have to send active-duty personnel, reserves, or (in the US) the National Guard to assist local agencies. The Home Guards in Denmark, Norway, and Sweden are currently the closest organized citizen-responder model, but because Home Guards involve military elements, they may not be palatable to all citizens. The Home Guards are also more highly trained than the citizen responders proposed here would be.

Citizens already help during crises. When COVID-19 struck the UK, the government issued a call for 250,000 volunteers to join a newly created "NHS [National Health Service] army" to help vulnerable citizens. In response, 750,000 Britons immediately signed up,[52] but because the call was issued during a crisis, the government lacked capacity to accommodate most of them. This again demonstrates the gap between citizens' willingness to assist and organized opportunities available.

Indeed, the challenge in involving civil society in crisis response is that, apart from the people with previous work experience in the respective field, volunteers mostly lack the skills for the tasks. That leads to situations in which well-intentioned offers pose a burden for emergency workers instead of helping them. Resilience training would address the recurring gap between citizens' willingness to help and skills to do so while signaling to adversaries that the public's involvement would reduce the effect of any attack.

Germany's Technisches Hilfswerk, a government contingencies agency that includes a volunteer force of some 80,000, assists in contingencies ranging from bridge ruptures to water contamination,[53] and many other countries have some form of disaster-relief volunteer organizations. In New Zealand, in turn, students assisting victims of the 2011 earthquake subsequently founded the Student Volunteer Army, whose members assist fellow citizens during a range of crises.[54] In Sweden, many people have in recent years joined volunteer search-and-rescue organizations such as Missing People, whose members are trained for the task and assist the police. These groups, however, have specific missions and membership and do not claim to by themselves form comprehensive societal resilience.

Singapore, a whole-of-society pioneer, takes a somewhat different approach, with total defense taught to the public on each Total Defence Day (which is on February 15, marking Singapore's fall to the Japanese in 1942). On each Total Defence Day, the "Important Message" signal of the public warning system is sounded to commemorate the day and remind the public of the system's different meanings. As the Singapore Civil Defence Force explains, Total Defence Day "is also an occasion to refamiliarise our people with the modern defence strategy of 'Total Defence' which Singapore has adopted to ensure our continued survival and security."[55]

Resilience training also matters because societal cohesion is declining. While communal activities are available to residents of all liberal democracies, civic participation is declining. In *Bowling Alone: The Collapse and Revival of American Community*, Robert Putnam documents this trend in the United States.[56] In addition, the rate of single-person households is increasing. For example, in the UK between 1999 and 2019, the number of people living alone grew by one-fifth, from 6.8 million to 8.2 million.[57] This fragmentation, atomization even, of society creates even more opportunities for gray-zone aggression. If a person, family, group, or business does not feel connected to wider society, they are unlikely to act in the interest of society. Through resilience training, citizens could learn practical skills that benefit themselves and their families and feel part of a national effort to keep their countries safe from threats that could cause real harm to their own lives.

Paradoxically, societal involvement in gray-zone defense and deterrence is thus a burden that creates purpose. In a society in which fewer people spend their working lives in uninterrupted career progressions than was the case two or three decades ago and in which artificial intelligence has replaced many tasks humans previously conducted, individuals need ways to express their contribution and therefore their place and value in society. Countries need societal resilience as part of deterrence, but the societal resilience effort also brings the enormous benefit of aiding societal cohesion.

The most important benefit of the resilience training, however, is that countries would have at their disposal a critical mass of people who would be not just alert citizens but also able, active players in emergencies ranging from serious national contingencies to minor ones such as traffic accidents. Because the training would be nonmilitary and involve no weapons, it would also be palatable to citizens who may be uneasy about the armed forces but who want to make a difference in their own lives and those of others. This citizen resolve, too, would help change adversaries' cost-benefit calculations.

Selective National Service in All Parts of Government Involved in Crisis Management. Another step on the ladder of involvement in national security is selective national service for secondary school graduates in all parts of government involved in crisis management. This concept, first proposed in an October 2019 report,[58] builds on the selective national service model Denmark, Norway, and Sweden use.[59] After the Cold War, Norway gradually reduced the number of young men doing military service. By 2016, about one-third of the country's around 30,000 male 19-year-olds were accepted for military service. That year, the country switched to gender-neutral national service, meaning all members of a year group are now assessed for national service even though the armed forces' needs remain the same, about 8,000 per year. In 2019, 7,996 young Norwegians were selected for national service[60] in different parts of the Norwegian armed forces, out of 59,234 19-year-olds.[61]

This selectivity, which equals a 13 percent acceptance rate, makes Norway's national service highly attractive to young Norwegians, and having served is an exceptionally strong entry on their resumes. Selectivity—a necessary path to pursue because the end of the Cold War meant Norway, like other countries, no longer needed large conscription-based armed forces—has thus turned national service from a burden on every Norwegian man into a highly desirable activity for which the Norwegian armed forces can select top-achieving young men and women. The success has made national service a prime source of recruitment for the armed forces: Around 25 percent of national service participants now opt for a military career.[62] In addition, the armed forces' attractiveness is reflected in surveys of favorite prospective employers among university students. In the 2020 survey, the armed forces ranked fourth among IT students, eighth among engineering students, 12th among liberal arts students, and 15th among business students (ahead of enterprises such as KPMG, the Oslo Stock Exchange, and Norway's Ministry of Finance).[63]

Other countries could build on this model, in which a national security need that at any rate does not require great quantities of people becomes, by virtue of its selectivity, an attractive proposition for young people. To meet the needs of gray-zone defense and deterrence, such a model should not be limited to the armed forces. Instead, all parts of the government involved in some aspect of national security—ranging from the armed forces to provision of health care—should be able to select a small group of secondary school graduates for training in a range of specializations. Sweden and Denmark have already expanded their national service systems to feature cyber specialization.[64]

The model could be set up similarly to the Norwegian one.

1. In their final year of secondary education, all young men and women are invited to the first round of selection, during which they fill out online self-assessments.

2. Based on the self-assessment results, a smaller number of candidates is invited for in-person tests covering their intelligence and physical and mental capabilities and for interviews with the government agencies involved.

3. Based on these tests, the government agencies involved—which can range from specialized military units to agencies providing health care—select the candidates of their choice.

4. Those selected are invited to spend 12 months in fast-track training and service with the respective government agency.

5. Upon finishing their service, they are entered into a reserve corps for the respective agency, which the agency can activate during crises.

Such a system would mean that all relevant parts of the government could access a reserve of specialists and would not need to improvise during crises. While the arrangement mirrors the armed forces' reserves model, the national security reserves' main attributes would be their specialization and selectivity, not large numbers.

Conversely, it would be an opportunity for every member of an annual cohort to be assessed on their individual merit, not their educational background. As a result, it would bring future opportunities for young people who may—perhaps because of their backgrounds or lack of access to a top education—otherwise have been overlooked by employers. The training during the first year and refresher training would provide them with valuable skills and, by virtue of having been selected for the program, would help them stand out in the labor market. While its prime purpose should obviously be defense and deterrence, selective national service would clearly also aid social mobility.

Informed and engaged citizens can make individual choices in the gray zone. They can decide whether to support a celebrity-endorsed firm with links to a hostile regime. They can choose to attend resilience training that will help them, their local communities, and the country in a crisis. They can seize the opportunity if offered a place in a highly selective national service program. Such involvement backs up whole-of-government efforts and helps build—and signal to adversaries—a wall of denial. In their efforts to deter gray-zone aggression, liberal democracies will benefit from empowered citizens. Indeed, the urgent issue of deterring gray-zone aggression through citizen participation may help liberal democracies counter the dangerous fragmentation first documented by Putnam.

Citizen engagement also offers a side benefit in foreign policy: With corps of citizens trained in basic resilience and specialized tasks, and with both groups part of a crisis response, Western governments could deploy volunteers from both groups to nonmilitary contingencies in other parts of the world. This would benefit the affected countries and help increase Western soft power, particularly as the West's rivals make virtually no such efforts.[65]

Involving the Private Sector

During his Senate confirmation hearings to be US secretary of defense, General Motors (GM) President Charles Wilson was asked whether he could make a decision that was in the interest of the United States but could harm GM (in which Wilson would retain stock). He responded,

> Yes, sir; I could. I cannot conceive of one because for years I thought what was good for our country was good for General Motors, and vice versa. The difference did not exist. Our company is too big. It goes with the welfare of the country. Our contribution to the Nation is quite considerable.[66]

What is good for GM is good for the United States. Similar sayings exist in many other countries. What is good for Volvo is good for Sweden. What is good for Nokia is good for Finland. What is good for BMW is good for Germany. During the Cold War and in previous eras, business leaders like Wilson also felt an obligation to their respective home countries' well-being, if nothing else because their businesses' success depended on their countries' success. In addition, with rare exceptions, executives were citizens of the countries in which their companies were based.

This generated some degree of allegiance to their respective home governments, even when businesses were under no legal obligation to show allegiance. In a 2007 interview, Helmut Schmidt—a Social Democrat and chancellor of Germany from 1974 to 1982—recounted one such example. In the late 1970s, he told the interviewer, the Iranian government had wanted to buy a sizable stake in Daimler-Benz.

> The ayatollah was waiting in Paris, and it was obvious that there would be a change of power. . . . I found it inappropriate that the pearl of German industry, which is what Daimler-Benz was, would end up in Iranian hands. I thought, this has to be prevented.[67]

Schmidt proceeded to ask Deutsche Bank, then a distinctly German company, to buy the stake.

> I said, it is in the patriotic interest that you buy this stake. You may have to keep the stake for many years . . . but you have to do it. And because they were good patriots, they did.[68]

Globalization has ushered in a new reality. Globe-spanning conglomerates may have their headquarters in a Western country but be led by top executives of different nationalities. McDonald's, perhaps the world's most recognized symbol of the United States, has a C-suite that, among others, features Britons and a Pole.[69] Top executives of the 21st century have included Indian-born Indra Nooyi at PepsiCo; Irishman Neville Isdell at Coca-Cola Company; German Klaus Kleinfeld at Alcoa Corporation, the US aluminum giant; British-Indian Anshu Jain, Briton John Cryan, and Swiss-born Josef Ackermann at Deutsche Bank; Indian-born Singaporean citizen Rajeev Suri at Nokia Corporation[70]; and the Swede Ola Källenius at the helm of Daimler.[71] In addition, companies ranging from global behemoths to midsize firms have operations in various countries and supply chains spanning even more countries. It would be a valid question to ask whether new market leaders such as Facebook, Netflix, and Spotify in any way represent their home countries or simply happen to be based there. Indeed, one could argue that some firms today are more powerful than many nation-states are.

Precisely such firms and indeed a cross section of Western private sectors are, as detailed in previous chapters, finding themselves unwitting participants in the increasing geopolitical confrontation. This presents a new reality for a generation of business leaders who have primarily viewed countries as markets or sources of production or supplies, not as sources of mutual confrontation. The dilemma facing businesses is if the "Davos Man" approach can be reconciled with the new reality of operating in a world of gray-zone aggression.

It can, if globalized businesses help liberal-world-order-abiding governments prevail. If such countries instead succumb to constant gray-zone aggression, neither the countries nor the businesses based in them will thrive. Unlike Deutsche Bank during Schmidt's chancellorship, firms may not be patriotically minded and may, if asked, refuse to do a good deed for their home countries. Every company will, however, carry out an action that benefits the company itself. If governments can offer their private sectors opportunities for engagement that benefit both national security and the businesses themselves, many would likely participate. This would be even more likely if consumers, corporate customers, and the wider public rewarded businesses for helping the country. In light of the rapidly growing distrust of China among Western citizens,[72] Western brands cooperating with China may soon suffer in the court of public opinion.

Government-Industry Leader Briefings. As with citizen engagement, such engagement could begin with a basic form of participation: regular consultations between business leaders and top government officials. Today, businesses receive, from consultancies and other private-sector services, regular updates on unrest, kidnap risks, and similar developments that can affect their operations. While this allows them to evaluate such tactical risks, they are on much less sure footing in strategic developments. Such strategic assessments have long been governments' domain. This has led to a situation in which, as Finnish executive Risto Penttilä notes, "Today, CEOs are more interested in listening to [retired US general] Jim Mattis than to the global head of McKinsey & Co."[73]

Regular consultations with key government officials would address executives' desire to better understand the changing geopolitical context in which their companies operate. The briefings would be off-the-record, unclassified, and available to invited top executives in all sectors. Government officials would share national security updates and discuss the context of these events, though the briefings would naturally not feature any details that could give participants commercial advantages. Instead, they would provide the overall picture of international developments that business leaders currently lack.

The objective would clearly not be to pressure business leaders toward particular actions—which would be questionable in a liberal democracy—but to help inform their decision-making. This way, executives would at least be aware of the nation's interests when making commercial decisions. For governments, the briefings would also be an opportunity to hear business leaders' accounts of the changing national security environment and help government decision makers understand what companies can and cannot do. The briefings would thus strengthen existing relationships between business leaders and the government and help business leaders understand their role in national resilience while giving top government officials a better understanding of the businesses' experiences in the geopolitical line of fire.

The briefing invitees could also include entertainment executives, academic leaders, religious leaders, and other civil-society leaders such as heads of NGOs and arts institutions. Not least because disinformation severely harms Western societies, the briefings should also involve social media executives.

Government-industry briefings, of course, do not preclude regulation. In the social media sector, Damian Collins—a Conservative member of the UK Parliament and former chair of its Digital, Culture, Media and Sport Committee—argued that regulation is necessary.

> We need a regulatory code for social media platforms, led by an agency like Ofcom. There also need to be independent bodies that can set standards. Banks can't launch new products without FCA [Financial Conduct Authority] approval. And if a bank fails to spot certain conduct, they can be fined. There should be something like "know your customer" for social media platforms.[74]

Marko Mihkelson, a member of Estonia's liberal Reform Party who chairs the Estonian parliament's foreign affairs committee, likewise suggested that some form of government oversight of social media platforms has now become unavoidable.

> Of course I like the internet, but on social media there are no checks and balances. Social media give a platform to those people in our societies who believe in conspiracy theories. They have always existed, but now they have a louder voice. The bottom line is: With social media, there's no quality control.[75]

Regardless of whether social media regulators are established in the short term, keeping leaders in all societal and business sectors informed of new gray-zone developments would benefit their understanding of the situation. While such leaders may be aware of activities touching their own entities, they cannot be expected to be familiar with the entirety of gray-zone aggression at any given time and may thus be unable to contextualize the activities intersecting with their own organizations.

Government-industry briefings would also be beneficial beyond exchanges of information. In isolation, organizations feel ill-equipped to identify, let alone address, interference and malign influence. Studio executives may, for example, be fully aware of the pressure to make films that have the best chances of pleasing Chinese censors but may not be familiar with the full extent of Chinese gray-zone aggression directed against Western countries. While governments of liberal democracies clearly cannot instruct the entertainment industry on how to create its entertainment content, they can keep it informed of the wider picture of malicious activities by hostile states.

The US government operates a small version of the proposed government-industry briefing program focused on cyber threats. Maj. Gen. Ed Wilson (ret.), who served as deputy assistant secretary of defense for cyber policy in the Donald Trump administration, pointed out that

> for the past few years we [the Department of Defense] have been inviting CEOs and COOs [chief operating officers] to events co-hosted by, together with the DOE [Department of

Energy], with DHS [Department of Homeland Security] participation. The purpose is simply to tell them about the threats we're seeing. We've also laid out sensors in cooperation with industry. A regional utility can't go toe to toe with Russia or China. DHS and Treasury have similar meetings. We want business leaders to understand the risk cyber aggression poses to their companies. Large companies have teams that can evaluate threats but smaller ones don't.[76]

The DOE explains that it works "to develop technologies, tools, exercises, and other resources to assist the energy sector in evaluating and improving their security posture, practices, and readiness."[77] As with the proposed national security consultations, the meetings form a "bi-directional sharing" of cyber-threat information.[78] An embryonic version of such consultations also exists in Finland and the UK, where the National Cyber Security Centre[79] exchanges information with key sectors and occasionally arranges meetings for top executives.

Artistic Side Benefits of National Security Awareness. In entertainment, consultations could yield a side benefit that may seem trivial but could have significant impact. To date, a small number of movies and TV drama series have featured gray-zone-aggression-like story lines. The Norwegian hit series *Occupied*[80] portrays a subversive attack on Norway that begins when a global energy crisis combined with climate change convince the country's prime minister to switch off its fossil-fuel production. His actions prompt gray-zone attacks by the EU and Russia. Steven Soderbergh's 2011 movie *Contagion*[81] features a pandemic of the kind that became reality with COVID-19. With its subversive features that can be found in random parts of everyday life, the gray zone lends itself to outstanding entertainment content, but filmmakers and entertainment executives lack insights into it. Through participation in government briefings, they could not only learn about how gray-zone aggression affects their own sector but also get ideas for new productions.

Indeed, entertainment content forms another way in which liberal democracies can strengthen resilience against gray-zone aggression. Millions of people on different continents have already watched *Occupied* or *Contagion* because each is outstanding entertainment. Neither *Occupied* nor *Contagion* was initiated by a government; indeed, government meddling harms the quality of content. Yet entertainment ideas resulting from government-industry gray-zone briefings—which could include feature films, TV drama series, and reality shows similar to Sweden's *Nedsläckt land* (*Blacked-Out Country*), which follows a group of people during an extended power cut[82]—could provide compelling entertainment and raise awareness of vital national security issues. To date, *Occupied* may well be most ordinary citizens' main source of information about gray-zone aggression.

Public Awareness and Corporate Behavior. Awareness of Beijing's pressure on Western film studios in particular is growing among the Western public. As recent Pew Research Center polling on global public opinion of China demonstrates, so is distrust of China.[83] As a result, close involvement with China poses a reputational risk to Western companies, similar to what was the case with South Africa's apartheid regime. Facing public pressure at home, many Western companies and institutional investors rescinded dealings with South Africa. While globalization has created a culture in which Western firms cooperate with authoritarian regimes for the sake of market access even as they shun committing to national efforts in their home countries, this model may no longer be viable. Indeed, close cooperation with authoritarian regimes may begin to backfire on Western firms.[84]

Disney's high-profile action drama *Mulan* is a case in point. Almost as soon as it was released in 2020, *Mulan*, which was considered a prospective blockbuster that could please the Chinese market, was greeted with enormous criticism. In posts that rapidly spread on social media, often using the hashtag #BoycottMulan, detractors pointed out that not only had the filming partially taken place in Xinjiang—where the Chinese government oppresses a minority—but also Disney, in the closing credits, even thanked authorities involved in the operation of Uyghur "reeducation" camps.[85] Instead of generating headlines for any artistic merits or box office success, *Mulan* generated controversy for Disney. This growing consumer awareness of Chinese pressure on Western firms can help Western countries trying to counter it.

Joint Military-Industry Gray-Zone Exercises. A more comprehensive part in private-sector engagement is joint military-industry gray-zone exercises, a step proposed in a September 2020 report of mine[86] and pioneered by the Czech Republic soon afterward.[87] While most businesses conduct crisis management exercises, such exercises concern tactical threats such as terrorist attacks or kidnappings of businesses' staff. Because gray-zone aggression is not directed against specific companies but affects them because they happen to be based in a particular country or because they are targets of convenience, it is virtually impossible for businesses to exercise for gray-zone threats on their own. Yet precisely because liberal democracies' private sectors cannot deflect such aggression, they are vulnerable targets.

Armed forces, in turn, constantly exercise but focus on threats involving sustained use of force by adversaries. They lack the capacity to defend the private sector against gray-zone threats, and doing so is not their focus. It is clearly in countries' interest that their private sectors not—unwittingly—provide adversaries with opportunities for gray-zone aggression, and equally it is in businesses' interest to minimize the effect of gray-zone aggression on their operations.

Joint military-industry gray-zone exercises would be led by the armed forces and include selected businesses and security-related government agencies such as the police. Some businesses would be identified and invited by the government based on their strategic importance for the country, while others would participate following an application procedure. Exercises would include only a small desktop component and instead primarily feature computer-simulated scenarios, which would regularly be updated to reflect gray-zone threats.

Unlike existing corporate crisis management exercises, which are often attended only by employees responsible for a firm's crisis management and are at any rate desktop exercises, the gray-zone exercises' different segments would involve representatives from all levels of a business, reflecting armed forces' exercise model. They would, of course, also involve government agencies with crisis responsibilities and senior political decision makers.

Firms completing the exercise would be granted an ISO 9000–style certification, which could be kept current through recurring participation.

Such certification would signal to shareholders that the company belongs to an elite class of companies in resilience and that shareholders can therefore have a high degree of confidence the firm will emerge from national and international contingencies with only limited damage. Considering the reputational, monetary, and stock-price damage suffered by businesses successfully targeted by gray-zone attacks, such certification would likely become a considerable asset and could become a feature of corporate annual reports in much the same way as environmental, social, and governance (ESG) standards.

Like all national security exercises, joint military-industry gray-zone exercises also signal to adversaries that aggression will not yield the hoped-for results. As the UK Ministry of Defence's Development, Concepts and Doctrine Centre notes, "An actor that repeatedly carries out actions that contribute to deterrence will build their credibility, both with those who are a direct recipient of their action and other observers."[88]

The Czech exercise initially involved the country's five largest defense companies, with further iterations to include energy, IT, health care, and food production. "We see industrial policy as part of not only economic welfare, but geopolitics and also defence and security," Deputy Minister for Defence Tomáš Kopečný told the *Financial Times*.

> This exercise is basically about creating [a] nexus between the military and civilian, between the government and private side....
>
> The very strategy that is being applied by Chinese state-affiliated investors is something that is targeting [Europe's] critical and strategic technologies.... It's definitely something that is decreasing our capability to defend ourselves, through us losing our technologies that are essential for defence.[89]

National Security Courses. Finnish-style national security courses represent a similarly ambitious option.[90] As in Finland, such a course would be an opportunity for employers in all parts of society to nominate promising mid-career leaders for national security education that also connects them with other leaders. For any country, it is invaluable when the top echelon in society—from members of parliament to heads of NGOs—mostly shares a basic understanding of national security and knows one another. This, too, contributes to creating a combined shield that signals to adversaries that a society is united in wanting to protect itself.

Finland's national defense course expressly does not aim to create a military-industrial complex; on the contrary, the fact that only 6 percent of the participants come from the armed forces—compared to 32 percent from the commercial sector; 19 percent from media, NGOs, and labor market organizations; and 12 percent from academia[91]—highlights the course's civilian nature. Such a focus should also be the goal of prospective national security courses. As with the Finnish course, the aim should clearly be to inform the participants about the country's national security background and current situation, not to try to influence any political convictions they may hold.

Business-Leader Allegiance. All three prospective forms of private-sector involvement proposed above—government-industry briefings, military-industry gray-zone exercises, and national security courses—are based on the assumption that private-sector and civil-society leaders will feel at least rudimentary allegiance to the country in which they and their organizations are based. How does one reconcile this with globalization, which features not just top personnel of other nationalities but also foreign ownership even of iconic firms? For example, that Volvo is now owned by China's Zhejiang Geely Holding Group[92] may invalidate the old saying that "what is good for Volvo is good for Sweden."

It is difficult. While foreign executives may feel an allegiance to their businesses' home countries, it cannot be assumed they will. For foreign-owned companies, the situation is even more challenging, as they have an obligation to consider their owners. If forced to choose, will such a business act in a way that favors its home government or its owner? The latter will likely win.

Yet it is in everyone's interest that liberal democracies continue to thrive. While they may have lost some of their innovation advantage—partially because of subversive economics—these countries remain the world's most desirable bases for businesses. They have rule of law, freedom from political interference in business activities, and highly educated and innovative populations. Indeed, having their headquarters in liberal democracies shields global businesses from the reach of the authoritarian governments whose interference they tolerate as the prize of operating in those governments' markets.

Turning the Cold War equation around, what is bad for Germany, Sweden, the UK, or the United States today is bad for the companies operating there. Indeed, because businesses are already targets of gray-zone aggression, they are painfully aware of the reality though not fully familiar with its extent. It is thus in business leaders' and businesses' interest to help keep their home countries safe.

Government-Owned Investment Funds. Considering the extent of subversive economics, an additional measure would contribute to the wall of denial: the creation of government-owned investment funds. In the 1970s, Schmidt could ask Deutsche Bank to buy a stake in Daimler-Benz as an act of patriotism. New legislation in many Western countries will, of course, require government approval for buyers from non-EU, non-NATO, and non–Five Eyes countries (depending on each country's legislation), but bans resulting from such legislation raise a new question: If a Chinese or other foreign firm is turned down, who will buy the stake? Many businesses will need some sort of recompense for not being allowed to accept a foreign investment. Solutions like the German government using its KfW bank to thwart a Chinese stake in a crucial energy provider are only patchwork solutions, as are direct government takeovers such as the UK government's bailout of the Royal Bank of Scotland, one of the country's largest banks, in 2008.[93]

As a first step, governments could strengthen today's rudimentary cooperation with private-sector investors. It would be based on not patriotic pleas but business opportunity. Foreign investors are interested in cutting-edge Western firms for their business potential (sometimes in combination with their national security utility). Through regular contact with private-sector investors, governments could steer investors' interest in the direction of businesses whose foreign offers it has blocked. This should obviously be done transparently so that no investor gains exclusive information.

Governments could also get involved as investors in their own right. Considering that the businesses whose foreign investors are likely to be blocked by many countries' recent foreign direct investment legislation are considered essential to the national interest, it is in the government's interest to invest in them. Indeed, precisely because such firms are vital to national security in the wider sense, government investments in them would not be a waste of taxpayer money. On the contrary, it could be a good investment. In June 2020, the European Commission published a white paper proposing an investment fund for this purpose,[94] though member states have not yet taken any concrete steps. Such investment funds would be a radical step for most Western governments that today take a highly hands-off approach to the private sector. Yet if the subversive economics aspect of globalization is to be minimized, something has to replace the subversive actors.

The same is true for venture capital (VC) investments. While US legislation now limits foreign VC investments by foreign nationals, many other Western countries lack such protection. Somewhat surprisingly, the US government is also more actively involved in the VC sector than any other Western government is, primarily through VC investors such as the CIA-affiliated In-Q-Tel[95] and the Army Venture Capital Initiative.[96] The Estonian government, in turn, owns the VC fund SmartCap,[97] while the UK government's National Security Strategic Investment Fund functions as a miniature In-Q-Tel.[98] In February 2021, the UK government also launched the Advanced Research and Invention Agency, whose £800 million fund chest will fund high-risk innovation similar to how the United States' Defense Advanced Research Projects Agency does.[99]

Since In-Q-Tel's launch in 1999, its investments have benefited US national security and generated financial returns that In-Q-Tel has reinvested. The same scenario appears likely for any further government-established VC funds. Indeed, government-supported VC firms similar to In-Q-Tel would not just benefit the startup community and with it national innovation and the economy but also be a good use of taxpayer money. Crucially, such funds could also reduce the attraction of not just foreign VC funds but also limited partners. This would, of course, be the case especially if startup entrepreneurs were conversant with the national security implications of accepting funding from VCs or limited partners with connections to regimes hostile to the West.

The Collective Benefit of Civil-Society Participation

Gray-zone exercises alone will clearly not change an adversary's cost-benefit calculation. Nor will government investment funds, resilience training, national defense courses, public awareness campaigns, or any of the other initiatives proposed above. Yet together, they can help create a wall of denial to deter other practices including IP theft, disinformation, and cyberattacks. None of the initiatives imposes a heavy burden on citizens or businesses; on the contrary, participating may benefit them and the country. As a wall of denial is a purely defensive act, these measures would also unlikely escalate tension with the West's adversaries.

Apart from public awareness campaigns and especially business-leader consultations, which could be initiated quickly, creating convincing resilience as outlined above would take time. In addition, it would need to be created under the intense scrutiny of hostile states that would also likely test any new initiatives as they were being set up and possibly use them as fodder for disinformation and misinformation. The time required may, however, be shorter than expected: The Czech Republic launched a gray-zone-exercise pilot project less than three months after the publication of the report on which it is based. Pilot projects would be a practical way of acting relatively quickly. Through such experimental steps, organizers can spot gaps at any early stage.

Another question is who would coordinate the efforts. This could be a resilience czar or, in larger countries, perhaps a group of resilience czars—respected leaders who could, not least through their personal standing in society, encourage participation. Seasoned former business leaders or civil-society leaders would be well-suited for this role.[100]

Building resilience against an adversary whose government can simply command action is undoubtedly a vexing task, but it is a key answer to helping keep liberal democracies safe. Voluntary participation in helping keep the country safe is, of course, what made Sweden's and Finland's Cold War total defense convincing even as they faced similar obstacles. With voluntary and multifaceted civil-society participation, liberal democracies can reduce the gray-zone opportunities for their adversaries, which may continue to possess intent and capability but whose ambitions will be thwarted if their opportunities are reduced.

Western countries should naturally also try to negotiate international gray-zone norms with their adversaries, but with societal resilience in place, they will be equipped to create a wall of denial against gray-zone aggression.

XI

Deterrence by Punishment

"I expect that we may come to a new respect for deterrence," Thomas Schelling said in his Nobel Memorial Prize in Economic Sciences lecture in 2005.[1] At that point, it was not yet obvious that gray-zone aggression would come to pose a major national security concern. Since then, liberal democracies have unquestionably gained a new respect—perhaps even a desire—for deterrence. As we have seen, the challenge they face is that existing forms of deterrence by punishment are ineffective against gray-zone aggression. This chapter discusses how to establish effective deterrence by punishment in the gray zone.

When Russia's interference with the 2016 US presidential election became clear, an expectation quickly took hold that the US government would punish Russia. According to this line of thinking, such a step would signal US strength and deter future attacks. Yet such logic is flawed. Aggression in the gray zone should be punished, but if a country's deterrence by punishment begins only *after* an attack, it is virtually useless. Indeed, the need to retaliate after disinformation campaigns, or any other incident of gray-zone aggression, is a sign that deterrence has failed. As with the threat of conventional aggression, signaling needs to happen before aggression occurs.

Admittedly, this is a tall order in the gray zone, where aggression constantly occurs because targeted countries have difficulty establishing what is a mere nuisance and what constitutes unacceptable aggression. In such a situation, what is even more difficult is how to communicate the intent to punish unacceptable aggression and what punishment to communicate beyond standard phrases pronouncing there will be a price to pay. It is unclear what, precisely, constitutes an intolerable level of gray-zone aggression, what the redline is, and how to communicate the redline and the prospective punishment.

Deterrence is, to again quote Dr. Strangelove, "the art of producing in the mind of the enemy the fear to attack."[2] Yet precisely because the aggression may be gradual and may not even be easily identifiable as aggression, it seems impossible to produce that fear. Deterrence by denial is predominantly passive in nature; it is designed to absorb blows and can therefore be established with little risk of causing provocation. In the gray zone, deterrence by denial is therefore best suited to counter legal forms of aggression. Against illegal forms of aggression, however, deterrence by denial is insufficient, as the targeted country must forcefully signal that prospective illegal acts will be avenged. Maj. Gen. Pekka Toveri (ret.), at the time of the interview the Finnish Defence Forces' chief of intelligence, observed that "building deterrence by resilience is good, but not a complete solution. That would leave us on the defensive while Russians and Chinese can choose the time and place of their attack."[3]

Another hurdle is, of course, the well-known challenge of how to establish that deterrence works when an absence of aggression can simply mean the adversary never intended to engage in aggression in the first place. Remarking on the absence of nuclear war since the end of World War II, Schelling noted in his Nobel Memorial Prize lecture,

> We have enjoyed sixty years without nuclear weapons exploded in anger.
> What a stunning achievement—or, if not achievement, what stunning good fortune.[4]

As discussed in previous chapters, the fundamental question of whether Cold War deterrence was effective still remains, though Schelling argued in his Nobel lecture that the Warsaw Pact deterred NATO from intervening in Hungary in 1956 and Czechoslovakia in 1968.[5] In the gray zone, the fact that aggression takes place means that, in general, there is no negative to prove. The challenge is instead to determine whether any shift in aggressive activity is because of deterrence or whether it instead reflects the adversary's changing interests.

In the gray zone, effective deterrence by punishment involves an intricate set of capabilities and signaling that must meet several requirements:

- The signaled response must be proportionate. If the threatened retaliation is out of proportion with the act of aggression, it is less credible

because the attacker knows that the attacked party is less likely to use it. This is why nuclear arsenals fail to deter gray-zone aggression.
- Conversely, the signaled response must be sufficiently strong so the adversary does not view the response as producing an acceptable loss to which it can then respond, which would risk an escalatory spiral.
- Targeted countries should signal punishment through military force in response to gray-zone aggression that causes loss of life. Military responses should, however, not be signaled as a response to gray-zone aggression not involving loss of life, which would also risk unnecessary escalation and cause liberal democracies to lose the moral high ground.
- Signaling (and prospective responses) must conform with liberal democracies' ethical standards and commitment to a rules-based international order.

Tools of Deterrence by Punishment

While it is clear which tools can be used to deter military aggression, it is much less clear which ones should be used for deterrence in the gray zone. Indeed, deterrence of gray-zone aggression is challenging because defense (and thus deterrence) often cannot mirror the aggression. While countries have, with varying success, deterred military aggression by fielding armed forces and equipment to match those of the prospective attacker, such steps are not possible in the gray zone. Subversive economics clearly cannot be deterred with the threat of even more subversive economics directed at the perpetrating country, nor can democracies facing state-sponsored disinformation campaigns change the perpetrating state's cost-benefit calculation by threatening to unleash disinformation campaigns in return.

The seemingly insolvable aspect of the defender's dilemma is that gray-zone aggression harms liberal democracies by exploiting their openness and using nefarious means not acceptable to liberal democracies. Maj. Gen. Ed Wilson (ret.) of the US Air Force, deputy assistant secretary of defense for cyber policy in the Donald Trump administration, observed that "countries like the United States will always be at a slight disadvantage compared to an authoritarian country. In a free society, the government can't command industry."⁶ To date, Western countries' main modes of deterrence by punishment in the gray zone have been targeted sanctions against individuals and companies and offensive cyber operations. As with all deterrence, it is difficult to know how effective these measures have been. Nevertheless, offensive cyber appears to have been at least partially successful as a deterrent, as neither China, Iran, nor Russia has disrupted critical national infrastructure in the United States or another NATO or EU member state even though they have the capability. During the Solar-Winds intrusion, for example, the perpetrators would have been able to also cause significant disruption but chose not to. Conversely, the fact that Russia has disrupted Ukrainian infrastructure proves that it does not fear any punishment Ukraine may have signaled.

The effect of personal and business sanctions is much harder to assess. Because they have become a standard retaliatory tool, such sanctions are firmly part of any aggressor's cost-benefit calculation. In response to Russia's aggression against Ukraine, Western countries quickly sanctioned Russian officials and companies. Russian officials and businesses have also been sanctioned in connection with cyber aggression and under Magnitsky Act legislation, which a number of Western countries have passed during the past decade and under which their governments can sanction Russian officials in connection with human rights abuses. In the United States, for example, Magnitsky legislation

> require[s] the President to identify the person(s) involved in the detention, abuse, or death of [Sergei] Magnitsky, and the ensuing cover-up, or those responsible for gross human rights violations against persons in Russia. Identified individuals are subject to blocking of assets under U.S. jurisdiction, prohibited from U.S. transactions, and denied entry into the United States.[7]

As of March 2020, the US government had sanctioned 690 Russian individuals in connection with the Ukraine conflict. It had also sanctioned Russian companies over the same matter and sanctioned at least 49 individuals in connection with cyber aggression and 55 under the Magnitsky Act.[8] The EU, in turn, has imposed Ukraine-related sanctions on 177 individuals and 48 entities.[9] Countries such as Australia and Canada have imposed similar sanctions. In early 2021, the EU also sanctioned 11 individuals and one research center over the jailing of opposition activist Alexey Navalny.[10] Personal sanctions typically comprise banning individuals from entering or transiting through the sanctioning country and freezing their assets in that country.

Criminal Justice and Visa Bans. Even though the sanctions include personal travel bans and asset freezes, it is disputable whether they have changed Russia's behavior. Indeed, judging from Russia's increasing assertiveness since 2014, the sanctions have had minimal effect. As with all deterrence, it is impossible to prove a negative: Russia could arguably have engaged in even more aggression had its leaders not been punished with sanctions. Nevertheless, even Russia's current level of gray-zone aggression suggests existing efforts have not been successful.

Indeed, sanctions on individuals and businesses are now so common, and the prospective targets chosen from such an easily definable group of leading officials and businesses, that the aggressor country can easily accomodate such details into its cost-benefit calculation. As a result, sanctions have become far too predictable, with the absence of a surprise element (and resulting fear) further diminishing any deterrent effect they may have had.

Yet while Western countries are constrained by their openness and the behavioral standards that guide liberal democracies, they also have advantages that their authoritarian adversaries lack: They have international credibility, are attractive countries to visit and live in, and have close and numerous allies. In gray-zone deterrence, they can use all these aspects.

Visas may seem a weak tool to use in deterrence. They are, however, important because they enormously benefit the individuals who receive them: Without visas, these individuals could not live and work in their country of choice. In the Schengen Area, a visa to one member state grants the recipient the right to travel to all member states. Visa approvals and the connected right to own property and open bank accounts are within the gift of the issuing country. This means visas can also be used to signal prospective punishment not of countries but of individuals of the deterrer's choosing. Western nations could enhance this effectiveness by signaling that not only may individuals involved in gray-zone aggression lose their right to visas but their family members and associates may too.

As a deterrent, current individual sanctions are largely toothless precisely because they are a predictable response and because they target a relatively small group of people. Indeed, Western governments' personal sanctions against key individuals sometimes give the impression that the governments could not think of another punishment. This is hardly effective deterrence. As Austin Long notes, "Cost/benefit calculation relies on known inputs, while much of deterrence rests on uncertainty about those inputs."[11] The way sanctions are currently used, the costs they impose are thus predictable and relatively painless.

That is a missed opportunity. Even within the confines of the relatively weak weapon of personalized sanctions, Western countries could use Herman Kahn's and Schelling's fear-and-surprise combinations and expand the number of people who may be targeted by personal sanctions. This tool, which includes visa bans, is even more powerful as foreign elites often receive long-term "golden visas" that give them, and usually their families, full residency rights in exchange for a sizable investment. In the UK, for example, Tier 1 investor visas are available to individuals who invest £2 million in the country.[12] Similar visas—popular among Chinese citizens—are available in the US for a $1.8 million investment (or $900,000 in a less desirable area).[13] Until 2020, Cyprus even offered immediate citizenship for €2.15 million, and, because the country is a member of the European Union, a Cypriot "golden passport" granted the recipient full EU citizen rights. The country ended its scheme in October 2020 after a corruption scandal.[14] While threatening to withhold golden visas as part of gray-zone deterrence could result in lost income, that figure will likely be significantly lower than the amount lost to the West because of gray-zone aggression would be.

To be sure, nobody wants a situation in which children are regularly punished for their parents' deeds. Yet any moral high ground connected to the children of, say, Russian officials is negated by the fact that, in many cases, their lifestyles are funded by their parents. Some family members may, as a result, also be party to asset concealment. "Where the parents may have been seen as parvenus, the progeny are unambiguously accepted as mainstays of high society.... They're regulars at Henley, Ascot and Annabel's," the British magazine *Tatler* reported in a 2020 feature about young, wealthy Russians in London, adding that they can be seen "on private planes, making peace signs outside the Kremlin, shooting in Gloucestershire, or with their Chanel handbags and sunglasses on rooftop pools overlooking the London skyline."[15] Except for one of the young Russians interviewed for the piece, the *Tatler* reporter noted, "Everyone I speak to says their father is a businessman, but most are vague about what that business entails."[16]

The individuals who take advantage of the West's hospitality even include the families of hostile countries' political leaders. Vladimir Putin's daughter Maria has lived and worked in the Netherlands,[17] and Xi Jinping's daughter (and only child), Mingze, graduated from Harvard University.[18] Anastasia Zheleznyak—daughter of Sergei Zheleznyak, who, as deputy State Duma speaker at the time of the annexation of Crimea, was placed on the EU sanctions list—remains in London, where she has attended university and now works for the BBC[19] and owns a company.[20] The 2016 Panama Papers leak of offshore accounts revealed, among other things, that Jia Qinglin's granddaughter Jasmine Li became the sole shareholder of two British Virgin Islands companies while studying at Stanford University in 2010. Her grandfather was at the time China's fourth-ranked official.[21]

The Chinese authorities' reaction to the Panama Papers leak points to extreme unease about such revelations involving potentially ill-gotten gains: Chinese authorities blocked access to reporting on holdings involving senior officials and their family members and deleted posts on the Chinese social media networks Weibo and WeChat.[22] This, too, provides clues about what kind of punishment signaling would be most successful. While naming and shaming countries that engage in gray-zone aggression has to date been minimally successful, naming and shaming hostile countries' leaders whose families live well-heeled lives in the West backed by mysterious assets has more potential. Gray-zone deterrence signaling could threaten forensic accounting to establish the source of such family members' wealth. During the 2020 election campaign, Joe Biden made a similar suggestion, writing that, if elected president, he would punish hostile governments found to have interfered with US elections with measures including "financial-sector sanctions, asset freezes, cyber responses, and the exposure of corruption."[23]

Western governments have been content to let adversary leaders' family members live in their countries not just as a generous gesture but also because they hoped the experience would create positive feelings. Hoping that the experience will indirectly rub off on hostile leaders is, however, a tenuous basis on which to continue pursuing this generosity.

Instead, Western governments should consider including in their deterrence signaling the prospective rejection of visas (tourist, work, business, study, and especially investor visas) for a larger group of officials and their family members and associates. Putin and his top officials know they are always the most likely recipients of sanctions and can adjust their cost-benefit calculations accordingly. If, however, visa bans—and the right to hold bank accounts and own property—were a sword of Damocles over the heads of more members of the elite, with no way for them to discern who might be targeted next, the adversary's cost-benefit calculation would likely change. Although more aggressive in nature, the threat of asset freezes could be used similarly, especially as individuals fearing asset freezes often transfer their assets to family members.

China has already gone far beyond such signaling. In March 2021, the Chinese government imposed an entry ban on a group of European legislators, the Political and Security Committee of the Council of the European Union, the Subcommittee on Human Rights of the European Parliament, the Mercator Institute for China Studies, and the Danish institute Alliance of Democracies Foundation. "The individuals concerned *and their families* are prohibited from entering the mainland, Hong Kong and Macao of China. They and companies and institutions associated with them are also restricted from doing business with China," China's Ministry of Foreign Affairs stated.[24] (Emphasis added.) It added that

> the Chinese side urges the EU side to reflect on itself, face squarely the severity of its mistake and redress it. It must stop lecturing others on human rights and interfering in their internal affairs. It must end the hypocritical practice of double standards and stop going further down the wrong path. Otherwise, China will resolutely make further reactions.[25]

Visa bans on family members are not a new concept. In the early 2000s, "smart sanctions"—which targeted elites, not just individuals involved in a specific act of aggression—were gaining traction, only to stall because of legal challenges. In the "Kadi I" and "Kadi II" cases in 2008 and 2013, respectively, the Court of Justice of the European Union ruled that smart sanctions could be subject to judicial review and that governments had to be able to present evidence for why an individual was being sanctioned.[26]

Retaliation poses another risk. Because, however, exceptionally few members of Western countries' elite want to live in the countries that are the West's main adversaries, threatening retaliation in visa bans would have limited effect. These adversary countries would, however, be able to threaten the expulsion of Western intelligence operatives active in their countries.

There is precedent in collective visa revocation. In 2009, Switzerland—in response to Libya holding two Swiss citizens hostage—canceled the Swiss visas of 186 Libyans, who, as a result, also lost access to the rest of the Schengen Area.[27] While EU member states criticized Switzerland for not having informed them before announcing the ban, no court struck it down. This also demonstrates the potential for countries jointly signaling visa bans as prospective punishment. Indeed, during the writing of this book, the Biden administration began denying and revoking visas to perpetrators of corruption, human rights abuses, or both—and extended the ban to the perpetrators' immediate families.[28]

As we have seen, an important part of gray-zone aggression is carried out not by governments but by various proxies. This means many individuals who have only a loose connection to the government and may feel little loyalty to it carry out subversive activities on its behalf, often for opportunistic reasons. This is different from soldiers, who have pledged loyalty to their country. Indeed, it stands to reason that proxies' loyalty to themselves trumps their loyalty to the government on whose behalf they operate (which may or may not be their own government).

Personalized deterrence messaging could, as a result, be directed against such individuals. The US Cyber Command's Defend Forward framework partially employs this approach, with operatives signaling to prospective attackers that they have been identified, implying—in the manner of *The Godfather*'s severed horse's head—that they stand to suffer consequences. This happened, for example, before the 2018 US midterm elections, when the US Cyber Command signaled to Russian disinformation operatives that the US government had identified them and was tracking their work.[29]

During the 2020 US presidential election campaign, the Cyber Command conducted more than 20 operations to block efforts by foreign countries to undermine the election. These efforts included shutting out a Russian troll farm and sending targeted messages to Russian cyber operatives and Russian elites who the US government believed were planning interference.[30] (Unfortunately for the United States, US citizens ended up doing as much or worse damage to the elections by sharing homegrown disinformation.)

The Cyber Command's strategy of persistent engagement, introduced in 2019, features constant, low-level threats against prospective perpetrators—the equivalent of neighborhood police officers conducting their beat and making occasional arrests. "Through persistent action and competing more effectively below the level of armed conflict, we can influence the calculations of our adversaries, deter aggression, and clarify the distinction between acceptable and unacceptable behavior in cyberspace," the Cyber Command states in its command vision.[31]

Similarly, the US government has in recent years also indicted numerous foreign nationals in connection with state-sponsored cyber aggression. In July 2020, for example, the US Department of Justice indicted two Chinese hackers, who had "in some instances acted for their own personal financial gain, and in others for the benefit of the MSS [Ministry of State Security] or other Chinese government agencies."[32] More recently, the European Union has sanctioned a small number of cyberattackers.[33]

Even though the individuals charged are highly unlikely to ever stand trial (as they would need to enter the United States to do so), the indictments and sanctions are punishment precisely because they prevent the individuals from entering the respective countries. Here, too, Western countries' attractiveness as a destination for tourism and residency is an asset that can be used in deterrence signaling. The most important recipients of the signaling are not the indicted attackers but other individuals who can be deterred because of the indictments. Similar to how the criminal justice system deters crime by signaling—through arrests and prosecutions—that those who engage in unlawful activities will pay a price, countries targeted by gray-zone aggression can signal to would-be perpetrators that they will personally pay a price. Such personalized deterrence is fundamentally different from traditional deterrence, which has been directed against countries.[34]

Yet despite these indictments, personalized deterrence targeting cyber and disinformation operators is not as effective as it could be. This is primarily because the criminal justice system is predictable. Western governments cannot charge attackers with random crimes; they can charge someone only with a crime to which the person can be linked beyond reasonable doubt. That clearly removes most of the surprise (and resulting fear) necessary for effective deterrence.

As with hostile states' officials and business associates and their families, Western governments could use visas to signal prospective punishment to individual cyber and disinformation operators. Individually and jointly, governments could use prospective permission, denials, and revocations of visas to signal to many individuals that they are being watched and that they can, at the discretion of the targeted government or its allies, lose the right to visit and live in one or more countries. In these cases, too, governments would need to consider the implications of visa denials, including the prospect of hostile governments retaliating with visa denials of their own. Nevertheless, like Switzerland in 2009, they may consider it an acceptable risk. The denial or revocation of visas would not need to be connected to a particular act of aggression. This also helps address the dilemma of attribution and so-called false-flag operations, in which gray-zone attackers (usually in cyberspace) conduct an operation pretending to represent another country.[35]

Imposition of Larger Costs. Targeted countries must clearly signal the threat of larger cost imposition than that from visa bans or individual indictments. They must possess the gray-zone equivalent of "overwhelming force." This is not an easy task. Part of the defender's dilemma is that a liberal democracy cannot build overwhelming force using the same means its rivals use, as some of these means are incompatible with the standards liberal democracies seek to uphold. As we have seen, some degree of interference by a hostile country and its proxies may also be unpreventable in liberal democracies.

Nonetheless, offense is possible even with these limitations. To borrow a phrase from the 2018 US National Defense Strategy, liberal democracies must "expand the competitive space."[36] Toveri suggested that Western countries need to establish hybrid capabilities that force the adversary to invest in its own defense much more than they are doing now. At least regarding the Russians, this would hurt them badly. And we have to remember that, when they're busy defending, they have less time to attack.[37]

Information operations provide one avenue. While Western governments should clearly not peddle disinformation (which would cause them to lose the moral high ground), there are ways to deter rivals by signaling the use of information campaigns that use only facts available in the public domain. To deter disinformation campaigns, a liberal democracy and its allies could threaten "second-strike communications," the information equivalent of the nuclear second-strike capability with which nuclear states seek to deter the first strike.[38] The information campaign might contain damaging information about the aggressor country's leaders and other representatives, including the existence of property ownership, bank accounts, and other assets in Western countries.

Disinformation would clearly be unacceptable, and classified information should not be revealed. Property ownership and many other categories are, however, publicly accessible, and the information is often damaging. Even when ownership is not in the respective person's name but organized through front companies, in many cases establishing links is possible.[39] As authoritarian rulers and their associates often use taxpayer funds for personal gains, revelations by Western organizations would harm such officials among their own populations, which are mostly unable to investigate such activity. The hypocrisy of top officials and their families enjoying the benefits of Western lifestyles at the citizenry's expense is not only a matter that, for moral reasons, deserves attention but also one that can be used for deterrence. In connection with its new visa-ban initiative, the Biden administration publicizes visa denials.[40] This, too, fits within second-strike communication.

The challenge in second-strike communication is how to reach the desired audience. Revelations about Western assets held by Kim Jong Un would, for example, be virtually impossible to bring to the attention of ordinary North Koreans (though members of the elite do have access to Western news outlets), while similar revelations involving Russian officials would be easier to convey to a Russian audience. A Russian-language video released on YouTube by Navalny in January 2021, documenting a lavish palace allegedly belonging to Putin, had by the end of February been viewed more than 113 million times.[41]

Either way, considering that resourceful citizens manage to share information even in authoritarian countries—as demonstrated by samizdat publications behind the Iron Curtain—second-strike communications are a tool that can produce in some leaders the fear to attack. As virtually every aspect of Western leaders' lives is already in the public domain, it would also be difficult for the adversary country to escalate in response.

Ideally, second-strike communications should be conducted not by Western governments but by independent media. No Western government can, of course, tell its media organizations what to report, but as reputable news outlets are also harmed by disinformation, it is in their interest to help deter these campaigns.

Unexplained wealth orders (UWOs) may seem like a bureaucratic tool. In reality, they are powerful because they can be used to seize foreign nationals' funds and because this information can be used in second-strike communications. Under the UK's Criminal Finances Act 2017, which targets individuals linked with serious crime or who hold public office outside Europe, UK law enforcement can

> apply for a court order requiring someone to explain their interest in property and how they obtained it. . . .
>
> UWOs provide an opportunity to confiscate assets without ever having to *prove* that the property was obtained from criminal activity.[42] (Emphasis in original.)

In December 2020, Zamira Hajiyeva, who is the wife of a jailed Azeri banker and who had spent £16 million at the luxury department store Harrods, lost her appeal against a UWO and could lose her £12 million London home and £10 million golf course.[43] While criminal justice should clearly be pursued on its own merits, the fact that well- and lesser-known officials from countries engaged in gray-zone aggression park unexplained wealth in the West should be addressed by seizing such assets and informing the individuals' fellow citizens about it.

The UK's response to the attempted murder of Sergei and Yulia Skripal forms another example of the sizable imposition of costs that can be used within the confines of liberal democracy. The UK government's retaliation began with Downing Street assembling a coalition of allies that expelled 342 Russian intelligence officers under diplomatic cover.[44] Journalists, in turn, did their own work, joined by newer investigative platforms such as Bellingcat. Soon the perpetrators had been named and shamed by Western media and will, as a result, never work abroad again. The video of Putin's alleged palace and the outing of the Skripals' would-be assassins were for all intents and purposes second-strike communications carried out by private individuals and organizations.

Long after the Skripal attack, it emerged that the UK government had also avenged the attack in other ways. Then–National Security Adviser Mark Sedwill told the *Times* in October 2020,

> We also took a series of other discreet measures including tackling some of the illicit money flows out of Russia, and covert measures as well. . . . The Russians know that they had to pay a higher price than they had expected for that operation.[45]

Knowing that you will have to pay a higher price than you consider acceptable is, of course, the purpose of all deterrence. In the case of the Skripal attack, the UK's deterrence clearly failed because the attack took place. The UK had failed to signal that Russia would have to pay an unacceptably high price for nerve agent attacks against individual people on UK soil. This, again, demonstrates the challenging nature of gray-zone deterrence: Because the aggressor can use any means, including ones never used before, the defender struggles to build defense against them and signal that the use will be avenged. Nevertheless, the UK's imaginative Skripal response forms a useful model for other countries' deterrence signaling. Is a nerve agent attack in the cards for them too? Nobody, of course, knows, and the exact nature of the aggression is less important in signaling deterrence by punishment. Of primary importance for Western governments is to communicate the general nature of retaliation—for example, that gray-zone aggression resulting in loss of life risks retaliation with military means.

Indeed, despite having been used after an attack rather than before, the UK government's punishment of Russia for the Skripal incident remains the best case study of gray-zone retaliation in recent years. Sedwill told the *Times*,

> We will use different techniques. We need to play to our strengths and focus our attention on their vulnerabilities. We are not going to conduct illegal operations, but there are things we can do. There are some vulnerabilities that we can exploit too.[46]

To be effective as deterrence, such asymmetric punishment needs constant signaling. While the defending country should clearly not reveal any details, it should be so specific that it can change the attacker's cost-benefit calculation. "We will respond in a time and manner of our choosing," a standard phrase used by Western governments after sundry attacks, is too generic for the adversary to use for a cost-benefit calculation, and signaling only after an incident is too late. Western governments, for example, should signal that they may target vulnerabilities such as illicit money flows that can be throttled via tools such as UWOs (which can be communicated to the public).

Offensive cyber operations are a frequently mentioned and much-used option. "Superiority through persistence seizes and maintains the initiative in cyberspace by continuously engaging and contesting adversaries and causing them uncertainty wherever they maneuver," the US Cyber Command explained in its 2018 command vision.[47] Offensive cyber has, in fact, long been treated as an all-around deterrent that can be used against all manner of aggression. Clearly, Western countries with offensive cyber capabilities (e.g., the United States and the UK) can inflict serious damage on their adversaries and those of their allies. They can do so in ways that are "responsible, targeted and proportionate, unlike those of some of our adversaries," as the UK signals intelligence agency puts it.[48]

Western countries are, in fact, unlikely to avenge hostile-state-sponsored cyber intrusion with overwhelming force in cyberspace. Even though responsible, targeted, and proportionate counterattacks can severely harm the organizations, networks, and individuals against whom they are directed, any use of cyber tools against an adversary removes some of their potency, as the adversary will be able to study at least part of them. This is certainly the lesson learned after the Stuxnet attack on Iran, which caused the country less damage than the attacker had hoped.[49]

Indeed, as the establishment of the US Cyberspace Solarium Commission in 2019 demonstrates, not even the United States has established effective cyber defense and deterrence. The commission proposes a "whole-of-nation framework" for cyber defense and deterrence including citizens, industry, and government that will provide what the commission calls "layered cyber deterrence," a combination of deterrence by denial and punishment.[50] This will "increase the costs and decrease the benefits that adversaries anticipate when planning cyberattacks against American interests," the commission rightly argues.[51]

Offensive cyber is, in other words, no *Wunderwaffe*. In fact, seemingly minute challenges affect even the most impressive offensive cyber capabilities. While US and British cyber warriors would, for example, be able to insert so-called Trojan horses into enemy networks and activate them whenever it is deemed necessary, David Omand warns that

> maintaining a "Trojan" capability of that sort is extremely difficult. Every patch to the target system, every change of configuration, has to be monitored in case it affects the malware, and can you really be sure that the owner of the system has not discovered the malware and how to disable it, so when it comes time to press the button nothing happens?[52]

The West's adversaries are, of course, familiar with this state of affairs and how it reduces offensive cyber's deterrent effect, not least because they face the same challenge.

Indeed, while offensive cyber is indispensable in gray-zone deterrence, Western governments' focus on it makes Western deterrence static and predictable and causes governments to neglect other existing and prospective forms of deterrence by punishment available to them. Adversaries, meanwhile, continue to innovate. Here, again, asymmetric deterrence— in which the defender signals that offenses can be punished using means different from those used by the aggressor—offers considerable potential as it incorporates the surprise-and-fear factor.

Part of the defender's dilemma is that gray-zone aggression indisputably imposes deterrence limitations on countries that adhere to international norms and criminal law. Their rivals, by contrast, have access to options they lack. This disadvantage can be turned around to trigger experimentation in deterrence by punishment that does not violate international norms. Indeed, liberal democracies should experiment as much in their gray-zone deterrence as their rivals experiment in aggression. This will allow liberal democracies to constantly cook a soup with changing ingredients and so keep prospective attackers on the back foot. A cyberattack does not have to be avenged—or deterred—with a cyberattack. In gray-zone deterrence, asymmetry is not just possible but also desirable.

Luxury Goods and More: Trade Suspension as a Tool. Access to a country's market can also be used in deterrence. As with visas and the right to hold bank accounts and own property, access to a country's market is within the gift of that country. A liberal democracy's government can, as a result, seek to deter gray-zone aggression by signaling to the offending government that aggression may result in loss of trade. Even China depends on Western countries for imports of key goods and components, and it certainly depends on Western markets to buy goods made in China. While a complete trade ban would violate World Trade Organization rules, liberal democracies could signal that they will adopt China's tactic of suspending imports of certain goods.

The intellectual property (IP) theft and counterfeiting discussed in Chapter VII, and the fact that the offending countries sell such goods back to the countries where their companies stole the IP, is certainly a valid reason for affected countries to threaten a trade ban. They should, however, not go as far as China did by suspending imports from to-be-punished countries based on procedural (and by all accounts fictitious) problems with the goods.[53] As liberal democracies strive to strengthen the rules-based international order, they would be unlikely to use threats so frivolously. If they did, aggressor governments would be unlikely to take them seriously, causing the deterrent signaling to lose its power. This, too, illustrates the defender's dilemma.

Western governments could instead offer carrots. While this gives the impression that an adversary is being rewarded for aggressive behavior, the UK Ministry of Defence's Development, Concepts and Doctrine Centre (DCDC) argues that "if this results in the adversary *not* conducting an unwelcome course of action, this is still a valid part of deterrence. A benefit of restraint can include the restoration of something lost to try to incentivise adversary restraint."[54] (Emphasis in original.) In 2003, the UN lifted its sanctions against Libya to incentivize good behavior, and the United States did so the following year. As DCDC notes, "The Iran nuclear deal is a similar encouragement."[55] During the Trump administration in particular, North Korea similarly received sweeteners to incentivize nuclear restraint. This, however, had the opposite effect, as Pyongyang simply proceeded with its nuclear plans.

Working with their private sectors, Western governments could also signal a measure that likewise does not violate international laws but would hit aggressor governments by targeting their citizens' increasingly Western consumption habits. As we have seen, Beijing in particular pressures Western film studios, fashion houses, and even athletes eager to be present on the Chinese market into pro-Beijing narratives. Western consumer goods and entertainment are also popular in Russia; indeed, Russia's and China's governments have managed to stay in power partly thanks to increasing prosperity and access to a Western lifestyle.[56] In Russia, 43 percent of millennials follow luxury brands on social networks, a 2018 McKinsey & Company and Condé Nast Russia report found.[57] Western governments and organizations (and personalities) in each sector—fashion houses, film studios, sports teams, and artists—could signal that they will no longer provide respective products to the aggressor country.

The sudden disappearance of Western fashion brands or movies from a country such as China or Russia would likely cause an unwelcome stir among key parts of the populace and would, as a result, rattle the regime. To be sure, a Western luxury boycott would clearly risk a retaliatory boycott by Chinese consumers. Such a Chinese consumer boycott occurred in 1999, after the United States erroneously bombed China's embassy in Belgrade. But, as Odd Arne Westad notes, "It lasted only a week."[58] A 2008 boycott of the French supermarket chain Carrefour over its owner's support of Tibet quietly petered out too.[59] In deterrence, Western governments—working with private sectors—could thus gamble that Beijing's and Moscow's barks are louder than their bites in the area of consumer products.

The same is true for supply chains more generally. As part of its Chinese trade policy, the Trump administration restricted exports to China of certain sensitive US products such as semiconductor components.[60] China, meanwhile, is trying to expand its self-sufficiency in areas in which it has, until now, relied on Western imports. Takeovers of Western firms are an important part of this effort. China is, however, still dependent on many Western goods, as is Russia. Western governments could, again working with their private sectors, signal that, in cases of significant gray-zone activity, they will suspend exports of certain products to the offending country. While a country faced with such a threat can certainly aim to develop self-sufficiency, no country can achieve complete autarky; gray-zone aggressors will thus be vulnerable to such threats.

The question is, of course, whether companies would agree to this type of cooperation, considering they would temporarily lose significant income if the threat were carried out. At the moment, it is unlikely, and a partial boycott would benefit only nonparticipating firms. Without corporate support for commercial boycotts, the deterrence signaling would be minimal and thus useless.

Yet precisely because these companies are themselves targeted by IP theft, bullying, and other gray-zone practices, it is in their interest to help stop these practices and allow globalization to function as intended. Thanks to briefings between the government and business leaders, executives would also be in a better position to understand aggression beyond what their own firms observe. The concept could also be expanded to other Western businesses, though the deterrence effect would be largest in sectors whose products the rival country cannot easily copy to a Western standard.

Threat of Kinetic Force. Seeking to find a way out of the defender's dilemma, Bart Groothuis, a Dutch member of the European Parliament, proposes what amounts to targeted deterrence using unlawful means. This is already practiced in cyberspace, where countries targeted by state-sponsored attacks retaliate in-kind. Groothuis, however, proposes that allied countries should also be able to avenge an unlawful attack with unlawful means.

> Therefore, the EU and NATO, together with their allies, should strive for a reinterpretation or legal development. A coalition of democratic countries could state in an international agreement that they reserve the right to take collective countermeasures if one of them falls victim to an internationally wrongful act.[61]

Such retaliation could be a last resort. However, Western governments signaling to gray-zone aggressors that their illegal actions will be avenged in-kind no longer occupy the moral high ground that separates Western democracies from their rivals. In addition, such collective commitment to illegal acts would further undermine the rules-based international order. A more promising approach may be to redefine what constitutes "wartime" in wartime powers—a change unlikely to happen quickly—and communicate this to adversaries.

The answer must instead be to innovate, exploiting surprise, fear, and the fact that Western countries are more attractive than their rivals are. Despite its limitations, the UK government's retaliation over the Skripal attack demonstrates what is possible with imagination and clever use of the West's levers. If, however, the West begins using the same illegal tools of gray-zone aggression that its adversaries use (or even signals that it will do so), it needlessly contributes to escalation in the gray zone. The US government's assassination of Qassem Soleimani in January 2020 clearly provided an excuse for adversaries to, in turn, assassinate US officials outside an armed conflict. Such assassination attempts may still occur.

The most consequential prospective punishment is, of course, military force. To date, only Israel has responded to gray-zone aggression with military action, as it did in 2019 when it bombed a Hamas building in the Gaza Strip in retaliation against a cyberattack.[62] Even though it is highly unlikely that Western countries would use military force to avenge gray-zone aggression, it must nevertheless remain an option. This is particularly the case with gray-zone aggression that leads to loss of life. The cyberattack on Mumbai in October 2020, which caused a power outage that left millions without power and caused the death of several residents, was initially thought to have been caused by China, but a government minister subsequently attributed the outage to human error. Whatever the cause of Mumbai's power cut, loss of life caused by cyberattacks remains a serious concern. India's Chief of Defence Staff Gen. Bipin Rawat subsequently said that "we know that China is capable of launching cyberattacks on us, and that can disrupt a large amount of our systems."[63] Given the prospect of cyberattacks claiming lives, Western governments should unequivocally signal that, should this kind of attack be directed against one of their countries and possible other allied countries, they will not hesitate to respond with military force.

In addition to signaling that gray-zone attacks causing loss of life may be avenged with military force (which is different from signaling that generic illegal gray-zone activities will be avenged this way), these governments should signal that they will reserve for themselves the right to decide against whom the force will be directed. Precision strikes are particularly useful in this context, as they allow the defending country to signal that it will strike directly involved individuals while minimizing innocent loss of life. This allows the defender to maintain the moral high ground.

The tools discussed here will have varying degrees of effectiveness, and some may not suit every country. In addition, decision makers may discover new deterrents. Either way, the objective should be to identify and use innovative tools not just because gray-zone deterrence allows for experimentation but also because the West's rivals constantly experiment. Regularly introducing new deterrents will strengthen the crucial surprise-and-fear element.

The Hedgehog Way of Latent Punishment. How does one build and communicate deterrence by punishment when aggression is latent, amorphous, and takes place below the threshold of armed conflict? How can governments build and signal deterrence when it is often difficult to pinpoint when aggression has taken place? When, exactly, does venture capital funding cross from cutthroat business to a gray-zone activity? At which step in an island-construction or "borderization" process should retaliation take place—that is, what should Western countries signal to any country contemplating such violations of neighboring territory?

Addressing threats posed by terrorism, asymmetric military strategies, and proliferation of weapons of mass destruction, Gen. Kevin Chilton and Greg Weaver made observations in 2009 that are equally relevant for gray-zone aggression.

> Peacetime activities can make use of deterrent means that take time to have their desired effects or that require repetition to be effective. They expand the range of deterrence options at our disposal. Conducting activities in peacetime also allows time to assess carefully the impact of our deterrence efforts and to adjust if they are ineffective or have unintended consequences.[64]

Although the peacetime-wartime distinction does not apply to gray-zone aggression, Chilton and Weaver's suggestion—in essence, to treat deterrence by punishment as a latent form of deterrence—holds great relevance. It answers the dilemma of when to retaliate—or preferably, to signal that retaliation will happen—when the aggression consists of a long string of minor activities, each of which individually does not warrant retaliation. Indeed, considering the fluidity of gray-zone forms of aggression (and in the case of cyberattacks and other somewhat more easily detectable forms of aggression, the difficulty of attributing them to sponsoring governments), liberal democracies should not link all their deterrence messaging to specific hostile actions. That makes latent deterrence a form of general deterrence, which signals that a nation—supported by allies through extended deterrence—will punish aggressors.

As Chilton and Weaver note, again referring to terrorism and asymmetric military strategies, "Conducting deterrence activities in peacetime may prevent the crisis from developing in the first place or may reduce the risk of waiting until we are in crisis to take deterrent action."[65] This is also a promising strategy in gray-zone deterrence. One might call it persistent engagement across the gray zone. Instead of signaling major punishment for specific acts, such latent deterrence can signal that targeted countries will punish behavior that forms part of a pattern and that they will decide the timing for doing so. Latent punishment, in other words, functions like

DETERRENCE BY PUNISHMENT 243

a hedgehog, which can deter low-intensity aggression that forms part of the environment but certainly cannot stave off major attacks. This means a seemingly small infraction—for example, an act of IP theft or the addition of one set of concrete infrastructure to a nonexistent island—may trigger limited retaliation.

Referring to offensive cyber, Omand describes how it might be used

> by hacking back, penetrating and disrupting the networks and systems of the attackers, to create difficulty and discomfort and make attacks more costly. Such persistent engagement is therefore a contribution to deterrence by denial. . . . But it is unlikely to cause an actual cessation of such activity, just as the threat of long prison sentences certainly inconveniences the few criminals that are caught and takes them temporarily out of circulation, but it does not stop criminals trying to commit crime. Nor does it stop them improving their techniques to lower the risk of being caught.[66]

Indeed, in the cyber domain, latent deterrence—akin to police stop-and-search methods—is perhaps the best use of offensive capabilities. While Israel frequently engages in larger-scale "hack backs" against its adversaries, China and Russia are indisputably more powerful cyber adversaries than the groups that attack Israel in cyberspace are.

Kahn's and Schelling's focus on fear and surprise is useful in the context of latent deterrence. Defending countries can take advantage of the uncertainty regarding when the threshold has been reached that will trigger retaliation, to signal that they alone decide when it has been reached. Because fear and surprise amplify the deterrent effect, the uncertainty regarding when the injured parties or their allies will respond may convince the aggressor that the risk of punishment whose timing and content is unknown supersedes the expected benefit.

Targeted countries must, however, communicate this is their intention. If they issue only vague pronouncements—such as "we will respond in a time and manner of our choosing"—their adversaries have little content to use in their cost-benefit calculations and may, as a result, ignore the deterrence signaling altogether. Defenders should instead signal what forms or levels of gray-zone aggression risk punishment and indicate what that punishment might be, again without providing details.

Signaling retaliation, however, may inadvertently cause escalation. Armed forces everywhere develop "escalate to de-escalate" strategies. The weakness of these strategies—that the adversary can choose to escalate in response rather than de-escalate—also plagues escalation in the gray zone. In the gray zone, the risk associated with latent deterrence by punishment is that it will lead the adversary to revise its cost-benefit calculation and will create a Hobbesian state in which globalization is impeded by constant low-intensity antagonism. If every act of gray-zone aggression is accompanied by latent deterrence by punishment (albeit against the very real forms of gray-zone aggression outlined in previous chapters), not only will it affect the globalized economy but also the punishment will no longer generate fear or surprise in the adversary. Indeed, the adversary may consider it the price for engaging in gray-zone aggression and respond by signaling escalatory punishment.

Tailored Deterrence. Latent deterrence is likely to change some cost-benefit calculations. Targeted countries, however, must also use a heavier deterrence arsenal to influence an adversary's cost-benefit calculation before a major act of aggression in such a way that the adversary cannot absorb the blow. This deterrence should be tailored to specific countries and thus complement hedgehog-style latent deterrence, which would not be potent enough to prevent, say, a crippling cyberattack or the construction of artificial islands. Schelling observes,

> Forcibly a country can repel and expel, penetrate and occupy, seize, exterminate, disarm and disable, confine, deny access, and directly frustrate intrusion or attack. It can, that is, if it has enough strength. "Enough" depends on how much an opponent has.[67]

Choosing from the tools discussed above and any prospective tools outlined by individual countries, Western governments could use the same tailored signaling that NATO countries employed vis-à-vis their different recipients during the Cold War. Now as then, the key point is to signal major punishment that will hurt the respective recipient. The threat of withheld microchip exports will, for example, frighten China more than it would North Korea. The latter is, in turn, likely to be rattled by Western governments signaling they will avenge cyberattacks that steal money with cyberattacks sabotaging North Korean currency holdings. Based on the presence of Russian and Chinese elites in Western countries, Russia and China are likely to change their cost-benefit calculations if Western countries communicate that, in cases of gray-zone aggression, they will revoke visas of individuals of their choosing. Both countries would also be vulnerable to the threat of withheld Western luxury goods, entertainment, or cutting-edge industrial components. That prospect would rattle Iran less than would the prospect of a massive cyberattack, as the country is already largely cut off from Western goods and makes do with ersatz products.

The question is, of course, what constitutes the gray-zone aggression that the West would seek to deter through tailored tools. Conventional military aggression is easier to deter because it is mostly clear when it occurs, but with gray-zone aggression, the deterrer must decide what constitutes an unacceptable measure of aggression. Which types (and what frequency) of gray-zone aggression cannot credibly be deterred through a hedgehog approach and instead require more-substantive threats of punishment?

Loss of life must fall into this category. If Western countries and their allies are seen accepting loss of life within their borders, it will imperil their governments' credibility vis-à-vis their own citizens and embolden adversaries. The protection of life is, of course, why governments monopolize violence. This means a cyberattack that results in loss of life must be treated as an armed attack, with tailored deterrence signaling that the targeted country and its allies may respond with military means.

Borderization, artificial island construction, and other border-alteration tricks also fall into this category, as the outcome is a permanent violation of another country's sovereignty. In addition, perpetrators of borderization and artificial island construction clearly view acquisition of additional territory in this manner as strategically important, as it is a major undertaking. To the aggressor countries, the threat of minor punishment can thus easily be accommodated in the cost-benefit calculation. The challenge with gray-zone border changes is, of course, that they are gradual and that there is, as a result, no clear point where defense and thus deterrence would be logical. In the case of China's island construction, even though it was clearly occurring and the US Navy urged the Barack Obama administration to intervene, the lack of an obvious "enough-is-enough" point caused the administration to prevaricate to the extent that the US government never forcefully intervened.

This muddled view in the gray zone, which makes it difficult for targeted countries to discern precisely what is occurring, is what makes gray-zone aggression so attractive. That makes it incumbent on defenders to specify—perhaps arbitrarily—what constitutes the point where enough is enough. For border alterations, the enough-is-enough point may be the first piece of infrastructure installed; for deadly cyberattacks, it may be when the first person dies (as opposed to when the targeted country has complete certainty regarding the identity of a sponsoring government, which may never materialize). Whatever the point is, Western governments and their allies should agree on it and communicate to the prospective perpetrator that they are united and will retaliate against gray-zone aggression that they consider crosses a line.

They should not, however, include the specific enough-is-enough point in their deterrence messaging. Doing so removes the fear factor. More importantly, if the deterrence signaling is not followed by action if the adversary proceeds with the aggression, the deterrence crumbles. As the US Cyberspace Solarium Commission notes, "Rather than clearly communicating an ultimatum to a target, which may tie their hands and create politically infeasible 'red lines,' states may prefer to retain strategic ambiguity and flexibility."[68]

Such a redline failure occurred in 2012, when President Obama sought to deter the Syrian government from using chemical weapons against its own citizens. "We have been very clear to the Assad regime that a red line for us is we start seeing a whole bunch of chemical weapons moving around or being utilized. That would change my calculus," he said.[69] Yet the following year, when the international community documented the Syrian government using chemical weapons against its own citizens, the US government failed to intervene. The Assad regime and the international community concluded that the Obama administration's redlines were not to be taken seriously.

Friends with Extended Deterrence. While Western countries spend considerable time bickering with one another, the fact that they have allies, however imperfect, is a key asset in deterrence. This is even more important because their adversaries have, at most, fleeting companions. Writing about conventional deterrence, Chilton and Weaver note that

> US friends and allies share our interest in deterrence success. Because of their different perspectives, different military capabilities, and different means of communication at their disposal, they offer much that can refine and improve our deterrence strategies and enhance the effectiveness of our deterrence activities. It is to our advantage (and theirs) to involve them more actively in "waging deterrence" in the twenty-first century.
>
> One of the most important contributions our friends and allies can make to our deterrence campaigns is to provide alternative assessments of competitors' perceptions. Allied insights into how American deterrence activities may be perceived by both intended and unintended audiences can help us formulate more effective plans.[70]

This is equally true for deterrence of gray-zone aggression. No Western country has access to every tool of punishment outlined above, and some may have additional tools. Just as in extended deterrence of conventional and nuclear threats, extended deterrence of gray-zone threats means allies benefit from the umbrella extended by others. The differences are that, in the gray zone, even small allies can extend umbrellas and even the United States can benefit from them doing so. Latvia and Portugal, for example, have golden-visa systems that attract many Russian citizens. Sweden and Germany are strong in high-tech manufacturing and could withhold vital exports, while Italy and France could suspend exports of luxury goods. Australia, too, could suspend exports. Companies in numerous countries produce entertainment content they could withhold. The United States and the UK bring particular strengths in offensive cyber and, of course, military power.

This whole-of-society approach makes extended deterrence more than just the sum of its member-state parts. Niklas Karlsson, a Social Democrat who serves as vice chair of the Swedish parliament's defense committee, pointed out that "to have any power whatsoever vis-à-vis China, you need allies. But even with allies we're smaller than China."[71] Collectively, however, Western countries, including their private sectors, can turn off the tap on a phenomenal range of goods and services that their adversaries take for granted, with governments inflicting additional damage through cyberattacks and even conventional military force. That damage would be stronger yet with selective national service programs in place, as governments could draw on graduates to help surge any punishment effort. All these capabilities should be communicated to adversaries.

Timing is also vitally important precisely because so many pieces of gray-zone aggression may seem trivial in isolation but collectively cause significant damage. In addition, just as a country that signals it will be able to mobilize only a week after an attack hardly changes an attacker's cost-benefit calculation, countries that signal they will need time to collectively determine how to respond to gray-zone aggression and then organize the response risk being unable to deter it. Indeed, such delayed reprisal would seem disconnected from the aggression and thus be ineffective.

Although the UK government managed to assemble a group of allies within days after the Skripal attack, responding to an easy-to-identify and easy-to-condemn attack on two individuals is far less challenging than is responding to other types of gray-zone aggression, in which the deed is gradual, invisible to the public, and potentially affecting far more people. By signaling unity and resolve, countries can make gray-zone aggression less likely. Again, if the deterrence signaling does not happen until after a serious case of aggression, it is too late. Today, however, Western allies' lack of coordination and collective resolve means they are unable to signal that they will collectively and speedily avenge aggression in the gray zone, as such signaling would not be taken seriously. There is, as a result, currently no extended deterrence below the level of armed conflict.

Useful first steps would be for willing countries to form a gray-zone defense coalition, establish a protocol and responses for gray-zone scenarios, and then exercise these procedures. Like military exercises, these steps would also play a part in deterrence signaling. With such a defense alliance in place, countries could respond much faster in case of a serious attack, and more importantly, they could also collectively signal their ability to act swiftly and collectively.

Extended deterrence is also vital if businesses are involved. Even companies that have operations in China and other gray-zone adversary countries or sell to those markets already lose considerable sums because of IP theft and cyber aggression and face serious disorder (and, again, money loss) when supply chains are disrupted or their imports or exports are suspended. They are, in other words, frenemies of countries that engage in gray-zone aggression. Their losses resulting from a range of gray-zone activities including IP theft, however, mean they will ultimately benefit if the activities subside because the West has demonstrated through convincing deterrence that it will not tolerate such activities. It is thus in these companies' interest to help even as they want to maintain friendly relations with every foreign market, especially China.

To be sure, as participation in the responses outlined above involves temporary loss of revenue, businesses are likely to hesitate. This is especially true for publicly listed ones that are measured on quarterly earnings. If governments introduce briefings between the government and business leaders, however, executives are more likely to understand the wider context of gray-zone aggression. As with citizen and business participation in resilience, it is vital for the respective governments to be fully transparent about the gray-zone aggression businesses are being asked to help counter.

In addition, extended deterrence means a significant number of Western countries could participate. That would make participation more palatable for businesses as their peers from many other countries could also participate, strengthening the power of deterrence and minimizing participating companies' exposure. Extended deterrence involving not just participating countries but also companies based in those countries would be the equivalent of threatening a general strike: Goods and services would simply not be delivered.

NATO's dual-track strategy, on which the alliance decided in 1979, has relevance for gray-zone aggression today. Just as it was vital for the alliance to counter Soviet stationing of nuclear weapons in East Germany while maintaining a disarmament dialogue, Western governments should respond to gray-zone aggression by China, Iran, North Korea, Russia (ordered alphabetically), and any future practitioners through not just deterrence but also dialogue. Credible deterrence, of course, ensures more-meaningful dialogue.

Concluding Reflections

As this book was nearing its completion, China Mobile—China's largest mobile network provider—awarded contracts as part of its massive 5G rollout. In a previous China Mobile contract round, Ericsson of Sweden had won 11 percent of the contract volume, but this time China Mobile awarded Ericsson a mere 2 percent.[1] Ericsson's Nordic rival Nokia, which had won nothing in the previous round, suddenly got a share of the desirable contract. Around the same time, Ericsson presented its latest quarterly results, and an odd picture emerged. Overall, Ericsson had done well, its global sales increasing by 8 percent since the same quarter the previous year. In China, though, sales had fallen.[2]

Ericsson's products had not deteriorated in quality: Its booming global sales were evidence of trust in its technology. Its fate on the Chinese market did, however, come as no surprise to those watching geopolitical developments. As discussed in this book, Chinese officials had been warning for months that Ericsson would suffer in China unless the Swedish Post and Telecom Authority (PTS) reversed its decision to exclude Huawei from Sweden's 5G network. When civil servants at the PTS failed to comply with Beijing's demands, Ericsson suddenly found itself virtually frozen out of China Mobile's massive 5G build-out and saw other sales fall in China. It was abundantly clear that Ericsson, a private company, was being punished for government decisions in Sweden, where it happens to be headquartered. Nokia's home country of Finland, meanwhile, had said nothing about excluding Huawei from its 5G network.

A short time later, in early August 2021, the oil tanker *Mercer Street*, traveling through the Gulf of Oman, was hit by a weapon thought to have been a drone. The attack killed the tanker's Romanian captain and a British security guard employed to help protect the ship against piracy. Why would someone attack a run-of-the-mill, Liberian-flagged oil tanker? The governments of Romania, the UK, and the United States soon concluded that Iran was behind the attack.[3] While the *Mercer Street* is owned by a Japanese firm, it is managed by London-based Zodiac Maritime, which is owned by Israeli billionaire Eyal Ofer. "You can attack a Japanese-owned, Liberian-flagged vessel simply because it's linked to an Israeli billionaire. It's a very useful way of launching deniable attacks that don't directly target your adversary," Cormac McGarry, a maritime analyst with the risk consultancy Control Risks, told me at the time.[4] Indeed, Iran and Israel have for the past couple years been engaging in a proxy conflict in which both sides harm civilian ships affiliated with the other country.

Both events—Ericsson's misfortune in China and the attack on the *Mercer Street*—demonstrate how gray-zone aggression is intensifying and how targeted countries struggle to respond to the aggression, let alone deter it. While China Mobile is ultimately owned by the Chinese government, it is a private company and has the right to award contracts as it wishes. It may be obvious to Ericsson, the Swedish government, other governments, and indeed everyone watching the drama unfold that Beijing was punishing Ericsson as a vulnerable proxy of the Swedish government, but Beijing has plausible deniability. So does Iran in the case of the *Mercer Street*.

The intensifying aggression against globalized businesses as witnessed during summer 2021 makes deterrence in the gray zone even more urgent. The policy suggestions for both deterrence by denial (including resilience) and deterrence by punishment are likely to be adopted by some countries and should help trigger an inspired discussion among policymakers in other countries—but also among business leaders and the wider public. If these three parts of Western societies do not work together, gray-zone aggression will continue to flourish.

Notes

Introduction

1. Andy Greenberg, "Chinese Hacking Spree Hit an 'Astronomical' Number of Victims," *Wired*, March 5, 2021, https://www.wired.com/story/china-microsoft-exchange-server-hack-victims/.

2. Fiona Hamilton, "Defence Chief Warns Attacks Online Could Lead to Real War," *Times*, January 11, 2021, https://www.thetimes.co.uk/edition/news/cyberattacks-risk-starting-a-war-defence-chief-says-onkg6fpt2.

3. Joe McDonald, "China Slaps 200% Tax on Australia Wine amid Tensions," Associated Press, November 27, 2020, https://apnews.com/article/beijing-global-trade-australia-coronavirus-pandemic-china-c0f921929c9c53af30da81ddd775ffe9.

4. Elisabeth Braw, "How China Took Western Tech Firms Hostage," *Foreign Policy*, January 19, 2021, https://foreignpolicy.com/2021/01/19/china-huawei-western-tech-hostages-national-firms/.

5. Reuters, "Norwegian Air's Lessors Take Majority Ownership," May 20, 2020, https://www.reuters.com/article/us-health-coronavirus-norwegianair/norwegian-airs-lessors-including-chinas-boc-take-main-ownership-idUSKBN22W0UP.

6. Reuters, "Norwegian Air's Lessors Take Majority Ownership."

7. I use the terms "West" and "Western" to mean Europe, North America, and Asia-Pacific liberal democracies including Japan and Australia.

8. North Atlantic Treaty Organization, Public Diplomacy Division, "Defence Expenditure of NATO Countries (2013–2019)," press release, November 29, 2019, https://www.nato.int/nato_static_fl2014/assets/pdf/pdf_2019_11/20191129_pr-2019-123-en.pdf.

9. Michael J. Mazarr, "The Essence of the Strategic Competition with China," *PRISM* 9, no. 1 (October 21, 2020), https://www.16af.af.mil/News/Article/2389108/the-essence-of-the-strategic-competition-with-china/.

10. Laura Silver, Kat Devlin, and Christine Huang, *Unfavorable Views of China Reach Historic Highs in Many Countries*, Pew Research Center, October 6, 2020, https://www.pewresearch.org/global/2020/10/06/unfavorable-views-of-china-reach-historic-highs-in-many-countries/.

11. Jeremy Kay, "Dalian Wanda Group Completes AMC Acquisition for $2.6bn," Screen Daily, September 4, 2012, https://www.screendaily.com/dalian-wanda-group-completes-amc-acquisition-for-26bn/5046096.article.

12. Klara Obermüller, ed., *Wir sind eigenartig, ohne Zweifel: Die kritischen Texte von Schweizer Schriftstellern über ihr Land* [*We're Peculiar, Without a Doubt: Critical Text by*

Swiss Authors About Their Country], Nagel & Kimche, https://files.hanser.de/Files/Article/ARTK_LPR_9783312003174_0001.pdf.

13. Yevgeny Vindman, "Is the SolarWinds Cyberattack an Act of War? It Is, If the United States Says It Is.," Lawfare, January 26, 2021, https://www.lawfareblog.com/solarwinds-cyberattack-act-war-it-if-united-states-says-it.

Chapter I—Defining and Identifying Gray-Zone Aggression

1. Philip Kapusta, "The Gray Zone," *Special Warfare* 28, no. 4 (October–December 2015): 20, https://www.soc.mil/SWCS/SWmag/archive/SW2804/GrayZone.pdf.
2. Frank G. Hoffman, *Conflict in the 21st Century: The Rise of Hybrid Wars*, Potomac Institute for Policy Studies, December 2007, 8, https://www.potomacinstitute.org/images/stories/publications/potomac_hybridwar_0108.pdf.
3. Erik Reichborn-Kjennerud and Patrick Cullen, "What Is Hybrid Warfare?," Norwegian Institute of International Affairs, January 2016, https://core.ac.uk/download/pdf/52131503.pdf.
4. Ewan Lawson (associate fellow, Royal United Services Institute for Defence and Security Studies), email to the author, December 17, 2020.
5. Mark Galeotti, "The Mythical 'Gerasimov Doctrine' and the Language of Threat," *Critical Studies on Security* 7, no. 2 (2019): 157–61, https://www.tandfonline.com/doi/full/10.1080/21624887.2018.1441623.
6. Oona A. Hathaway and Scott J. Shapiro, *The Internationalists: How a Radical Plan to Outlaw War Remade the World* (New York: Simon & Schuster, 2018).
7. Patrick J. Cullen and Erik Reichborn-Kjennerud, *MCDC Countering Hybrid Warfare Project: Understanding Hybrid Warfare*, Multinational Capability Development Campaign, January 2017, https://assets.publishing.service.gov.uk/government/uploads/system/uploads/attachment_data/file/647776/dar_mcdc_hybrid_warfare.pdf.
8. Reichborn-Kjennerud and Cullen, "What Is Hybrid Warfare?"
9. European Centre of Excellence for Countering Hybrid Threats, "Hybrid Threats as a Concept," https://www.hybridcoe.fi/hybrid-threats-as-a-phenomenon/. This definition is also semantically questionable, as the word "hybrid" denotes a matter composed of different elements.
10. Sean Aday et al., *Hybrid Threats: A Strategic Communications Perspective*, NATO Strategic Communications Centre of Excellence, April 8, 2019, 11, https://stratcomcoe.org/publications/hybrid-threats-a-strategic-communications-perspective/79.
11. Lyle J. Morris et al., *Gaining Competitive Advantage in the Gray Zone: Response Options for Coercive Aggression Below the Threshold of Major War*, RAND Corporation, 2019, 16, https://www.rand.org/pubs/research_reports/RR2942.html.
12. Morris et al., *Gaining Competitive Advantage in the Gray Zone*, 27.
13. Renee Dudley and Daniel Golden, "The Colonial Pipeline Ransomware Hackers Had a Secret Weapon: Self-Promoting Cybersecurity Firms," *MIT Technology Review*, May 24, 2021, https://www.technologyreview.com/2021/05/24/1025195/colonial-pipeline-ransomware-bitdefender/; and BBC, "JBS: FBI Says Russia-Linked

Group Hacked Meat Supplier," June 3, 2021, https://www.bbc.com/news/world-us-canada-57338896.

14. CEO of a major European telecoms infrastructure company, telephone interview with the author, March 4, 2020.

15. Jaqueline Balcer Bednarska, "Kina hotar med motåtgärder efter beslutet om att blocka Huawei och ZTE i 5G-nätet" [China Threatens Countermeasures After the Decision to Block Huawei and ZTE in the 5G Network], Sveriges Television, October 21, 2020, https://www.svt.se/nyheter/kina-hotar-med-motatgarder-efter-beslutet-om-att-blocka-huawei-och-zte-i-5g-natet.

16. Reuters, "China Urges Britain to 'Correct Its Mistakes' on Hong Kong Visas," October 23, 2020, https://www.reuters.com/article/us-hong-kong-security-britain-visa/china-urges-britain-to-correct-its-mistakes-on-hong-kong-visas-idUSKBN2780LF.

17. Garry White, "'Kowtowing' HSBC Is Caught in the US Deglobalisation Crossfire," *Telegraph*, June 13, 2020, https://www.telegraph.co.uk/business/2020/06/13/kowtowing-hsbc-caught-us-deglobalisation-crossfire/.

18. Kathrin Hille, "'Wolf Warrior' Diplomats Reveal China's Ambitions," *Financial Times*, May 11, 2020, https://www.ft.com/content/7d500105-4349-4721-b4f5-179de6a58f08.

19. Standing Committee to Advise the Department of State on Unexplained Health Effects on US Government Employees and Their Families at Overseas Embassies, *An Assessment of Illness in U.S. Government Employees and Their Families at Overseas Embassies* (Washington, DC: National Academies Press, 2020), https://www.nap.edu/read/25889/chapter/1.

20. Guðmundur J. Guðmundsson, "The Cod and the Cold War," *Scandinavian Journal of History* 31, no. 2 (2006): 97–118, https://www.tandfonline.com/doi/abs/10.1080/03468750600604184.

21. Renee Cluff, "China's Plan to Build a Fish Processing Facility in the Torres Strait Raises Alarm over Fishing, Border Security," ABC Far North, December 16, 2020, https://amp.abc.net.au/article/12985504.

22. Elisabeth Braw, "Back to the Finland Station," *Foreign Affairs*, June 18, 2015, https://www.foreignaffairs.com/articles/finland/2015-06-18/back-finland-station.

23. Jenna Emtö, "Staten ska få bättre koll på utlänningars fastighetsköp—ett nytt lagförslag som ger staten förkörsrätt på strategiskt viktiga fastigheter tar oss tillbaka till 90-talet" [The Government to Gain Better Scrutiny of Foreigners' Property Purchases—Proposed New Legislation Giving the Government Buying Priority for Strategically Important Properties Takes Us Back to the '90s], Svenska Yle, September 25, 2018, https://svenska.yle.fi/artikel/2018/09/25/staten-ska-fa-battre-koll-pa-utlanningars-fastighetskop-ett-nytt-lagforslag-som.

24. UK Government Communications Headquarters, "National Cyber Force Transforms Country's Cyber Capabilities to Protect the UK," November 19, 2020, https://www.gchq.gov.uk/news/national-cyber-force.

25. Elisabeth Braw, "From Schools to Total Defence Exercises: Best Practices in Greyzone Deterrence," Royal United Services Institute for Defence and Security Studies, November 15, 2019, https://rusi.org/publication/rusi-newsbrief/schools-total-defence-exercises-best-practices-greyzone-deterrence.

26. See, for example, US Department of Justice, Office of Public Affairs, "Seven International Cyber Defendants, Including 'Apt41' Actors, Charged in Connection with Computer Intrusion Campaigns Against More Than 100 Victims Globally," press release, September 16, 2020, https://www.justice.gov/opa/pr/seven-international-cyber-defendants-including-apt41-actors-charged-connection-computer.

27. Hannah Beech, "China's Sea Control Is a Done Deal, 'Short of War with the U.S.,'" *New York Times*, September 20, 2018, https://www.nytimes.com/2018/09/20/world/asia/south-china-sea-navy.html.

28. Mark Montgomery (retired rear admiral, US Navy), telephone interview with the author, April 21, 2020.

29. Sun Tzu, *The Art of War*, trans. Lionel Giles, Internet Classics Archive, http://classics.mit.edu/Tzu/artwar.html.

Chapter II—2014: A Decisive Year

1. Frank G. Hoffman, *Conflict in the 21st Century: The Rise of Hybrid Wars*, Potomac Institute for Policy Studies, December 2007, https://www.potomacinstitute.org/images/stories/publications/potomac_hybridwar_0108.pdf.

2. Patrick J. Cullen and Erik Reichborn-Kjennerud, *MCDC Countering Hybrid Warfare Project: Understanding Hybrid Warfare*, Multinational Capability Development Campaign, January 2017, 17, https://assets.publishing.service.gov.uk/government/uploads/system/uploads/attachment_data/file/647776/dar_mcdc_hybrid_warfare.pdf.

3. Radio Free Europe/Radio Liberty provides a photographic timeline. See Lucie Steinzova and Kateryna Oliynyk, "The Sparks of Change: Ukraine's Euromaidan Protests," Radio Free Europe/Radio Liberty, November 21, 2018, https://www.rferl.org/a/ukraine-politics-euromaidan-protests/29608541.html.

4. BBC, "Crimea Referendum: Voters 'Back Russia Union,'" March 16, 2014, https://www.bbc.co.uk/news/world-europe-26606097.

5. US Army Special Operations Command, *"Little Green Men": A Primer on Modern Russian Unconventional Warfare, Ukraine 2013–2014*, 31, https://www.jhuapl.edu/Content/documents/ARIS_LittleGreenMen.pdf.

6. Danielle Wiener-Bronner, "Ukraine's Pro-Russia 'Militia' Look Suspiciously Like Veteran Russian Soldiers," *Atlantic*, April 21, 2014, https://www.theatlantic.com/international/archive/2014/04/ukraine-soldiers-russian/360969/.

7. Balkan Devlen (senior fellow, Macdonald-Laurier Institute), email to the author, February 4, 2021.

8. Organization for Security and Co-operation in Europe, "January–March 2020 Trends and Observations from the Special Monitoring Mission to Ukraine," April 15, 2020, https://www.osce.org/special-monitoring-mission-to-ukraine/450175.

9. Jim Nichol, *Russia-Georgia Conflict in August 2008: Context and Implications for U.S. Interests*, Congressional Research Service, March 3, 2009, https://fas.org/sgp/crs/row/RL34618.pdf.

10. Damien McGuinness, "How a Cyber Attack Transformed Estonia," BBC, April 27, 2017, https://www.bbc.com/news/39655415.

11. Pål Jonson (chairman, Committee on Defence, Swedish Parliament), telephone interview with the author, June 25, 2020.

12. European Council and Council of the European Union, "Timeline—EU Restrictive Measures in Response to the Crisis in Ukraine," December 16, 2020, https://www.consilium.europa.eu/en/policies/sanctions/ukraine-crisis/history-ukraine-crisis/; and US Department of the Treasury, "Ukraine-/Russia-Related Sanctions," https://www.treasury.gov/resource-center/sanctions/Programs/pages/ukraine.aspx.

13. North Atlantic Treaty Organization, "Defence Expenditure of NATO Countries (2013–2019)," press release, November 29, 2019, https://www.nato.int/cps/en/natohq/news_171356.htm.

14. North Atlantic Treaty Organization, "Trident Juncture 2018," October 29, 2018, https://www.nato.int/cps/en/natohq/157833.htm.

15. Jen Judson, "COVID-19 Dampens European Exercise, but US Army Chief Says All Is Not Lost," *Defense News*, March 18, 2020, https://www.defensenews.com/smr/army-modernization/2020/03/18/covid-19-dampens-european-exercise-but-army-chief-says-all-is-not-lost/.

16. Elisabeth Braw, *Competitive National Service: How the Scandinavian Model Can Be Adapted by the UK*, Royal United Services Institute for Defence and Security Studies, October 23, 2019, https://rusi.org/publication/occasional-papers/competitive-national-service-how-scandinavian-model-can-be-adapted-uk.

17. Oona A. Hathaway and Scott J. Shapiro, *The Internationalists: How a Radical Plan to Outlaw War Remade the World* (New York: Simon & Schuster, 2018).

18. Barclay Ballard, "Crimea Doesn't Pay: Assessing the Economic Impact of Russia's Annexation," *World Finance*, October 28, 2019, https://www.worldfinance.com/special-reports/crimea-doesnt-pay-assessing-the-economic-impact-of-russias-annexation.

19. Robert M. Lee, Michael J. Assante, and Tim Conway, *Analysis of the Cyber Attack on the Ukrainian Power Grid*, SANS Institute and Electricity Information Sharing and Analysis Center, March 18, 2016, https://www.cybermongol.ca/uploads/1/1/9/8/119816416/darkenergy-ukrainepowergrid.pdf.

20. Andy Greenberg, "New Clues Show How Russia's Grid Hackers Aimed for Physical Destruction," *Wired*, September 12, 2019, https://www.wired.com/story/russia-ukraine-cyberattack-power-grid-blackout-destruction/.

21. Todd C. Helmus et al., *Russian Social Media Influence: Understanding Russian Propaganda in Eastern Europe*, RAND Corporation, 2018, 15, https://www.rand.org/pubs/research_reports/RR2237.html.

22. BBC, "MH17: Four Charged with Shooting Down Plane over Ukraine," June 19, 2019, https://www.bbc.co.uk/news/world-europe-48691488.

23. NATO Strategic Communications Centre of Excellence, *Analysis of Russia's Information Campaign Against Ukraine*, 2015, 13, https://www.stratcomcoe.org/download/file/fid/77757.

24. NATO Strategic Communications Centre of Excellence, *Analysis of Russia's Information Campaign Against Ukraine*, 13.

25. Ian Traynor, "Russia Accused of Unleashing Cyberwar to Disable Estonia," *Guardian*, May 16, 2007, https://www.theguardian.com/world/2007/may/17/topstories3.russia.

26. Lawrence Freedman, *The Future of War: A History* (London: Penguin, 2017), 66.
27. Helmus et al., *Russian Social Media Influence*, 15.
28. Lyse Doucet, "Qasem Soleimani: US Kills Top Iranian General in Baghdad Air Strike," BBC, January 3, 2020, https://www.bbc.com/news/world-middle-east-50979463.

Chapter III—Gray-Zone Aggression, a National Security Threat

1. HM Government, *Global Britain in a Competitive Age: The Integrated Review of Security, Defence, Development and Foreign Policy*, March 2021, 3, https://assets.publishing.service.gov.uk/government/uploads/system/uploads/attachment_data/file/969402/The_Integrated_Review_of_Security__Defence__Development_and_Foreign_Policy.pdf.
2. UK Cabinet Office, *National Risk Register of Civil Emergencies, 2017 Edition*, September 2017, 34, https://assets.publishing.service.gov.uk/government/uploads/system/uploads/attachment_data/file/644968/UK_National_Risk_Register_2017.pdf.
3. UK Department of Health and Social Care, "UK Pandemic Preparedness," November 5, 2020, https://www.gov.uk/government/publications/uk-pandemic-preparedness/uk-pandemic-preparedness.
4. Ukraine might be considered an exception to this, though there is not a clear consensus that it is a full-fledged member of the Western community.
5. BBC, "China Bans BBC World News from Broadcasting," February 12, 2021, https://www.bbc.co.uk/news/world-asia-china-56030340.
6. Damelya Aitkhozhina, "Russian Court Rules to Jail Navalny," Human Rights Watch, February 2, 2021, https://www.hrw.org/news/2021/02/02/russian-court-rules-jail-navalny.
7. Ed Wilson (retired major general, US Air Force), telephone interview with the author, May 7, 2020.
8. Chris Inglis (former deputy director, US National Security Agency), telephone interview with the author, April 21, 2020.
9. Giedrimas Jeglinskas (assistant secretary-general for executive management, NATO), telephone interview with the author, July 1, 2020.
10. David Ljunggren, "China Poses Serious Strategic Threat to Canada, Says Canadian Spy Agency Head," Reuters, February 9, 2021, https://www.reuters.com/article/us-china-canada/china-poses-serious-strategic-threat-to-canada-says-canadian-spy-agency-head-idUSKBN2A92VH.
11. Erik Reichborn-Kjennerud and Patrick Cullen, "What Is Hybrid Warfare?," Norwegian Institute of International Affairs, January 2016, https://core.ac.uk/download/pdf/52131503.pdf.
12. Senior executive in the Finnish critical national infrastructure sector, telephone interview with the author, November 29, 2019.
13. Swedish Security Service, "Främmande makt utnyttjar brister i svenskt säkerhetsskydd" [Foreign Powers Exploit Shortcomings in Swedish Security], press release, January 11, 2021, https://www.sakerhetspolisen.se/ovrigt/pressrum/aktuellt/aktuellt/2021-01-11-frammande-makt-utnyttjar-brister-i-svenskt-sakerhetsskydd.html.

14. Netherland General Intelligence and Security Service, "Nederlandse veiligheidsbelangen kwetsbaar voor activiteiten andere landen" [Dutch Security Interests Vulnerable to Activities by Other Countries], press release, February 3, 2021, https://www.aivd.nl/actueel/nieuws/2021/02/03/nederlandse-veiligheidsbelangen-kwetsbaar-voor-activiteiten-andere-landen.

15. Erik Brandsma (former CEO, Jämtkraft), telephone interview with the author, November 29, 2019.

16. CEO of a major European telecommunications company, telephone interview with the author, March 11, 2020. The CEO asked not to be named, to be able to speak freely.

17. Jeglinskas, telephone interview.

18. Dominykas Tučkus (former director of infrastructure and development, Ignitis Group), telephone interview with the author, February 21, 2020.

19. Thomas Grove, "Belarus Plane Diversion: What Happened to the Ryanair Flight and Who Is Roman Protasevich?," *Wall Street Journal*, May 26, 2021, https://www.wsj.com/articles/belarus-ryanair-plane-lukashenko-protasevich-11621874251.

20. Baltic News Service, "Lithuanian PM Calls Lukashenko 'Migrants and Drugs' Threats Absurd," Lithuanian National Radio and Television, May 27, 2021, https://www.lrt.lt/en/news-in-english/19/1418870/lithuanian-pm-calls-lukashenko-migrants-and-drugs-threats-absurd.

21. William James, Daphne Psaledakis, and Robin Emmott, "West Hits Belarus with New Sanctions over Ryanair 'Piracy,'" Reuters, June 21, 2021, https://www.reuters.com/world/europe/west-hits-belarus-with-new-sanctions-over-ryanair-piracy-2021-06-21/.

22. Republic of Lithuania, Ministry of the Interior, State Border Guard Service, "The First Team of Frontex Officers Starts Patrolling the Border with Belarus," July 1, 2021, http://www.pasienis.lt/eng/The-first-team-of-frontex-officers-starts-patrolling-the-border-with-belarus.

23. Andrius Sytas, "Lithuania Says Belarus Is Flying in Migrants, Plans Border Barrier," Reuters, July 7, 2021, https://www.reuters.com/world/europe/lithuania-build-barrier-belarus-border-stop-migrants-says-pm-2021-07-07/.

24. Benas Gerdžiūnas et al., "Baghdad to Lithuania: How Belarus Opened New Migration Route to EU," EURACTIV, July 15, 2021, https://www.euractiv.com/section/global-europe/news/baghdad-to-lithuania-how-belarus-opened-new-migration-route-to-eu/.

25. Jeglinskas, telephone interview.

26. US Department of Defense, *Summary of the 2018 National Defense Strategy of the United States of America: Sharpening the American Military's Competitive Edge*, 2018, 5, https://dod.defense.gov/Portals/1/Documents/pubs/2018-National-Defense-Strategy-Summary.pdf.

27. UK Ministry of Defence, Development, Concepts and Doctrine Centre, *Deterrence: The Defence Contribution*, Joint Doctrine Note 1/19, February 2019, 18, https://assets.publishing.service.gov.uk/government/uploads/system/uploads/attachment_data/file/860499/20190204-doctrine_uk_deterrence_jdn_1_19.pdf.

28. UK Ministry of Defence, Development, Concepts and Doctrine Centre, *Deterrence*, 27.

29. In 2020, Toby Harris, a member of the UK House of Lords, launched the National Preparedness Commission, comprising leaders from business, politics, and academia, to raise critical national infrastructure preparedness. I am one of the commission's members. See National Preparedness Commission, website, https://nationalpreparednesscommission.uk/.

30. Erin Douglas, "Texas Was 'Seconds and Minutes' away from Catastrophic Monthslong Blackouts, Officials Say," Texas Tribune, February 18, 2021, https://www.texastribune.org/2021/02/18/texas-power-outages-ercot/.

31. Jens Stoltenberg, "Keynote Speech" (speech, Global Security 2020 Bratislava Forum, Bratislava, Slovakia, October 7, 2020), https://www.nato.int/cps/en/natohq/opinions_178605.htm.

32. US Congress has tried to decide, to date unsuccessfully, whether and how to compel social media platforms to better regulate misinformation and disinformation. See, for example, Cristiano Lima and Steven Overly, "Senate Hearing Flashes Signs of Action on Regulating Tech," *Politico*, November 17, 2020, https://www.politico.com/news/2020/11/17/facebook-twitter-senate-hearing-437116.

33. US Department of Agriculture, Economic Research Service, "Agricultural Trade," August 20, 2019, https://www.ers.usda.gov/data-products/ag-and-food-statistics-charting-the-essentials/agricultural-trade/.

34. Christine Crudo Blackburn et al., "Commentary: COVID-19 Exposes US Reliance on China for Pharmaceuticals and Medical Devices," CNA, February 19, 2020, https://www.channelnewsasia.com/news/commentary/covid-19-wuhancoronavirus-china-us-medical-medicine-supply-chain-12441770.

35. The Donald Trump administration created the so-called entity list, which prevented US companies from selling to or buying from companies included on it. The companies on the list are "reasonably believed to be involved, or to pose a significant risk of becoming involved, in activities contrary to the national security or foreign policy interests of the United States." See US Department of Commerce, Bureau of Industry and Security, "Addition of Entities to the Entity List, Revision of Entry on the Entity List, and Removal of Entities from the Entity List," *Federal Register* 85, no. 246 (December 22, 2020): 83416–32, https://www.federalregister.gov/documents/2020/12/22/2020-28031/addition-of-entities-to-the-entity-list-revision-of-entry-on-the-entity-list-and-removal-of-entities. As such, the list is more akin to unilateral sanctions than wanton disruption of supply chains. For further details on security of supply, see Elisabeth Braw, "Securing Supplies: How to Prevent Another COVID-19 Breakdown," American Enterprise Institute, June 10, 2021, https://www.aei.org/research-products/report/securing-supplies-how-to-prevent-another-covid-19-breakdown/.

36. Per Henricsson, "300 miljoner européer surfar med Huawei" [300 Million Europeans Surf with Huawei], *Elektroniktidningen*, February 8, 2021, https://etn.se/index.php/67649.

37. Senior executive in the Finnish critical national infrastructure sector, telephone interview.

Chapter IV—Is Sponsorship an Act of Aggression? Use of Licit Means in the Gray Zone

1. TV4, "Zara Larsson om Huawei: 'Inte den smartaste dealen jag gjort'" [Zara Larsson on Huawei: "Not the Smartest Deal I've Done"], August 4, 2020, https://www.tv4.se/nyhetsmorgon/klipp/zara-larsson-om-huawei-inte-den-smartaste-dealen-jag-gjort-13285006.
2. Matilda Ekeblad, "Varför springer du Kinas ärenden, Zara Larsson?" [Why Do You Do China's Bidding, Zara Larsson?], *Expressen*, August 4, 2020, https://www.expressen.se/debatt/varfor-springer-du-kinas-arenden-zara-larsson/.
3. Sean Aday et al., *Hybrid Threats: A Strategic Communications Perspective*, NATO Strategic Communications Centre of Excellence, April 8, 2019, 38, https://stratcomcoe.org/publications/hybrid-threats-a-strategic-communications-perspective/79.
4. For further information, see Pratik Jakhar, "Confucius Institutes: The Growth of China's Controversial Cultural Branch," BBC, September 7, 2019, https://www.bbc.com/news/world-asia-china-49511231.
5. Harry Krejsa, "Under Pressure: The Growing Reach of Chinese Influence Campaigns in Democratic Societies," Center for a New American Security, 2018, 8, https://www.jstor.org/stable/pdf/resrep20457.pdf.
6. Vytautas Leškevičius (former Lithuanian ambassador, NATO), email to the author, March 11, 2021.
7. Leškevičius, email.
8. *Baltic Times*, "Vilnius Court Hearing Dispute over Moscow House Gets SSD Involved in Case," February 27, 2020, https://www.baltictimes.com/vilnius_court_hearing_dispute_over_moscow_house_gets_ssd_involved_in_case/.
9. Jojje Olsson, "Stjärnorna som lånar sig till Kinas regim" [The Stars Who Lend Themselves Out to China's Regime], *Expressen*, April 23, 2019, https://www.expressen.se/kultur/ide/stjarnorna-som-lanar-sig-till-kinas-regim/.
10. BBC, "Football Star Griezmann Severs Ties with Huawei over Uighurs," December 10, 2020, https://www.bbc.co.uk/news/world-europe-55265989.
11. BBC, "Huawei: Uighur Surveillance Fears Lead PR Exec to Quit," December 16, 2020, https://www.bbc.co.uk/news/technology-55332671.
12. PTS, "Four Companies Approved for Participation in the 3.5 GHz and 2.3 GHz Auctions," press release, October 20, 2020, https://www.pts.se/en/news/press-releases/2020/four-companies-approved-for-participation-in-the-3.5-ghz-and-2.3-ghz-auctions/. For more on China's pressure on Sweden, see Chapter VI.
13. This is discussed in Chapter V.
14. Authoritarian countries' mix of popular culture and great-power politics has long posed a dilemma to liberal democracies, perhaps best highlighted by Nazi Germany hosting the 1936 Olympics.
15. See, for example, People's Republic of China, Ministry of Foreign Affairs, "Ambassador Gui Congyou Gives Exclusive Interview with Dagens Industri on Current China-Sweden Relations," December 19, 2019, https://www.fmprc.gov.cn/mfa_eng/wjb_663304/zwjg_665342/zwbd_665378/t1726265.shtml.

16. Jack Denton, "Ericsson Has a Big Problem in China and the Stock Is Falling. Here's What to Know.," *Barron's*, July 16, 2021, https://www.barrons.com/articles/ericsson-has-a-big-problem-in-china-and-the-stock-is-falling-heres-what-to-know-51626442650.

17. Ericsson, "Ericsson Reports Second Quarter Results 2021," press release, July 16, 2021, https://www.ericsson.com/en/press-releases/2021/7/ericsson-reports-second-quarter-results-2021.

18. Score and Change, "Overview of the 2020/2021 Premier League Sponsors," March 15, 2021, https://www.scoreandchange.com/overview-of-the-2020-2021-premier-league-sponsors/.

19. Rod McGuirk, "Huawei Ends Sports Sponsor Deal over Australia 'Trade War,'" Associated Press, August 31, 2020, https://apnews.com/article/virus-outbreak-global-trade-technology-sports-asia-national-rugby-league-8c1e2c5dc3f03be44357c7fb8af4919b.

20. McGuirk, "Huawei Ends Sports Sponsor Deal over Australia 'Trade War.'"

21. Nord Stream 2, "Sports," https://www.nord-stream2.com/responsibility-sponsoring/sports/.

22. Gazprom, "UEFA Champions League," https://www.gazprom-football.com/sponsorship/uefa-champions-league/.

23. Simon Chadwick and Paul Widdop, "Russia Is Flexing Its Sports Sponsorship Muscles," Asia and the Pacific Policy Society, December 20, 2017, https://www.policyforum.net/russia-is-flexing-its-sports-sponsorship-muscles/.

24. For a good overview, see Edoardo Bressanelli et al., *Institutions and Foreign Interferences*, European Parliament, Directorate-General for Internal Policies, Policy Department for Citizens' Rights and Constitutional Affairs, June 2020, https://www.europarl.europa.eu/thinktank/en/document.html?reference=IPOL_STU(2020)655290.

25. Danielle Zurtzleben, "Did Fake News on Facebook Help Elect Trump? Here's What We Know," National Public Radio, April 11, 2018, https://www.npr.org/2018/04/11/601323233/6-facts-we-know-about-fake-news-in-the-2016-election.

26. Dan Sabbagh, Luke Harding, and Andrew Roth, "Russia Report Reveals UK Government Failed to Investigate Kremlin Interference," *Guardian*, July 21, 2020, https://www.theguardian.com/world/2020/jul/21/russia-report-reveals-uk-government-failed-to-address-kremlin-interference-scottish-referendum-brexit.

27. Amar Toor, "France Has a Fake News Problem, but It's Not as Bad as the US," Verge, April 21, 2017, https://www.theverge.com/2017/4/21/15381422/france-fake-news-election-russia-oxford-study.

28. John B. Whitton, "Cold War Propaganda," *American Journal of International Law* 45, no. 1 (January 1951): 151, https://www.cambridge.org/core/journals/american-journal-of-international-law/article/cold-war-propaganda/FD4E98F49AE175545A642926A68B62CB.

29. Samantha Bradshaw, Hannah Bailey, and Philip N. Howard, *Industrialized Disinformation: 2020 Global Inventory of Organized Social Media Manipulation*, University of Oxford, Oxford Internet Institute, Computational Propaganda Project, 2021, 1, https://comprop.oii.ox.ac.uk/wp-content/uploads/sites/127/2021/01/CyberTroop-Report20-FINALv.3.pdf.

30. Bradshaw, Bailey, and Howard, *Industrialized Disinformation*, i.

31. European External Action Service, "EEAS Special Report Update: Short Assessment of Narratives and Disinformation Around the COVID-19 Pandemic (Update December 2020–April 2021)," EUvsDisinfo, April 28, 2021, https://euvsdisinfo.eu/eeas-special-report-update-short-assessment-of-narratives-and-disinformation-around-the-covid-19-pandemic-update-december-2020-april-2021/.

32. BBC, "China Refuses to Apologise to Australia for Fake Soldier Image," December 1, 2020, https://www.bbc.co.uk/news/world-asia-china-55140848.

33. *Report of the Select Committee on Intelligence United States Senate on Russian Active Measures Campaigns and Interference in the 2016 U.S. Election—Volume 5: Counterintelligence Threats and Vulnerabilities*, 116-XX, 116th Cong., 1st sess., https://www.intelligence.senate.gov/sites/default/files/documents/report_volume5.pdf.

34. Robert S. Mueller III, *Report on the Investigation into Russian Interference in the 2016 Presidential Election*, vol. 1, US Department of Justice, March 2019, https://www.justice.gov/storage/report.pdf.

35. *Report of the Select Committee on Intelligence United States Senate on Russian Active Measures Campaigns and Interference in the 2016 U.S. Election—Volume 2: Russia's Use of Social Media with Additional Views*, 116-XX, 116th Cong., 1st sess., 3, https://www.intelligence.senate.gov/sites/default/files/documents/Report_Volume2.pdf.

36. Jānis Garisons (state secretary, Latvia Ministry of Defence), telephone interview with the author, April 11, 2020.

37. Mindaugas Ubartas (CEO, Infobalt), telephone interview with the author, January 13, 2020.

38. Ubartas, telephone interview.

39. BBC, "Hackers Post Fake Stories on Real News Sites 'to Discredit Nato,'" July 30, 2020, https://www.bbc.co.uk/news/technology-53594440.

40. Ojārs Kalniņš (vice chair, Foreign Affairs Committee, Latvian Parliament), telephone interview with the author, June 25, 2020.

41. Mindaugas Ubartas (CEO, Infobalt), telephone interview with the author, February 26, 2020.

42. Diego A. Martin, Jacob N. Shapiro, and Julia G. Ilhardt, "Trends in Online Foreign Influence Efforts," Princeton University, Empirical Studies of Conflict Project, August 5, 2020, 3, https://drive.google.com/file/d/18QIENHZslNIoKvOu72iEjG6RgWL1Dww_/view.

43. Martin, Shapiro, and Ilhardt, "Trends in Online Foreign Influence Efforts," 3.

44. Martin, Shapiro, and Ilhardt, "Trends in Online Foreign Influence Efforts," 8.

45. Quint Forgey and Nahal Toosi, "Biden Delivers a Warning to Putin over Ransomware Attacks," *Politico*, July 9, 2021, https://www.politico.com/news/2021/07/09/biden-putin-ransomware-attack-498956.

46. Paolo Alli (former president, NATO Parliamentary Assembly), telephone interview with the author, June 25, 2020.

47. Elisabeth Braw, "The EU Is Abandoning Italy in Its Hour of Need," *Foreign Policy*, March 14, 2020, https://foreignpolicy.com/2020/03/14/coronavirus-eu-abandoning-italy-china-aid/.

48. Mark Scott, "Chinese Diplomacy Ramps Up Social Media Offensive in COVID-19 Info War," *Politico*, April 29, 2020, https://www.politico.eu/article/china-

disinformation-covid19-coronavirus/.

49. Elisabeth Braw, "Beware of Bad Samaritans," *Foreign Policy*, March 30, 2020, https://foreignpolicy.com/2020/03/30/russia-china-coronavirus-geopolitics/.

50. Francesco De Palo, "W la Cina! Il sondaggio Swg che non ti aspetti. Parla Pier Ferdinando Casini" [Long Live China! The SWG Poll You Didn't Expect. Pier Ferdinando Casini Speaks], *Formiche*, April 7, 2020, https://formiche.net/2020/04/cina-usa-sondaggio-swg-casini-ventura/.

51. Katherine Butler, "Coronavirus: Europeans Say EU Was 'Irrelevant' During Pandemic," *Guardian*, June 24, 2020, https://www.theguardian.com/world/2020/jun/23/europeans-believe-in-more-cohesion-despite-eus-covid-19-failings.

52. Kathy Frankovic, "Are the US Elections Safe from Foreign Interference? Americans Aren't Sure," YouGov, February 28, 2020, https://today.yougov.com/topics/international/articles-reports/2020/02/28/us-elections-foreign-interference-poll.

53. Alexander Nieves, "Poll: 60 Percent of Americans Say Russia Meddled in 2016 Election," *Politico*, July 18, 2018, https://www.politico.com/story/2018/07/18/poll-russia-meddling-election-mueller-investigation-730529.

54. Zack Budryk, "Poll: Just 16 Percent Say Democracy Is Working Well in US," *Hill*, February 8, 2021, https://thehill.com/blogs/blog-briefing-room/news/537790-poll-just-16-percent-say-democracy-is-working-well-in-us.

55. Michael Savage, "49% of Voters Believe Kremlin Interfered in Brexit Referendum," *Guardian*, July 26, 2020, https://www.theguardian.com/world/2020/jul/26/49-of-voters-believe-kremlin-interfered-in-brexit-referendum-russia-report.

56. Oxford Reference, s.v. "Thomas Theorem," https://www.oxfordreference.com/view/10.1093/oi/authority.20110803104247382.

57. Elisabeth Braw, "Putin Seeks to Influence Radical Parties in Bid to Destabilise Europe," *Newsweek*, January 9, 2015, https://www.newsweek.com/2015/01/16/putins-envoys-seek-influence-european-radicals-297769.html.

58. Braw, "Putin Seeks to Influence Radical Parties in Bid to Destabilise Europe."

59. Federiga Bindi, "Why Did Italy Embrace the Belt and Road Initiative?," Carnegie Endowment for International Peace, May 20, 2019, https://carnegieendowment.org/2019/05/20/why-did-italy-embrace-belt-and-road-initiative-pub-79149.

60. Paolo Alli (former president, NATO Parliamentary Assembly), telephone interview with the author, June 22, 2020.

61. Charles Parton, *China-UK Relations: Where to Draw the Border Between Influence and Interference?*, Royal United Services Institute for Defence and Security Studies, February 20, 2019, 13, https://rusi.org/publication/occasional-papers/china-uk-relations-where-draw-border-between-influence-and.

62. Damian Collins (former chairman, Digital, Culture, Media and Sport Committee, UK Parliament), telephone interview with the author, June 7, 2020.

63. UK Parliament, House of Commons, Digital, Culture, Media and Sport Committee, *Disinformation and 'Fake News': Final Report*, February 18, 2019, https://publications.parliament.uk/pa/cm201719/cmselect/cmcumeds/1791/179112.htm.

64. Pekka Toveri (former chief of intelligence, Finnish Defence Forces), telephone interview with the author, April 2, 2020.

65. David Child, "Fighting Fake News: The New Front in the Coronavirus

Battle," Al Jazeera, April 13, 2020, https://www.aljazeera.com/news/2020/04/fighting-fake-news-front-coronavirus-battle-200413164832300.html.

66. Todd C. Frankel, "A Majority of the People Arrested for Capitol Riot Had a History of Financial Trouble," *Washington Post*, February 10, 2021, https://www.washingtonpost.com/business/2021/02/10/capitol-insurrectionists-jenna-ryan-financial-problems/.

67. US National Intelligence Council, *Foreign Threats to the 2020 US Federal Elections*, March 10, 2021, i, https://www.dni.gov/files/ODNI/documents/assessments/ICA-declass-16MAR21.pdf.

68. Bressanelli et al., *Institutions and Foreign Interferences*, 24.

69. Bressanelli et al., *Institutions and Foreign Interferences*, 45–46.

70. Bressanelli et al., *Institutions and Foreign Interferences*, 46.

71. Kalniņš, telephone interview.

72. Niklas Karlsson (vice chair, Committee on Defence, Swedish Parliament), telephone interview with the author, August 11, 2020.

73. Toveri, telephone interview.

74. In Western countries, it is legal for former government officials, legislators, and government ministers to join the boards or staff of foreign-owned companies as long as they have been out of office for a specified period of time. This issue is discussed in Chapter V.

75. Pekka Toveri (former chief of intelligence, Finnish Defence Forces), email to the author, February 8, 2021.

Chapter V—Subversive Economics: When Business as Usual Enters the Gray Zone

1. Although subversive economics also includes currency manipulation—which can, with some difficulty, be described as legal—this chapter focuses on subversive economic actions conducted through businesses.

2. Matthew P. Goodman, "Predatory Economics and the China Challenge," Center for Strategic and International Studies, November 21, 2017, https://www.csis.org/analysis/predatory-economics-and-china-challenge.

3. US Department of Defense, *Summary of the 2018 National Defense Strategy of the United States of America: Sharpening the American Military's Competitive Edge*, 2018, https://dod.defense.gov/Portals/1/Documents/pubs/2018-National-Defense-Strategy-Summary.pdf.

4. John A. C. Conybeare, "Managing International Trade Conflicts: Explanations and Prescription," *Journal of International Affairs* 42, no. 1 (Fall 1988): 75, https://www.jstor.org/stable/24357202?seq=1.

5. Conybeare, "Managing International Trade Conflicts," 75.

6. José Niño, "Tariffs: A History of Repeated Failure," American Institute for Economic Research, March 12, 2018, https://www.aier.org/article/tariffs-a-history-of-repeated-failure/.

7. World Trade Organization, "A Unique Contribution," https://www.wto.org/english/thewto_e/whatis_e/tif_e/disp1_e.htm.

8. James McBride, Andrew Chatzky, and Anshu Siripurapu, "What's Next for the WTO?," Council on Foreign Relations, February 16, 2021, https://www.cfr.org/backgrounder/whats-next-wto.

9. Jennifer Rankin, "EU Opens WTO Case Against Trump's Steel and Aluminium Tariffs," *Guardian*, June 1, 2018, https://www.theguardian.com/business/2018/jun/01/eu-starts-retaliation-against-donald-trumps-steel-and-aluminium-tariffs.

10. Andrea Shalal and David Lawder, "As Trump Takes Aim at EU Trade, European Officials Brace for Fight," Reuters, February 11, 2020, https://www.reuters.com/article/us-usa-trade-europe-analysis-idUSKBN2051AK.

11. McBride, Chatzky, and Siripurapu, "What's Next for the WTO?"

12. Elisabeth Braw, "Don't Let China Steal Your Steel Industry," *Foreign Policy*, May 19, 2020, https://foreignpolicy.com/2020/05/19/dont-let-china-steal-your-steel-industry/.

13. US Department of the Interior, US Geological Survey, *Mineral Commodity Summaries 2019*, February 28, 2019, 112–13, https://prd-wret.s3-us-west-2.amazonaws.com/assets/palladium/production/atoms/files/mcs2019_all.pdf.

14. Hong Kong Means Business, "Belt and Road Gets Indonesian Boost," June 8, 2018, https://hkmb.hktdc.com/en/1X0AE6D5/market-spotlight/Belt-and-Road-Gets-Indonesian-Boost.

15. Nickel Institute, "Stainless Steel: The Role of Nickel," https://www.nickelinstitute.org/about-nickel/stainless-steel.

16. Braw, "Don't Let China Steal Your Steel Industry."

17. Braw, "Don't Let China Steal Your Steel Industry."

18. Ashutosh Pandey, "Double Whammy for EU as China Slaps Anti-Dumping Tax on Stainless Steel," Deutsche Welle, July 22, 2019, https://www.dw.com/en/double-whammy-for-eu-as-china-slaps-anti-dumping-tax-on-stainless-steel/a-49701786.

19. Reuters, "OmniVision to Be Bought by Chinese Investors in $1.9 Billion Deal," Vox, May 1, 2015, https://www.vox.com/2015/5/1/11562246/omnivision-to-be-bought-by-chinese-investors-in-1-9-billion-deal. Shortly before that acquisition, OmniVision Technologies had been acquired by a Chinese consortium. See OmniVision Technologies, "OmniVision to Be Acquired by Hua Capital Management, CITIC Capital and GoldStone Investment for $29.75 per Share in Cash," press release, Cision PR Newswire, April 30, 2015, https://www.prnewswire.com/news-releases/omnivision-to-be-acquired-by-hua-capital-management-citic-capital-and-goldstone-investment-for-2975-per-share-in-cash-300075052.html.

20. Annegret Kramp-Karrenbauer, "Speech by AKK: Presentation of the Steuben Schurz Media Award" (speech, October 26, 2020), https://www.bmvg.de/en/news/speech-akk-presentation-steuben-schurz-media-award-3856630.

21. Birgitta Forsberg, "Staten sålde spjutspetsbolag till Kina—under radarn" [The Government Sold Cutting-Edge Firms to China—Under the Radar], *Svenska Dagbladet*, December 18, 2018, https://www.svd.se/staten-salde-spjutspetsbolag-till-kina--trots-militara-kopplingar.

22. Sebastian Sprenger, "German Government Buys Stake in Defense Supplier Hensoldt," *Defense News*, March 29, 2021, https://www.defensenews.com/industry/2021/03/29/german-government-buys-stake-in-defense-supplier-hensoldt/.

23. Emily Feng, "How China Acquired Mastery of Vital Microchip Technology," *Financial Times*, January 29, 2019, https://www.ft.com/content/7cfb2f82-1ecc-11e9-b126-46fc3ad87c65.

24. For EU member states, any non-EU member state is considered a foreign country, as the EU operates as a single market.

25. UK House of Commons, Defence Committee and Business, Energy and Industrial Strategy Committee, "Oral Evidence: National Security and Investment White Paper," October 30, 2018, http://data.parliament.uk/writtenevidence/committeeevidence.svc/evidencedocument/business-energy-and-industrial-strategy-committee/national-security-and-investment/oral/92148.html.

26. Rob Davies, "David Cameron's UK-China Fund 'Struggling to Attract Investors,'" *Guardian*, May 1, 2019, https://www.theguardian.com/business/2019/may/01/david-cameron-uk-china-fund-struggling-to-attract-investors.

27. Pål Jonson (chairman, Committee on Defence, Swedish Parliament), video interview with the author, July 25, 2020. Sweden passed fast-track legislation in late 2020.

28. NTB, "Russisk oppkjøp av motorfabrikk får Forsvaret til å reagere" [Russian Acquisition of Engine Factory Causes the Norwegian Defense Forces to React], *Forsvarets Forum*, February 22, 2021, https://forsvaretsforum.no/flo-russland-sjoforsvaret/russisk-oppkjop-av-motorfabrikk-far-forsvaret-til-a-reagere/184135.

29. State Council of the People's Republic of China, "'Made in China 2025' Plan Issued," May 19, 2015, http://english.www.gov.cn/policies/latest_releases/2015/05/19/content_281475110703534.htm.

30. Jost Wübbeke et al., *Made in China 2025: The Making of a High-Tech Superpower and Consequences for Industrial Countries*, Mercator Institute for China Studies, December 2016, 11, https://www.chinafile.com/library/reports/made-china-2025.

31. Wübbeke et al., *Made in China 2025*, 6.

32. Wübbeke et al., *Made in China 2025*, 6.

33. Nikolaus Doll and Gerhard Hegmann, "Fall Kuka schürt die Angst vor China" [The Case of Kuka Sturs Up China Fears], *Die Welt*, November 27, 2018, https://www.welt.de/wirtschaft/article184525100/Midea-Fall-Kuka-wird-zum-Suendenfall-fuer-den-Standort-D.html.

34. Mikko Huotari and Agatha Kratz, *Beyond Investment Screening: Expanding Europe's Toolbox to Address Economic Risks from Chinese State Capitalism*, Bertelsmann Stiftung, October 2019, 11–12, https://www.bertelsmann-stiftung.de/fileadmin/files/BSt/Publikationen/GrauePublikationen/DA_Studie_ExpandEurope_2019.pdf.

35. Kirsty Needham, "Special Report: COVID Opens New Doors for China's Gene Giant," Reuters, August 5, 2020, https://www.reuters.com/article/us-health-coronavirus-bgi-specialreport/special-report-covid-opens-new-doors-for-chinas-gene-giant-idUSKCN2511CE.

36. Kirsty Needham, "Exclusive: China Gene Firm Providing Worldwide COVID Tests Worked with Chinese Military," Reuters, January 30, 2021, https://www.reuters.com/article/us-china-genomics-military-exclusive/exclusive-china-gene-firm-providing-worldwide-covid-tests-worked-with-chinese-military-idUSKBN29Z0HA.

37. *60 Minutes*, "China's Push to Control Americans' Health Care Future," CBS, January 31, 2021, https://www.cbsnews.com/news/biodata-dna-china-collection-60-minutes-2021-01-31/.

38. Louise Callaghan, "Coronavirus: Sweden Was Dragging Its Heels, So I Created 'the Monster' to Save Us," *Times*, April 19, 2020, https://www.thetimes.co.uk/article/coronavirus-sweden-was-dragging-its-heels-so-i-created-the-monster-to-save-us-r89lnp3lz.

39. Jerker Hellström, "Kinas politiska prioriteringar: militär-civil fusion och konsekvenser för Sverige" [China's Political Priorities: Military-Civil Fusion and Consequences for Sweden], Swedish Defence Research Agency, January 1, 2019, https://www.foi.se/rapportsammanfattning?reportNo=FOI%20Memo%206649.

40. Peter J. Williamson and Anand Raman, "The Globe: How China Reset Its Global Acquisition Agenda," *Harvard Business Review* (April 2011), https://hbr.org/2011/04/the-globe-how-china-reset-its-global-acquisition-agenda.

41. Agatha Kratz et al., *Chinese FDI in Europe: 2019 Update*, Rhodium Group and Mercator Institute for China Studies, April 2020, 7, https://merics.org/sites/default/files/2020-05/MERICSRhodium%20GroupCOFDIUpdate2020.pdf.

42. While such investments increased significantly around 2015, the year did not form a clear demarcation line in Chinese acquisition strategy; on the contrary, investments and acquisitions had already begun migrating toward high-tech targets. The reason for Western attention to the practice around 2015 is, as Derek Scissors noted, likely connected to the fact that Western countries were becoming key targets around that time. Derek Scissors (senior fellow, American Enterprise Institute), email to the author, January 23, 2021.

43. National Electric Vehicle Sweden, "Evergrande Group New Main Owner in NEVS AB," press release, January 15, 2019, https://www.mynewsdesk.com/nevs-int/pressreleases/evergrande-group-new-main-owner-in-nevs-ab-2946341.

44. Emma Foehringer Merchant, "Maxeon Aims to 'Outgrow the Market' After Splitting from SunPower," Greentech Media, November 19, 2019, https://www.greentechmedia.com/articles/read/maxeon-aims-to-outgrow-the-market-after-splitting-from-sunpower.

45. Peter Clarke, "OmniVision Bought Quietly by China's Will Semiconductor," eeNews Europe, May 24, 2019, https://www.eenewsanalog.com/news/omnivision-bought-quietly-chinas-will-semiconductor.

46. Mark Lewis, "Norway's Salmon Rot as China Takes Revenge for Dissident's Nobel Prize," *Independent*, October 23, 2011, https://www.independent.co.uk/news/world/europe/norway-s-salmon-rot-china-takes-revenge-dissident-s-nobel-prize-2366167.html.

47. Connie Loizos, "Serial Entrepreneurs Rick Marini and Michael Levit Are Selling Companies to China—for a Lot of Money," TechCrunch, November 1, 2016, https://techcrunch.com/2016/11/01/serial-entrepreneurs-rick-marini-and-michael-levit-are-selling-companies-to-china-for-a-lot-of-money/.

48. Jerker Hellström, Oscar Almén, and Johan Englund, *Kinesiska bolagsförvärv i Sverige: en kartläggning* [Chinese Acquisitions in Sweden: A Survey], Swedish Defence Research Agency, November 27, 2019, https://www.foi.se/rest-api/report/

FOI%20Memo%206903#:~:text=Det%20f%C3%B6rsta%20st%C3%B6rre%20kinesiska%20f%C3%B6rv%C3%A4rvet,Filmstaden%20ing%C3%A5r)%20och%20hotellf%C3%B6retaget%20Radisson.

49. American Enterprise Institute and Heritage Foundation, China Global Investment Tracker, July 2021, https://www.aei.org/china-global-investment-tracker/.

50. Nasdaq Helsinki Oy, "National Silicon Industry Group Announces a Voluntary Recommended Public Tender Offer for All Shares and Option Rights in Okmetic OYJ," press release, GlobeNewswire, April 1, 2016, https://www.globenewswire.com/news-release/2016/04/01/824958/0/en/NATIONAL-SILICON-INDUSTRY-GROUP-ANNOUNCES-A-VOLUNTARY-RECOMMENDED-PUBLIC-TENDER-OFFER-FOR-ALL-SHARES-AND-OPTION-RIGHTS-IN-OKMETIC-OYJ.html.

51. Guy Faulconbridge, "UK Urged to Stop China Taking Control of Imagination Tech: Lawmaker," Reuters, April 14, 2020, https://www.reuters.com/article/us-china-britain-imaginationtechnologies-idUSKCN21W1FW.

52. Kane Wu and Prakash Chakravarti, "Chinese Chipmaker Tsinghua Unigroup to Buy France's Linxens for $2.6 Billion: Sources," Reuters, July 25, 2018, https://uk.reuters.com/article/us-linxens-m-a-tsinghua-unigroup/chinese-chipmaker-tsinghua-unigroup-to-buy-frances-linxens-for-2-6-billion-sources-idUKKBN1KF0B1.

53. MP Biomedicals, "Acquisition of MP Biomedicals by Valiant Co. Ltd," press release, March 18, 2016, https://www.mpbio.com/uk/aquisition-of-mp-biomedicals-by-valiant-co.-ltd.

54. Jon Russell, "Alibaba Acquires German Big Data Startup Data Artisans for $103M," TechCrunch, January 8, 2019, https://techcrunch.com/2019/01/08/alibaba-data-artisans/.

55. Romaco Group, "Truking Acquires 75.1 Percent of Romaco Shares," press release, July 13, 2017, https://www.romaco.com/en/press-news-exhibitions/news/archive/2017/details/?tx_news_pi1%5Bnews%5D=307&cHash=612f8d2ab29d30c14be4eeb0218de018.

56. Jones Day, "Takeover of Biotest AG by Chinese Strategic Investor Creat Group," January 2018, https://www.jonesday.com/en/practices/experience/2018/01/takeover-of-biotest-ag-by-chinese-strategic-investor-creat-group.

57. BioSpace, "Shanghai's SARI Pays $359M for Italian Cancer Biopharma NMS," December 29, 2017, https://www.biospace.com/article/releases/sari-announced-today-it-has-entered-into-an-agreement-to-acquire-the-90-percent-interests-in-group-nms-nerviano-medical-sciences/.

58. Datenna, China-EU FDI Radar, "Factsheet: Germany." The fact sheet is available upon request.

59. Kratz et al., *Chinese FDI in Europe*.

60. Mindaugas Ubartas (CEO, Infobalt), telephone interview with the author, March 10, 2020.

61. David Cogman, Paul Gao, and Nick Leung, "Making Sense of Chinese Outbound M&A," McKinsey & Company, July 3, 2017, https://www.mckinsey.com/business-functions/strategy-and-corporate-finance/our-insights/making-sense-of-chinese-outbound-m-and-a.

62. Kratz et al., *Chinese FDI in Europe*, 12.

63. Datenna, China-EU FDI Radar, "Factsheet: Germany."

64. Datenna, "The Acquisition of Ampleon (NXP Power Division)," https://www.datenna.com/the-acquisition-of-the-nxp-power-division/.
65. Samantha Hoffman and Elsa Kania, "Huawei and the Ambiguity of China's Intelligence and Counter-Espionage Laws," Strategist, September 13, 2018, https://www.aspistrategist.org.au/huawei-and-the-ambiguity-of-chinas-intelligence-and-counter-espionage-laws/.
66. Richard McGregor, "How the State Runs Business in China," *Guardian*, July 25, 2019, https://www.theguardian.com/world/2019/jul/25/china-business-xi-jinping-communist-party-state-private-enterprise-huawei.
67. Datenna, "The Acquisition of Linxens," https://www.datenna.com/the-acquisition-of-linxens/.
68. Feng, "How China Acquired Mastery of Vital Microchip Technology."
69. Echo Wang and Carl O'Donnell, "Exclusive: Behind Grindr's Doomed Hookup in China, a Data Misstep and Scramble to Make Up," Reuters, May 22, 2019, https://www.reuters.com/article/us-usa-china-grindr-exclusive-idUSKCN1SS10H.
70. Wang and O'Donnell, "Exclusive: Behind Grindr's Doomed Hookup in China, a Data Misstep and Scramble to Make Up."
71. Wang and O'Donnell, "Exclusive: Behind Grindr's Doomed Hookup in China, a Data Misstep and Scramble to Make Up."
72. Echo Wang, Alexandra Alper, and Chibuike Oguh, "Exclusive: Winning Bidder for Grindr Has Ties to Chinese Owner," Reuters, June 2, 2020, https://www.reuters.com/article/us-grindr-m-a-sanvicente-exclusive/exclusive-winning-bidder-for-grindr-has-ties-to-chinese-owner-idUSKBN2391AI.
73. Feng, "How China Acquired Mastery of Vital Microchip Technology."
74. European Commission, "EU and China Reach Agreement in Principle on Investment," press release, December 30, 2020, https://ec.europa.eu/commission/presscorner/detail/en/IP_20_2541.
75. Intellectual property theft is discussed in Chapter VII.
76. Patrick Wintour, "China Is Breaking Hong Kong Treaty with UK, Says Dominic Raab," *Guardian*, November 12, 2020, https://www.theguardian.com/world/2020/nov/12/china-is-breaking-hong-kong-treaty-with-uk-says-dominic-raab.
77. Alex Joske, *The China Defence Universities Tracker*, Australian Strategic Policy Institute, International Cyber Policy Centre, November 25, 2019, https://www.aspi.org.au/report/china-defence-universities-tracker.
78. Elsa B. Kania and Lorand Laskai, *Myths and Realities of China's Military-Civil Fusion Strategy*, Center for a New American Security, January 2021, 4, https://s3.us-east-1.amazonaws.com/files.cnas.org/documents/Myths-and-Realities-of-China%E2%80%99s-Military-Civil-Fusion-Strategy_FINAL-min.pdf.
79. Lorand Laskai, "Civil-Military Fusion: The Missing Link Between China's Technological and Military Rise," Council on Foreign Relations, January 29, 2018, https://www.cfr.org/blog/civil-military-fusion-missing-link-between-chinas-technological-and-military-rise.
80. Laskai, "Civil-Military Fusion."
81. Emily de La Bruyère and Nathan Picarsic, "How to Beat China's Military-Civil Fusion," *American Interest*, June 22, 2020, https://www.the-american-interest.

com/2020/06/22/how-to-beat-chinas-military-civil-fusion/.

82. White House, "United States Strategic Approach to the People's Republic of China," May 20, 2020, 7, https://china.usembassy-china.org.cn/wp-content/uploads/sites/252/U.S.-Strategic-Approach-to-The-Peoples-Republic-of-China-Report-5.24v1.pdf.

83. RT, "5 Russian Billionaires Who Are Also Sports Clubs Owners," March 5, 2016, https://www.rt.com/sport/334678-russian-billionaires-sports-clubs/.

84. Elisabeth Braw, "Can Putin's Professional Hockey League Challenge the NHL?," *Foreign Policy*, April 1, 2016, https://foreignpolicy.com/2016/04/01/the-troubled-rebirth-of-russian-hockey-kontinental-hockey-league-playoffs/.

85. Deutsche Welle, "North Korean Embassy Hostel in Berlin Locks Its Doors," May 29, 2020, https://www.dw.com/en/north-korean-embassy-hostel-in-berlin-locks-its-doors/a-53622706.

86. Elisabeth Braw, "Back to the Finland Station," *Foreign Affairs*, June 18, 2015, https://www.foreignaffairs.com/articles/finland/2015-06-18/back-finland-station.

87. Rachel Ellehuus, "Strange Birds in the Archipelago: Finland's Legislation on Foreign Real Estate Investment," Center for Strategic and International Studies, April 7, 2020, https://www.csis.org/blogs/kremlin-playbook-spotlight/strange-birds-archipelago-finlands-legislation-foreign-real-estate.

88. UK Intelligence and Security Committee of Parliament, *Russia*, July 21, 2020, 15, https://isc.independent.gov.uk/wp-content/uploads/2021/01/20200721_HC632_CCS001_CCS1019402408-001_ISC_Russia_Report_Web_Accessible.pdf.

89. United Nations Conference on Trade and Development, *Review of Maritime Transport 2018*, 2018, https://unctad.org/webflyer/review-maritime-transport-2018.

90. Reuters, "China, Greece Agree to Push Ahead with COSCO's Piraeus Port Investment," November 11, 2019, https://www.reuters.com/article/us-greece-china/china-greece-agree-to-push-ahead-with-coscos-piraeus-port-investment-idUSKBN1XL1KC.

91. Silvia Amaro, "China Bought Most of Greece's Main Port and Now It Wants to Make It the Biggest in Europe," CNBC, November 15, 2019, https://www.cnbc.com/2019/11/15/china-wants-to-turn-greece-piraeus-port-into-europe-biggest.html.

92. Zeno Saracino, "Porto di Trieste protagonista del Made in Italy in Cina, siglato accord" [Port of Trieste, Protagonist of Made in Italy in China, Accord Signed], Trieste. News, November 6, 2019, https://www.triesteallnews.it/2019/11/06/porto-di-trieste-protagonista-del-made-in-italy-in-cina-siglato-accordo/.

93. Francesca Ghiretti, "Demystifying China's Role in Italy's Port of Trieste," *Diplomat*, October 15, 2020, https://thediplomat.com/2020/10/demystifying-chinas-role-in-italys-port-of-trieste/.

94. Charlie Lyons Jones and Raphael Veit, *Leaping Across the Ocean: The Port Operators Behind China's Naval Expansion*, Australian Strategic Policy Institute, February 2021, 10, https://s3-ap-southeast-2.amazonaws.com/ad-aspi/2021-02/Leaping%20across%20the%20ocean.pdf.

95. Lyons Jones and Veit, *Leaping Across the Ocean*, 11.

96. Ojārs Kalniņš (vice chair, Foreign Affairs Committee, Latvian Parliament), telephone interview with the author, June 25, 2020.

97. ERR, "Estonia and Lithuania to Attend 17+1 Summit on Lower Level,"

February 7, 2021, https://news.err.ee/1608100870/estonia-and-lithuania-to-attend-17-1-summit-on-lower-level.

98. Stuart Lau, "Lithuania Pulls Out of China's '17+1' Bloc in Eastern Europe," *Politico*, May 21, 2021, https://www.politico.eu/article/lithuania-pulls-out-china-17-1-bloc-eastern-central-europe-foreign-minister-gabrielius-landsbergis/.

99. US Department of State, "The Chinese Communist Party's Military-Civil Fusion Policy," https://2017-2021.state.gov/military-civil-fusion//index.html.

100. Gordon Lubold and Dawn Lim, "Trump Bars Americans from Investing in Firms That Help China's Military," *Wall Street Journal*, November 12, 2020, https://www.wsj.com/articles/trump-bars-americans-from-investing-in-firms-that-help-chinas-military-11605209431.

101. European Commission, "EU Foreign Investment Screening Mechanism Becomes Fully Operational," press release, October 9, 2020, https://ec.europa.eu/commission/presscorner/detail/en/ip_20_1867.

102. Government Offices of Sweden, Ministry of Justice, "Ny lag stärker det internationella samarbetet avseende utländska direktinvesteringar" [New Law Strengthens International Cooperation Regarding Foreign Direct Investment], press release, October 1, 2020, https://www.regeringen.se/pressmeddelanden/2020/10/ny-lag-starker-det-internationella-samarbetet-avseende-utlandska-direktinvesteringar/.

103. Alec Burnside et al., "Increased Regulatory Scrutiny of Foreign Direct Investments in the Healthcare Sector," JD Supra, July 29, 2020, https://www.jdsupra.com/legalnews/increased-regulatory-scrutiny-of-42895/.

104. Petr Müller, Adam Přerovský, and Petr Zákoucký, "The Czech Republic's New Act on Foreign Direct Investment," JD Supra, February 12, 2021, https://www.jdsupra.com/legalnews/the-czech-republic-s-new-act-on-foreign-6935584/.

105. UK Department for Business, Energy and Industrial Strategy, "New Powers to Protect UK from Malicious Investment and Strengthen Economic Resilience," press release, November 11, 2020, https://www.gov.uk/government/news/new-powers-to-protect-uk-from-malicious-investment-and-strengthen-economic-resilience.

106. Farhad Jalinous et al., "CFIUS Finalizes New FIRRMA Regulations," White & Case, January 22, 2020, https://www.whitecase.com/publications/alert/cfius-finalizes-new-firrma-regulations.

107. Anahita Thoms and Yeelen Bihn, "Neue Regeln bei der Investitionskontrolle" [New Roles for Investment Scrutiny], Kompass, April 29, 2019, http://www.bakermckenzie-kompass.de/neue-regeln-bei-der-investitionskontrolle-das-aendert-sich-fuer-erwerber-und-zielunternehmen/. The government decision was made in 2018, entering into force in 2019.

108. Pekka Toveri (former chief of intelligence, Finnish Defence Forces), telephone interview with the author, April 1, 2020.

109. Defense Advanced Research Projects Agency, website, https://www.darpa.mil/.

110. In-Q-Tel, website, https://www.iqt.org/.

111. DHVC, "Partnering with Innovators," https://www.dh.vc/.

112. Heather Somerville, "China's Penetration of Silicon Valley Creates Risks for Startups," Reuters, June 28, 2018, https://www.reuters.com/article/us-usa-china-techinvesting-insight/chinas-penetration-of-silicon-valley-creates-risks-for-

startups-idUSKBN1JP08V.

113. Elisabeth Braw, "How China Is Buying Up the West's High-Tech Sector," *Foreign Policy*, December 3, 2020, https://foreignpolicy.com/2020/12/03/how-china-is-buying-up-the-wests-high-tech-sector/.

114. TusPark UK, website, https://www.tuspark.co.uk/.

115. Puhua Capital, website, http://www.puhuacapital.com/.

116. Business Wire, "Perspectum Closes $36M Financing Round Co-Led by Blue Venture Fund and HealthQuest Capital," April 14, 2020, https://www.businesswire.com/news/home/20200414005078/en/Perspectum-Closes-36M-Financing-Round-co-led-by-Blue-Venture-Fund-and-HealthQuest-Capital.

117. FinSMEs, "Inotec AMD Secures £7M in Funding," February 19, 2020, https://www.finsmes.com/2020/02/inotec-amd-secures-7m-in-funding.html.

118. Mark Kleinman, "British Genomics Start-Up Congenica Sells Stake to China's Tencent," Sky News, November 9, 2020, https://news.sky.com/story/british-genomics-start-up-congenica-sells-stake-to-chinas-tencent-12127498.

119. Somerville, "China's Penetration of Silicon Valley Creates Risks for Startups."

120. Sabrina Yuan and Art Dicker, "The Real Impact of CFIUS on Venture Capital in Silicon Valley," China-US Focus, June 27, 2019, https://www.chinausfocus.com/finance-economy/the-real-impact-of-cfius-on-venture-capital-in-silicon-valley.

121. Braw, "How China Is Buying Up the West's High-Tech Sector."

122. The World Council of Churches, officially a nonpolitical body, was such an organization. This is documented in, for example, Elisabeth Braw, *God's Spies: The Stasi's Cold War Espionage Campaign Inside the Church* (Grand Rapids, MI: William B. Eerdmans, 2019).

123. Stuart Lau and Jakob Hanke Vela, "EU Deal Cements China's Advantage in Media War," *Politico*, March 13, 2021, https://www.politico.eu/article/eu-trade-deal-china-media-war-industry-soft-power/.

124. National Council of Applied Economic Research, *Elite Capture and Corruption: Concepts and Definitions*, October 2009, https://www.academia.edu/237917/Elite_Capture_and_Corruption_Concepts_and_Definitions.

125. Deborah Haynes, "China 'Trying to Influence Elite Figures in British Politics', Dossier Claims," Sky News, July 7, 2020, https://news.sky.com/story/china-trying-to-influence-elite-figures-in-british-politics-dossier-claims-12022695.

126. There were some cases of business cooperation. Through sometimes clandestine import-export arrangements with West German firms, for example, East Germany's Bureau of Commercial Coordination earned billions of desperately needed deutsche marks, the West German hard currency.

127. Huawei, "Huawei Technologies UK Appoints Sir Michael Rake to Its Board," press release, April 14, 2020, https://www.huawei.com/uk/news/uk/2020/huawei-technologies-uk-appoints-sir-michael-rake-to-its-board.

128. Leo Kelion, "Huawei 5G Kit Must Be Removed from UK by 2027," BBC, July 14, 2020, https://www.bbc.co.uk/news/technology-53403793. Another high-profile board member, Michael Rake, resigned in February 2021. See Mark Kleinman, "Former BT Chair Rake Quits Huawei UK Board After a Year," Sky News, February 15, 2021, https://news.sky.com/story/former-bt-chair-rake-quits-huawei-uk-board-after-a-year-12218780.

129. Stefan Boscia, "HSBC's Head of Public Affairs Leads Pro-China Lobbying Push," *City A.M.*, June 14, 2020, https://www.cityam.com/hsbcs-head-of-public-affairs-leads-pro-china-lobbying-push/.
130. Nord Stream, "Our Shareholders' Committee," https://www.nord-stream.com/about-us/our-shareholders-committee/.
131. Nord Stream, "Our Shareholders," https://www.nord-stream.com/about-us/our-shareholders/.
132. Vladimir Soldatkin, "Russian Oil Giant Rosneft Appoints Former Austrian Foreign Minister to Its Board," Reuters, June 2, 2021, https://www.reuters.com/business/energy/russian-oil-giant-rosneft-appoints-former-austrian-foreign-minister-its-board-2021-06-02/.
133. Frida Sundkvist, "Reinfeldts miljonavtal med diktaturen Kina" [Reinfeldt's Million Deal with the Dictatorship of China], *Expressen*, February 20, 2020, https://www.expressen.se/nyheter/reinfeldts-miljonavtal-med-diktaturen-kina.
134. See, for example, UK Parliament, "MPs and Second Jobs," https://www.parliament.uk/business/publications/research/key-issues-parliament-2015/parliament-politics/mp-second-jobs/.
135. UK Intelligence and Security Committee of Parliament, *Russia*, 16.
136. Charles Parton, *UK Relations with China*, China Research Group, November 2, 2020, https://chinaresearchgroup.org/values-war.
137. Helen Warrell, "Tory Group in Push for Watchdog to Counter Chinese Interference," *Financial Times*, November 1, 2020, https://www.ft.com/content/4ee90cca-3992-4b06-adob-8463afb959ef.
138. Henry Farrell and Abraham L. Newman, "Choke Points," *Harvard Business Review* (January–February 2020), https://hbr.org/2020/01/choke-points.

Chapter VI—Coercion, Bullying, and Subversion of Civil Society

1. Xi Jinping, "Special Address" (speech, World Economic Forum, Davos Agenda, virtual, January 25, 2021), Xinhua, http://www.xinhuanet.com/english/2021-01/25/c_139696610.htm.
2. Odd Arne Westad, *Restless Empire: China and the World Since 1750* (New York: Random House, 2012), 352.
3. Westad, *Restless Empire*, 352.
4. Helen Davidson, "China Ambassador Makes Veiled Threat to Hong Kong–Based Canadians," *Guardian*, October 16, 2020, https://www.theguardian.com/world/2020/oct/16/china-ambassador-makes-veiled-threat-to-hong-kong-based-canadians.
5. Guy Faulconbridge and Martin Quin Pollard, "China Warns UK: 'Dumping' Huawei Will Cost You," Reuters, July 15, 2020, https://www.reuters.com/article/us-britain-huawei-trump-idUSKCN24G0LF.
6. Ivar Kolstad, "Too Big to Fault? Effects of the 2010 Nobel Peace Prize on Norwegian Exports to China and Foreign Policy" (working paper, Chr. Michelsen Institute, Bergen, Norway, 2016), https://www.cmi.no/publications/5805-too-big-to-fault.

7. BBC, "China Warns UK Not to Offer Citizenship to Hong Kong Residents," October 23, 2020, https://www.bbc.co.uk/news/world-asia-china-54655285.

8. Didi Tang, "China Says It Will No Longer Recognise BNO Passports for Hong Kong Residents," *Times*, January 29, 2021, https://www.thetimes.co.uk/article/china-says-it-will-no-longer-recognise-bno-passports-for-hong-kong-residents-3ghxhj38j.

9. Joyce Huang, "China, Czech Republic at Odds After Czech Officials Visit Taiwan," Voice of America, September 5, 2020, https://www.voanews.com/east-asia-pacific/china-czech-republic-odds-after-czech-officials-visit-taiwan.

10. Raphael Satter and Nick Carey, "China Threatened to Harm Czech Companies over Taiwan Visit: Letter," Reuters, February 19, 2020, https://www.reuters.com/article/us-china-czech-taiwan/china-threatened-to-harm-czech-companies-over-taiwan-visit-letter-idUSKBN20D0G3.

11. Satter and Carey, "China Threatened to Harm Czech Companies over Taiwan Visit."

12. Jari Tanner, "Sweden Summons Chinese Envoy over 'Lightweight Boxer' Remark," Associated Press, January 18, 2020, https://apnews.com/article/c4985d0264489bbc48678f6b7817b2dd.

13. Charles Parton, *China-UK Relations: Where to Draw the Border Between Influence and Interference?*, Royal United Services Institute for Defence and Security Studies, February 2019, 29, https://rusi.org/sites/default/files/20190220_chinese_interference_parton_web.pdf.

14. Parton, *China-UK Relations*, 29.

15. Reuters, "China Says No Excuses for Foreign Officials Meeting Dalai Lama," October 21, 2017, https://www.reuters.com/article/us-china-congress-tibet/china-says-no-excuses-for-foreign-officials-meeting-dalai-lama-idUSKBN1CQ057.

16. Erik Reichborn-Kjennerud and Patrick Cullen, "What Is Hybrid Warfare?," Norwegian Institute of International Affairs, January 2016, 1, https://core.ac.uk/download/pdf/52131503.pdf.

17. Kolstad, "Too Big to Fault? Effects of the 2010 Nobel Peace Prize on Norwegian Exports to China and Foreign Policy."

18. YLE News, "Russia Threatens Response If Finland and Sweden Join NATO," Barents Observer, July 25, 2018, https://thebarentsobserver.com/en/security/2018/07/russia-threatens-response-if-finland-and-sweden-join-nato.

19. Stanislav L. Tkachenko and Antongiulio de' Robertis, "New Diplomacy of the Russian Federation: Coercion and Dialogue," *Rivista di Studi Politici Internazionali* 83, no. 4 (October–December 2016): 553–66, https://www.jstor.org/stable/pdf/44427822.pdf.

20. Toby Helm, "Pressure from Trump Led to 5G Ban, Britain Tells Huawei," *Guardian*, July 18, 2020, https://www.theguardian.com/technology/2020/jul/18/pressure-from-trump-led-to-5g-ban-britain-tells-huawei; and US Mission Brazil, "Fact Sheet: The Clean Network Safeguards America's Assets," US Embassy and Consulates in Brazil, August 13, 2020, https://br.usembassy.gov/the-clean-network-safeguards-americas-assets/.

21. Elizabeth Rosenberg et al., *America's Use of Coercive Economic Statecraft*, Center for a New American Security, December 17, 2020, https://www.cnas.org/publications/reports/americas-use-of-coercive-economic-statecraft.

22. *Encyclopædia Britannica*, s.v. "Marcus Porcius Cato," November 13, 2008, https://www.britannica.com/biography/Marcus-Porcius-Cato-Roman-statesman-234-149-BC#ref215402.
23. George W. Bush, "War Ultimatum Speech" (speech, White House, Washington, DC, March 17, 2003), *Guardian*, https://www.theguardian.com/world/2003/mar/18/usa.iraq.
24. William Burr and Jeffrey P. Kimball, "Nixon, Kissinger, and the Madman Strategy During Vietnam War," National Security Archive, May 29, 2015, https://nsarchive2.gwu.edu/nukevault/ebb517-Nixon-Kissinger-and-the-Madman-Strategy-during-Vietnam-War/.
25. Reuters, "China Urges Sweden to Reverse Its Huawei, ZTE Ban to Avoid Harming Its Companies," October 21, 2020, https://www.reuters.com/article/ctech-us-sweden-huawei-china-idCAKBN2760W1-OCATC.
26. Elisabeth Braw, "How China Took Western Tech Firms Hostage," *Foreign Policy*, January 19, 2021, https://foreignpolicy.com/2021/01/19/china-huawei-western-tech-hostages-national-firms/.
27. *Dagens Nyheter*, "Ericssons vd Börje Ekholm bekräftar påtryckningar från Kina" [Ericsson CEO Börje Ekholm Confirms Pressure from China], January 6, 2021, https://www.dn.se/ekonomi/ericssons-vd-borje-ekholm-bekraftar-patryckningar-fran-kina/.
28. Braw, "How China Took Western Tech Firms Hostage."
29. Shen Weiduo, Chen Qingqing, and Zhao Juecheng, "Exclusive: Sweden Faces 'Last Chance' on Ericsson's Fate in China over 5G Equipment Test Involvement After Huawei Fallout: Source," *Global Times*, May 10, 2021, https://www.globaltimes.cn/page/202105/1223089.shtml.
30. Ericsson, "Ericsson Reports Second Quarter Results 2021," press release, July 16, 2021, https://www.ericsson.com/en/press-releases/2021/7/ericsson-reports-second-quarter-results-2021.
31. Supantha Mukherjee, "Nokia Wins First 5G Radio Contract in China, Ericsson Loses Ground," Reuters, July 19, 2021, https://www.reuters.com/technology/nokia-wins-first-5g-radio-contract-china-2021-07-19/.
32. Ray Le Maistre, "Ericsson Takes a Hit in China Mobile's Latest 5G Contract Awards . . . and Nokia Gets a Slice of the Pie," TelecomTV, July 19, 2021, https://www.telecomtv.com/content/5g/ericsson-takes-a-hit-in-china-mobile-s-latest-5g-contract-awards-and-nokia-gets-a-slice-of-the-pie-41994/.
33. Eva Dou, "China's State Media Outlets Call for Boycott of H&M for Avoiding Xinjiang Cotton," *Washington Post*, March 24, 2021, https://www.washingtonpost.com/world/chinas-state-media-calls-for-boycott-of-handm-for-avoiding-xinjiang-cotton/2021/03/24/41a3ef4a-8d07-11eb-aff6-4f720ca2d479_story.html.
34. Terry Nguyen, "Why Chinese Shoppers Are Boycotting H&M, Nike, and Other Major Retailers," Vox, March 30, 2021, https://www.vox.com/the-goods/2021/3/30/22358750/chinese-shoppers-boycott-h-m-nike.
35. Caroline Vakil, "CEO: 'Nike Is a Brand That Is of China and for China,'" *Hill*, June 26, 2021, https://thehill.com/business-a-lobbying/business-a-lobbying/560386-ceo-nike-is-a-brand-that-is-of-china-and-for-china.
36. Vendela Ögren, "Barcelona stoppar H&M som sponsor" [Barcelona Blocks

H&M as a Sponsor], *Expressen*, July 20, 2021, https://www.expressen.se/sport/fotboll/barcelona-stoppar-hochm-som-sponsor/.

37. Eamon Barrett, "China Is Ramping Up Its Other Big Trade War," *Fortune*, November 4, 2020, https://fortune.com/2020/11/04/china-australia-trade-war/.

38. Saheli Roy Choudhury, "Here's a List of the Australian Exports Hit by Restrictions in China," CNBC, December 17, 2020, https://www.cnbc.com/2020/12/18/australia-china-trade-disputes-in-2020.html.

39. Daniel Hurst, "How Much Is China's Trade War Really Costing Australia?," *Guardian*, October 27, 2020, https://www.theguardian.com/australia-news/2020/oct/28/how-much-is-chinas-trade-war-really-costing-australia.

40. Colin Packham, "Australia Says World Needs to Know Origins of COVID-19," Reuters, September 25, 2020, https://www.reuters.com/article/us-health-coronavirus-australia-china-idUSKCN26H0oT.

41. Joe McDonald, "China Slaps 200% Tax on Australia Wine amid Tensions," Associated Press, November 27, 2020, https://apnews.com/article/beijing-global-trade-australia-coronavirus-pandemic-china-c0f921929c9c53af30da81ddd775ffe9.

42. Reuters, "Taiwan Urges People to Eat More Pineapples After China Bans Imports amid Campaign of 'Intimidation,'" ABC News, February 26, 2021, https://www.abc.net.au/news/2021-02-27/china-bans-taiwan-pineapple-imports-independence-intimidation/13199504.

43. Hurst, "How Much Is China's Trade War Really Costing Australia?"

44. Kolstad, "Too Big to Fault? Effects of the 2010 Nobel Peace Prize on Norwegian Exports to China and Foreign Policy."

45. Kolstad, "Too Big to Fault? Effects of the 2010 Nobel Peace Prize on Norwegian Exports to China and Foreign Policy."

46. David M. Hart, *The Impact of China's Production Surge on Innovation in the Global Solar Photovoltaics Industry*, Information Technology and Innovation Foundation, October 5, 2020, https://itif.org/publications/2020/10/05/impact-chinas-production-surge-innovation-global-solar-photovoltaics.

47. Nevertheless, in June 2021, Australia said it would lodge a World Trade Organization complaint against China over the wine tariffs.

48. Bloomberg, "China Trade Row Has Cost Australia $3 Billion in Lost Exports," January 21, 2021, https://www.bloomberg.com/news/articles/2021-01-21/china-trade-row-has-cost-australia-3-billion-in-lost-exports.

49. BBC, "Canadians Kovrig and Spavor 'Have Not Been Tried' in China," December 10, 2020, https://www.bbc.com/news/world-asia-china-55250144.

50. Gerry Shih, "China Withholds Verdict on Second Canadian Man amid Frigid Ties with U.S. and Canada," *Washington Post*, March 22, 2021, https://www.washingtonpost.com/world/asia_pacific/china-detained-canadians-kovrig-trial/2021/03/22/75feb0b4-8ab3-11eb-a33e-da28941cb9ac_story.html.

51. Sarah Zheng, "Chinese Court Sentences Canadian Michael Spavor to 11 Years After Finding Him Guilty of Spying," *South China Morning Post*, August 11, 2021, https://www.scmp.com/news/china/diplomacy/article/3144606/chinese-court-sentences-canadian-michael-spavor-11-years-after.

52. Leyland Cecco, "Canada Risks Being Outplayed in Feud over Citizens Jailed

in China," *Guardian*, June 23, 2020, https://www.theguardian.com/world/2020/jun/23/canada-risks-being-outplayed-in-feud-over-citizens-jailed-in-china.

53. Lucia Binding, "Nazanin Zaghari-Ratcliffe Jailed for Another Year in Iran over 'Propaganda Activities,'" Sky News, April 27, 2021, https://news.sky.com/story/nazanin-zaghari-ratcliffe-jailed-for-another-year-in-iran-over-propaganda-activities-reports-12287545.

54. Binding, "Nazanin Zaghari-Ratcliffe Jailed for Another Year in Iran over 'Propaganda Activities.'"

55. Patrick Wintour, "MoD and Foreign Office Clash over £400m Debt Linked to Zaghari-Ratcliffe Release," *Guardian*, May 28, 2019, https://www.theguardian.com/uk-news/2019/may/28/mod-and-foreign-office-clash-over-400m-debt-linked-to-zaghari-ratcliffe-release.

56. Jamie Dettmer, "Fears Mount over Fate of 15 Britons and Americans Detained in Iran," Voice of America, January 7, 2020, https://www.voanews.com/middle-east/voa-news-iran/fears-mount-over-fate-15-britons-and-americans-detained-iran.

57. Meghan Keneally, "Otto Warmbier's Family Wins $500M Judgment in Case Against North Korea," ABC News, December 24, 2018, https://abcnews.go.com/International/otto-warmbiers-family-wins-500m-judgment-case-north/story?id=60001728.

58. Anna Fifield, "North Korea Issued $2 Million Bill for Comatose Otto Warmbier's Care," *Washington Post*, April 25, 2019, https://www.washingtonpost.com/world/asia_pacific/north-korea-issued-2-million-bill-for-comatose-otto-warmbiers-care/2019/04/25/0e8022a0-66ad-11e9-a698-2a8f808c9cfb_story.html.

59. Questionable detainment of foreign nationals is not exclusively practiced by authoritarian regimes. The United States' Guantanamo Bay detention camp squarely qualifies as such.

60. Alan Cullison, "Stalin-Era Secret Police Documents Detail Arrest, Execution of Americans," *Los Angeles Times*, November 9, 1997, https://www.latimes.com/archives/la-xpm-1997-nov-09-mn-51910-story.html.

61. Pew Research Center, "International Migrants by Country," January 30, 2019, https://www.pewresearch.org/global/interactives/international-migrants-by-country/.

62. Bernard Gwertzman, "Reagan Lifts Sanctions on Sales for Soviet Pipeline; Reports Accord with Allies," *New York Times*, November 14, 1982, https://www.nytimes.com/1982/11/14/world/reagan-lifts-sanctions-on-sales-for-soviet-pipeline-reports-accord-with-allies.html.

63. Kenneth Katzman, *Iran Sanctions*, Congressional Research Service, April 6, 2021, https://fas.org/sgp/crs/mideast/RS20871.pdf.

64. Timothy Gardner and Daphne Psaledakis, "Exclusive: U.S. Tells European Companies They Face Sanctions Risk on Nord Stream 2 Pipeline," Reuters, January 12, 2021, https://www.reuters.com/article/us-usa-nord-stream-2-sanctions-exclusive/exclusive-u-s-tells-european-companies-they-face-sanctions-risk-on-nord-stream-2-pipeline-idUSKBN29I0CN.

65. Elisabeth Braw, "How Washington's Nord Stream Strategy Could Backfire," *Politico*, January 22, 2021, https://www.politico.eu/article/us-nord-stream-gas-pipeline-sanctions-europe-joe-biden-russia-germany/.

66. Bojan Pancevski and Brett Forrest, "U.S.-German Deal on Russia's Nord Stream 2 Pipeline Expected Soon," *Wall Street Journal*, July 20, 2021, https://www.wsj.com/articles/u-s-german-deal-on-russian-natural-gas-pipeline-expected-soon-11626813466.

67. Mario Damen, "The European Union and Its Trade Partners," European Parliament, October 2020, https://www.europarl.europa.eu/factsheets/en/sheet/160/the-european-union-and-its-trade-partners.

68. Swedish National Defense College, Center for Total Defense and Society's Security, *Förutsättningar för krisberedskap och totalförsvar i Sverige* [*Conditions for Crisis Preparedness and Total Defense in Sweden*], 2019 ed., 150, https://www.fhs.se/centrum-for-totalforsvar-och-samhallets-sakerhet/forskning/publikationer/forutsattningar-for-krisberedskap-och-totalforsvar-i-sverige.html.

69. Deepa Seetharaman, "Automakers Face Paint Shortage After Japan Quake," Reuters, March 25, 2011, https://www.reuters.com/article/us-japan-pigment/automakers-face-paint-shortage-after-japan-quake-idUSTRE72P04B20110326.

70. Norwegian Directorate for Civil Protection, *Risikoanalyse av legemiddelmangel: Krisescenarioer 2018—analyser av alvorlige hendelser som kan ramme Norge* [*Risk Analysis of Food Shortage: Crisis Scenarios 2018—Analyses of Serious Events That Can Affect Norway*], 2018, 4, https://www.dsb.no/globalassets/dokumenter/rapporter/risikoanalyse_av_legemiddelmangel.pdf.

71. Michael Peel and Henry Sanderson, "EU Sounds Alarm on Critical Raw Materials Shortages," *Financial Times*, August 31, 2020, https://www.ft.com/content/8f153358-810e-42b3-a529-a5a6d0f2077f?shareType=nongift.

72. Wayne M. Morrison, "Trade Dispute with China and Rare Earth Elements," Congressional Research Service, June 28, 2019, https://crsreports.congress.gov/product/pdf/IF/IF11259.

73. Kenji Kawase, "China Worries over Rare-Earth Supply Disruption from Myanmar Coup," *Nikkei*, March 4, 2021, https://asia.nikkei.com/Spotlight/Comment/China-worries-over-rare-earth-supply-disruption-from-Myanmar-coup.

74. Nabeel A. Mancheri et al., "Effect of Chinese Policies on Rare Earth Supply Chain Resilience," *Resources, Conservation and Recycling* 142 (March 2019): 101–12, https://www.sciencedirect.com/science/article/pii/S092134491830435X.

75. Sun Yu and Demetri Sevastopulo, "China Targets Rare Earth Export Curbs to Hobble US Defence Industry," *Financial Times*, February 16, 2021, https://www.ft.com/content/d3ed83f4-19bc-4d16-b510-415749c032c1.

76. BBC, "China Resumes Rare Earth Exports to Japan," November 24, 2010, https://www.bbc.co.uk/news/business-11826870.

77. Julian Ryall, "Japan Moves to Secure Rare Earths to Reduce Dependence on China," *South China Morning Post*, August 17, 2020, https://www.scmp.com/week-asia/politics/article/3097672/japan-moves-secure-rare-earths-reduce-dependence-china.

78. Katherin Machalek, "Factsheet: Russia's NGO Laws," Freedom House, https://freedomhouse.org/sites/default/files/Fact%20Sheet_0.pdf.

79. Edoardo Bressanelli et al., *Institutions and Foreign Interferences*, European Parliament, Directorate-General for Internal Policies, Policy Department for Citizens' Rights and Constitutional Affairs, June 2020, 64, https://www.europarl.europa.eu/thinktank/en/document.html?reference=IPOL_STU(2020)655290.

80. FinCEN Files, "FinCEN Files: Tory Donor Lubov Chernukhin Linked to $8m Putin Ally Funding," BBC, September 21, 2020, https://www.bbc.co.uk/news/uk-54228079.

81. UK Intelligence and Security Committee of Parliament, *Russia*, July 21, 2020, 16, https://isc.independent.gov.uk/wp-content/uploads/2021/01/20200721_HC632_CCS001_CCS1019402408-001_ISC_Russia_Report_Web_Accessible.pdf.

82. Scott Neuman and Cory Turner, "Harvard, Yale Accused of Failing to Report Hundreds of Millions in Foreign Donations," National Public Radio, February 13, 2020, https://www.npr.org/2020/02/13/805548681/harvard-yale-targets-of-education-department-probe-into-foreign-donations.

83. Science News, "United States Charges Prominent Harvard Chemist with Failing to Disclose China Ties," *Science*, January 28, 2020, https://www.sciencemag.org/news/2020/01/us-charges-prominent-harvard-chemist-failing-disclose-china-ties.

84. US Senate, Committee on Homeland Security and Governmental Affairs, Permanent Subcommittee on Investigations, *China's Impact on the U.S. Education System*, February 27, 2019, 70, https://www.hsgac.senate.gov/imo/media/doc/PSI%20Report%20China's%20Impact%20on%20the%20US%20Education%20System.pdf.

85. Merlyn Thomas, "University Accepted over £6 Million from Wanted Ukrainian Oligarch," *Varsity*, February 26, 2017, https://www.varsity.co.uk/news/12328.

86. Matt Dathan and Charlie Parker, "Oxford Renames 120-Year-Old Wykeham Professorship for Tencent, Chinese Software Company," *Times*, February 9, 2021, https://www.thetimes.co.uk/article/student-watchdog-vows-to-tackle-national-security-threat-from-university-links-to-china-c7jjzgks9. Tencent is also highlighted in Chapter V.

87. Charlie Parker, Matt Dathan, and Nicola Woolcock, "Tencent: Tech Giant Backed by Beijing Funded Cambridge Research," *Times*, February 10, 2021, https://www.thetimes.co.uk/article/tencent-firm-with-links-to-chinese-state-funds-cambridge-studies-6bp8kmsvs.

88. Tom Simonite, "China Stakes Its Claim to Quantum Supremacy," *Wired*, December 3, 2020, https://www.wired.com/story/china-stakes-claim-quantum-supremacy/.

89. Casey Michel and David Szakonyi, "America's Cultural Institutions Are Quietly Fueled by Russian Corruption," *Foreign Policy*, October 30, 2020, https://foreignpolicy.com/2020/10/30/americas-cultural-institutions-are-quietly-fueled-by-russian-corruption/. Several think tanks, including the American Enterprise Institute, do not accept foreign donations.

90. Michel and Szakonyi, "America's Cultural Institutions Are Quietly Fueled by Russian Corruption."

91. It should be noted, again, that liberal democracies fund a wide range of initiatives in other countries.

92. BBC, "'Hello Greta!': Justin Trudeau 'Fields Call from Pranksters,'" November 24, 2020, https://www.bbc.co.uk/news/world-us-canada-55062943.

93. Caroline Davies, "Prince Harry Thought He Was Talking to Greta Thunberg, Russian Pranksters Claim," *Guardian*, March 12, 2020, https://www.theguardian.com/uk-news/2020/mar/12/prince-harry-thought-he-was-talking-to-greta-thunberg-russian-pranksters-claim.

94. Natasha Bertrand, "Lindsey Graham Dishes on Trump in Hoax Calls with Russians," *Politico*, October 10, 2019, https://www.politico.com/news/2019/10/10/lindsey-graham-trump-hoax-call-043991.

95. Associated Press, "UK Slams Russian Pranksters over Boris Johnson Call," May 24, 2018, https://apnews.com/article/e8a8c6b08f2a43c096eaff52ffd57842.

96. Reuters, "When Virtual Turns Fake: Danish Politicians 'Meet' Belarusian Opposition Figure," October 8, 2020, https://www.reuters.com/article/us-denmark-belarus/when-virtual-turns-fake-danish-politicians-meet-belarusian-opposition-figure-idUSKBN26T2V4.

97. BBC, "'Hello Greta!'"

98. Paolo Alli (former president, NATO Parliamentary Assembly), telephone interview with the author, May 25, 2020.

99. *Report of the Select Committee on Intelligence United States Senate on Russian Active Measures Campaigns and Interference in the 2016 U.S. Election—Volume 5: Counterintelligence Threats and Vulnerabilities*, 116-XX, 116th Cong., 1st sess., https://www.intelligence.senate.gov/sites/default/files/documents/report_volume5.pdf. See, for example, pages 185–86.

100. Christina Wilkie, "Colonial Pipeline Paid $5 Million Ransom One Day After Cyberattack, CEO Tells Senate," CNBC, June 9, 2021, https://www.cnbc.com/2021/06/08/colonial-pipeline-ceo-testifies-on-first-hours-of-ransomware-attack.html.

101. Jacob Bunge, "JBS Paid $11 Million to Resolve Ransomware Attack," *Wall Street Journal*, June 9, 2021, https://www.wsj.com/articles/jbs-paid-11-million-to-resolve-ransomware-attack-11623280781.

102. Lee Mathews, "North Korea–Linked Hackers Are Now Spreading Their Own Ransomware," *Forbes*, July 29, 2020, https://www.forbes.com/sites/leemathews/2020/07/29/north-korea-hackers-lazarus-vhd-ransomware/.

103. This section was primarily written by Áine Josephine Tyrrell.

104. Leila Abboud and Jonathan Eley, "Coronavirus Wreaks Havoc on Luxury and Fashion Groups," *Financial Times*, February 21, 2020, https://www.ft.com/content/85ce-58be-534b-11ea-8841-482eed0038b1.

105. Reuters, "Christian Dior Criticized over China Map, Apologizes, Upholds 'One China,'" October 16, 2019, https://www.reuters.com/article/us-china-dior-politics/christian-dior-criticized-over-china-map-apologizes-upholds-one-china-idUSKBN1WW096.

106. Isabel Togoh, "Luxury Brands Want to Attract Chinese Consumers. But Why Do They Keep Getting It So Wrong?," *Forbes*, August 24, 2019, https://www.forbes.com/sites/isabeltogoh/2019/08/24/luxury-brands-want-to-attract-chinese-consumers-but-why-do-they-keep-getting-it-so-wrong/?sh=25e69f006a6e.

107. Togoh, "Luxury Brands Want to Attract Chinese Consumers."

108. James Tager, *Made in Hollywood, Censored by Beijing: The U.S. Film Industry and Chinese Government Influence*, PEN America, August 5, 2020, 2, https://pen.org/wp-content/uploads/2020/09/Made_in_Hollywood_Censored_by_Beiing_Report_FINAL.pdf.

109. Thomson Reuters Practical Law, s.v. "Publicity Department of the Communist Party of China (CPCPD)," https://uk.practicallaw.thomsonreuters.com/w-015-2153.

110. Tager, *Made in Hollywood, Censored by Beijing*, ii.

111. Edward Wong, "Xi Jinping's News Alert: Chinese Media Must Serve the Party," *New York Times*, February 22, 2016, https://www.nytimes.com/2016/02/23/world/asia/china-media-policy-xi-jinping.html.

112. Ng Yik-tung, Yeung Mak, and Yang Fan, "China's Central Propaganda Department Takes Over Regulation of All Media," Radio Free Asia, March 21, 2018, https://www.rfa.org/english/news/china/china-propaganda-03212018140841.html.

113. Tager, *Made in Hollywood, Censored by Beijing*, iii.

114. Benjamin Lee, "China Continues to Exert Damaging Influence on Hollywood, Report Finds," *Guardian*, August 5, 2020, https://www.theguardian.com/film/2020/aug/05/china-hollywood-films-damaging-impact-report.

115. Tager, *Made in Hollywood, Censored by Beijing*, iv.

116. Tager, *Made in Hollywood, Censored by Beijing*, 3.

117. David S. Cohen, "'Transformers': A Splendidly Patriotic Film, If You Happen to Be Chinese (Opinion)," *Variety*, July 3, 2014, https://variety.com/2014/film/columns/transformers-age-of-extinction-patriotic-for-china-1201257030/.

118. Justin Chang, "'Transformers 4' vs. 'Snowpiercer': What Michael Bay and Bong Joon-ho Have in Common," *Variety*, July 1, 2014, https://variety.com/2014/film/news/transformers-4-vs-snowpiercer-what-michael-bay-and-bong-joon-ho-have-in-common-1201256360/.

119. Amanda Macias and Lauren Feiner, "AG Barr Slams U.S. Tech Companies for Becoming 'Pawns of Chinese Influence,'" CNBC, July 16, 2020, https://www.cnbc.com/2020/07/16/barr-slams-us-tech-for-becoming-pawns-of-chinese-influence.html.

120. Macias and Feiner, "AG Barr Slams U.S. Tech Companies for Becoming 'Pawns of Chinese Influence.'"

121. Amy Qin and Audrey Carlsen, "How China Is Rewriting Its Own Script," *New York Times*, November 18, 2018, https://www.nytimes.com/interactive/2018/11/18/world/asia/china-movies.html.

122. Mark Hughes, "Red Dawn Film Replaces Chinese Villains with North Koreans," *Telegraph*, November 22, 2012, https://www.telegraph.co.uk/culture/film/film-news/9697307/Red-Dawn-film-replaces-Chinese-villains-with-North-Koreans.html.

123. Shelby Rose and Jessie Yeung, "Tencent-Backed 'Top Gun' Cuts Taiwan Flag from Tom Cruise's Jacket," CNN, July 22, 2019, https://www.cnn.com/2019/07/22/media/top-gun-flags-intl-hnk/index.html.

124. Gabrielle Sierra, James Tager, and Aynne Kokas, "China's Starring Role in Hollywood," January 6, 2021, in *Why It Matters*, podcast, https://www.cfr.org/podcasts/chinas-starring-role-hollywood.

125. Marvel Entertainment, "Ancient One," https://www.marvel.com/characters/ancient-one.

126. Edward Wong, "'Doctor Strange' Writer Explains Casting of Tilda Swinton as Tibetan," *New York Times*, April 26, 2016, https://www.nytimes.com/2016/04/27/world/asia/china-doctor-strange-tibet.html.

127. Mark Alan Burger, "That Time Brad Pitt Was Banned from China," *Interview Magazine*, December 20, 2019, https://www.interviewmagazine.com/film/that-time-brad-pitt-was-banned-in-china-seven-years-in-tibet.

128. Patrick Brzeski, "Martin Scorsese's 'The Irishman' Lands Distributor in China,"

Hollywood Reporter, August 16, 2016, https://www.hollywoodreporter.com/news/martin-scorseses-irishman-lands-distributor-china-920231.

129. Ben Cohen, Erich Schwartzel, and James T. Areddy, "NBA Stars Study Hollywood's Playbook in China," *Wall Street Journal*, October 12, 2019, https://www.wsj.com/articles/nba-stars-study-hollywoods-playbook-in-china-11570852864.

130. Vincent Ni, "John Cena 'Very Sorry' for Saying Taiwan Is a Country," *Guardian*, May 25, 2021, https://www.theguardian.com/world/2021/may/26/john-cena-very-sorry-for-saying-taiwan-is-a-country.

131. Tatiana Siegel, "Richard Gere's Studio Exile: Why His Hollywood Career Took an Indie Turn," *Hollywood Reporter*, April 18, 2017, https://www.hollywoodreporter.com/features/richard-geres-studio-exile-why-his-hollywood-career-took-an-indie-turn-992258.

132. American Civil Liberties Union, "Film Censorship: Noteworthy Moments in History," https://www.aclu.org/files/multimedia/censorshiptimeline.html.

133. Tager, *Made in Hollywood, Censored by Beijing*, ii.

134. Nazvi Careem, "NBA No 1 in China Ahead of Premier League and Champions League in Survey of Internet Users; CSL Not in the Top 10," *South China Morning Post*, May 14, 2019, https://www.scmp.com/sport/china/article/3010184/nba-no-1-china-ahead-premier-league-and-champions-league-survey.

135. Jonah Blank, "China Bends Another American Institution to Its Will," *Atlantic*, October 10, 2019, https://www.theatlantic.com/international/archive/2019/10/nba-victim-china-economic-might/599773/.

136. Blank, "China Bends Another American Institution to Its Will."

137. James T. Areddy and Ben Cohen, "NBA vs. China: The Power Struggle Behind the Standoff," *Wall Street Journal*, October 8, 2019, https://www.wsj.com/articles/nba-vs-china-the-power-struggle-behind-the-standoff-11570557671.

138. Laura He, "China Suspends Business Ties with NBA's Houston Rockets over Hong Kong Tweet," CNN, October 7, 2019, https://edition.cnn.com/2019/10/07/business/houston-rockets-nba-china-daryl-morey/index.html.

139. Associated Press, "Rockets' General Manager's Hong Kong Comments Anger China," October 7, 2019, https://apnews.com/article/asia-pacific-tx-state-wire-china-daryl-morey-houston-rockets-0a660e9e10664e31bf6ee359c22058cf.

140. Associated Press, "Rockets Working to Mend Ties with China After Executive's Hong Kong Tweet," NBA Media Ventures, October 7, 2019, https://www.nba.com/news/cba-suspends-cooperation-rockets.

141. Ben Cohen, "The NBA Feels a Backlash in China After a Tweet Supporting Hong Kong," *Wall Street Journal*, October 7, 2019, https://www.wsj.com/articles/the-nba-feels-a-backlash-in-china-after-a-tweet-supporting-hong-kong-11570396236?mod=article_inline.

142. Tilman Fertitta (@TilmanJFertitta), "Listen . . . . @dmorey does NOT speak for the @HoustonRockets. Our presence in Tokyo is all about the promotion of the @NBA internationally and we are NOT a political organization. @espn," Twitter, October 4, 2019, 11:54 p.m., https://twitter.com/TilmanJFertitta/status/1180330287957495809.

143. Lauren Teixeira, "K-Pop's Big China Problem," *Foreign Policy*, July 30, 2019, https://foreignpolicy.com/2019/07/30/k-pops-big-china-problem/.

144. Agence France-Presse, "BTS Worth $5b a Year to South Korean Economy," *Straits Times*, December 20, 2018, https://www.straitstimes.com/lifestyle/entertainment/bts-worth-5b-a-year-to-south-korean-economy.
145. Teixeira, "K-Pop's Big China Problem."
146. Defense Media Activity, DOD News, "US to Deploy THAAD Missile Battery to South Korea," US Army, September 16, 2016, https://www.army.mil/article/171316.
147. Xinhua, "China Voices Resolute Opposition to THAAD Deployment in ROK," People's Daily Online, February 27, 2017, http://en.people.cn/n3/2017/0227/c90000-9183211.html.
148. Teixeira, "K-Pop's Big China Problem."
149. Jack Lau, "Tzuyu of Twice: Beautiful, Youngest Band Member Wants to Be Known for More Than Just Her Good Looks," *South China Morning Post*, April 1, 2020, https://www.scmp.com/lifestyle/entertainment/article/3077878/tzuyu-twice-beautiful-youngest-band-member-wants-be-known.
150. *Korea Times*, "Should K-Pop Stars Be Mindful of Chinese Nationalism, or Risk Cyberbullying and Losing a Profitable Market by Saying What They Think?," *South China Morning Post*, September 16, 2020, https://www.scmp.com/lifestyle/entertainment/article/3101713/should-k-pop-stars-be-mindful-chinese-nationalism-or-risk.
151. BBC, "BTS in Trouble in China over Korean War Comments," October 13, 2020, https://www.bbc.com/news/world-asia-54513408.
152. Arthur Tam, "China Went Up Against a K-Pop Giant—and Lost," *Washington Post*, October 26, 2020, https://www.washingtonpost.com/opinions/2020/10/26/bts-china-spat-korean-war/.
153. BBC, "BTS in Trouble in China over Korean War Comments."

Chapter VII—Gradual Border Alterations and Surreptitious Fishing: Use of Illicit Means

1. Even the *Tallinn Manual on the International Law Applicable to Cyber Warfare*, a set of rules put together by an international group of distinguished legal experts, has failed to reign in government-supported hostilities in cyberspace, primarily because it is not law. See Michael N. Schmitt, ed., *Tallinn Manual on the International Law Applicable to Cyber Warfare* (New York: Cambridge University Press, 2013), https://issuu.com/nato_ccd_coe/docs/tallinnmanual. There is also a subsequent *Tallinn Manual 2.0 on the International Law Applicable to Cyber Operations*.
2. World Economic Forum, "Securing a Common Future in Cyberspace," YouTube, January 24, 2018, https://www.youtube.com/watch?v=Tqe3K3D7TnI.
3. A.P. Moller-Maersk, "Ocean Transport," https://www.maersk.com/transportation-services/ocean-transport.
4. World Economic Forum, "Securing a Common Future in Cyberspace."
5. A.P. Moller-Maersk, "Ocean Transport."
6. Rae Ritchie, "Maersk: Springing Back from a Catastrophic Cyber-Attack," *I—Global Intelligence for Digital Leaders*, August 2019, https://www.i-cio.com/

management/insight/item/maersk-springing-back-from-a-catastrophic-cyber-attack.

7. Andy Greenberg, "The Untold Story of NotPetya, the Most Devastating Cyberattack in History," *Wired*, August 22, 2018, https://www.wired.com/story/notpetya-cyber-attack-ukraine-russia-code-crashed-the-world/.

8. Danny Palmer, "Ransomware: The Key Lesson Maersk Learned from Battling the NotPetya Attack," ZDNet, April 29, 2019, https://www.zdnet.com/article/ransomware-the-key-lesson-maersk-learned-from-battling-the-notpetya-attack/.

9. David Voreacos, Katherine Chiglinsky, and Riley Griffin, "Merck Cyberattack's $1.3 Billion Question: Was It an Act of War?," Bloomberg, December 3, 2019, https://www.bloomberg.com/news/features/2019-12-03/merck-cyberattack-s-1-3-billion-question-was-it-an-act-of-war.

10. World Economic Forum, "Securing a Common Future in Cyberspace."

11. Greenberg, "The Untold Story of NotPetya, the Most Devastating Cyberattack in History."

12. Nadiya Kostyuk, "How Ukraine's Government Has Struggled to Adapt to Russia's Digital Onslaught," Council on Foreign Relations, August 29, 2018, https://www.cfr.org/blog/how-ukraines-government-has-struggled-adapt-russias-digital-onslaught.

13. White House, "Statement from the Press Secretary," press release, February 15, 2018, https://2017-2021-translations.state.gov/2018/02/15/statement-from-the-press-secretary-3/index.html.

14. UK Foreign and Commonwealth Office and National Cyber Security Centre, "Foreign Office Minister Condemns Russia for NotPetya Attacks," February 15, 2018, https://www.gov.uk/government/news/foreign-office-minister-condemns-russia-for-notpetya-attacks.

15. US Department of Justice, Office of Public Affairs, "Six Russian GRU Officers Charged in Connection with Worldwide Deployment of Destructive Malware and Other Disruptive Actions in Cyberspace," press release, October 19, 2020, https://www.justice.gov/opa/pr/six-russian-gru-officers-charged-connection-worldwide-deployment-destructive-malware-and.

16. Patrick Reevell, "What to Know About the Russia-Linked Hackers Accused of Stealing COVID Vaccine Data," ABC News, July 16, 2020, https://abcnews.go.com/International/russia-linked-hackers-accused-stealing-covid-vaccine-data/story?id=71819152.

17. UK National Cyber Security Centre, "Advisory: APT29 Targets COVID-19 Vaccine Development," July 16, 2020, https://www.ncsc.gov.uk/news/advisory-apt29-targets-covid-19-vaccine-development.

18. Chris Inglis (former deputy director, US National Security Agency), telephone interview with the author, April 21, 2020.

19. Ellen Nakashima and Philip Rucker, "U.S. Declares North Korea Carried Out Massive WannaCry Cyberattack," *Washington Post*, December 19, 2017, https://www.washingtonpost.com/world/national-security/us-set-to-declare-north-korea-carried-out-massive-wannacry-cyber-attack/2017/12/18/509deb1c-e446-11e7-a65d-1acofd7f097e_story.html.

20. Erik Brandsma (former CEO, Jämtkraft), telephone interview with the author, November 29, 2019.

21. Inglis, telephone interview.
22. Joe Tidy, "SolarWinds Orion: More US Government Agencies Hacked," BBC, December 15, 2020, https://www.bbc.co.uk/news/technology-55318815.
23. Ellen Nakashima and Craig Timberg, "Russian Government Hackers Are Behind a Broad Espionage Campaign That Has Compromised U.S. Agencies, Including Treasury and Commerce," *Washington Post*, December 14, 2020, https://www.washingtonpost.com/national-security/russian-government-spies-are-behind-a-broad-hacking-campaign-that-has-breached-us-agencies-and-a-top-cyber-firm/2020/12/13/d5a53b88-3d7d-11eb-9453-fc36ba051781_story.html.
24. Krebs on Security, "At Least 30,000 U.S. Organizations Newly Hacked via Holes in Microsoft's Email Software," March 5, 2021, https://krebsonsecurity.com/2021/03/at-least-30000-u-s-organizations-newly-hacked-via-holes-in-microsofts-email-software/.
25. David Smith and Vincent Ni, "US Condemns China for 'Malicious' Cyberattacks, Including Microsoft Hack," *Guardian*, July 20, 2021, https://www.theguardian.com/technology/2021/jul/19/microsoft-exchange-hack-us-biden-administration-china.
26. Andrew Jeong, "North Korean Hackers Are Said to Have Targeted Companies Working on Covid-19 Vaccines," *Wall Street Journal*, December 2, 2020, https://www.wsj.com/articles/north-korean-hackers-are-said-to-have-targeted-companies-working-on-covid-19-vaccines-11606895026.
27. Jeff Stone, "Australia Blames a State Actor for Major Disruptions. China Is Already Denying It.," CyberScoop, June 19, 2020, https://www.cyberscoop.com/australia-cyber-attack-china-trade-scott-morrison/.
28. Lucas Ropek, "France Just Suffered a SolarWinds-Style Cyberattack," Gizmodo, February 16, 2021, https://gizmodo.com/france-just-suffered-a-solarwinds-style-cyberattack-1846276808/amp.
29. Nora Buli, "Norway Says Cyber Attack on Parliament Carried Out from China," Reuters, July 19, 2021, https://www.reuters.com/world/china/norway-says-march-cyber-attack-parliament-carried-out-china-2021-07-19/.
30. David E. Sanger and Emily Schmall, "China Appears to Warn India: Push Too Hard and the Lights Could Go Out," *New York Times*, February 28, 2021, https://www.nytimes.com/2021/02/28/us/politics/china-india-hacking-electricity.html.
31. Sean Lyngaas, "Grid Regulator Warns Utilities of Risk of SolarWinds Backdoor, Asks How Exposed They Are," CyberScoop, December 23, 2020, https://www.cyberscoop.com/nerc-alert-solarwinds-grid-russia/.
32. Inglis, telephone interview.
33. Netherland General Intelligence and Security Service, "Nederlandse veiligheidsbelangen kwetsbaar voor activiteiten andere landen" [Dutch Security Interests Vulnerable to Activities by Other Countries], press release, February 3, 2021, https://www.aivd.nl/actueel/nieuws/2021/02/03/nederlandse-veiligheidsbelangen-kwetsbaar-voor-activiteiten-andere-landen.
34. Recorded Future, Insikt Group, *Chinese State-Sponsored Group 'RedDelta' Targets the Vatican and Catholic Organizations*, July 28, 2020, https://www.recordedfuture.com/reddelta-targets-catholic-organizations/.
35. Reuters, "BASF, Siemens, Henkel, Roche Target of Cyber Attacks," July 24, 2019,

https://www.reuters.com/article/us-germany-cyber/basf-siemens-henkel-roche-target-of-cyber-attacks-idUSKCN1UJ147.

36. Nalani Fraser et al., "APT41: A Dual Espionage and Cyber Crime Operation," FireEye, August 7, 2019, https://www.fireeye.com/blog/threat-research/2019/08/apt41-dual-espionage-and-cyber-crime-operation.html.

37. For recent cases, see, for example, Zak Doffman, "Forget Russia—Iranian Hackers Behind Malicious New Cyber Attacks, Warns New Report," *Forbes*, November 12, 2020, https://www.forbes.com/sites/zakdoffman/2020/11/12/forget-russia-iranian-hackers-behind-malicuous-new-cyber-attacks-warns-new-report/?sh=605a78bb309a.

38. US Department of Justice, Office of Public Affairs, "Three North Korean Military Hackers Indicted in Wide-Ranging Scheme to Commit Cyberattacks and Financial Crimes Across the Globe," press release, February 17, 2021, https://www.justice.gov/opa/pr/three-north-korean-military-hackers-indicted-wide-ranging-scheme-commit-cyber-attacks-and.

39. US Department of Justice, Office of Public Affairs, "Three North Korean Military Hackers Indicted in Wide-Ranging Scheme to Commit Cyberattacks and Financial Crimes Across the Globe."

40. David Omand, "The Future of Deterrence" (eighth Sir Michael Quinlan Memorial Lecture, King's College London, London, January 21, 2020), https://thestrandgroup.kcl.ac.uk/event/the-eighth-sir-michael-quinlan-memorial-lecture/.

41. Hiscox, *Hiscox Cyber Readiness Report* 2020, https://www.hiscox.co.uk/sites/uk/files/documents/2020-06/Hiscox_Cyber_Readiness_Report_2020_UK.PDF.

42. Samu Konttinen has since become CEO of Viria Group.

43. Samu Konttinen (former CEO, F-Secure Corporation), telephone interview with the author, June 3, 2020.

44. Harriet Moynihan, *The Application of International Law to State Cyberattacks: Sovereignty and Non-Intervention*, Chatham House, Royal Institute of International Affairs, December 2019, 2, https://www.chathamhouse.org/sites/default/files/publications/research/2019-11-29-Intl-Law-Cyberattacks.pdf.

45. Pekka Toveri (former chief of intelligence, Finnish Defence Forces), telephone interview with the author, April 2, 2020.

46. Toveri, telephone interview.

47. Daniel I. Wolf, "Reasons for Communicating Clearly with Your Insurer Regarding the Scope of Coverage Before Purchasing Cyber Insurance," *National Law Review* 10, no. 155 (June 3, 2020), https://www.natlawreview.com/article/reasons-communicating-clearly-your-insurer-regarding-scope-coverage-purchasing-cyber.

48. Gary D. Brown, *State Cyberspace Operations: Proposing a Cyber Response Framework*, Royal United Services Institute for Defence and Security Studies, September 2020, 3, https://rusi.org/sites/default/files/rusi_pub_184_op_strategic_military_operations_final_web_version.pdf.

49. Senior executive of a leading European telecoms provider, telephone interview with the author, March 10, 2020. The executive spoke on the condition of anonymity, to be able to speak freely.

50. Doffman, "Forget Russia—Iranian Hackers Behind Malicious New Cyber Attacks, Warns New Report."

51. Dan Sabbagh, "Insurers 'Funding Organised Crime' by Paying Ransomware Claims," *Guardian*, January 24, 2021, https://www.theguardian.com/technology/2021/jan/24/insurers-funding-organised-by-paying-ransomware-claims.

52. Quint Forgey and Nahal Toosi, "Biden Delivers a Warning to Putin over Ransomware Attacks," *Politico*, July 9, 2021, https://www.politico.com/news/2021/07/09/biden-putin-ransomware-attack-498956.

53. Ed Wilson (retired major general, US Air Force), telephone interview with the author, April 21, 2020.

54. Catalin Cimpanu, "Ransomware Attack Cripples Vancouver Public Transportation Agency," ZDNet, December 4, 2020, https://www.zdnet.com/article/ransomware-attack-cripples-vancouver-public-transportation-agency/.

55. Ron Shinkman, "Rising Hospital Ransomware Attacks Could Endanger Patients, Hit Bottom Lines Hard, Moody's Says," Healthcare Dive, May 27, 2021, https://www.healthcaredive.com/news/rising-hospital-ransomware-attacks-could-endanger-patients-hit-bottom-line/600896/.

56. Lawrence Abrams, "Dutch Supermarkets Run Out of Cheese After Ransomware Attack," BleepingComputer, April 12, 2021, https://www.bleepingcomputer.com/news/security/dutch-supermarkets-run-out-of-cheese-after-ransomware-attack/.

57. BBC, "Ransomware Halts Classes for 115,000 Baltimore Pupils," November 30, 2020, https://www.bbc.co.uk/news/technology-55129564.

58. Lily Hay Newman, "Atlanta Spent $2.6M to Recover from a $52,000 Ransomware Scare," *Wired*, April 23, 2018, https://www.wired.com/story/atlanta-spent-26m-recover-from-ransomware-scare/.

59. Konttinen, telephone interview.

60. Konttinen, telephone interview.

61. Dustin Volz and Robert McMillan, "Suspected Russian Hack Said to Have Gone Undetected for Months," *Wall Street Journal*, December 15, 2020, https://www.wsj.com/articles/suspected-russian-hack-said-to-have-gone-undetected-for-months-11607974376.

62. Konttinen, telephone interview.

63. Kevin Brown (managing director, BT Security), telephone interview with the author, March 6, 2020.

64. Brad Smith, "A Moment of Reckoning: The Need for a Strong and Global Cybersecurity Response," Microsoft, December 17, 2020, https://blogs.microsoft.com/on-the-issues/2020/12/17/cyberattacks-cybersecurity-solarwinds-fireeye/.

65. Smith, "A Moment of Reckoning."

66. Craig Timberg et al., "On the List: Ten Prime Ministers, Three Presidents and a King," *Washington Post*, July 20, 2021, https://www.washingtonpost.com/world/2021/07/20/heads-of-state-pegasus-spyware/.

67. Konttinen, telephone interview.

68. Elisabeth Braw, "The Temptation for Cyber Attackers to Become Short-Sellers," *Financial Times*, January 5, 2021, https://www.ft.com/content/59949478-65e1-45bd-8c24-873c241cd3f1.

69. In its final report, the US Cyberspace Solarium Commission proposes that the US and its allies promote responsible behavior in cyberspace, deny benefits to aggressors

(i.e., improve resilience), and impose more costs on attackers. See US Cyberspace Solarium Commission, *Our Strategy*, March 2020, https://www.solarium.gov/report. This book outlines new deterrence options in Chapters X and XI.

70. US Office of the Secretary of State, Policy Planning Staff, *The Elements of the China Challenge*, December 2020, 10, https://www.state.gov/wp-content/uploads/2020/11/20-02832-Elements-of-China-Challenge-508.pdf.

71. Senior executive in the Finnish critical national infrastructure sector, telephone interview with the author, February 21, 2020.

72. Eben Kaplan, "The Uneasy U.S.-Chinese Trade Relationship," Council on Foreign Relations, April 19, 2006, https://www.cfr.org/backgrounder/uneasy-us-chinese-trade-relationship.

73. US Commission on the Theft of American Intellectual Property, *The IP Commission Report*, National Bureau of Asian Research, May 2013, 10, https://www.nbr.org/wp-content/uploads/pdfs/publications/IP_Commission_Report.pdf.

74. US Commission on the Theft of American Intellectual Property, *The IP Commission Report*, 3.

75. US Commission on the Theft of American Intellectual Property, *The IP Commission Report*, 2.

76. Wilson, telephone interview.

77. Frank Ertesvåg, "PST-sjef for kontra-etterretning: En del naivitet i utdanningssektoren" [PST-Head of Counterintelligence: Some Naivete in the Educational Sector], *Verdens Gang*, February 4, 2021, https://www.vg.no/nyheter/innenriks/i/KyPgKM/pst-sjef-for-kontra-etterretning-en-del-naivitet-i-utdanningssektoren.

78. White House, Office of the Press Secretary, "Fact Sheet: President Xi Jinping's State Visit to the United States," press release, September 25, 2015, https://obamawhitehouse.archives.gov/the-press-office/2015/09/25/fact-sheet-president-xi-jinpings-state-visit-united-states.

79. Daniel Paltiel, "G20 Communiqué Agrees on Language to Not Conduct Cyber Economic Espionage," Center for Strategic and International Studies, November 16, 2015, https://www.csis.org/blogs/strategic-technologies-blog/g20-communiqu%C3%A9-agrees-language-not-conduct-cyber-economic.

80. Adam Segal et al., *Hacking for Ca$h*, Australian Strategic Policy Institute, International Cyber Policy Centre, September 25, 2018, 8, https://www.aspi.org.au/report/hacking-cash.

81. Jack Stubbs, Joseph Menn, and Christopher Bing, "Inside the West's Failed Fight Against China's 'Cloud Hopper' Hackers," Reuters, June 26, 2019, https://www.reuters.com/investigates/special-report/china-cyber-cloudhopper/.

82. Reuters, "Chinese Employees Stole Corporate Secrets from Dutch Semiconductor Maker, Newspaper Reports," *Japan Times*, April 11, 2019, https://www.japantimes.co.jp/news/2019/04/11/business/tech/chinese-employees-stole-corporate-secrets-dutch-semiconductor-maker-newspaper-reports/.

83. Reuters, "U.S. Court Rules in Favor of Dutch ASML in IP Theft Case Against Xtal," May 4, 2019, https://www.reuters.com/article/us-asml-holding-xtal-court/u-s-court-rules-in-favor-of-dutch-asml-in-ip-theft-case-against-xtal-idUSKCN1SA0A3.

84. Paul Wiseman, "In Trade Wars of 200 Years Ago, the Pirates Were

Americans," Associated Press, March 28, 2019, https://apnews.com/article/b40414d22f2248428ce11ff36b88dc53.

85. Wiseman, "In Trade Wars of 200 Years Ago, the Pirates Were Americans."

86. *United States of America v. Huawei Device Co. Ltd.*, No. CR19-010 (RSM), 12 (W.D. Wash. January 16, 2019), https://www.justice.gov/opa/press-release/file/1124996/download.

87. *United States of America v. Huawei Device Co. Ltd.*, 14.

88. Catalin Cimpanu, "FBI Is Investigating More Than 1,000 Cases of Chinese Theft of US Technology," ZDNet, February 9, 2020, https://www.zdnet.com/article/fbi-is-investigating-more-than-1000-cases-of-chinese-theft-of-us-technology/.

89. US Senate, Committee on Homeland Security and Governmental Affairs, Permanent Subcommittee on Investigations, *Threats to the U.S. Research Enterprise: China's Talent Recruitment Plans*, November 18, 2019, 1, https://www.hsgac.senate.gov/imo/media/doc/2019-11-18%20PSI%20Staff%20Report%20-%20China's%20Talent%20Recruitment%20Plans.pdf.

90. Netherland General Intelligence and Security Service, "Nederlandse veiligheidsbelangen kwetsbaar voor activiteiten andere landen" [Dutch Security Interests Vulnerable to Activities by Other Countries].

91. European Commission, *Report on the Protection and Enforcement of Intellectual Property Rights in Third Countries*, April 27, 2021, 4, https://trade.ec.europa.eu/doclib/docs/2021/april/tradoc_159553.pdf.

92. European Commission, *Report on the Protection and Enforcement of Intellectual Property Rights in Third Countries*, 5.

93. European Commission, *Report on the Protection and Enforcement of Intellectual Property Rights in Third Countries*, 6.

94. European Commission, *Report on the Protection and Enforcement of Intellectual Property Rights in Third Countries*, 6.

95. *United States of America v. Zhang Zhang-Gui*, No. 13CR3132-H (S.D. Cal. October 25, 2018), https://www.justice.gov/opa/press-release/file/1106491/download.

96. Robert Hackett, "Chinese Hacking: The Plane Made from Stolen Tech?—Cyber Saturday," *Fortune*, October 19, 2019, https://fortune.com/2019/10/19/chinese-hacking-plane-stolen-tech-cyber-saturday/.

97. US Department of Justice, Office of Public Affairs, "Two Chinese Hackers Working with the Ministry of State Security Charged with Global Computer Intrusion Campaign Targeting Intellectual Property and Confidential Business Information, Including COVID-19 Research," press release, July 21, 2020, https://www.justice.gov/opa/pr/two-chinese-hackers-working-ministry-state-security-charged-global-computer-intrusion.

98. US Department of Justice, Office of Public Affairs, "Researcher Pleaded Guilty to Conspiring to Steal Scientific Trade Secrets from Ohio Children's Hospital to Sell in China," press release, July 30, 2020, https://www.justice.gov/opa/pr/researcher-pleaded-guilty-conspiring-steal-scientific-trade-secrets-ohio-children-s-hospital.

99. Odd Arne Westad, *Restless Empire: China and the World Since 1750* (London: Vintage, 2013), 41.

100. Daniel Rechtschaffen, "How China's Legal System Enables Intellectual Property Theft," *Diplomat*, November 11, 2020, https://thediplomat.com/2020/11/how-chinas-

legal-system-enables-intellectual-property-theft/.

101. European Commission, *Report on the Protection and Enforcement of Intellectual Property Rights in Third Countries*, 11.

102. Casey Tonkin, "China Hacking Australia 'Not Remotely Surprising,'" Information Age, August 21, 2020, https://ia.acs.org.au/article/2020/china-hacking-australia-not-remotely-surprising.html.

103. Xi Jinping, "Special Address" (speech, World Economic Forum, Davos Agenda, virtual, January 25, 2021), Xinhua, http://www.xinhuanet.com/english/2021-01/25/c_139696610.htm.

104. Theresa May, "Statement on the Salisbury Investigation" (speech, UK Parliament, London, September 5, 2018), https://www.gov.uk/government/speeches/pm-statement-on-the-salisbury-investigation-5-september-2018.

105. Lyse Doucet, "Qasem Soleimani: US Kills Top Iranian General in Baghdad Air Strike," BBC, January 3, 2020, https://www.bbc.co.uk/news/world-middle-east-50979463.

106. Madeleine G. Kalb, "The C.I.A. and Lumumba," *New York Times*, August 2, 1981, https://www.nytimes.com/1981/08/02/magazine/the-cia-and-lumumba.html.

107. Ana Swanson and Edward Wong, "Report Points to Microwave 'Attack' as Likely Source of Mystery Illnesses That Hit Diplomats and Spies," *New York Times*, March 4, 2021, https://www.nytimes.com/2020/12/05/business/economy/havana-syndrome-microwave-attack.html.

108. US Standing Committee to Advise the Department of State on Unexplained Health Effects on US Government Employees and Their Families at Overseas Embassies, *An Assessment of Illness in U.S. Government Employees and Their Families at Overseas Embassies* (Washington, DC: National Academies Press, 2020), https://www.nap.edu/catalog/25889/an-assessment-of-illness-in-us-government-employees-and-their-families-at-overseas-embassies.

109. Lara Seligman, Andrew Desiderio, and Erin Banco, "U.S. Probing Suspected Directed-Energy Attack on Government Personnel in Miami," *Politico*, April 29, 2021, https://www.politico.com/amp/news/2021/04/29/directed-energy-attack-probe-485086.

110. Olivia Gazis, "U.S. Conducting Intelligence Review of 'Havana Syndrome' Incidents, as Suspected CIA Cases Rise," CBS News, May 6, 2021, https://www.cbsnews.com/news/energy-attack-intelligence-review-cia/.

111. Adam Entous, "Vienna Is the New Havana Syndrome Hotspot," *New Yorker*, July 16, 2021, https://www.newyorker.com/news/news-desk/vienna-is-the-new-havana-syndrome-hotspot.

112. Tara Davenport, "Island-Building in the South China Sea: Legality and Limits," *Asian Journal of International Law* 8, no. 1 (January 2018): 76, https://www.cambridge.org/core/journals/asian-journal-of-international-law/article/abs/islandbuilding-in-the-south-china-sea-legality-and-limits/442BCFEF6A8AA7E75B1AEA5ADCFB139C.

113. Ethan Meick, *China's First Airstrip in the Spratly Islands Likely at Fiery Cross Reef*, US-China Economic and Security Review Commission, December 18, 2014, 1, https://www.uscc.gov/sites/default/files/Research/Staff%20Report_China's%20First%20Airstrip%20in%20the%20Spratly%20Islands%20Likely%20at%20Fiery%20Cross%20Reef_12%2018%202014.pdf.

114. BBC, "South China Sea: What's China's Plan for Its 'Great Wall of Sand'?," July 14, 2020, https://www.bbc.co.uk/news/world-asia-53344449.
115. Davenport, "Island-Building in the South China Sea," 77.
116. Davenport, "Island-Building in the South China Sea," 76.
117. Bill Hayton, "Two Years On, South China Sea Ruling Remains a Battleground for the Rules-Based Order," Chatham House, Royal Institute of International Affairs, July 11, 2018, https://www.chathamhouse.org/2018/07/two-years-south-china-sea-ruling-remains-battleground-rules-based-order.
118. Hayton, "Two Years On, South China Sea Ruling Remains a Battleground for the Rules-Based Order."
119. Mark Montgomery (retired rear admiral, US Navy), telephone interview with the author, April 21, 2020.
120. Erik Reichborn-Kjennerud and Patrick Cullen, "What Is Hybrid Warfare?," Norwegian Institute of International Affairs, January 2016, https://core.ac.uk/download/pdf/52131503.pdf.
121. Edward Boyle, "Borderization in Georgia: Sovereignty Materialized," *Eurasia Border Review*, forthcoming, 2, https://papers.ssrn.com/sol3/papers.cfm?abstract_id=3274407.
122. Robert Barnett, "China Is Building Entire Villages in Another Country's Territory," *Foreign Policy*, May 7, 2021, https://foreignpolicy.com/2021/05/07/china-bhutan-border-villages-security-forces/.
123. Tony Long et al., "Approaches to Combatting Illegal, Unreported and Unregulated Fishing," *Nature Food* 1 (July 2020): 389–91, https://www.nature.com/articles/s43016-020-0121-y.
124. Ryan C. Berg, "China's Hunger for Seafood Is Now Latin America's Problem," *Foreign Policy*, October 30, 2020, https://foreignpolicy.com/2020/10/30/chinas-hunger-for-seafood-is-now-latin-americas-problem/.
125. Yuri Garcia, "Ecuador Says Some Chinese Vessels Near Galapagos Have Cut Communications Systems," Reuters, August 18, 2020, https://www.reuters.com/article/us-ecuador-environment-china/ecuador-says-some-chinese-vessels-near-galapagos-have-cut-communications-systems-idUSKCN25E2XI.
126. Berg, "China's Hunger for Seafood Is Now Latin America's Problem."
127. Sofia Tomacruz, "Timeline: China's Vessels Swarming Julian Felipe Reef, West PH Sea," Rappler, April 30, 2021, https://www.rappler.com/newsbreak/iq/timeline-china-vessels-julian-felipe-reef-west-philippine-sea-2021.
128. CNN Philippines, "Video Shows over a Hundred Chinese Ships Around Julian Felipe Reef," YouTube, March 26, 2021, https://www.youtube.com/watch?v=RI7GbWmM9EI.
129. Ian Urbina, "How China's Expanding Fishing Fleet Is Depleting the World's Oceans," Yale Environment 360, August 17, 2020, https://e360.yale.edu/features/how-chinas-expanding-fishing-fleet-is-depleting-worlds-oceans.
130. Reuters, "France, South Pacific Nations to Combat 'Predatory' Fishing as China Extends Reach," CNN, July 20, 2021, https://edition.cnn.com/2021/07/20/asia/france-south-pacific-fishing-china-intl-hnk/index.html.
131. Africa Times, "NGO Says Iranian Boats Are Illegally Fishing in Somali Waters,"

June 30, 2020, https://africatimes.com/2020/06/30/ngo-says-iranian-boats-are-illegally-fishing-in-somali-waters/.

132. Derek Grossman and Logan Ma, "A Short History of China's Fishing Militia and What It May Tell Us," RAND Corporation, April 6, 2020, https://www.rand.org/blog/2020/04/a-short-history-of-chinas-fishing-militia-and-what.html.

133. Ben Bordelon, "Boost Coast Guard Fleet for Pacific Partnerships," Breaking Defense, December 14, 2020, https://breakingdefense.com/2020/12/boost-coast-guard-fleet-for-pacific-partnerships/.

134. Michelle Nichols, "U.S. and China Spar over Racism at United Nations," Reuters, March 19, 2021, https://www.reuters.com/article/us-usa-china-un/u-s-and-china-spar-over-racism-at-united-nations-idUSKBN2BB29E.

135. Reuters, "Taiwan Says Has Spent Almost $900 Million Scrambling Against China This Year," October 7, 2020, https://uk.reuters.com/article/us-taiwan-security/taiwan-says-has-spent-almost-900-million-scrambling-against-china-this-year-idUSKBN26S0K6.

136. Ben Blanchard, "Taiwan Reports Large Incursion by Chinese Air Force," Reuters, January 23, 2021, https://www.reuters.com/article/us-taiwan-china-security/taiwan-reports-large-incursion-by-chinese-air-force-idUSKBN29S0BK.

137. Figures provided by the office of the NATO spokesperson.

138. North Atlantic Treaty Organization, "NATO Intercepts Hundreds of Russian Military Jets in 2020," December 28, 2020, https://www.nato.int/cps/en/natohq/news_180551.htm.

139. North Atlantic Treaty Organization, "NATO Intercepts Hundreds of Russian Military Jets in 2020."

140. BBC, "Turkey's Downing of Russian Warplane—What We Know," December 1, 2015, https://www.bbc.com/news/world-middle-east-34912581.

141. Riho Terras (former chief of defense, Estonian Defence Forces), video interview with the author, January 19, 2021.

142. Woon Wei Jong, "Over 100 Mainland Chinese Sand Dredgers 'Surround' Matsu Islands," ThinkChina, October 27, 2020, https://www.thinkchina.sg/over-100-mainland-chinese-sand-dredgers-surround-matsu-islands.

143. Yimou Lee, "China's Latest Weapon Against Taiwan: The Sand Dredger," Reuters, February 5, 2021, https://www.reuters.com/article/us-taiwan-china-security/chinas-latest-weapon-against-taiwan-the-sand-dredger-idUSKBN2A51EJ.

144. Elisabeth Braw, "Balts Say Russian Navy Bullying Undersea Cable Crews," Radio Free Europe/Radio Liberty, May 5, 2015, https://www.rferl.org/a/russia-bullying-undersea-baltic-cable/26996165.html.

145. Jonathan Marcus, "Stena Impero: Seized British Tanker Leaves Iran's Waters," BBC, September 27, 2019, https://www.bbc.com/news/world-middle-east-49849718.

146. UN Conference on Trade and Development, *Review of Maritime Transport 2019* (New York: United Nations Publications, 2019), https://www.un-ilibrary.org/content/books/9789210043021.

147. International Chamber of Shipping, "Shipping and World Trade: Global Supply and Demand for Seafarers," https://www.ics-shipping.org/shipping-fact/shipping-and-world-trade-global-supply-and-demand-for-seafarers/.

148. Braw, "Balts Say Russian Navy Bullying Undersea Cable Crews."

Chapter VIII—Producing Fear in the Enemy's Mind: Adapting Cold War Deterrence for Gray-Zone Aggression

1. Westminster Abbey choirboy, in discussion with the author, July 7, 2020.
2. Acc3ssd, "Dr. Strangelove: Deterrence," YouTube, May 28, 2009, https://www.youtube.com/watch?v=nSRtgqqixUY.
3. US Department of Defense, Office of the Chairman of the Joint Chiefs of Staff, *DOD Dictionary of Military and Associated Terms*, December 2020, https://www.jcs.mil/Portals/36/Documents/Doctrine/pubs/dictionary.pdf.
4. UK Ministry of Defence, Development, Concepts and Doctrine Centre, *Deterrence: The Defence Contribution, Joint Doctrine Note 1/19*, February 2019, 23, https://assets.publishing.service.gov.uk/government/uploads/system/uploads/attachment_data/file/860499/20190204-doctrine_uk_deterrence_jdn_1_19.pdf.
5. UK Ministry of Defence, Development, Concepts and Doctrine Centre, *Deterrence*, 25.
6. See Elisabeth Braw, "The SolarWinds Hack Doesn't Demand a Violent Response," Defense One, December 31, 2020, https://www.defenseone.com/ideas/2020/12/solarwinds-hack-doesnt-demand-violent-response/171105/.
7. UK Ministry of Defence, Development, Concepts and Doctrine Centre, *Deterrence*, 26.
8. UK Ministry of Defence, Development, Concepts and Doctrine Centre, *Deterrence*, 16.
9. Riho Terras (former chief of defense, Estonian Defence Forces), telephone interview with the author, January 19, 2021.
10. Terras, telephone interview.
11. In the 1960s, a secret arrangement between Sweden and the United States included assistance if Sweden were invaded. Since it can be assumed that the Soviet Union knew about this agreement, Sweden can be said to have enjoyed a version of extended deterrence.
12. Thucydides, *History of the Peloponnesian War*, ed. Benjamin Jowett (Oxford, UK: Clarendon Press, 1881), book 4, chap. 59, http://www.perseus.tufts.edu/hopper/text?doc=Perseus%3Atext%3A1999.04.0105%3Abook%3Dintroduction.
13. Thucydides, *History of the Peloponnesian War*, book 4, chap. 62.
14. See Barry R. Schneider, "Deterrence and Saddam Hussein: A Case Study of the 1990–1991 Gulf War," in *Deterrence in the Twenty-First Century: Proceedings*, ed. Anthony C. Cain (Montgomery, AL: Air University Press, 2010), 156–57, https://media.defense.gov/2017/Apr/05/2001727306/-1/-1/0/B_0118_DETERRENCE_TWENTYFIRST_CENTURY.PDF.
15. Jeffrey Record, *Japan's Decision for War in 1941: Some Enduring Lessons*, Strategic Studies Institute, February 2009, 25, https://www.hsdl.org/?view&did=38470.

16. Lawrence Freedman, *Strategy: A History* (New York: Oxford University Press, 2013), 157.

17. Frederick S. Dunn, "The Common Problem," in *The Absolute Weapon: Atomic Power and World Order*, ed. Bernard Brodie et al. (New Haven, CT: Yale Institute of International Studies, 1946), 12, https://www.osti.gov/opennet/servlets/purl/16380564.

18. Bernard Brodie, "Implications for Military Policy," in *The Absolute Weapon: Atomic Power and World Order*, ed. Bernard Brodie et al. (New Haven, CT: Yale Institute of International Studies, 1946), 62, https://www.osti.gov/opennet/servlets/purl/16380564.

19. Freedman, *Strategy*, 163.

20. Kevin Chilton and Greg Weaver, "Waging Deterrence in the Twenty-First Century," in *Deterrence in the Twenty-First Century: Proceedings*, ed. Anthony C. Cain (Montgomery, AL: Air University Press, 2010), 75, https://media.defense.gov/2017/Apr/05/2001727306/-1/-1/0/B_0118_DETERRENCE_TWENTYFIRST_CENTURY.PDF.

21. The Stasi's infiltration of churches is documented in Elisabeth Braw, *God's Spies: The Stasi's Cold War Espionage Campaign Inside the Church* (Grand Rapids, MI: William B. Eerdmans, 2019).

22. Erhard Geissler and Robert Hunt Sprinkle, "Disinformation Squared: Was the HIV-from-Fort-Detrick Myth a Stasi Success?," *Politics and the Life Sciences* 32, no. 2 (Fall 2013): 2–99, https://www.jstor.org/stable/43287281?read-now=1&refreqid=excelsior%3A56e55fe8647a0062ce9512dea9ffdb88&seq=1#page_scan_tab_contents.

23. Radio Free Europe/Radio Liberty, "History," https://pressroom.rferl.org/history.

24. Glenn Diesen, "Yes Prime Minister—Salami Tactics and Nuclear Deterrent," YouTube, https://www.youtube.com/watch?v=0861Ka9TtT4.

25. Nobel Media, "Thomas C. Schelling: Biographical," https://www.nobelprize.org/prizes/economic-sciences/2005/schelling/biographical/.

26. Nobel Media, "Thomas C. Schelling: Facts," https://www.nobelprize.org/prizes/economic-sciences/2005/schelling/facts/.

27. Freedman, *Strategy*, 163.

28. Nobel Media, "Thomas C. Schelling: Facts."

29. Henry A. Kissinger, *A World Restored: Metternich, Castlereagh and the Problems of Peace 1812–1822* (Boston, MA: Houghton Mifflin, 1957).

30. Robert D. Kaplan, *The Coming Anarchy: Shattering the Dreams of the Post Cold War* (New York: Random House, 2000), 129.

31. See Thomas C. Schelling, *The Strategy of Conflict* (Cambridge, MA: Harvard University Press, 1981), 207–29.

32. See Austin Long, *Deterrence—from Cold War to Long War: Lessons from Six Decades of RAND Research* (Santa Monica, CA: RAND Corporation, 2008), 7, https://www.rand.org/pubs/monographs/MG636.html.

33. John J. Mearsheimer, *Conventional Deterrence* (Ithaca, NY: Cornell University Press, 1983), 59.

34. Terras, telephone interview.

35. Lawrence Freedman, "Framing Strategic Deterrence: Old Certainties, New Ambiguities," in *Deterrence in the Twenty-First Century: Proceedings*, ed. Anthony C. Cain (Montgomery, AL: Air University Press, 2010), 246, https://media.defense.gov/2017/Apr/05/2001727306/-1/-1/0/B_0118_DETERRENCE_TWENTYFIRST_CENTURY.PDF.

36. Adam Lowther, "Framing Deterrence in the Twenty-First Century: Conference Summary," in *Deterrence in the Twenty-First Century: Proceedings*, ed. Anthony C. Cain (Montgomery, AL: Air University Press, 2010), 8, https://media.defense.gov/2017/Apr/05/2001727306/-1/-1/0/B_0118_DETERRENCE_TWENTYFIRST_CENTURY.PDF.
37. Long, *Deterrence—from Cold War to Long War*, 54.
38. Long, *Deterrence—from Cold War to Long War*, 57.
39. US Department of State, Office of the Historian, Foreign Service Institute, *Foreign Relations of the United States, 1981–1988, volume IV, Soviet Union, January 1983–March 1985*, 458, https://static.history.state.gov/frus/frus1981-88v04/pdf/frus1981-88v04.pdf.
40. US Department of State, Office of the Historian, Foreign Service Institute, *Foreign Relations of the United States, 1981–1988, volume IV, Soviet Union, January 1983–March 1985*, 458.
41. Kissinger, *A World Restored*, 22.
42. Francis Fukuyama, "A World Restored: Europe After Napoleon," *Foreign Affairs* 76, no. 5 (September–October 1997), https://www.foreignaffairs.com/reviews/capsule-review/1997-09-01/world-restored-europe-after-napoleon.
43. Keith B. Payne, "On Nuclear Deterrence and Assurance," in *Deterrence in the Twenty-First Century: Proceedings*, ed. Anthony C. Cain (Montgomery, AL: Air University Press, 2010), 81, https://media.defense.gov/2017/Apr/05/2001727306/-1/-1/0/B_0118_DETERRENCE_TWENTYFIRST_CENTURY.PDF.
44. A good example of a key intelligence asset delivering decisive information relating to a leader's thinking around a potential war is Ashraf Marwan, Gamal Abdel Nasser's son-in-law, who spied on both Nasser and Nasser's successor, Anwar Sadat, for the Mossad. East Germany and thus the Soviet Union gained similarly invaluable insights in the early 1970s, when the East German agent Günther Guillaume worked as a close aide to West German Chancellor Willy Brandt. Guillaume had access to voluminous secret information, including letters from US President Richard Nixon regarding NATO's nuclear strategy.
45. Thomas C. Schelling, *Arms and Influence* (New Haven, CT: Yale University Press, 1966), 35.
46. Long, *Deterrence—from Cold War to Long War*, 15.
47. *Frontline*, "Oral History: Tariq Aziz," Public Broadcasting Service, https://www.pbs.org/wgbh/pages/frontline/gulf/oral/aziz/1.html.
48. *Frontline*, "Oral History: Tariq Aziz."
49. *Frontline*, "Oral History: Tariq Aziz."
50. Geoff Blake, "The 1991 Gulf War a BBC Production," YouTube, February 8, 2019, https://www.youtube.com/watch?v=8zQT5WB_nHE&t=1747s.
51. Quoted in Record, *Japan's Decision for War in 1941*, 40–41.
52. Schneider, "Deterrence and Saddam Hussein," 162.
53. Phoenix, "Staatsakt für Helmut Schmidt: Henry Kissinger hält Rede am 23.11.2015" [State Ceremony for Helmut Schmidt: Henry Kissinger Delivers Speech on November 23, 2015], YouTube, November 23, 2015, https://www.youtube.com/watch?v=-nz-2qM9qpA.
54. Former cabinet minister of an EU member state, email to the author, January 6, 2021.

55. The relatively frank exchanges between the Soviet Union's ambassador to the United States, Anatoly Dobrynin, and US officials were an exception.

56. If US interrogators queried Saddam Hussein and Tariq Aziz during their detention following the 2003 US invasion of Iraq about which US deterrence moves had influenced their actions, the Iraqis' answers are not in the public record.

57. See, for example, US Department of State, Office of the Historian, Foreign Service Institute, "The Cuban Missile Crisis, October 1962," https://history.state.gov/milestones/1961-1968/cuban-missile-crisis.

58. George Robertson (former secretary-general, NATO), email to the author, January 5, 2021.

59. Pekka Toveri (former chief of intelligence, Finnish Defence Forces), email to the author, January 12, 2021.

60. Toveri, email.

61. Phil Mattingly, Clare Foran, and Zachary Cohen, "Pelosi Says She Spoke to Gen. Milley About Trump and the Nuclear Codes," CNN, January 8, 2021, https://edition.cnn.com/2021/01/08/politics/house-speaker-joint-chiefs-milley/index.html.

62. Thomas C. Schelling, "An Astonishing Sixty Years: The Legacy of Hiroshima" (Nobel Memorial Prize in Economic Sciences lecture, Royal Swedish Academy of Sciences, Stockholm, Sweden, December 8, 2005), https://www.nobelprize.org/uploads/2018/06/schelling-lecture.pdf.

63. White House, "Remarks by President Barack Obama in Prague as Delivered," press release, April 5, 2009, https://obamawhitehouse.archives.gov/the-press-office/remarks-president-barack-obama-prague-delivered.

64. For further details on no-first-use policies, see Union of Concerned Scientists, "No-First-Use Policy Explained," May 7, 2020, https://www.ucsusa.org/resources/no-first-use-explained.

65. Chilton and Weaver, "Waging Deterrence in the Twenty-First Century," 73.

66. HM Government, *Global Britain in a Competitive Age: The Integrated Review of Security, Defence, Development and Foreign Policy*, March 2021, 77, https://assets.publishing.service.gov.uk/government/uploads/system/uploads/attachment_data/file/969402/The_Integrated_Review_of_Security__Defence__Development_and_Foreign_Policy.pdf.

67. UK Ministry of Defence, Development, Concepts and Doctrine Centre, *Deterrence*, 29.

68. Mark Montgomery (retired rear admiral, US Navy), telephone interview with the author, April 21, 2020.

69. North Atlantic Treaty Organization, "North Atlantic Treaty," April 4, 1949, https://www.nato.int/cps/en/natolive/official_texts_17120.htm.

70. Andrew F. Krepinevich Jr., *The Decline of Deterrence*, Hudson Institute, March 2019, 42, https://s3.amazonaws.com/media.hudson.org/Krepinevich%20Decline%20of%20Deterrence%20final%20WEB.pdf.

71. Krepinevich Jr., *The Decline of Deterrence*, 42.

72. Krepinevich Jr., *The Decline of Deterrence*, 42.

73. Krepinevich Jr., *The Decline of Deterrence*, 9.

74. Elisabeth Braw, "The Case for Joint Military-Industry Greyzone Exercises," Royal United Services Institute for Defence and Security Studies, September 28, 2020, https://rusi.org/publication/briefing-papers/joint-military-industry-greyzone-exercises.

75. Helen Warrell, "Czech Republic Turns to War-Games to Build Cyber Defences," *Financial Times*, February 18, 2021, https://www.ft.com/content/8c018644-3866-4f69-9105-d3c0e68ca491.

76. Artis Pabriks, "How Latvia Accomplishes Comprehensive Defence," Royal United Services Institute for Defence and Security Studies, June 25, 2020, https://rusi.org/commentary/how-latvia-accomplishes-comprehensive-defence.

77. Elisabeth Braw, "The Return of the Military Draft," Atlantic Council, February 15, 2017, https://www.atlanticcouncil.org/in-depth-research-reports/issue-brief/the-return-of-the-draft/.

78. Elisabeth Braw, "What 'The Godfather' Can Teach Us About Fighting Cyber Attacks," *Financial Times*, April 23, 2019, https://www.ft.com/content/5e167af8-65bd-11e9-b809-6f0d2f5705f6.

79. Elisabeth Braw and Gary Brown, "Personalised Deterrence of Cyber Aggression," *RUSI Journal* 165, no. 2 (2020): 48–54, https://www.tandfonline.com/doi/full/10.1080/03071847.2020.1740493.

80. UK Government Communications Headquarters, "National Cyber Force Transforms Country's Cyber Capabilities to Protect the UK," November 19, 2020, https://www.gchq.gov.uk/news/national-cyber-force.

81. Cynthia Brumfield, "26 Cyberspace Solarium Commission Recommendations Likely to Become Law with NDAA Passage," CSO, December 14, 2020, https://www.csoonline.com/article/3601120/26-cyberspace-solarium-commission-recommendation-likely-to-become-law-with-ndaa-passage.html.

Chapter IX—Cold War Swedish and Finnish Total Defense as Deterrence

1. Erich Ludendorff, *Der totale Krieg* [*The Total War*] (Munich, Germany: Ludendorffs Verlag, 1935), 5, https://archive.org/details/Ludendorff-Erich-Der-totale-Krieg/page/n5/mode/2up. Ludendorff's analysis of previous wars was not entirely accurate. As Jan Willem Honig notes, total war had emerged in Napoleonic times. Thinking about total defense thus began before Nazi Germany's use of total war, though the Nazis' total war dramatically accelerated it. See Jan Willem Honig, "The Idea of Total War: From Clausewitz to Ludendorff," in *The Pacific War as Total War: Proceedings of the 2011 International Forum on War History* (Tokyo, Japan: National Institute for Defence Studies, 2012), https://www.researchgate.net/profile/Jan_Willem_Honig/publication/301220150_'The_Idea_of_Total_War_From_Clausewitz_to_Ludendorff'/links/570d0ea908ae3199889b49a5/The-Idea-of-Total-War-From-Clausewitz-to-Ludendorff.pdf.

2. For the connection between Ludendorff's theory and those of Carl von Clausewitz, see Honig, "The Idea of Total War."

3. Ernst Forsthoff, *Der totale Staat* [*The Total State*] (Hamburg, Germany: Hanseatische Verlagsanstalt, 1933).

4. Lawrence Freedman, *The Future of War: A History* (New York: PublicAffairs, 2017), 67.

5. Ludendorff, having succumbed to conspiracy thinking of fantastical proportions, never played an official role in the Third Reich despite embracing right-wing radicalism early on.

6. Norbert F. Pötzl, "Wie Goebbels sein Publikum aufpeitschte—und verachtete" [How Goebbels Whipped Up—and Despised—His Audience], *Der Spiegel*, February 18, 2018, https://www.spiegel.de/geschichte/sportpalast-rede-von-joseph-goebbels-wollt-ihr-den-totalen-krieg-a-1193427.html.

7. Honig, "The Idea of Total War," 29.

8. Swedish Armed Forces, "Värnplikten genom åren" [Military Service Through the Years], https://www.forsvarsmakten.se/sv/information-och-fakta/var-historia/artiklar/varnplikt-under-109-ar/.

9. Swedish National Defense College, Center for Total Defense and Society's Security, *Förutsättningar för krisberedskap och totalförsvar i Sverige* [*Conditions for Crisis Preparedness and Total Defense in Sweden*], 2019 ed., 20, https://www.fhs.se/centrum-for-totalforsvar-och-samhallets-sakerhet/forskning/publikationer/forutsattningar-for-krisberedskap-och-totalforsvar-i-sverige.html; and Bo Richard Lundgren, "Totalförsvarets tillkomst och utveckling" [The Origins and Development of Total Defense], in *Totalförsvaret under Sveriges kalla krig* [*Total Defense During Sweden's Cold War*], ed. Gunnart Artéus and Herman Fältström (Stockholm, Sweden: Swedish Royal Society of Naval Sciences, 2011), 27, http://fokk.eu/files/2017/11/31-Totalfo%CC%88rsvaret-under-Sveriges-kalla-krig.pdf.

10. Swedish National Defense College, Center for Total Defense and Society's Security, *Förutsättningar för krisberedskap och totalförsvar i Sverige* [*Conditions for Crisis Preparedness and Total Defense in Sweden*], 15.

11. Per Larsson, Christoffer Wedebrand, and Carl Denward, *Personal för ett nytt civilt försvar: Förutsättningar, problem och möjligheter* [*Civil Defense Personnel Planning: Prerequisites, Problems, and Possibilities*], Swedish Defence Research Agency, December 2018, 19, https://www.foi.se/rest-api/report/FOI-R--4675--SE.

12. The Lottakåren was inspired by Finland's Lotta Svärd movement, which took on similar tasks; it was named after the heroic Lotta Svärd, a fictional character in a famous Finnish poem who follows her husband into battle and, after he is killed, stays to care for other soldiers.

13. Lundgren, "Totalförsvarets tillkomst och utveckling" [The Origins and Development of Total Defense], 27.

14. Swedish Government Official Report, *Totalförsvarsplikt och frivillighet* [*Total Defense Duty and Voluntariness*], 2009, 23, https://www.regeringen.se/49bb47/contentassets/23fa098fd8c240a5b080e2afd14a7ccb/totalforsvarsplikt-och-frivillighet-sou-200963.

15. Swedish National Defense College, Center for Total Defense and Society's Security, *Förutsättningar för krisberedskap och totalförsvar i Sverige* [*Conditions for Crisis Preparedness and Total Defense in Sweden*], 21. In the early 1900s, the UK established a

system similar to the gray slips of paper, known as D-notices. The system, now formally known as the DSMA Notice System, is still operating. See DSMA Notice System, website, https://dsma.uk/.

16. Available from Clarence Lööw, "Om kriget kommer—1943" [If War Comes—1943], Skymningsläge, July 11, 2015, https://www.skymningslage.se/om-kriget-kommer-1943/.

17. Swedish National Defense College, Center for Total Defense and Society's Security, *Förutsättningar för krisberedskap och totalförsvar i Sverige* [*Conditions for Crisis Preparedness and Total Defense in Sweden*], 26.

18. Mischa Hietanen, "Stella Polaris—en mytomspunnen operation" [Stella Polaris—a Fabled Operation], Svenska Yle, September 27, 2012, https://svenska.yle.fi/artikel/2012/09/27/stella-polaris-en-mytomspunnen-operation.

19. Jan Joel Andersson, *Försvarsindustrins säkerhetspolitiska roll: från hårt stål till mjuk makt?* [*The Defense Industry's Security Policy Role: From Hard Steel to Soft Power?*], Swedish Institute of International Affairs, May 2009, 13, https://www.ui.se/globalassets/ui.se-eng/publications/ui-publications/forsvarsindustrins-sakerhetspolitiska-roll-fran-hart-stal-till-mjuk-makt-min.pdf.

20. This figure does not include strategic bombers. Bertil Wennerholm, "Fjärde flygvapnet i världen? Doktrinutveckling i det svenska flygvapnet i försvarsbesluten 1942–1958. Underlag, beslut och genomförande i nationellt och internationellt perspektiv." [The World's Fourth-Largest Air Force? Doctrinal Development in the Swedish Air Force in the (Quadrennial) Defense Policy Decisions 1942–1958. Basis, Decision, and Implementation in a National and International Perspective.], *Försvaret och det kalla kriget* 8 (2006), https://web.archive.org/web/20180804014643/http://fokk.eu/files/2017/11/08-Fja%CC%88rde-flygvapnet-i-va%CC%88rlden.pdf.

21. Swedish Royal Ministry of the Interior, *Om kriget kommer* [*If War Comes*], Swedish Armed Forces, 1961, 2, https://www.forsvarsmakten.se/siteassets/5-information-och-fakta/historia/psykforsvarets-historia/om-kriget-kommer-1961.komprimerad.pdf.

22. Swedish Armed Forces, "Hesa Fredrik" [Coarse Fredrik], https://www.forsvarsmakten.se/sv/information-och-fakta/var-historia/artiklar/hesa-fredrik/.

23. Swedish Armed Forces, "Frivilliga försvarsorganisationer" [Volunteer Defense Organizations], https://www.forsvarsmakten.se/sv/organisation/frivilliga-forsvarsorganisationer/.

24. Rune Dahlén, "Totalförsvarets planering för skydd av befolkning, statsledning, produktion och kommunikation" [Total Defense Planning for the Protection of the Population, the Government, Production, and Communications], in *Totalförsvaret under Sveriges kalla krig* [*The Role of Total Defense During Sweden's Cold War*], ed. Gunnart Artéus and Herman Fältström (Stockholm, Sweden: Swedish Royal Society of Naval Sciences, 2011), 49, http://fokk.eu/files/2017/11/31-Totalfo%CC%88rsvaret-under-Sveriges-kalla-krig.pdf.

25. Per Larsson, *Civilbefälhavare—en övergripande historisk belysning* [*Civilian Commander in Chief—an Overall Historical Examination*], Swedish Defence Research Agency, August 2019, 10, https://www.foi.se/rest-api/report/FOI-R--4795--SE.

26. Morgan Jönsson, *En introduktion till totalförsvar: För dig som undrar vad det är och varför det behövs* [*An Introduction into Total Defense: For Those Curious About What It Is*

and Why It Is Needed], County Administrative Board of Kalmar County, 2019, 8, https://www.lansstyrelsen.se/download/18.26f506e0167c605d5695356e/1552466961000/En%20introduktion%20till%20totalf%C3%B6rsvar_tillg%C3%A4nglighetsanpassad.pdf.

27. Tekniskt Magasin, "Vi går under Jorden (1959)" [Let's Go Underground (1959)], YouTube, https://www.youtube.com/watch?v=k_I9Ew-sZAw.

28. Swedish National Defense College, Center for Total Defense and Society's Security, *Förutsättningar för krisberedskap och totalförsvar i Sverige* [*Conditions for Crisis Preparedness and Total Defense in Sweden*], 25.

29. Swedish National Defense College, Center for Total Defense and Society's Security, *Förutsättningar för krisberedskap och totalförsvar i Sverige* [*Conditions for Crisis Preparedness and Total Defense in Sweden*], 19.

30. Swedish Armed Forces, "Om kriget kom, avsnitt 6, 'Det totala försvaret'" [If War Came, Episode 6, "The Total Defense"], YouTube, March 7, 2017, https://www.youtube.com/watch?v=SLPZtEmMOyc&t=2s.

31. Bengt Nylander and Wilhelm Agrell, *Det som inte har berättats: 25 år vid SÄPOs kontraspionage* [*What Has Not Been Told: 25 Years at SÄPO Counterintelligence*] (Stockholm, Sweden: Medströms Bokförlag, 2016), 75–76.

32. Swedish Government Official Report, *Näringslivets roll inom totalförsvaret* [*The Role of Business Within Total Defense*], 2019, 88, https://www.regeringen.se/4ad9c6/globalassets/regeringen/dokument/forsvarsdepartementet/sou/sou-2019-51-naringslivets-roll-inom-totalforsvaret.pdf.

33. Swedish Government Official Report, *Näringslivets roll inom totalförsvaret* [*The Role of Business Within Total Defense*], 88.

34. Swedish National Defense College, Center for Total Defense and Society's Security, *Förutsättningar för krisberedskap och totalförsvar i Sverige* [*Conditions for Crisis Preparedness and Total Defense in Sweden*], 48.

35. Bo Hugemark (retired colonel, Swedish Armed Forces), in discussion with the author, January 30, 2021.

36. A similar scenario occurred when "little green men" appeared in eastern Ukraine. The hit Norwegian television show *Occupied* also includes a similar scenario. When the Soviet Whiskey-class submarine ran aground close to the Swedish coast in 1981, it was first spotted by a private citizen.

37. Björn Körlof, "Mental beredskap. Ett nytt koncept inom totalförsvaret" [Mental Preparedness. A New Concept Within Total Defense], in *Sverige—Värt att skydda: Ett sårbart samhälle kräver ett modernt civilt försvar* [*Sweden—Worth Protecting: A Vulnerable Society Demands Modern Total Defense*], ed. Thomas Hörberg (Stockholm, Sweden: Royal Swedish Academy of War Sciences, 2017), 267.

38. Körlof, "Mental beredskap. Ett nytt koncept inom totalförsvaret" [Mental Preparedness. A New Concept Within Total Defense], 267.

39. Swedish National Defense College, Center for Total Defense and Society's Security, *Förutsättningar för krisberedskap och totalförsvar i Sverige* [*Conditions for Crisis Preparedness and Total Defense in Sweden*], 43. Real defense expenditures were likely much higher, as expenditures for many civil defense aspects were included in the Ministry of Defence's budget.

40. Albert Resis, ed., *Molotov Remembers: Inside Kremlin Politics—Conversations with*

Felix Chuev (Chicago: Ivan R. Dee, 1993), 10.

41. René Nyberg, "Paasikivi in Moscow," Paasikivi-Seura, https://jkpaasikivi.fi/en/paasikivi-in-moscow-2/.

42. Pekka Visuri, *Evolution of the Finnish Military Doctrine 1945–1985*, Finnish War College, 1990, 26, https://www.doria.fi/bitstream/handle/10024/119958/FDS%201%20OCR.pdf.

43. Juhana Aunesluoma and Johanna Rainio-Niemi, "Neutrality as Identity? Finland's Quest for Security in the Cold War," *Journal of Cold War Studies* 18, no. 4 (Fall 2016): 53, https://researchportal.helsinki.fi/en/publications/neutrality-as-identity-finlands-quest-for-security-in-the-cold-wa.

44. Throughout the Cold War, Soviet recognition of Finnish neutrality was shaky, and in the late 1960s, Moscow withdrew its recognition of Finnish neutrality altogether.

45. Vesa Tynkkynen and Petteri Jouko, *Towards East or West? Defence Planning in Finland 1944–1966*, Finnish National Defence University, 2007, 29, https://www.doria.fi/bitstream/handle/10024/119978/FDS%2017%20OCR.pdf.

46. Visuri, *Evolution of the Finnish Military Doctrine 1945–1985*, 23.

47. Visuri, *Evolution of the Finnish Military Doctrine 1945–1985*, 23.

48. Visuri, *Evolution of the Finnish Military Doctrine 1945–1985*, 28.

49. Tynkkynen and Jouko, *Towards East or West?*, 29.

50. Tynkkynen and Jouko, *Towards East or West?*, 35.

51. Aila Virtanen, Anna-Maija Lämsä, and Tuomo Takala, "The War Heroine in the Finnish Organization—Lotta Svärd," *Management Research and Practice* 9, no. 2 (June 2017): 12, http://mrp.ase.ro/no92/f1.pdf.

52. Aunesluoma and Rainio-Niemi, "Neutrality as Identity?," 63.

53. Aunesluoma and Rainio-Niemi, "Neutrality as Identity?," 66.

54. Aunesluoma and Rainio-Niemi, "Neutrality as Identity?," 66.

55. Statistics Finland, Findicator, "Försvarsviljan" [Commitment to Defense], December 14, 2020, https://findikaattori.fi/sv/77.

56. Statistics Finland, Findicator, "Försvarsviljan" [Commitment to Defense].

57. Arto Räty (former director, Finnish National Defence Course), in discussion with the author, January 20, 2020.

58. Räty, in discussion with the author.

59. A few other countries, such as Lithuania, have in recent years introduced adapted versions of the course.

60. Pekka Toveri (former chief of intelligence, Finnish Defence Forces), telephone interview with the author, January 19, 2021.

61. Riho Terras (former chief of defense, Estonian Defence Forces), video interview with the author, January 19, 2021.

62. Tynkkynen and Jouko, *Towards East or West?*, 70.

63. Toveri, telephone interview.

64. Tynkkynen and Jouko, *Towards East or West?*, 90.

65. Anders Kilander and Stefan Winiger, "USA backade upp Sverige under kalla kriget" [The United States Backed Sweden Up During the Cold War], Sveriges Radio, December 20, 2002, https://sverigesradio.se/artikel/162540. In 1952, Sweden also signed a memorandum of understanding with the United States that allowed Sweden to buy

US military equipment. See Joel Andersson, *Försvarsindustrins säkerhetspolitiska roll: från hårt stål till mjuk makt?* [*The Defense Industry's Security Policy Role: From Hard Steel to Soft Power?*], 20.

66. Pekka Toveri (former chief of intelligence, Finnish Defence Forces), email to the author, January 12, 2021.

67. Terras, video interview.

68. Terras, video interview.

69. Niklas Karlsson (vice chair, Committee on Defence, Swedish Parliament), telephone interview with the author, August 11, 2020.

Chapter X—Building a Wall of Denial Against Gray-Zone Aggression

1. Klara Obermüller, ed., *Wir sind eigenartig, ohne Zweifel: Die kritischen Texte von Schweizer Schriftstellern über ihr Land* [*We're Peculiar, Without a Doubt: Critical Text by Swiss Authors About Their Country*], Nagel & Kimche, https://files.hanser.de/Files/Article/ARTK_LPR_9783312003174_0001.pdf.

2. North Atlantic Treaty Organization, "North Atlantic Treaty," April 4, 1949, https://www.nato.int/cps/en/natolive/official_texts_17120.htm.

3. Other countries, notably Norway and Denmark, built similar systems. Sweden's and Finland's approach is, however, selected here as a basis for learning.

4. Wolf-Diether Roepke and Hasit Thankey, "Resilience: The First Line of Defence," NATO Review, February 27, 2019, https://www.nato.int/docu/review/articles/2019/02/27/resilience-the-first-line-of-defence/index.html.

5. Roepke and Thankey, "Resilience."

6. Elisabeth Braw, "Producing Fear in the Enemy's Mind: How to Adapt Cold War Deterrence for Gray Zone Aggression," American Enterprise Institute, March 9, 2021, https://www.aei.org/research-products/report/producing-fear-in-the-enemys-mind-how-to-adapt-cold-war-deterrence-for-gray-zone-aggression/; and Elisabeth Braw, "The Defender's Dilemma: Defining, Identifying, and Deterring Gray-Zone Aggression," American Enterprise Institute, February 8, 2021, https://www.aei.org/research-products/report/the-defenders-dilemma-defining-identifying-and-deterring-gray-zone-aggression/.

7. Lyle J. Morris et al., *Gaining Competitive Advantage in the Gray Zone: Response Options for Coercive Aggression Below the Threshold of Major War*, RAND Corporation, 2019, 140, https://www.rand.org/pubs/research_reports/RR2942.html.

8. HM Government, UK Cabinet Office, *National Security Capability Review*, March 2018, 2, https://assets.publishing.service.gov.uk/government/uploads/system/uploads/attachment_data/file/705347/6.4391_CO_National-Security-Review_web.pdf.

9. HM Government, UK Cabinet Office, *National Security Capability Review*, 11.

10. Niklas Karlsson (vice chair, Committee on Defence, Swedish Parliament), telephone interview with the author, August 11, 2020.

11. UK Civil Defence Association, "Brief History of UK Civil Defence," https://civildefenceassociation.uk/history/.

12. Ole Wæver et al., *Identity, Migration and the New Security Agenda in Europe* (New York: St. Martin's Press, 1993), 23.
13. HM Government, *Global Britain in a Competitive Age: The Integrated Review of Security, Defence, Development and Foreign Policy*, March 2021, 3, https://assets.publishing.service.gov.uk/government/uploads/system/uploads/attachment_data/file/969402/The_Integrated_Review_of_Security_Defence_Development_and_Foreign_Policy.pdf.
14. HM Government, *Global Britain in a Competitive Age*, 88.
15. HM Government, *Global Britain in a Competitive Age*, 99.
16. Carl Rådestad and Oscar Larsson, "Responsibilization in Contemporary Swedish Crisis Management: Expanding 'Bare Life' Biopolitics Through Exceptionalism and Neoliberal Governmentality," *Critical Policy Studies* 14, no. 1 (October 9, 2018): 92, https://www.tandfonline.com/doi/full/10.1080/19460171.2018.1530604?af=R.
17. Federal Government of Germany, *White Paper on German Security Policy and the Future of the Bundeswehr*, German Federal Ministry of Defence, June 2016, 39, https://www.gmfus.org/publications/white-paper-german-security-policy-and-future-bundeswehr.
18. Rådestad and Larsson, "Responsibilization in Contemporary Swedish Crisis Management."
19. Elisabeth Braw, *Competitive National Service: How the Scandinavian Model Can Be Adapted by the UK*, Royal United Services Institute for Defence and Security Studies, October 23, 2019, https://rusi.org/explore-our-research/publications/occasional-papers/competitive-national-service-how-the-scandinavian-model-can-be-adapted-by-the-uk.
20. Finnish National Audiovisual Institute, *Finnish Media Education: Promoting Media and Information Literacy in Finland*, https://kavi.fi/sites/default/files/documents/mil_in_finland.pdf.
21. Government of Finland, Security Committee, *Security Strategy for Society*, 2018, 5, https://turvallisuuskomitea.fi/wp-content/uploads/2018/04/YTS_2017_english.pdf.
22. Government of Finland, Security Committee, *Security Strategy for Society*, 7–8.
23. Government Offices of Sweden, *Inrättande av Myndigheten för psykologiskt försvar* [*Establishment of the Agency for Psychological Defense*], March 18, 2021, https://www.regeringen.se/rattsliga-dokument/kommittedirektiv/2021/03/dir.-202120/.
24. Gerhard Wheeler, "Northern Composure: Initial Observations from Sweden's Total Defence 2020 Exercise," Royal United Services Institute for Defence and Security Studies, September 3, 2020, https://rusi.org/commentary/northern-composure-initial-observations-swedens-total-defence-2020-exercise.
25. Government of Denmark, *Udenrigs- og Sikkerhedspolitisk Strategi, 2017–2018* [*Foreign and Security Policy Strategy, 2017–2018*], June 14, 2017, https://www.regeringen.dk/publikationer-og-aftaletekster/udenrigs-og-sikkerhedspolitisk-strategi-for-2017-2018/.
26. Republic of Estonia, Ministry of Defence, *National Security Concept 2017*, 8, https://www.kaitseministeerium.ee/sites/default/files/elfinder/article_files/national_security_concept_2017_0.pdf.
27. Estonian Defence League, "Estonian Defence League's Cyber Unit," https://www.kaitseliit.ee/en/cyber-unit. For further details, see Elisabeth Braw, "Everyone Together Now: Creating a Resilient Society in an Age of Cyber Threats," Macdonald-

Laurier Institute, June 2021, https://macdonaldlaurier.ca/files/pdf/20210601_Everyone_together_now_Braw_COMMENTARY_FWeb.pdf.

28. Elisabeth Braw, "How We Can Tackle the Next Invisible Enemy," *Times*, April 14, 2020, https://www.thetimes.co.uk/article/how-we-can-tackle-the-next-invisible-enemy-flqqpzww6.

29. Artis Pabriks, "How Latvia Accomplishes Comprehensive Defence," Royal United Services Institute for Defence and Security Studies, June 25, 2020, https://rusi.org/commentary/how-latvia-accomplishes-comprehensive-defence.

30. Pabriks, "How Latvia Accomplishes Comprehensive Defence."

31. US Cyberspace Solarium Commission, *Our Strategy*, March 2020, 5, https://www.solarium.gov/report.

32. Lucy Williamson, "France's Raw Recruits Sign Up for Return of National Service," BBC, June 26, 2019, https://www.bbc.co.uk/news/world-europe-48755605.

33. Elisabeth Braw, "Ask What You Can Do for Your Country," *Foreign Policy*, August 4, 2020, https://foreignpolicy.com/2020/08/04/national-service-germany-usa-ask-what-you-can-do-for-your-country/.

34. Guna Gavrilko (head of the structure and military personnel development planning section, Latvian Ministry of Defence), telephone interview with the author, summer 2020; and Ilze Leimane (head of the planning section of the cadet force of Latvia, Latvian Ministry of Defence), telephone interview with the author, summer 2020.

35. For further information about this incident, see Gordon H. McCormick, *Stranger Than Fiction: Soviet Submarine Operations in Swedish Waters*, Project Air Force, January 1990, 4–9, https://apps.dtic.mil/dtic/tr/fulltext/u2/a238953.pdf.

36. Ojārs Kalniņš (vice chair, Foreign Affairs Committee, Latvian Parliament), telephone interview with the author, June 25, 2020.

37. Monika Garbačiauskaitė-Budrienė (CEO, Lithuanian National Radio and Television), email to the author, January 15, 2020.

38. Garbačiauskaitė-Budrienė, email.

39. I outlined this proposal in Elisabeth Braw, "Citizen Alienation and the Political and Media Elite" (working paper, University of Oxford, Reuters Institute for the Study of Journalism, Oxford, UK, August 2014), https://reutersinstitute.politics.ox.ac.uk/sites/default/files/2018-01/Citizen%20alienation%20and%20the%20political%20and%20media%20elite.pdf.

40. Tokyo Metropolitan Government, "Disaster Prevention Information," https://www.metro.tokyo.lg.jp/english/guide/bosai/index.html.

41. SF72, "Earthquake," https://www.sf72.org/hazard/earthquake.

42. Kieran Dent, Ben Westwood, and Miguel Segoviano, "Stress Testing of Banks: An Introduction," *Bank of England Quarterly Bulletin* Q3 (2016), https://www.bankofengland.co.uk/-/media/boe/files/quarterly-bulletin/2016/stress-testing-of-banks-an-introduction.pdf.

43. Ben Lefebvre, "Biden Implores Drivers 'Don't Panic' as Colonial Pipeline Ramps Up Deliveries," *Politico*, May 13, 2021, https://www.politico.com/news/2021/05/13/colonial-pipeline-deliveries-488025.

44. Fox 5 Digital Team, "East Coast Gas Shortage: Gas Prices in DC, Maryland and Virginia," Fox 5 Washington DC, May 14, 2021, https://www.fox5dc.com/news/

east-coast-gas-shortage-impact-on-dc-maryland-and-virginia-pumps.amp.

45. Elisabeth Braw, "We Must Learn What to Do If the Lights Go Out," *Times*, May 10, 2019, https://www.thetimes.co.uk/article/we-must-learn-what-to-do-if-the-lights-go-out-xlcph6cqt.

46. See, for example, ShakeOut, website, https://www.shakeout.org/.

47. Phil Helsel and Yuliya Talmazan, "Texas Water Shortage Adds to Power Crisis as New Winter Storm Moves in," NBC News, February 18, 2021, https://www.nbcnews.com/news/us-news/texas-contending-water-nightmare-top-power-crisis-n1258208.

48. BBC, "Russian Trolls' Chief Target Was 'Black US Voters' in 2016," October 9, 2019, https://www.bbc.co.uk/news/technology-49987657.

49. ITV, "Covid: Almost 620,000 Told to Isolate amid 'Pingdemic'—Highest Ever Figure," July 22, 2021, https://www.itv.com/news/2021-07-22/almost-620000-told-to-isolate-amid-pingdemic-highest-ever-figure.

50. Tom Knowles, "Plague of NHS App Pings Means We May Have to Call on Army, Says Tory MP Tobias Ellwood," *Times*, July 23, 2021, https://www.thetimes.co.uk/article/plague-of-nhs-app-pings-means-we-may-have-to-call-on-army-says-tory-mp-tobias-ellwood-d67fonp5s.

51. Kevin Roose, "What Is QAnon, the Viral Pro-Trump Conspiracy Theory?," *New York Times*, June 15, 2021, https://www.nytimes.com/article/what-is-qanon.html.

52. Ewan Somerville, "750,000 People Sign Up to Join NHS Volunteer Army in Less Than a Week," *Evening Standard*, March 29, 2020, https://www.standard.co.uk/news/health/coronavirus-nhs-army-applications-royal-voluntary-service-a4400821.html.

53. German Federal Ministry of the Interior, Technisches Hilfswerk, "Overview," https://www.thw.de/EN/THW/Overview/overview_node.html.

54. Student Volunteer Army, website, https://sva.org.nz/.

55. Singapore Civil Defence Force, "What Is Total Defence," https://www.scdf.gov.sg/home/community-volunteers/community-preparedness/total-defence.

56. Robert D. Putnam, *Bowling Alone: The Collapse and Revival of American Community* (New York: Simon & Schuster, 2000).

57. UK Office for National Statistics, "Families and Households in the UK: 2019," November 15, 2019, https://www.ons.gov.uk/peoplepopulationandcommunity/birthsdeathsandmarriages/families/bulletins/familiesandhouseholds/2019.

58. Braw, *Competitive National Service*.

59. Lithuania has selective national service, though it admits a higher percentage than Denmark, Norway, and Sweden do.

60. Norwegian Armed Forces, Årsrapport 2019 [*Annual Report 2019*], 2019, https://www.forsvaret.no/aktuelt-og-presse/publikasjoner/forsvarets-arsrapport/Forsvaret-aarsrapport2019_web.pdf/_/attachment/inline/7cd7c737-ddad-4ac3-a97f-742b9dc6d6e3:ebcecbe81a552443e801808d49391bbab240e570/Forsvaret-aarsrapport2019_web.pdf.

61. Statisics Norway, "Fakta om befolkningen" [Facts About the Population], https://www.ssb.no/befolkning/faktaside/befolkningen.

62. Information provided by the Norwegian Armed Forces.

63. Universum, "Norway," https://universumglobal.com/rankings/norway/.

64. See Norwegian Armed Forces, "Cyberværneplikt" [Cyber Defense], https://karriere.forsvaret.dk/varnepligt/varnepligten/cybervarnepligt/; and Swedish Armed Forces, "Försvarsmakten utbildar cybersoldater" [The Armed Forces Trains Cyber Soldiers], February 15, 2019, https://www.forsvarsmakten.se/sv/aktuellt/2019/02/forsvarsmakten-utbildar-cybersoldater/.

65. As previously noted, China's personal protective equipment deliveries during the first COVID-19 wave were modest and contained a significant amount of faulty products. In addition, the recipient countries had in many cases purchased a large share of the goods, making it a commercial arrangement rather than assistance.

66. Ellen Terrell, "When a Quote Is Not (Exactly) a Quote: General Motors," Library of Congress, April 22, 2016, https://blogs.loc.gov/inside_adams/2016/04/when-a-quote-is-not-exactly-a-quote-general-motors/.

67. Satellite, "Helmut Schmidt im Gespräch mit Ulrich Wickert" [Helmut Schmidt in Conversation with Ulrich Wickert], YouTube, November 26, 2016, https://www.youtube.com/watch?v=i18VPjFcsLQ&t=1137s.

68. Satellite, "Helmut Schmidt im Gespräch mit Ulrich Wickert" [Helmut Schmidt in Conversation with Ulrich Wickert].

69. McDonald's, "Our Leadership," https://corporate.mcdonalds.com/corpmcd/our-company/who-we-are/our-leadership.html.

70. Elisabeth Braw, "Will American Firms Put America First?," *Foreign Policy*, February 21, 2020, https://foreignpolicy.com/2020/02/21/davos-wef-will-american-companies-put-america-first/.

71. Daimler, "Ola Källenius: Chairman of the Board of Management of Daimler AG and Mercedes-Benz AG," https://www.daimler.com/company/corporate-governance/board-of-management/kaellenius/.

72. Laura Silver, Kat Devlin, and Christine Huang, *Unfavorable Views of China Reach Historic Highs in Many Countries*, Pew Research Center, October 6, 2020, https://www.pewresearch.org/global/2020/10/06/unfavorable-views-of-china-reach-historic-highs-in-many-countries/.

73. Elisabeth Braw, "Military Knowhow Can Help Business Navigate a Hostile World," *Financial Times*, March 21, 2021, https://www.ft.com/content/91768471-f991-40ef-a976-448568600b0f.

74. Damian Collins (former chairman, Digital, Culture, Media and Sport Committee, UK Parliament), telephone interview with the author, June 8, 2020.

75. Marko Mihkelson (chair, Foreign Affairs Committee, Estonian Parliament), telephone interview with the author, June 10, 2020.

76. Ed Wilson (retired major general, US Air Force), telephone interview with the author, June 25, 2020.

77. US Department of Energy, Office of Cybersecurity, Energy Security, and Emergency Response, "Energy Sector Cybersecurity Preparedness," https://www.energy.gov/ceser/activities/cybersecurity-critical-energy-infrastructure/energy-sector-cybersecurity.

78. US Department of Energy, Office of Cybersecurity, Energy Security, and Emergency Response, "Energy Sector Cybersecurity Preparedness."

79. UK National Cyber Security Centre, website, https://www.ncsc.gov.uk/.

80. Karianne Lund, Jo Nesbø, and Erik Skjoldbjærg, dirs., *Occupied* (Sweden: Yellow Bird, 2015).

81. Steven Soderbergh, dir., *Contagion* (Burbank, CA: Warner Bros. Pictures, 2011).

82. Björn Östlund, dir., *Nedsläckt land [Blacked-Out Country]* (Sweden: Sveriges Television, 2019).

83. Silver, Devlin, and Huang, *Unfavorable Views of China Reach Historic Highs in Many Countries*.

84. Elisabeth Braw, "Why Western Companies Should Leave China," *Foreign Policy*, February 17, 2021, https://foreignpolicy.com/2021/02/17/why-western-companies-should-leave-china/.

85. Ryan Faughnder and Alice Su, "How Disney's 'Mulan' Became One of 2020's Most Controversial Movies," *Los Angeles Times*, September 11, 2020, https://www.latimes.com/entertainment-arts/business/story/2020-09-11/disneys-mulan-debuts-in-china-heres-why-its-controversial.

86. Elisabeth Braw, "The Case for Joint Military-Industry Greyzone Exercises," Royal United Services Institute for Defence and Security Studies, September 28, 2020, https://rusi.org/publication/briefing-papers/joint-military-industry-greyzone-exercises.

87. Helen Warrell, "Czech Republic Turns to War-Games to Build Cyber Defences," *Financial Times*, February 18, 2021, https://www.ft.com/content/8c018644-3866-4f69-9105-d3c0e68ca491.

88. UK Ministry of Defence, Development, Concepts and Doctrine Centre, *Deterrence: The Defence Contribution, Joint Doctrine Note 1/19*, February 2019, 50, https://assets.publishing.service.gov.uk/government/uploads/system/uploads/attachment_data/file/860499/20190204-doctrine_uk_deterrence_jdn_1_19.pdf.

89. Warrell, "Czech Republic Turns to War-Games to Build Cyber Defences."

90. Lithuania has a similar course, as does Sweden, the concept's originator.

91. The percentages were provided by Arto Räty (former director, Finnish National Defence Course), email to the author, April 12, 2019.

92. Reuters, "Geely to Deepen Ties with Volvo, Plans to List Under One Umbrella," February 10, 2020, https://www.reuters.com/article/us-volvo-cars-m-a-geely-automobile/geely-to-deepen-ties-with-volvo-plans-to-list-under-one-umbrella-idUSKBN2041D5.

93. Emma Rumney, "UK Government Plans to Sell Remaining RBS Stake by 2024," Reuters, October 29, 2018, https://www.reuters.com/article/uk-britain-economy-rbs/uk-government-plans-to-sell-remaining-rbs-stake-by-2024-idUKKCN1N32E7.

94. European Commission, *White Paper on Levelling the Playing Field as Regards Foreign Subsidies*, June 17, 2020, https://ec.europa.eu/competition/international/overview/foreign_subsidies_white_paper.pdf.

95. In-Q-Tel, website, https://www.iqt.org/about-iqt/.

96. Army Venture Capital Initiative, website, http://armyvci.org/.

97. SmartCap, website, https://smartcap.ee/.

98. National Security Strategic Investment Fund, website, http://www.british-business-bank.co.uk/national-security-strategic-investment-fund/.

99. UK Department for Business, Energy and Industrial Strategy, "UK to Launch New Research Agency to Support High Risk, High Reward Science," press release, February 19, 2021, https://www.gov.uk/government/news/uk-to-launch-new-research-

agency-to-support-high-risk-high-reward-science.

100. In the UK, the House of Lords offers an ideal selection of respected leaders from which resilience czars could be selected.

Chapter XI—Deterrence by Punishment

1. Thomas C. Schelling, "An Astonishing Sixty Years: The Legacy of Hiroshima" (Nobel Memorial Prize in Economic Sciences lecture, Royal Swedish Academy of Sciences, Stockholm, Sweden, December 8, 2005), 374, https://www.nobelprize.org/uploads/2018/06/schelling-lecture.pdf.

2. Acc3ssd, "Dr. Strangelove: Deterrence," YouTube, May 28, 2009, https://www.youtube.com/watch?v=nSRtgqqixUY.

3. Pekka Toveri (former chief of intelligence, Finnish Defence Forces), telephone interview with the author, April 1, 2020.

4. Schelling, "An Astonishing Sixty Years," 365.

5. Schelling, "An Astonishing Sixty Years," 374.

6. Ed Wilson (retired major general, US Air Force), telephone interview with the author, June 25, 2020.

7. Michael A. Weber and Edward J. Collins-Chase, "The Global Magnitsky Human Rights Accountability Act," Congressional Research Service, October 28, 2020, https://crsreports.congress.gov/product/pdf/IF/IF10576.

8. Dianne E. Rennack and Cory Welt, "U.S. Sanctions on Russia: An Overview," Congressional Research Service, June 7, 2021, https://fas.org/sgp/crs/row/IF10779.pdf.

9. European Council and Council of the European Union, "EU Restrictive Measures in Response to the Crisis in Ukraine," June 23, 2021, https://www.consilium.europa.eu/en/policies/sanctions/ukraine-crisis/.

10. Robin Emmott and Sabine Siebold, "EU to Sanction Four Russians over Navalny, Including Prosecutors," Reuters, February 22, 2021, https://www.reuters.com/article/us-russia-politics-navalny-eu-idUSKBN2AM0M2.

11. Austin Long, *Deterrence—from Cold War to Long War: Lessons from Six Decades of RAND Research* (Santa Monica, CA: RAND Corporation, 2008), 8, https://www.rand.org/pubs/monographs/MG636.html.

12. UK Government, "Investor Visa (Tier 1)," https://www.gov.uk/tier-1-investor.

13. Anne Machalinksi, "Golden Visas: The Investment Migration Industry Evolves Globally," *Penta*, August 24, 2020, https://www.barrons.com/articles/golden-visas-the-investment-migration-industry-evolves-globally-01598279613.

14. BBC, "Cyprus to Suspend 'EU Golden Passports' Scheme," October 13, 2020, https://www.bbc.com/news/world-europe-54522299.

15. Francesca Carington, "Meet the Crazy Rich Russians Who Grew Up in London," *Tatler*, July 22, 2020, https://www.tatler.com/article/wealthy-russians-in-london.

16. Carington, "Meet the Crazy Rich Russians Who Grew Up in London."

17. Caroline Bankoff, "Putin's Daughter Reportedly Flees Home in the Netherlands amid Anger over MH17," Intelligencer, July 25, 2014, https://nymag.com/intelligencer/2014/07/putins-daughter-reportedly-flees-netherlands.html.

18. Evan Osnos, "What Did China's First Daughter Find in America?," *New Yorker*, April 6, 2015, https://www.newyorker.com/news/news-desk/what-did-chinas-first-daughter-find-in-america.
19. Elisabeth Braw, "Educating Their Children Abroad Is the Russian Elite's Guilty Secret," *Newsweek*, July 30, 2014, https://www.newsweek.com/2014/08/08/educating-their-children-abroad-russian-elites-guilty-secret-261909.html.
20. UK Companies House, "Entwined Productions Ltd," https://find-and-update.company-information.service.gov.uk/company/10825053.
21. Juliette Garside and David Pegg, "Panama Papers Reveal Offshore Secrets of China's Red Nobility," *Guardian*, April 6, 2016, https://www.theguardian.com/news/2016/apr/06/panama-papers-reveal-offshore-secrets-china-red-nobility-big-business.
22. Garside and Pegg, "Panama Papers Reveal Offshore Secrets of China's Red Nobility."
23. John Verhovek, "Biden Warns Against Foreign Interference in US Elections: 'I Am Putting the Kremlin and Other Foreign Governments on Notice,'" ABC News, July 20, 2020, https://abcnews.go.com/Politics/biden-warns-foreign-interference-us-elections-putting-kremlin/story?id=71886014.
24. Ministry of Foreign Affairs of the People's Republic of China, "Foreign Ministry Spokesperson Announces Sanctions on Relevant EU Entities and Personnel," March 22, 2021, https://www.fmprc.gov.cn/mfa_eng/xwfw_665399/s2510_665401/t1863106.shtml.
25. Ministry of Foreign Affairs of the People's Republic of China, "Foreign Ministry Spokesperson Announces Sanctions on Relevant EU Entities and Personnel."
26. Menelaos Markakis, "Kadi II: Fundamental Rights and International Terrorism," Oxford Human Rights Hub, August 23, 2013, https://ohrh.law.ox.ac.uk/kadi-ii-fundamental-rights-and-international-terrorism/.
27. Daniel Flynn, "Libya and Swiss Close to Ending Visa Dispute: Italy," Reuters, February 17, 2010, https://www.reuters.com/article/idUSTRE61G3C020100217?edition-redirect=ca.
28. Nahal Toosi, "Biden Targets Children, Spouses in Visa Crackdown on World's Villains," *Politico*, July 7, 2021, https://www.politico.com/news/2021/07/07/oligarch-visa-bans-498336.
29. Julian E. Barnes, "U.S. Begins First Cyberoperation Against Russia Aimed at Protecting Elections," *New York Times*, October 23, 2018, https://www.nytimes.com/2018/10/23/us/politics/russian-hacking-usa-cyber-command.html.
30. Mark Pomerleau, "US Military Conducted 2 Dozen Cyber Operations to Head Off 2020 Election Meddling," *C4ISRNET*, March 25, 2021, https://www.c4isrnet.com/cyber/2021/03/25/us-military-conducted-2-dozen-cyber-operations-to-head-off-2020-election-meddling/.
31. US Cyber Command, *Achieve and Maintain Cyberspace Superiority: Command Vision for US Cyber Command*, 2018, 6, https://www.cybercom.mil/Portals/56/Documents/USCYBERCOM%20Vision%20April%202018.pdf?ver=2018-06-14-152556-010.
32. US Department of Justice, Office of Public Affairs, "Two Chinese Hackers Working with the Ministry of State Security Charged with Global Computer Intrusion Campaign Targeting Intellectual Property and Confidential Business Information, Including

COVID-19 Research," press release, July 21, 2020, https://www.justice.gov/opa/pr/two-chinese-hackers-working-ministry-state-security-charged-global-computer-intrusion.

33. European Council and Council of the European Union, "EU Imposes the First Ever Sanctions Against Cyber-Attacks," press release, July 30, 2020, https://www.consilium.europa.eu/en/press/press-releases/2020/07/30/eu-imposes-the-first-ever-sanctions-against-cyber-attacks/.

34. Elisabeth Braw and Gary Brown, "Personalised Deterrence of Cyber Aggression," *RUSI Journal* 165, no. 2 (2020): 48–54, https://www.tandfonline.com/doi/abs/10.1080/03071847.2020.1740493.

35. See, for example, Jack Stubbs and Christopher Bing, "Hacking the Hackers: Russian Group Hijacked Iranian Spying Operation, Officials Say," Reuters, October 21, 2019, https://www.reuters.com/article/us-russia-cyber/hacking-the-hackers-russian-group-hijacked-iranian-spying-operation-officials-say-idUSKBN1X00AK.

36. US Department of Defense, *Summary of the 2018 National Defense Strategy of the United States of America: Sharpening the American Military's Competitive Edge*, 2018, 5, https://dod.defense.gov/Portals/1/Documents/pubs/2018-National-Defense-Strategy-Summary.pdf.

37. Toveri, telephone interview.

38. Elisabeth Braw, "Second Strike Communications," Royal United Services Institute for Defence and Security Studies, May 17, 2019, https://rusi.org/publication/rusi-newsbrief/second-strike-communications.

39. Investigations regarding property and company ownership are regularly carried out by firms in the due diligence sector.

40. Toosi, "Biden Targets Children, Spouses in Visa Crackdown on World's Villains."

41. Alexey Navalny, "Putin's Palace. History of World's Largest Bribe," YouTube, January 19, 2021, https://www.youtube.com/watch?v=ipAnwilMncI.

42. Ali Shalchi, *Unexplained Wealth Orders*, UK Parliament, House of Commons Library, January 8, 2021, https://commonslibrary.parliament.uk/research-briefings/cbp-9098/.

43. Dominic Casciani, "Harrods Mega-Spender Loses Supreme Court Challenge," BBC, December 21, 2020, https://www.bbc.com/news/uk-55389134.

44. Alia Chughtai and Mariya Petkova, "Skripal Case Diplomatic Expulsions in Numbers," Al Jazeera, April 3, 2018, https://www.aljazeera.com/news/2018/4/3/skripal-case-diplomatic-expulsions-in-numbers. Diplomatic expulsions are usually avenged by the other country, as in this case when Russia responded by expelling Western diplomats.

45. Tom Newton Dunn, "Mark Sedwill: 'We Always Hit Back Hard. Russia Paid a High Price for Salisbury Poisonings,'" *Times*, October 24, 2020, https://www.thetimes.co.uk/edition/news/mark-sedwill-we-always-hit-back-hard-russia-paid-a-high-price-for-salisbury-poisonings-5v3n3hngk.

46. Newton Dunn, "Mark Sedwill."

47. US Cyber Command, *Achieve and Maintain Cyberspace Superiority*, 6.

48. UK Government Communications Headquarters, "National Cyber Force Transforms Country's Cyber Capabilities to Protect the UK," November 19, 2020, https://www.gchq.gov.uk/news/national-cyber-force.

49. Kim Zetter, "An Unprecedented Look at Stuxnet, the World's First Digital Weapon," *Wired*, November 3, 2014, https://www.wired.com/2014/11/countdown-to-zero-day-stuxnet/.

50. US Cyberspace Solarium Commission, *Our Strategy*, March 2020, 23, https://www.solarium.gov/report.

51. US Cyberspace Solarium Commission, *Our Strategy*, 24.

52. David Omand, "The Future of Deterrence" (eighth Sir Michael Quinlan Memorial Lecture, King's College London, London, January 21, 2020), https://thestrandgroup.kcl.ac.uk/event/the-eighth-sir-michael-quinlan-memorial-lecture/.

53. Reuters, "Taiwan Urges People to Eat More Pineapples After China Bans Imports amid Campaign of 'Intimidation,'" ABC News, February 26, 2021, https://www.abc.net.au/news/2021-02-27/china-bans-taiwan-pineapple-imports-independence-intimidation/13199504.

54. UK Ministry of Defence, Development, Concepts and Doctrine Centre, *Deterrence: The Defence Contribution, Joint Doctrine Note 1/19*, February 2019, 39, https://assets.publishing.service.gov.uk/government/uploads/system/uploads/attachment_data/file/860499/20190204-doctrine_uk_deterrence_jdn_1_19.pdf.

55. UK Ministry of Defence, Development, Concepts and Doctrine Centre, *Deterrence*, 39.

56. Regarding China, see Xiaotong Jin et al., "Why Chinese Elites Buy What They Buy: The Signalling Value of Conspicuous Consumption in China," *International Journal of Market Research* 57, no. 6 (November 1, 2015): 877–908, https://journals.sagepub.com/doi/abs/10.2501/IJMR-2015-041#articleCitationDownloadContainer.

57. Anita Gigovskaya, Alexander Sukharevsky, and Vitaly Gordon, *Mathematics of the Luxury Market in Russia: Growth Potential and Consumer Behavior*, McKinsey & Company and Condé Nast Russia, May 2018, 32, https://www.mckinsey.com/~/media/McKinsey/Featured%20Insights/Europe/Mathematics%20of%20the%20luxury%20market%20in%20Russia/Mathematics-of-the-luxury-market-in-Russia.pdf.

58. Odd Arne Westad, *Restless Empire: China and the World Since 1750* (London: Vintage, 2013), 398.

59. Carrefour left China in 2019, though for reasons unrelated to the boycott. See Warren Shoulberg, "Carrefour Is the Latest Victim of the China Retail Syndrome," *Forbes*, June 24, 2019, https://www.forbes.com/sites/warrenshoulberg/2019/06/24/carrefour-is-the-latest-victim-of-the-china-retail-syndrome/?sh=6c8dcbe82037.

60. Laurens Cerulus and Jakob Hanke Vela, "Europe Looks to Go It Alone on Microchips amid US-China Clash," *Politico*, February 19, 2021, https://www.politico.eu/article/europe-seeks-to-decouple-from-us-china-chip-war/.

61. Bart Groothuis, "Proposal for Collective Countermeasures" (unpublished material, February 16, 2021), PDF document.

62. Catalin Cimpanu, "In a First, Israel Responds to Hamas Hackers with an Air Strike," ZDNet, May 5, 2019, https://www.zdnet.com/article/in-a-first-israel-responds-to-hamas-hackers-with-an-air-strike/.

63. Fiona Cunningham, "Was China Behind Last October's Power Outage in India? Here's What We Know.," *Washington Post*, April 29, 2021, https://www.washingtonpost.com/politics/2021/04/29/was-china-behind-last-octobers-power-outage-india-

heres-what-we-know/.

64. Kevin Chilton and Greg Weaver, "Waging Deterrence in the Twenty-First Century," in *Deterrence in the Twenty-First Century: Proceedings*, ed. Anthony C. Cain (Montgomery, AL: Air University Press, 2010), 67, https://media.defense.gov/2017/Apr/05/2001727306/-1/-1/0/B_0118_DETERRENCE_TWENTYFIRST_CENTURY.PDF.

65. Chilton and Weaver, "Waging Deterrence in the Twenty-First Century," 67.

66. Omand, "The Future of Deterrence."

67. This quotation can be found in Lawrence Freedman, *Strategy: A History* (New York: Oxford University Press, 2013), 162.

68. US Cyberspace Solarium Commission, *Our Strategy*, 27.

69. Ben Rhodes, "Inside the White House During the Syrian 'Red Line' Crisis," *Atlantic*, June 3, 2018, https://www.theatlantic.com/international/archive/2018/06/inside-the-white-house-during-the-syrian-red-line-crisis/561887/.

70. Chilton and Weaver, "Waging Deterrence in the Twenty-First Century," 68–69.

71. Niklas Karlsson (vice chair, Committee on Defence, Swedish Parliament), telephone interview with the author, August 11, 2020.

Concluding Reflections

1. Ray Le Maistre, "Ericsson Takes a Hit in China Mobile's Latest 5G Contract Awards . . . and Nokia Gets a Slice of the Pie," TelecomTV, July 19, 2021, https://www.telecomtv.com/content/5g/ericsson-takes-a-hit-in-china-mobile-s-latest-5g-contract-awards-and-nokia-gets-a-slice-of-the-pie-41994/.

2. Ericsson, "Ericsson Reports Second Quarter Results 2021," press release, July 16, 2021, https://www.ericsson.com/en/press-releases/2021/7/ericsson-reports-second-quarter-results-2021.

3. North Atlantic Treaty Organization, "Statement by the Acting NATO Spokesperson on the Mercer Street Vessel Attack," August 3, 2021, https://www.nato.int/cps/en/natohq/news_186010.htm.

4. Elisabeth Braw, "Attacks on Gulf Shipping Leave the Global Economy Vulnerable," Politico.eu, August 5, 2021, https://www.politico.eu/article/gulf-shipping-attacks-leave-global-economy-vulnerable-trade/.

About the Author

Elisabeth Braw is a senior fellow at the American Enterprise Institute (AEI), where she focuses on defense against emerging national security challenges, such as hybrid and gray-zone threats. She is also a columnist with *Foreign Policy*, where she writes on national security and the globalized economy, and a member of the UK's National Preparedness Commission. Before joining AEI, Braw was a senior research fellow at the Royal United Services Institute for Defence and Security Studies in London, where she founded its modern deterrence project. She has also been an associate fellow at the European Leadership Network, a senior fellow at the Atlantic Council, and a senior consultant at Control Risks, a global risk consultancy. Braw started her career as a journalist working for Swedish newspapers and has reported on Europe for publications such as the *Christian Science Monitor* and *Newsweek*. She is often published in the *Economist*, *Foreign Affairs*, the *Times*, and the *Wall Street Journal*, among other publications. She is also the author of *God's Spies: The Stasi's Cold War Espionage Campaign Inside the Church* (William B. Eerdmans, 2019). A frequent speaker at national security and business conferences, Braw often appears on various international media.

Index

Aalbersberg, Pieter-Jaap, 30
Able Archer nuclear exercise, 154–55
Afghanistan, 44, 152
Agriculture, 89–90
Ahmad, Tariq, 111
AI. *See* Artificial intelligence
Alli, Paolo, 49, 51, 100–1
Allies, 246–49
AMC movie theater, 5
Anti-Corruption Data Collective, 99
A.P. Moller-Maersk, 110–12
APT29, 112–14
Arab Spring revolutions, 10
Artificial intelligence (AI), 40, 64, 71
Artificial islands, South China Sea, 18–19, 132–33, 149, 245–46
Artists, 38, 40–42
  See also Film industry
Assad regime, 246
Assassinations
  espionage and, 130–32
  physical harm and attempts of, 130–32
  by poisoning, 17–18, 27, 130–31, 234–35
  of Soleimani, 25, 131, 240
Athletes, 38, 40–42, 72
Atomic bomb, 147–48

Attal, Gabriel, 195
Aunesluoma, Juhana, 178–79
Australia
  Afghanistan and, 44
  China and, 1, 17, 44, 89–91, 129, 276n47
  disinformation in, 44
  on IP theft, 129
Authoritarian countries, 10, 55, 168–69, 260n14
  See also specific countries
Aviation
  China and, 1–2
  harassment in national airspace and, 137–41, 245–46
  Malaysian Airlines Flight 17 and, 24
  NATO on, 138–39
  piracy, 33
  Russia and, 138–39
Aziz, Tariq, 157, 296n56

"Bad Samaritanism," 3–4, 49
Baltic Air Policing (BAP), 138
Baltic Sea, 139–40
Baltic states, 6
  civil defense in, 193–94
  deterrence in, 165–66, 193–94
  disinformation in, 45–47
  energy infrastructure in, 32–33

NATO and, 22, 33–34, 46–47, 85–86
Russia and, 2, 33–34, 45–47, 138–40
United States and, 85–86
See also specific countries
Banking, 15, 217, 233
Banks, Adam, 110
BAP. *See* Baltic Air Policing
Barr, William, 105
Basketball, 106–7
BBC ban, 27
Beijing Jianguang Asset Management, 67
Belarus, 32–33
Belgium, 2
Belt and Road Initiative, 50–51, 54, 73–74
Bergen Engines, 61
BGI Group, 63
Bhutan, 135
Biden, Joe, 1, 44, 94
  deterrence by, 48–49
  Russia and, 48–49, 118
  on visas, 229
Biotechnology, 63, 64, 65–66
Blackmail, 69, 83
Blomberg, Hanne, 124
Bluffing, 156–58
BOC Aviation, 2
Border disputes
  "borderization" and, 135–36, 189, 245
  Crimea's annexation and, 2, 8–9, 20, 21–22, 52, 135
  for Georgia, 135
  harassment in national airspace and territorial waters, 137–41, 245–46
  territorial violations, harassment, and, 132–37
Bowling Alone (Putnam), 203–4
Brandsma, Erik, 30, 112
Bressanelli, Edoardo, 53
Brexit, 50, 52
British spinning machine, 125–26
Brodie, Bernard, 148
Brown, Gary, 117
Brown, Kevin, 120–21
Browne, John, 80
BT Security, 120–21
Bullying, 83
Bush, George H. W., 157, 158
Bush, George W., 87, 158
Business
  artistic side benefits of national security awareness, 212–13
  banking and, 15, 217, 233
  boycotts, 88, 213, 238–39
  business-leader allegiance and, 216–17
  civic financing and, 97–99
  coercion in, 87–91
  Cold War and, 79–80
  corporate behavior and public awareness, 213
  deterrence and, 207–19, 244–45, 247–49
  foreign investments and, 59–67, 69–70, 72–74, 79, 98–99, 216–18
  globalization and, 55–57, 208–9, 239

INDEX 317

government-industry leader
briefings and, 209–12
government-owned
investments and, 217–18
gray-zone aggression and, 1–2,
4–5, 13, 35–36
intellectual property theft and,
4, 237
joint military-industry gray-
zone exercises, 214–15
K companies and, 174
national security courses and,
215–16
national security threats and,
35–36, 59–82
private sector and, 207–19
sponsorship, 41–42
startups and VC funding, 13, 64,
76–79, 218
strategic investments in, 13,
59–67
subversive economics and,
56–82
Warsaw Pact and, 79–80
Business acquisitions, 4, 14, 208
of AMC movie theater, 5
by China, 1–2, 5, 59–82, 216,
267n42
corporate appointments and,
79–81, 264n74
intellectual property and,
68–69
know your buyer in, 67–70
law and, 39, 60–61, 67–68, 74–76
legislation, policy, and, 74–78
MCF strategy and, 72

of Norwegian Air Shuttle, 1–2
by Russia, 61
of semiconductor firms, 59–61,
64–65, 67
subversive economics and,
59–82
VC funding and, 64, 76–79, 218

CAI. *See* Comprehensive
Agreement on Investment
Cambridge Analytica, 51–52
Cambridge University, 99
Cameron, David, 61
Canada, 28, 83–84, 91, 100
Capitol insurrection, US, 1, 44, 52,
160
"Captured elite," 79–80
Carbon dioxide levies, 31–32
Carter, Nick, 1
Carthage, 87
Castro, Fidel, 83
Cato the Censor, 87
CCP. *See* Chinese Communist
Party
Celebrities, 38, 40–42, 105–6, 108,
212–13
Censorship, 5, 105–6
Central Propaganda Department,
103–4
CESSPIT, 115–16
Chemical weapons, 246
Chernukhin, Lubov, 98
Chilton, Kevin, 148, 242, 247
China
artificial islands constructed by,
18–19, 132–33, 149, 245–46

Australia and, 1, 17, 44, 89–91, 129, 276n47
aviation and, 1–2
BBC ban in, 27
Belt and Road Initiative in, 50–51, 54, 73–74
business acquisitions by, 1–2, 5, 59–82, 216, 267n42
Canada and, 28, 91
censorship in, 5, 105–6
Central Propaganda Department and, 103–4
civic financing and foreign donations from, 98–99
coercive diplomacy in, 83–87
Confucius Institutes in, 39
COVID-19 and, 3–5, 48–49, 89, 306n65
Cuba and, 83
cyberattacks and, 1, 13, 24, 114–16, 121, 163–66
Czech Republic and, 84–85
disinformation from, 43–44, 51
education in, 39
energy infrastructure and, 60
Europe and, 1–2, 4–5, 50–51, 58–59, 66, 70, 74–75, 79
film industry and, 5, 103–6
fisheries and, 17, 135–37
foreign investments and, 59–67, 98–99
geopolitics and, 28–29
Germany and, 5, 59, 62, 66
Greece and, 73–74
Hong Kong and, 70, 80, 83–84
Huawei and, 1, 15, 37, 38, 40–41, 84–85, 87–89, 250
IP theft by, 115, 123–30, 237
Italy and, 4–5, 48–49, 50–51, 74
Japan and, 96, 134
on K-pop, 107–8
Latin America and, 136
Lithuania and, 66
Made in China 2025 plan and, 61–62, 65
MCF strategy of, 70–72
"mystery illnesses" in, 15, 131
National Intelligence Law in, 67–68
Netherlands and, 114–15
Norway and, 1–2, 84–85, 90, 113, 250
Norwegian Air Shuttle and, 1–2
Opium Wars and, 137
Pew Research Center on, 4
rare earth minerals in, 95–96
sanctions against, 88
semiconductor firms and, 59–61, 64–65, 67, 70
"16+1" platform in, 74–75
South China Sea and, 18–19, 132–33, 149, 245–46
Southeast Asia and, 12–13, 132–34, 136
sports and, 72, 106–7
supply chains and, 94–96
Sweden and, 1, 15, 38, 40–41, 54, 59–65, 70, 85–89, 250
Taiwan and, 84, 89, 102–3, 105–6, 108, 137–39
Thousand Talents program in, 127

Torres Strait and, 17
United Kingdom and, 60–61, 70, 79–81, 84
United States and, 1, 5, 28, 58, 71–72, 98–99, 127–28, 239
Uyghurs and, 40, 88, 213
VC funding and, 76–79
See also Cyberattacks; Subversive economics
China Global Investment Tracker, 65–66
China Mobile, 250
China Research Group, 81
Chinese Communist Party (CCP), 49, 51, 63, 68, 71–72, 103–4
Chisholm, Alex, 60
Citizenship, 225–31
Civic financing, 97–99
Civil Contingencies Agency (MSB), 193
Civil defense
  in Baltic states, 193–94
  civil preparedness and, 186
  Cold War, civil society, and, 22, 172–84, 192–93
  in Finland, 176–84, 192–93, 216
  selective national service and, 204–7
  in Sweden, 22, 169–70, 172–75, 182–84, 193
Civil Defence Corps, UK, 188
Civil society
  business, private sector, and, 207–19
  Cold War, civil defense, and, 22, 172–84, 192–93
  collective benefit of civil-society participation, 219–20
  COVID-19 and, 196
  resilience and, 193–95, 199–204
  as resource for deterrence, 185–93, 195–220
  selective national service and, 204–7
  whole-of-society wall approach, 185–93, 247–48
  World War II and, 191
Civilians
  business boycotts by, 88, 213, 238–39
  civilian maritime crews, 137–41
  coercion of, 91–93
  detainment, of private citizens, and, 91–92, 277n59
  deterrence, denial, and, 195–220
  loss of life and, 245–46
  public awareness campaigns and, 197–99
  societal stress testing and, 199–200
  volunteering and, 203, 221
Clean Network agenda, 86
CNI. *See* Critical national infrastructure
Cod wars, 16–17
Coercion
  blackmail and, 69, 83
  bullying and, 83
  in business, 87–91
  civic financing and, 97–99
  through diplomacy, 83–87

through influencing and
    popular culture, 102–8
public humiliation and,
    100–102
through sanctions, 93–94
supply-chain disruption and,
    94–96
using private citizens for, 91–93
Cogman, David, 66
Cohen, David S., 104
Cold War, 28, 102
    business and, 79–80
    civil society, civil defense, and,
        22, 172–84, 192–93
    disinformation during, 42–43
    foreign investments and, 61
    subversive economics during,
        57, 79
    Warsaw Pact and, 46, 79–80,
        143, 148, 149, 154, 159, 177–78
Cold War deterrence, 143, 190, 222
    in Finland, 145–46, 152, 170–71,
        175–84, 197
    lessons from, 161–67, 182–84
    in Sweden, 145–46, 152, 172–75,
        197, 293n11
    understanding adversary in,
        154–56
Collins, Damian, 51, 210
Colonial Pipeline attack, 13, 35–36,
    119, 195, 199
Combined gray-zone aggression,
    48–51
Comprehensive Agreement on
    Investment (CAI), 70, 79
Confucius Institutes, 39

Cong Peiwu, 83–84
Contagion (film), 212–13
Continuation War, 175–76
"Convenience trap," 16, 196
Conybeare, John, 57
Corporate appointments, 79–81,
    264n74
Corporate behavior, 213
COSCO Shipping, 73–74
Cost-related punishments, 231–37
COVID-19, 1–2, 189, 201
    China and, 3–5, 48–49, 89,
        306n65
    civil society and, 196
    disinformation about, 51
    government vulnerability and,
        4, 26
    Gray-zone aggression and, 3–4
    in Italy, 4–5, 48–49
    NATO on, 49
    origins of, 26
    Russia and, 48–49
    supply chains and, 95–96
    testing, 63
    in UK, 51
    vaccines and, 43–44, 89
Credible deterrence, 156–58
Crimea, 2, 8–9, 20, 21–23, 52, 135
Criminal justice, 225–31, 233
Crisis management, 194–95,
    199–200
    resilience testing and, 200–204
    selective national service and,
        204–7
Critical national infrastructure
    (CNI), 29, 36

Croatia, 2
Cuba, 15, 83, 131
Cuban missile crisis, 159–60
Cullen, Patrick, 9, 10–11, 20, 28–29, 85, 134–35
Cyber Command, US, 166, 229–30
Cyber weapons, 144
Cyberattacks
   on A.P. Moller-Maersk, 110–12
   by APT29, 112–14
   from China, 1, 13, 24, 114–16, 121, 163–66
   on Colonial Pipeline, US, 13, 35–36, 119, 195, 199
   cyber aggression and overview of, 110–23
   deterrence of, 18, 48, 113, 116–17, 119–23, 229–30, 235–37, 240–41, 243, 283n1
   disinformation and, 3, 4
   on energy infrastructure, 23, 113–14, 120, 240–41
   espionage and, 114–15
   in Estonia, 24
   "hack backs" and, 243
   by hacktivists, 120–21
   improving security and, 24–25
   increase in, 118–23
   on infrastructure, 119
   insurance for, 116–17
   IP theft and, 4, 70, 123–30, 189
   on Irish national health care system, 13
   on JBS meat-processing plant, 13
   of Kyivoblenergo, 23
   law and cyber governance, 115–18
   Mumbai cyberattack, 241–42
   by NotPetya, 38, 110–12, 117
   by NSO Group, 121–22
   public humiliation and, 101
   ransomware attacks and, 13, 18, 35–36, 48, 101, 118–19, 195, 199
   by RedDelta, 115
   Russian, 1, 2, 13, 23–24, 38, 110–14, 116–23, 143, 223–25
   social media and, 119, 121–22
   on SolarWinds, 113–14, 120, 143
   on Sony Pictures, 101
   on supply chains, 110–12, 113
   types of, 118
   WannaCry attack, 112
Cyberspace Solarium Commission, US, 112, 163–66, 194–95, 236, 246, 287n69
Czech Republic, 84–85, 165, 214–15, 219

Dalai Lama, 85, 105
Dalian Wanda Group, 5
Daru, 17
Data, user, 69
Datenna, 66–67
DCDC. *See* Development, Concepts and Doctrine Centre
DCMS. *See* Digital, Culture, Media and Sport Committee
Defender Europe 2020, 22
Defense spending, 2
Denial
   business, private sector, and, 207–19

civil society as resource for, 185–93
civilian involvement in, 195–220
deterrence by, 21–22, 185–220, 222
public awareness campaigns and, 197–99
resilience and, 193–95, 199–204
selective national service and, 204–7
societal stress testing and, 199–200
whole-of-society wall of, 185–93
Denmark, 193, 204–5
Department of Energy (DOE), 211–12
Destabilization, 9
Detainment, of private citizens, 91–92, 277n59
Deterrence, 6, 16–19
in Baltic states, 165–66, 193–94
by Biden, 48–49
by bluffing, 156–58
business and, 207–19, 244–45, 247–49
civil society as resource for, 185–93, 195–220
credible, 156–58
of cyberattacks, 18, 48, 113, 116–17, 119–23, 229–30, 235–37, 240–41, 243, 283n1
by denial, 21–22, 185–220, 222
of disinformation, 45–46, 202, 210–11, 219, 232–33
dissuasion and, 185
escalate to de-escalate strategies in, 244
in Estonia, 145, 194
forms of, 142–46
friends with extended, 246–49
in Germany, 144–45
intent and, 159–61
of IP theft, 128–30, 237
irony of success in, 53–55
leadership and, 158–59
in Lithuania, 166
by military, 144, 240–41
NATO on, 151–53, 185–86, 249
nuclear, 93–94, 144–55, 161–62, 238
by posturing, 156–58
psychology of, 142, 146–50
by punishment, 152, 166, 221–49
of ransomware attacks, 48
resilience and, 51–53, 122–23, 172, 185–86, 193–95, 199–204, 249
retaliation and, 143–45
selective national service and, 204–7
tailored, 244–46
theories on, 150, 151–54
understanding the adversary and, 154–56
in United Kingdom, 142–44, 149, 152, 162–63, 187–91, 233–35
in World War II, 146–48, 152, 157–58
See also Cold War deterrence
Development, Concepts and Doctrine Centre (DCDC), 34–35, 142–44, 163, 215, 238

Dicker, Art, 78
Digital, Culture, Media and Sport Committee (DCMS), 51–52
Diplomacy
  allies and, 246–49
  coercive, 83–87
  global governance and, 1–2
  vaccine, 43–44, 89
Disinformation
  in Australia, 44
  in Baltic states, 45–47
  about Brexit, 52
  Chinese, 43–44, 51
  during Cold War, 42–43
  in combined gray-zone aggression, 48–51
  cost-related punishments for, 232–33
  about COVID-19, 51
  cyberattacks and, 3, 4
  deterrence of, 45–46, 202, 210–11, 219, 232–33
  early, 8
  elections and, 42–45, 46, 50, 52–53, 229–30
  on Facebook, 51
  fake news and, 29, 42, 46
  free speech and, 42
  on health, 149
  law and, 42–43, 47–48, 51
  media and, 12
  NATO on, 24, 46–47
  overview of, 42–48
  resilience to, 51–52
  Russian, 23–24, 42–48, 50, 221, 229–34
  on social media, 44–45, 51, 210–11, 259n32
  trust eroded by, 28, 50
  in Ukraine, 23–24
  during World War II, 46
Disney, 105–6, 213
Dissuasion, 185
D-notices, 298n15
DOE. *See* Department of Energy
Drone attacks, 250–51
Drug smuggling, 128
Dunn, Frederick, 147–48
Duterte, Rodrigo, 134

Economics, 56–57, 133, 150
  See also Subversive economics
Economist, 50
Economy, 55, 123–24
Education, 195
  in China, 39
  foreign donations and, 99
  on gray-zone aggression, 37
  national security courses and, 215–16
EEZ. *See* Exclusive economic zone
EFP. *See* Enhanced Forward Presence, NATO
Ekholm, Börje, 1, 87–88
Elections
  Capitol insurrection and, 1, 44, 52, 160
  disinformation and, 42–45, 46, 50, 52–53, 229–30
  in Europe, 52–53
  Facebook and, 14
  Russia and, 14, 42, 44–45, 50, 52,

221, 229–30
    in United States, 1, 14, 44, 52, 160, 221, 229–30
The Elements of the China Challenge (US State Department), 123
Elite capture, 79–80
Energy infrastructure
    in Baltic states, 32–33
    carbon dioxide levies and, 31–32
    China and, 60
    cyberattacks on, 23, 113–14, 120, 240–41
    DOE and, 211–12
    energy market and, 31–33, 80
    Kyivoblenergo and, 23
    in Lithuania, 31–33
    nuclear power plants and, 31–32
    in Texas, 35–36
Enhanced Forward Presence, NATO (EFP), 22, 153, 159
Enterprise Act (2002), 60–61
Ericsson, 1, 41, 88, 250
Escalation, 28, 244
Espionage, 91–92
    assassinations and, 130–32
    cyberattacks and, 114–15
    intellectual property and, 128
Estonia, 211
    deterrence in, 145, 194
    Russia and, 22, 24, 138–39, 159–60, 184
Europe
    China and, 1–2, 4–5, 50–51, 58–59, 66, 70, 74–75, 79
    Defender Europe 2020 and, 22
    defense spending in, 2
    elections in, 52–53
    infrastructure in, 13
    rare earth minerals in, 95–96
    Russia and, 12, 50
    Ukraine and, 20–21, 22
    See also specific countries
European Centre of Excellence for Countering Hybrid Threats, 11–12
Exclusive economic zone (EEZ), 133

Facebook, 14, 51, 208
Facial recognition software, 40
Fake news, 29, 42, 46
    See also Disinformation
Family, 226–31
Farrell, Henry, 82
FCMA treaty. *See* Friendship, Cooperation, and Mutual Assistance treaty
FDF. *See* Finnish Defence Forces
Fear, 142, 175, 198, 226
Film industry
    artistic side benefits of national security awareness and, 212–13
    China and, 5, 103–6
    popular culture and, 103–6, 212–13
Finland, 11–12, 18, 54, 85–86
    CNI in, 29
    Cold War deterrence in, 145–46, 152, 170–71, 175–84, 197
    Continuation War and, 175–76
    Germany and, 175–76

INDEX 325

military and civil defense in, 176–84, 192–93, 216
National Defence Course in, 179–80
Russia and, 17, 73, 301n44
Security Strategy for Society report in, 193
Winter War in, 170–71, 175–77, 181
World War II and, 175–76, 181–82
Finnish Defence Forces (FDF), 181
FIRRMA. *See* Foreign Investment Risk Review Modernization Act
Fisheries, 17, 90, 135–37
Fitzgibbon, Joel, 89–90
5G network, 1, 15, 86, 250
   See also Huawei
Foreign and Security Policy Strategy, Denmark, 193
Foreign donations, 96–99
Foreign Investment Risk Review Modernization Act (FIRRMA) (2018), 75–78
Foreign investments, 216–18
   CAI and, 70, 79
   China and, 59–67, 98–99
   China Global Investment Tracker on, 65–66
   Cold War and, 61
   extent of, 63–67
   national security threats and, 69
   subversive economics and, 59–67, 69–70, 72–74
Fragogiannis, Kostas, 73–74

France, 50, 113, 136
   Linxens and, 65, 68, 69–70
Free speech, 42
Freedman, Lawrence, 147, 148, 153
Friends with extended deterrence, 246–49
Friendship, Cooperation, and Mutual Assistance (FCMA) treaty, 176
F-Secure Corporation, 116
Fukuyama, Francis, 155
Fusion Doctrine, UK, 187

Galápagos Islands, 136
Game theory, 150
Gao, Paul, 66
Garbačiauskaitė-Budrienė, Monika, 198
Gaslighting, geopolitical, 29, 132
Geistige Landesverteidigung (GLV), 178
General Motors (GM), 207
Genome sequencing, 63
Geopolitical gaslighting, 29, 132
Geopolitics, 18–19, 20, 28–29
   of contested waters, 132–35, 137–41
George Washington, USS, 18–19, 134
Georgia, 22, 112, 135, 181, 184
Gerasimov, Valery, 10
Gerasimov doctrine, 10
Gere, Richard, 106
Germany, 191, 247, 272n126
   China and, 5, 59, 62, 66
   deterrence in, 144–45
   Finland and, 175–76

326 THE DEFENDER'S DILEMMA

Nazi, 168–70, 172, 175–76, 260n14, 297n1, 298n5
Russia and, 16, 50
Soviet Union and, 16
Sweden and, 169–70, 172
Global Britain in a Competitive Age (UK strategy), 26, 162–63
Global governance, 1–2, 10
Globalization, 16
business and, 55–57, 208–9, 239
economy and, 55
national security threats and, 35
subversive economics and, 56–57, 61–62
supply chains and, 36–37, 94–95
travel and, 92–93
GLV. *See Geistige Landesverteidigung*
GM. *See General Motors*
The Godfather (film), 166
Gorbachev, Mikhail, 159
Government Information Board (SIS), 170
Government vulnerability
COVID-19 and exposing, 4, 26
in liberal democracies, 14, 17, 37, 38
national security threats and, 26–37
Government-industry leader briefings, 209–12
Government-owned investments, 217–18
Graham, Lindsey, 100
Gray-zone aggression
blended nature of, 30, 34
business and, 1–2, 4–5, 13, 35–36

combined means of, 48–51
"convenience trap" and, 16, 196
COVID-19 and, 3–4
decisive year of 2014 and, 20–25
defining, 8–13, 245–46
education on, 37
foreign investments as, 59–67
hybrid threats and, 8–12
identifying, 13–16, 39–40, 245–46
joint military-industry gray-zone exercises for, 214–15
law and, 14–15, 54, 240, 283n1
loss of life and, 245–46
military and, 17, 21
as national security threats, 26–37
NATO's list of, 38–39
in peacetime, 2, 5, 8–9, 242–43
public awareness of, 14
real estate and, 17, 72–74
through sponsorship, 38–55
strategic investments in, 13, 59–67
through subversive economics, 56–82
synchronized attack packages and, 10
See also specific countries; specific topics
Greece, 73–74
Griezmann, Antoine, 40, 42
Grindr, 69
Groothuis, Bart, 239–40
Guillaume, Günther, 295n44
Gulf War, 157, 158

INDEX

"Hack backs," 243
Hacktivists, 120–21
Hajiyeva, Zamira, 233
Halder, Franz, 169
Hamilton, Alexander, 125–26
Hanban, 99
Harassment
    maritime, 139–41, 196, 250–51
    in national airspace and territorial waters, 137–41
    piracy and, 33, 250–51
    territorial violations and, 132–37
Harris, Toby, 259n29
Harry (Prince), 100
Hathaway, Oona, 10
Havana syndrome, 15, 131
Hayton, Bill, 133–34
Health, 13
    disinformation on, 149
    medical experimentation and, 149
    medical research and, 128
    medical supplies and, 36, 49, 95, 110–11, 306n65
    "mystery illnesses" and Havana syndrome on, 15, 131
    poisoning and, 17–18, 27, 130–31, 234–35
    vaccine diplomacy and, 43–44, 89
    See also COVID-19
Hedgehog way of latent punishment, 241–44
Hellström, Jerker, 64
henkinen maanpuolustus (HMP), 178–79
Hermocrates, 146
Hideki Tojo, 24
History of the Peloponnesian War (Thucydides), 146
Hitler, Adolf, 169–70
HMP. *See henkinen maanpuolustus*
Hockey, 72
Hoffman, Frank, 9, 11–12, 20
Hollywood, California, 103–6
Hong Kong, 70, 80, 83–84
Honig, Jan Willem, 297n1
Hoover, Herbert, 57
Horizontal escalation, 28
Houston Rockets, 107
Huawei, 37
    IP theft by, 126
    in Sweden, 1, 15, 38, 40–41, 87–89, 250
    in United Kingdom, 15, 80, 84
Huotari, Mikko, 62–63
Hussein, Saddam, 157, 158, 296n56
Hybrid threats
    definition of, 253n9
    destabilization and, 9
    gray-zone aggression and, 8–12
    hybrid warfare and, 8–9, 11, 20–22
    media and, 12
    NATO's list of, 12

Iceland, 16–17
If War Comes pamphlet, 170, 172, 194
Ilhardt, Julia, 47
India, 240–41
Industrialized Disinformation (Oxford Internet Institute), 43

Influencers, 55, 102–8
Information, 18–19
    national security threats and, 197–98
    operations and campaigns, 232
    social media and access to, 43
    warfare, 45–46
    See also Disinformation
Infrastructure
    CNI, 29, 36
    in Crimea, 23
    cyberattacks on, 119
    in Europe, 13
    national security threats and, 29–37
    Russian cyberattacks on, 23, 31–33
    telecom, 1, 13, 15, 30, 40–41, 86, 250
    See also Energy infrastructure
Inglis, Chris, 28, 112–14
In-Q-Tel, 218
Insurance, 116–17
Intellectual property (IP)
    business acquisitions and, 68–69
    espionage and, 128
    medical research and, 128
    responding to threats to, 124–25
Intellectual property (IP) theft, 4, 70, 189
    Chinese, 115, 123–30, 237
    cyberattacks and, 123–30
    deterrence of, 128–30, 237
    outside of cyberspace, 125–26
    Russian, 123–25

Intent, 159–61
Investments
    foreign, 59–67, 69–70, 72–74, 79, 98–99, 216–18
    government-owned, 217–18
    property purchases and, 17, 72–74
    strategic, 13, 59–67
    VC funding and, 13, 64, 76–79, 218
    See also Business acquisitions
IP. See Intellectual property
Iran, 25, 91–92, 94, 144, 164, 208, 251
Iraq, 87, 157, 158, 296n56
Irish national health care system, 13
Iron Curtain, 102, 233
Israel, 121–22, 240, 251
Italy, 4–5, 48–49, 50–51, 74

Japan, 251
    China and, 96, 134
    rare earth minerals in, 96
    United States and, 146–47
    World War II and, 146–47, 157–58
JBS meat-processing plant, 13
JCPOA. See Joint Comprehensive Plan of Action
Jeglinskas, Giedrimas, 28, 31, 34
Jia Qinglin, 227
Johnson, Boris, 26, 100, 189
Joint Comprehensive Plan of Action (JCPOA), 94
Joint military-industry gray-zone exercises, 214–15

Jones, Charlie Lyons, 74
Jonson, Pål, 22, 61
Jouko, Petteri, 182

K companies, 174
Kahn, Herman, 151, 156, 226, 243
Kalniņš, Ojārs, 46–47, 53, 197–98
Kania, Elsa, 70
Kaplan, Robert, 151
Karlsson, Niklas, 54, 184, 188, 247–48
Karolinska Institute, 63
Kerch Strait Bridge, 23
Kinetic force, 239–41
Kissinger, Henry, 151, 155, 158–59
Kneissl, Karin, 80
Kolstad, Ivar, 85, 90
Konttinen, Samu, 116–20
Kopečný, Tomáš, 215
Körlof, Björn, 174–75
Kovrig, Michael, 91
K-pop, 107–8
Kramp-Karrenbauer, Annegret, 59
Kratz, Agatha, 62–63, 64, 66
Krepinevich, Andrew, Jr., 164–65
Kubera, Jaroslav, 84–85
Kubrick, Stanley, 142
KUKA robotics firm, 62–63
Kunlun, 69
Kurds, 100
Kuwait, 157
Kuznetsov, Vladimir, 100–101
Kyivoblenergo, 23

Labor force, 202–3, 216
Larsson, Oscar, 190–92
Larsson, Zara, 38, 40, 42
Laskai, Lorand, 70
Latin America, 136
Latvia, 18, 165–66, 194, 195
  Russia and, 2, 45, 247
Law
  business acquisitions and, 39,
    60–61, 67–68, 74–76
  cyber governance and, 115–18
  disinformation and, 42–43,
    47–48, 51
  gray-zone aggression and,
    14–15, 54, 240, 283n1
  maritime, 133–34, 136
  sponsorship and, 39–40
  Vienna Convention and, 131–32
  on war and peace, 5, 109
Lawson, Ewan, 9
Layton, Edwin, 157–58
Leadership
  business-leader allegiance and,
    216–17
  deterrence and, 158–59
  government-industry leader
    briefings, 209–12
  personality and, 158–59
Lega–Five Star Movement, 51
Legislation
  on business acquisitions, 74–78
Magnitsky, 224
Leškevičius, Vytautas, 39–40
Leung, Nick, 66
Leyen, Ursula von der, 70
Li Chen, 128
Liberal democracies, 3, 5, 10–11
  media in, 47
  openness as disadvantage in, 14

subversive economics and,
  56–57, 81–82
vulnerabilities of, 14, 17, 37, 38
Libya, 229, 238
Linxens, 65, 68, 69–70
Lithuania
  Belarus and, 33
  China and, 66
  deterrence in, 166
  energy infrastructure in, 31–33
  Military in, 22
  public awareness campaigns
    in, 198
  Russia and, 34, 39–40, 45–46,
    139–41
Liu Xiaobo, 84
Liu Xiaoming, 84
Long, Austin, 154, 156, 226
Lorenzana, Delfin, 136
Loss of life, 245–46
Lottakåren, 169, 298n12
Lowther, Adam, 154
Ludendorff, Erich, 168–69, 297n1,
  298n5
Lukashenko, Alexander, 33
Luxury goods, 102–3, 127, 237–39,
  244–45, 247

Macron, Emmanuel, 112, 136
Made in China 2025 plan, 61–62, 65
Magnitsky legislation, 224
Malaysian Airlines Flight 17, 24
Mannerheim, Carl Gustaf, 171
Maritime harassment, 139–41, 196,
  250–51
Maritime law, 133–34, 136

Martin, Ciaran, 122
Martin, Diego, 47
Marwan, Ashraf, 295n44
Mattis, James, 9
Mazarr, Michael, 2–3
MCF strategy. *See* Military-Civil
  Fusion strategy
McGarry, Cormac, 251
McGregor, Richard, 68
Mearsheimer, John, 153
Media
  BBC ban and, 27
  DCMS and, 51–52
  disinformation and, 12
  hybrid threats and, 12
  in liberal democracies, 47
  public awareness campaigns
    and, 198–99
  quality and quantity in, 47
  in Russia, 47
  See also Social media
Medical experimentation, 149
Medical research, 128
Medical supplies, 36, 49, 95, 110–11,
  306n65
Meng Wanzhou, 91
Mercer Street tanker, 250–51
Merck pharmaceuticals, 110–11
Metropolitan Museum of Art, 102
Metternich, Klemens von, 155
Microsoft Exchange servers, 1
Midea Group, 62–63
Mihkelson, Marko, 211
Military, 14
  Crimea's annexation and, 21–22
  defense spending and, 2

deterrence by, 144, 240–41
in Finland, 176–84, 192–93, 216
gray-zone aggression and, 17, 21
in Lithuania, 22
selective national service and, 204–7
in Sweden, 22, 169–70, 172–75, 182–84, 193
transport, 36
See also Civil defense
Military-Civil Fusion (MCF) strategy, 70–72
Military-Industrial Courier, 10
Milley, Mark, 160
Minger, Rudolf, 5, 185
Mobile networks, 1, 13, 15, 30, 40–41, 86, 250
See also Huawei
Molotov, Vyacheslav, 176
Mondelēz, 117
Money laundering, 73, 99
Montgomery, Mark, 18, 134, 163–64
Morey, Daryl, 107
Morris, Lyle, et al., 12–13, 187
Morrison, Scott, 89–90
Moscow Houses, 39–40
MSB. *See* Civil Contingencies Agency
Mueller, Robert, 44–45
Mulan (film), 213
Mumbai cyberattack, 241–42
"Mystery illnesses," 15, 131

Napoleon Bonaparte, 155
Nasser, Gamal Abdel, 295n44
National Academies of Sciences, Engineering, and Medicine, US, 15
National airspace, 137–41
National Coordinator for Counterterrorism and Security, 30
National Cyber Force, UK, 18
National Defence Course, Finland, 179–80
National Defense Strategy, US, 34
National Intelligence Law (2017), 67–68
National Security Agency, US, 28
National Security Concept 2017 report, 193–94
National Security Council, US (NSC), 131
National security courses, 215–16
National security threats
  business and, 35–36, 59–82
  energy market and, 31–33
  foreign investments and, 69
  globalization and, 35
  government vulnerability and, 26–37
  gray-zone aggression as, 26–37
  information and, 197–98
  infrastructure and, 29–37
  pandemics as, 26–27
  public awareness campaigns and, 197–99
  by terrorism, 242
  Trump administration on, 27–28, 211–12, 259n35
  to UK, 34–35
  to US, 27–28, 34, 69

user data and, 69
See also specific threats
NATO. *See* North Atlantic Treaty Organization
Navalny, Alexey, 27, 225
NavTech, 59, 60
Nazi Germany, 168–70, 172, 175–76, 260n14, 297n1, 298n5
Netherlands, 30, 114–15
New Zealand, 203
Newman, Abraham, 82
NGOs. *See* nongovernmental organizations
Nixon, Richard, 87
Nobel Memorial Prize, 150, 161, 221, 222
Nobel Peace Prize, 84, 85, 90
Nokia, 250
Nongovernmental organizations (NGOs), 97, 195, 200
Nord Stream pipeline, 80, 94
North Atlantic Treaty Organization (NATO), 2, 17, 178
  on aviation, 138–39
  Baltic states and, 22, 33–34, 46–47, 85–86
  on civil preparedness, 186
  on COVID-19, 49
  Cuban missile crisis and, 159–60
  on deterrence, 151–53, 185–86, 249
  on disinformation, 24, 46–47
  EFP, 22, 153, 159
  on gray-zone aggression, 38–39
  on hybrid threats, 12
  pranksters and, 100–1
  Strategic Communications Centre of Excellence, 12, 38–39
North Korea, 92, 101, 107–8, 115, 164, 232–33, 238
Norway, 61
  China and, 1–2, 84–85, 90, 113, 250
  selective national service in, 204–6
Norwegian Air Shuttle, 1–2
Norwegian fisheries, 90
NotPetya, 38, 110–12, 117
Novichok nerve agent, 130–31
  See also Poisoning
NSC. *See* National Security Council, US
NSO Group, 121–22
Nuclear deterrence, 93–94, 144–55, 161–62, 238
Nuclear power plants, 31–32
Nuclear weapons, 147–50, 154–55, 161–62

Obama, Barack, 125, 161–62, 245–46
Occupied (television series), 212, 300n36
Ofer, Eyal, 251
Oil embargo, 147
Omand, David, 115, 243
OmniVision Technologies, 65
Opium smuggling, 128
Opium Wars, 137

Oxford Internet Institute, 43
Oxford University, 99

Paasikivi, Juho Kusti, 177
Pabriks, Artis, 194
Panama Papers, 227
Pandemics, 26–27
    See also COVID-19
Papua New Guinea, 17
Parton, Charles, 51, 85
Payne, Keith, 155–56
Peacetime distinctions, 2, 8–9, 109, 242–43
Pearl Harbor, 146–47
Pegasus, 121–22
Pelosi, Nancy, 160
Personality of leadership, 158–59
Pew Research Center, 4
Philippines, 133–34, 136
Piracy, 33, 250–51
Pitt, Brad, 105
Poisoning
    of Navalny, 27
    in UK, 17–18, 130–31, 234–35
Poland, 2
Politics
    CCP and, 49, 51, 63, 68, 71–72, 103–4
    civic financing and, 97–99
    corporate appointment and, 80–81, 264n74
    pranksters and, 100–1
    subversive economics and, 74–76, 80–81
    trade and, 57–58
Pompeo, Mike, 56–57
Popular culture
    athletes in, 38, 40–42, 72
    in authoritarian countries, 260n14
    celebrities in, 38, 40–42, 105–6, 108, 212–13
    coercion through, 102–8
    film industry and, 103–6, 212–13
    K-pop and, 107–8
    sports and, 106–7
Port of Piraeus, 73–74
Port of Trieste, 74
Portugal, 247
Posturing, 156–58
Pranksters, 100–2
Predatory economics, 56–57
    See also Subversive economics
Private citizens. *See* Civil society; Civilians
Private sector. *See* Business
Property purchases, 17, 72–74
Protasevich, Roman, 33
Psychology
    of deterrence, 142, 146–50
    of intent, 159–61
PTS. *See* Swedish Post and Telecom Authority
Public awareness
    campaigns, 197–99
    corporate behavior and, 213
    of gray-zone aggression, 14
Public humiliation, 100–2, 227
Pulsed radio frequency energy, 15, 131
Punishment
    through cost impositions, 231–37

through criminal justice,
  225–31, 233
deterrence by, 152, 166, 221–49
  by friends with extended
    deterrence, 246–49
  hedgehog way of, 241–44
  by kinetic force, 239–41
  tailored deterrence and, 244–46
  tools, 223–49
  trade suspension, 237–39
  through visa bans, 225–31
  See also sanctions
Putin, Vladimir, 98, 118, 156, 160, 227
Putnam, Robert, 203–4

QAnon conspiracies, 202
Quantum technology, 99

Rådestad, Carl, 190–92
Radio broadcasting, 149
Rainio-Niemi, Johanna, 178–79
Ransomware attacks, 18
  Colonial Pipeline attack, 13, 35–36, 119, 195, 199
  deterrence of, 48
  increase in, 118–19
  on JBS meat-processing plant, 13
  public humiliation and, 101
Rare earth minerals, 95–96
Rawat, Bipin, 241
Reagan, Ronald, 93–94
Real estate, 17, 72–74
Record, Jeffrey, 146–47
RedDelta, 115

Reichborn-Kjennerud, Erik, 9, 10–11, 20, 28–29, 85, 134–35
Reinfeldt, Fredrik, 80
Resilience
  civil society and, 193–95, 199–204
  denial and, 193–95, 199–204
  deterrence and, 51–53, 122–23, 172, 185–86, 193–95, 199–204, 249
  to disinformation, 51–52
  early efforts at creating, 51–53
  societal stress testing and, 199–200
  training courses, 200–204
Retaliation, 143–45
Reverse interference, 50
Robertis, Antongiulio de', 86
Robertson, George, 159–60
Robotics, 62–63, 126
Roepke, Wolf-Diether, 186
Romans, 87
Rosneft Oil Company, 80
Russia
  aviation and, 138–39
  Baltic states and, 2, 33–34, 45–47, 138–40
  Belarusian air traffic control and, 33
  Biden and, 48–49, 118
  Brexit and, 50
  business acquisitions by, 61
  Canada and, 100
  civic financing and foreign donations from, 97–99
  coercive diplomacy in, 86

COVID-19 and, 48–49
Crimea's annexation and, 2, 8–9, 20, 21–22, 52, 135
disinformation in, 23–24, 42–48, 50, 221, 229–34
elections and, 14, 42, 44–45, 50, 52, 221, 229–30
energy market and, 31–33, 80
Estonia and, 22, 24, 138–39, 159–60, 184
Europe and, 12, 50
Finland and, 17, 73, 301n44
Georgia and, 22, 112, 135, 184
Gerasimov doctrine and, 10
Germany and, 16, 50
Latvia and, 2, 45, 247
Lithuania and, 34, 39–40, 45–46, 139–41
on Malaysian Airlines Flight 17, 24
media in, 47
Moscow Houses in, 39–40
"mystery illnesses" and, 15, 131
nuclear power plants in, 31–32
poisonings by, 17–18, 27, 130–31, 234–35
property purchases by, 17, 72–74
reverse interference in, 50
sanctions against, 22, 93–94, 224–25
social media and, 44–45
subversive economics and, 61, 72
Ukraine and, 2, 9, 20–24, 38, 111–12, 224, 300n36
United Kingdom and, 17–18, 73, 98, 100, 234–35
United States and, 13, 14, 28, 110–12, 221, 224–25, 229–30
visas and, 226–27
See also Cold War; Disinformation
Russian cyberattacks, 1, 2, 13, 143, 223–25
by APT29, 112–14
in Estonia, 24
on infrastructure, 23, 31–33
IP theft and, 123–25
by NotPetya, 38, 110–12, 117
overview of, 110–14, 116–23
in Ukraine, 38, 111–12

Sanctions
against Belarus, 33
against China, 88
coercion through, 93–94
effects of, 224, 226
overview of, 93–94
against Russia, 22, 93–94, 224–25
against South Africa, 93
trade and, 89–91
by United States, 88, 93–94, 224–26, 238
for Uyghur treatment, 88
visas and, 228–29
Sapega, Sofia, 33
Schelling, Thomas, 148, 150, 156, 161, 221, 222, 226, 243
Schmidt, Helmut, 144–45, 208
Schmitt, Michael N., 116, 283n1
Schneider, Barry, 158
Schumer, Chuck, 124

Scissors, Derek, 267n42
Scorsese, Martin, 105–6
Security Strategy for Society report, 193
Sedwill, Mark, 234
Selective national service, 204–7
Semiconductor firms, 59–61, 64–65, 67, 70
Separatists, 22–23
"17+1" platform, 74–75
Shapiro, Jacob, 47
Shapiro, Scott, 10
Shelters, 172–73
Shipping, 73–74, 110–12, 140–41
　See also Supply chains
Shoigu, Sergei, 85–86
Silex Microsystems, 59–60
Singapore, 203
SIS. *See* Government Information Board
Sissi units, 181–82
"16+1" platform, 74–75
Skripal, Sergei and Yulia, 17–18, 129–30, 234–35
Smith, Brad, 121
Smoot-Hawley Tariff Act, 57
Snabe, Jim Hagemann, 110, 111
Social media, 69
　cyberattacks and, 119, 121–22
　disinformation on, 44–45, 51, 210–11, 259n32
　Facebook, 14, 51, 208
　influencers and, 55, 103
　information and, 43
　Russia and, 44–45
Societal stress testing, 199–200

Solar panels, 59, 65
SolarWinds, 1, 113–14, 120, 143
Soleimani, Qassem, 25, 131, 240
Sony Pictures cyberattack, 101
South Africa, 93
South China Sea, 18–19, 132–33, 149, 245–46
South Korea, 85, 107–8
Southeast Asia, 12–13, 132–34, 136
　See also specific countries
Soviet Union. *See* Cold War
Spavor, Michael, 91
Spigot, 65
Sponsorship
　business, 41–42
　combined gray-zone aggression and, 48–51
　gray-zone aggression through, 38–55
　law and, 39–40
　of Western artists and athletes, 40–42
Sports
　athletes, 38, 40–42, 72
　basketball, 106–7
　China and, 72, 106–7
　hockey, 72
　popular culture and, 106–7
Stainless steel, 58–59
State Grid Corporation of China, 60
Stena Impero (UK ship), 140
Stoltenberg, Jens, 36
Stolyarov, Alexey, 100–1
Strait of Hormuz, 140
Strategic Communications Centre

of Excellence, NATO, 12, 38–39
Subversive economics
business acquisitions and, 59–82
business and, 56–82
China's MCF strategy and, 70–72
during Cold War, 57, 79
corporate appointments and, 80–81, 264n74
foreign investments and, 59–67, 69–70, 72–74
globalization and, 56–57, 61–62
liberal democracies and, 56–57, 81–82
overview of, 56–57
politics and, 74–76, 80–81
property purchases in, 72–74
Russia and, 61, 72
trade disputes and, 57–59
Trump administration on, 56–57
VC funding and, 76–79
Sun Tzu, 19
Supply chains, 16
China and, 94–96
COVID-19 and, 95–96
cyberattacks on, 110–12, 113
disruption of, 94–96, 259n35
globalization and, 36–37, 94–95
shipping and, 73–74, 110–12, 140–41
trade and, 94–96
Swartz, Vivien Yang, 63
Sweden, 2, 18, 247, 298n15

China, Huawei and, 1, 15, 38, 40–41, 85, 87–89, 250
China's Belt and Road Initiative and, 54
China's investments in, 59–65, 70
Cold War deterrence in, 145–46, 152, 172–75, 197, 293n11
Germany and, 169–70, 172
If War Comes pamphlet in, 170, 172, 194
Military and civil defense in, 22, 169–70, 172–75, 182–84, 193
MSB in, 193
World War II and, 169–70, 172, 175
Swedish Post and Telecom Authority (PTS), 250
Swedish Security Service, 29–30
Switzerland, 5, 229
Synchronized attack packages, 10
Syria, 92, 246

Tager, James, 103–4
Tailored deterrence, 244–46
Taiwan, 84, 89, 102–3, 105–6, 108, 137–39
Tallinn Manual on the International Law Applicable to Cyber Warfare (Schmitt), 116, 283n1
Tariffs, 1, 57–59, 89, 276n47
Tatler magazine, 226–27
Telecom infrastructure, 1, 13, 15, 30, 40–41, 86, 250
See also Huawei
Terras, Riho, 138–39, 145, 153, 181, 184

Territorial conquest, 22–23, 245–46
  See also Border disputes
Terrorism, 242
Texas energy infrastructure, 35–36
Thankey, Hasit, 186
Thousand Talents program, 127
Thucydides, 146
Thunberg, Greta, 100
Tianjin Zhonghuan
  Semiconductor, 65
Tibet, 85, 105
Tillerson, Rex, 56–57
Tkachenko, Stanislav, 86
TMH International, 61
T-Mobile, 126
Torres Strait, 17
Total Defence Day, 203
The Total War (Der totale Krieg)
  (Ludendorff), 168
Totalitarianism, 168–69
Toveri, Pekka, 52, 54–55, 76, 116, 160, 181–83, 231–32
Trade
  luxury goods and, 102–3, 127, 237–39, 244–45, 247
  maritime harassment and, 140–41
  oil embargo and, 147
  politics and, 57–58
  sanctions and, 89–91
  subversive economics and, 57–59
  supply chains and, 94–96
  suspension punishments, 237–39
  tariffs and, 1, 57–59, 89, 276n47
  WTO and, 57–58, 90
Travel, 92–93
Trojan War, 8, 16, 19
Trudeau, Justin, 100
Trump, Donald, 1, 44, 160
Trump administration
  China and, 5, 58, 127–28, 239
  coercive diplomacy by, 86
  on national security threats, 27–28, 211–12, 259n35
  sanctions by, 94
  on subversive economics, 56–57
Trust, 28, 50, 175
Tugendhat, Tom, 81
Turkey, 100, 138
Turnbull, Malcolm, 129
Tynkkynen, Vesa, 182

Ubartas, Mindaugas, 45–46
UFWD. *See* United Front Work Department
UK. *See* United Kingdom
Ukraine
  disinformation in, 23–24
  Europe and, 20–21, 22
  hybrid warfare in, 9, 11, 20–22
  Kyivoblenergo in, 23
  NotPetya cyberattack in, 38
  Russia and, 2, 9, 20–24, 38, 111–12, 224, 300n36
  Russian cyberattacks in, 38, 111–12
  separatists in, 22, 23
Unexplained wealth orders (UWOs), 233
Unfavorable Views of China Reach Historic Highs in Many Countries (Pew Research Center), 4

United Front Work Department
    (UFWD), 51
United Kingdom (UK)
    Brexit and, 50, 52
    British spinning machine from,
        125–26
    China and, 60–61, 70, 79–81, 84
    Civil Defence Corps in, 188
    cod wars and, 16–17
    COVID-19 in, 51
    DCDC in, 34–35, 142–44, 163,
        215, 238
    deterrence in, 142–44, 149, 152,
        162–63, 187–91, 233–35
    D-notices in, 298n15
    Enterprise Act and, 60–61
    Fusion Doctrine and, 187
    *Global Britain in a Competitive
        Age* strategy and, 26, 162–63
    Hong Kong and, 70, 80, 84
    Huawei in, 15, 80, 84
    Iran and, 91–92
    National Cyber Force in, 18
    national security threats to,
        34–35
    Opium Wars and, 137
    pandemic exercises in, 26–27
    poisoning in, 17–18, 130–31,
        234–35
    resilience training in, 201–4
    Russia and, 17–18, 73, 98, 100,
        234–35
    visas and, 226–27
    World War II in, 188
United States (US)
    Baltic states and, 85–86

    Capitol insurrection in, 1, 44,
        52, 160
    China and, 1, 5, 28, 58, 71–72,
        98–99, 127–28, 239
    civic financing and foreign
        donations in, 97–99
    Clean Network agenda, 86
    coercive diplomacy by, 86–87
    Colonial Pipeline attack in, 13,
        35–36, 119, 195, 199
    Cyber Command in, 166,
        229–30
    Cyberspace Solarium
        Commission in, 112, 163–66,
        194–95, 236, 246, 287n69
    DOE in, 211–12
    elections in, 1, 14, 44, 52, 160,
        221, 229–30
    FIRRMA and, 75–78
    Grindr and national security
        of, 69
    Hollywood and film industry
        in, 103–6
    IP theft and, 123–30
    Japan and, 146–47
    JBS meat-processing plant in,
        13
    National Academies of
        Sciences, Engineering, and
        Medicine in, 15
    National Defense Strategy of, 34
    National Security Agency in, 28
    national security threats to,
        27–28, 34, 69
    NSC in, 131
    oil embargo and, 147

rare earth minerals in, 95–96
Russia and, 13, 14, 28, 110–12, 221, 224–25, 229–30
sanctions by, 88, 93–94, 224–26, 238
semiconductor firms in, 65
Soleimani and, 25, 131
Texas energy infrastructure in, 35–36
VC funding in, 77–79, 218
See also specific topics
User data, 69
UWOs. *See* Unexplained wealth orders
Uyghurs, 40, 88, 213

Vaccine diplomacy, 43–44, 89
VC funding. *See* Venture capital funding
Veit, Raphael, 74
Venezuela, 40
Venture capital (VC) funding, 13, 64, 76–79, 218
Vienna Convention, 131–32
Vietnam War, 87
Vigneault, David, 28
Vindman, Yevgeny, 5
Visas, 225–31
Visuri, Pekka, 177
Volunteering, 203, 221
Vystrčil, Miloš, 84

Wæver, Ole, et al., 189
Wang Yi, 84
WannaCry attack, 112
War
  avoidance of, 147–48
  changes in warfare, 22–23, 164
  cod wars, 16–17
  Continuation War and, 175–76
  declarations of, 5, 10, 164
  gray-zone aggression and, 5
  Gulf War, 157, 158
  hybrid, 8–9, 11, 20–22
  information warfare and, 45–46
  law on, 5, 109
  Opium Wars, 137
  peacetime distinctions from, 2, 8–9, 109, 242–43
  placement system, 173–74
  territorial conquest and, 22–23
  Trojan War, 8, 16, 19
  Vietnam War, 87
  Winter War, 170–71, 175–77, 181
  World War I, 168
  See also Cold War; World War II
Warmbier, Otto, 92
Warsaw Pact, 46, 79–80, 143, 148, 149, 154, 159, 177–78
Wealth, 227, 233
Weaver, Greg, 148, 242, 247
Westad, Odd Arne, 238
Westminster Abbey, 142
Westphalian system, 10
"Whataboutism," 29
WhatsApp, 121–22
Whitton, John, 42–43
Whole-of-society approach, 185–93, 247–48
WikiLeaks, 101
Willersdorf, Sarah, 103

Wilson, Charles, 207
Wilson, Ed, 27–28, 118–19, 124, 211–12, 223
Wine dumping, 1, 89
Winter War, 170–71, 175–77, 181
Women, 169, 298n12
A World Restored (Kissinger), 151, 155
World Trade Organization (WTO), 57–58, 90
World War I, 168
World War II, 5, 27, 168, 297n1
   civil society and, 191
   deterrence in, 146–48, 152, 157–58
   disinformation during, 46
   Finland and, 175–76, 181–82
   Japan and, 146–47, 157–58
   Sweden and, 169–70, 172, 175
   in United Kingdom, 188
Wray, Christopher, 126–27
WTO. *See* World Trade Organization
Wübbeke, Jost, et al., 62

Xi Jinping, 49, 67–68, 71, 129–30

Yanukovych, Viktor, 20–21
Yemen, 92
YouGov, 50
Yuan, Sabrina, 78

Zaghari-Ratcliffe, Nazanin, 91–92
Zhang Gaoli, 71
Zhao Lijian, 15, 44, 87
Zheleznyak, Anastasia, 227

BOARD OF TRUSTEES

DANIEL A. D'ANIELLO, Chairman
Chairman and Cofounder
The Carlyle Group

CLIFFORD S. ASNESS
Managing and Founding Principal
AQR Capital Management LLC

THE HONORABLE
RICHARD B. CHENEY

PETER H. COORS
Vice Chairman of the Board
Molson Coors Brewing Company

HARLAN CROW
Chairman
Crow Holdings

RAVENEL B. CURRY III
Chief Investment Officer
Eagle Capital Management LLC

KIMBERLY O. DENNIS
President and CEO
Searle Freedom Trust

DICK DEVOS
President
The Windquest Group

ROBERT DOAR
President; Morgridge Scholar
American Enterprise Institute

MARTIN C. ELTRICH III
Partner
AEA Investors LP

JOHN V. FARACI
Chairman and CEO, Retired
International Paper Company

TULLY M. FRIEDMAN
Chairman and Co-CEO
FFL Partners LLC

CHRISTOPHER B. GALVIN
Chairman
Harrison Street Capital LLC

HARVEY GOLUB
Chairman and CEO, Retired
American Express Company
Chairman, Miller Buckfire

ROBERT F. GREENHILL
Founder and Chairman
Greenhill & Co. Inc.

FRANK J. HANNA
CEO
Hanna Capital LLC

JOHN K. HURLEY
Founder and Managing Partner
Cavalry Asset Management

JOANNA F. JONSSON
Partner
Capital Group

BRUCE KOVNER
Chairman
CAM Capital

MARC S. LIPSCHULTZ
Cofounder and President
Owl Rock Capital Partners

JOHN A. LUKE JR.
Chairman
WestRock Company

PAT NEAL
Chairman of the Executive Committee
Neal Communities

ROSS PEROT JR.
Chairman
Hillwood Development Company

GEOFFREY S. REHNERT
Co-Chief Executive Officer
Audax Group

KEVIN B. ROLLINS
CEO, Retired
Dell Inc.

MATTHEW K. ROSE
Retired CEO/Chairman
BNSF Railway

EDWARD B. RUST JR.
Chairman Emeritus
State Farm Insurance Companies

WILSON H. TAYLOR
Chairman Emeritus
Cigna Corporation

WILLIAM H. WALTON
Managing Member
Rockpoint Group LLC

EMERITUS TRUSTEES

PAUL F. OREFFICE
D. GIDEON SEARLE
MEL SEMBLER
HENRY WENDT

OFFICERS

ROBERT DOAR
President; Morgridge Scholar

JASON BERTSCH
Executive Vice President

SUZANNE GERSHOWITZ
Vice President, Administration and Counsel

JOHN CUSEY
Vice President, Communications

YUVAL LEVIN
Senior Fellow; Beth and Ravenel Curry
Chair in Public Policy; Director, Social, Cultural,
and Constitutional Studies;
Editor in Chief, National Affairs

KORI SCHAKE
Senior Fellow; Director, Foreign and
Defense Policy Studies

MICHAEL R. STRAIN
Senior Fellow; Arthur F. Burns Scholar
in Political Economy; Director,
Economic Policy Studies

RYAN STREETER
Senior Fellow; Director, Domestic Policy Studies

RESEARCH STAFF

SAMUEL J. ABRAMS
Nonresident Senior Fellow

BETH AKERS
Senior Fellow

J. JOEL ALICEA
Nonresident Fellow

JOSEPH ANTOS
Senior Fellow; Wilson H. Taylor Scholar
in Health Care and Retirement Policy

LEON ARON
Senior Fellow

KIRSTEN AXELSEN
Nonresident Fellow

JOHN P. BAILEY
Nonresident Senior Fellow

The American Enterprise Institute for Public Policy Research

AEI is a nonpartisan, nonprofit research and educational organization. The work of our scholars and staff advances ideas rooted in our commitment to expanding individual liberty, increasing opportunity, and strengthening freedom.

The Institute engages in research; publishes books, papers, studies, and short-form commentary; and conducts seminars and conferences. AEI's research activities are carried out under four major departments: Domestic Policy Studies, Economic Policy Studies, Foreign and Defense Policy Studies, and Social, Cultural, and Constitutional Studies. The resident scholars and fellows listed in these pages are part of a network that also includes nonresident scholars at top universities.

The views expressed in AEI publications are those of the authors; AEI does not take institutional positions on any issues.

CLAUDE BARFIELD
Senior Fellow

MICHAEL BARONE
Senior Fellow Emeritus

ROBERT J. BARRO
Nonresident Senior Fellow

J. HOWARD BEALES III
Visiting Senior Fellow

MICHAEL BECKLEY
Nonresident Senior Fellow

ERIC J. BELASCO
Nonresident Senior Fellow

ANDREW G. BIGGS
Senior Fellow

JASON BLESSING
Jeane Kirkpatrick Visiting Research Fellow

DAN BLUMENTHAL
Senior Fellow; Director, Asian Studies

KARLYN BOWMAN
Distinguished Senior Fellow

HAL BRANDS
Senior Fellow

ELISABETH BRAW
Senior Fellow

ALEX BRILL
Senior Fellow

ARTHUR C. BROOKS
President Emeritus

RICHARD BURKHAUSER
Nonresident Senior Fellow

JAMES C. CAPRETTA
Senior Fellow; Milton Friedman Chair

TIMOTHY P. CARNEY
Senior Fellow

AMITABH CHANDRA
John H. Makin Visiting Scholar

THOMAS CHATTERTON WILLIAMS
Nonresident Fellow

LYNNE V. CHENEY
Distinguished Senior Fellow

JAMES W. COLEMAN
Nonresident Senior Fellow

MATTHEW CONTINETTI
Senior Fellow

ZACK COOPER
Senior Fellow

JAY COST
Gerald R. Ford Nonresident Senior Fellow

DANIEL A. COX
Senior Fellow

SADANAND DHUME
Senior Fellow

GISELLE DONNELLY
Senior Fellow

MICHAEL BRENDAN DOUGHERTY
Nonresident Fellow

ROSS DOUTHAT
Nonresident Fellow

COLIN DUECK
Nonresident Senior Fellow

MACKENZIE EAGLEN
Senior Fellow

NICHOLAS EBERSTADT
Henry Wendt Chair in Political Economy

MAX EDEN
Research Fellow

JEFFREY EISENACH
Nonresident Senior Fellow

EMILY ESTELLE
Research Fellow

ANDREW FERGUSON
Nonresident Fellow

JOHN G. FERRARI
Nonresident Senior Fellow

JOHN C. FORTIER
Senior Fellow

JOSEPH B. FULLER
Nonresident Senior Fellow

SCOTT GANZ
Research Fellow

R. RICHARD GEDDES
Nonresident Senior Fellow

ROBERT P. GEORGE
Nonresident Senior Fellow

JOSEPH W. GLAUBER
Nonresident Senior Fellow

JONAH GOLDBERG
Fellow; Asness Chair in Applied Liberty

BARRY K. GOODWIN
Nonresident Senior Fellow

SCOTT GOTTLIEB, MD
Senior Fellow

PHIL GRAMM
Nonresident Senior Fellow

WILLIAM C. GREENWALT
Nonresident Senior Fellow

JIM HARPER
Nonresident Senior Fellow

WILLIAM HAUN
Nonresident Fellow

ROBERT B. HELMS
Senior Fellow Emeritus

FREDERICK M. HESS
Senior Fellow; Director,
Education Policy Studies

CHRISTINA HOFF SOMMERS
Senior Fellow Emeritus

R. GLENN HUBBARD
Nonresident Senior Fellow

HOWARD HUSOCK
Senior Fellow

BENEDIC N. IPPOLITO
Senior Fellow

MARK JAMISON
Nonresident Senior Fellow

MATT JENSEN
Director, Open Source Policy Center

FREDERICK W. KAGAN
Senior Fellow; Director,
Critical Threats Project

STEVEN B. KAMIN
Senior Fellow

LEON R. KASS, MD
Senior Fellow Emeritus

KLON KITCHEN
Senior Fellow

STEVEN E. KOONIN
Nonresident Senior Fellow

KEVIN R. KOSAR
Senior Fellow

ROBERT KULICK
Visiting Fellow

PAUL H. KUPIEC
Senior Fellow

DESMOND LACHMAN
Senior Fellow

DANIEL LYONS
Nonresident Senior Fellow

NAT MALKUS
Senior Fellow; Deputy Director,
Education Policy Studies

ORIANA SKYLAR MASTRO
Nonresident Senior Fellow

JOHN D. MAURER
Nonresident Fellow

MICHAEL MAZZA
Nonresident Fellow

RACHEL M. MCCLEARY
Nonresident Senior Fellow

ELAINE MCCUSKER
Senior Fellow

BRUCE D. MEYER
Nonresident Senior Fellow

THOMAS P. MILLER
Senior Fellow

M. ANTHONY MILLS
Senior Fellow

TIMOTHY J. MURIS
Visiting Senior Fellow

CHARLES MURRAY
F. A. Hayek Chair Emeritus in
Cultural Studies

NEIL NARANG
Jeane Kirkpatrick Visiting Fellow

SITA NATARAJ SLAVOV
Nonresident Senior Fellow

STEPHEN D. OLINER
Senior Fellow; Senior Adviser,
AEI Housing Center; State Farm
James Q. Wilson Scholar

NORMAN J. ORNSTEIN
Senior Fellow Emeritus

BRENT ORRELL
Senior Fellow

AJIT PAI
Nonresident Fellow

MARK J. PERRY
Senior Fellow

TOBIAS PETER
Research Fellow; Director of Research,
AEI Housing Center

JAMES PETHOKOUKIS
Senior Fellow; Editor, AEIdeas Blog;
DeWitt Wallace Chair

EDWARD J. PINTO
Senior Fellow; Director, AEI Housing Center

DANIELLE PLETKA
Distinguished Senior Fellow

KENNETH M. POLLACK
Senior Fellow

KYLE POMERLEAU
Senior Fellow

ROBERT PONDISCIO
Senior Fellow

RAMESH PONNURU
Nonresident Senior Fellow

ANGELA RACHIDI
Senior Fellow; Rowe Scholar

DALIBOR ROHAC
Senior Fellow

JEFFREY A. ROSEN
Nonresident Fellow

IAN ROWE
Senior Fellow

MICHAEL RUBIN
Senior Fellow

PAUL RYAN
Distinguished Visiting Fellow
in the Practice of Public Policy

SALLY SATEL, MD
Senior Fellow

ERIC SAYERS
Nonresident Fellow

NAOMI SCHAEFER RILEY
Senior Fellow

DIANA SCHAUB
Nonresident Senior Fellow

ANNA SCHERBINA
Nonresident Senior Fellow

GARY J. SCHMITT
Senior Fellow

DEREK SCISSORS
Senior Fellow

NEENA SHENAI
Nonresident Fellow

DAN SLATER
Nonresident Fellow

VINCENT H. SMITH
Nonresident Senior Fellow

CHRIS STIREWALT
Senior Fellow

BENJAMIN STOREY
Visiting Fellow

JENNA SILBER STOREY
Visiting Fellow

IVANA STRADNER
Jeane Kirkpatrick Visiting Research Fellow

BRET SWANSON
Nonresident Senior Fellow

SHANE TEWS
Nonresident Senior Fellow

MARC A. THIESSEN
Senior Fellow

SEAN TRENDE
Nonresident Fellow

TUNKU VARADARAJAN
Nonresident Fellow

STAN VEUGER
Senior Fellow

ALAN D. VIARD
Senior Fellow Emeritus

PHILIP WALLACH
Senior Fellow

PETER J. WALLISON
Senior Fellow Emeritus

MARK J. WARSHAWSKY
Senior Fellow

MATT WEIDINGER
Senior Fellow; Rowe Scholar

GREGORY S. WEINER
Nonresident Senior Fellow

ADAM J. WHITE
Senior Fellow

W. BRADFORD WILCOX
Nonresident Senior Fellow

SCOTT WINSHIP
Senior Fellow; Director, Poverty Studies

PAUL WOLFOWITZ
Senior Fellow

JOHN YOO
Nonresident Senior Fellow

KAREN E. YOUNG
Nonresident Senior Fellow

KATHERINE ZIMMERMAN
Fellow

BENJAMIN ZYCHER
Senior Fellow

www.ingramcontent.com/pod-product-compliance
Lightning Source LLC
Chambersburg PA
CBHW021818300426
44114CB00009BA/221